Developing Solutions with Microsoft® InfoPath™

Patrick Halstead, Matthew Blain,
and Vani Mandava-Teredesai

PUBLISHED BY
Microsoft Press
A Division of Microsoft Corporation
One Microsoft Way
Redmond, Washington 98052-6399

Library of Congress Control Number: 2004113264

Printed and bound in the United States of America.

1 2 3 4 5 6 7 8 9 QWT 8 7 6 5 4 3

Distributed in Canada by H.B. Fenn and Company Ltd.

A CIP catalogue record for this book is available from the British Library.

Microsoft Press books are available through booksellers and distributors worldwide. For further information about international editions, contact your local Microsoft Corporation office or contact Microsoft Press International directly at fax (425) 936-7329. Visit our Web site at www.microsoft.com/mspress. Send comments to mspinput@microsoft.com.

Acquisitions Editors: Robin Van Steenburgh and Ben Ryan
Project Editor: Kathleen Atkins
Copy Editor: Ina Chang
Indexer: Virginia Bess

Body Part No. X10-87039

To Naoko

やっと終わったぞ！気晴らしに里帰りしようね。

To Ankur

My hero

To Mom and Dad

Thanks for getting me the VIC-20 I wanted when I was in third grade!

Contents at a Glance

Table of Contents

Acknowledgments

We couldn't have written this book without the assistance of many people. We are especially indebted to Greg Collins for the superb technical review work that he did, without which the quality of this book would have undoubtedly suffered. In addition, we would like to thank the following people:

- **Members of the Microsoft Press editorial team:** Kathleen Atkins, project editor; Robin Van Steenburgh and Ben Ryan, acquisitions editors; Devon Musgrave, developmental editor; and Ina Chang, copy editor
- **Members of the InfoPath team:** Rajesh Jha, Paul Lorimer, Nathaniel Stott, Joshua Bell, Silviu Ifrim, Jane Kim, Laurent Mollicone, Claudio Caldato, Ed Essey, Rodrigo Lode, Kamaljit Bath, Christian Stark, Alessandro Catorcini, Nora Selim, David Snow, Kalpita Deobhakta, Adriana Neagu, Scott Roberts, and Rick Severson
- **From the BizTalk team:** Scott Woodgate
- **Reviewers:** Greg Collins, Rick Severson (thank you, again!), Roger Jennings, and Jim Cantwell
- **Friends:** Nina Ramsey, Constantin Stanciu

Matthew would also like to thank his coauthors for inviting him aboard this project. He also appreciates the support and encouragement of his coworkers at Serriform, including Alessandro, Gabriele, Scott, Jason, Jon, Dan, and Tom.

Introduction

Today we are in the midst of a sea change brought about by Web services, structured data, and database integration. These technologies improve data processing for the enterprise and thereby enable many powerful new features such as faster fulfillment, document workflow, and business intelligence. But the new infrastructure doesn't address how to get office workers' data. Going the last mile to their desks—those important leaf nodes of the organization—is currently the job of a vast array of proprietary solutions and custom Web pages. Users have no standardized user interface for entering their data. Most businesses still use paper forms as the first step in the data entry process. Microsoft Office InfoPath aims to plug in the office worker to the many new business processes that information technology enables. InfoPath offers an on ramp for structured data entry and attempts to do for information technology what the browser has achieved for Web pages.

What is the value proposition? Businesses incur huge costs developing custom solutions for data entry, fixing mistakes in that data entry, and finally getting the data in the right format for databases, line-of-business processes, and other applications. InfoPath addresses each of these pain points. As a member of Microsoft Office, InfoPath presents a familiar user interface. For data entry, InfoPath checks the format and values when the data is entered, preventing errors from getting into the data in the first place. Best of all, InfoPath adopts emerging XML standards and as a result integrates out of the box with Web services, databases, Web servers, and Microsoft BizTalk.

To be more concrete, let's contrast this new technology with an earlier approach—using a word processor. Suppose you wanted to develop a form for entering real estate appraisals. In the word processor era, you would have simply created a word processor document and saved it to your hard drive. Data was unstructured and based on a proprietary format. After saving the document, you could print it or send it to a coworker, but business processes could not act on it. Today, you can upload the appraisal to a Web service or Web site and have it available for viewing and editing. Business processes on the Web site can mine, or extract, data from the document to do sales history and tax record checks by querying online databases. The Internet has enabled more integration. Full text search isn't enough to enable complete data integration. We need structured data, and InfoPath has come to the rescue.

What Is InfoPath?

You've probably heard that InfoPath is a replacement for paper forms, but what exactly is it? InfoPath is both a designer for creating forms as well as an editor for displaying them for being filled out. Microsoft FrontPage designs Web pages, while Microsoft Internet Explorer displays them. InfoPath does both—it both designs and displays XML forms.

When you define a form in InfoPath, InfoPath creates a form template for it. The form template does not accompany the XML form. Rather, the form template exists in a separate file with an .xsn extension (for XML solution). When you open an InfoPath XML form, InfoPath loads the form template associated with it and uses the contents to determine how to display the form. Figure I-1 depicts this process.

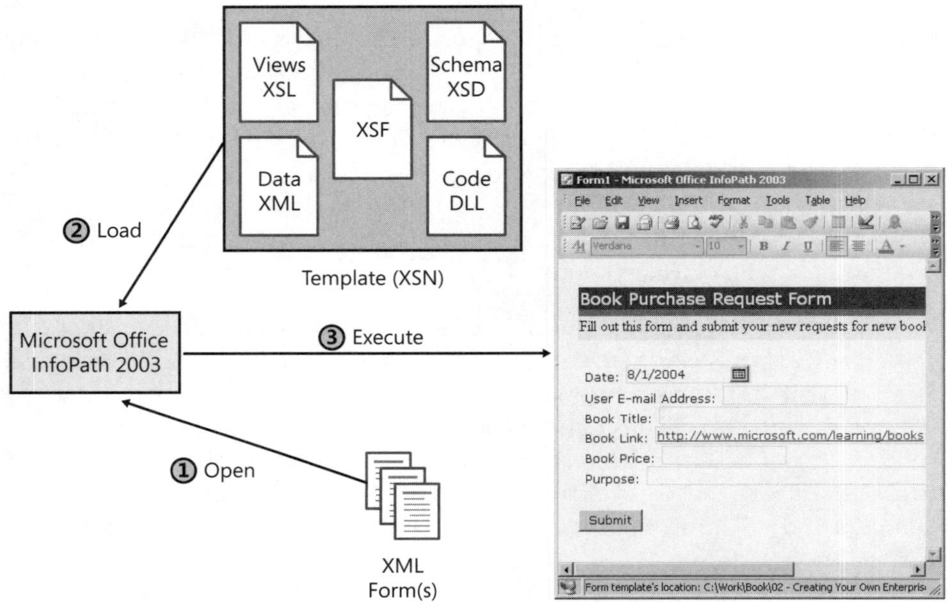

Figure I-1 InfoPath separates the form's data from its description.

XML Forms

InfoPath forms are documents stored in XML format. The forms are pure data, with one exception. The addition of a processing instruction at the beginning of the .xml file tells Microsoft Windows to open the file"using InfoPath. Here's an example of a form:

```
<?xml version="1.0" encoding="UTF-8"?>
<?mso-infoPathSolution
 solutionVersion="1.0.0.38"
 PIVersion="1.0.0.0"
 href="http://testserver/infopathtemplates/Book%20Purchases.xsn"
 name="urn:schemas-microsoft-com:office:infopath:Book-Purchases:-myXSD-2004-02-18T23-56-55"
 productVersion="11.0.6357" ?>
<?mso-application progid="InfoPath.Document"?>
<my:myFields
 xmlns:xsi="http://www.w3.org/2001/XMLSchema-instance"
 xmlns:xhtml="http://www.w3.org/1999/xhtml"
```

```
 xmlns:my="http://schemas.microsoft.com/office/infopath/2003/myXSD/2004-02-18T23-56-55"
 xmlns:xd="http://schemas.microsoft.com/office/infopath/2003"
 xml:lang="en-us">
    <my:Requests>
        <my:Date>2004-08-01</my:Date>
        <my:EmailAddress>patrick.halstead@infopathdev.com</my:EmailAddress>
        <my:BookTitle>Developing Solutions With InfoPath</my:BookTitle>
        <my:BookLink><a xmlns="http://www.w3.org/1999/xhtml"
         href="http://www.microsoft.com/learning/books">
         http://www.microsoft.com/learning/books</a>
        </my:BookLink>
        <my:BookPrice xsi:nil="true"></my:BookPrice>
        <my:Purpose>Prototype company forms in InfoPath.</my:Purpose>
        <my:Approved>false</my:Approved>
    </my:Requests>
</my:myFields>
```

The InfoPath processing instruction, *mso-infoPathSolution*, contains a few attributes that describe the version of the form template (*solutionVersion*), where it's located (*href*), what it's called (*name*), and what version of InfoPath was used to create the form (*ProductVersion*).

Form Templates

When you open an InfoPath XML form, InfoPath loads the form template to figure out how to initially process and display the XML data. The form template is a compressed package of files consisting of the following:

- **Views (.xsl)** The views describe how the form looks—in other words, how to display it. InfoPath supports multiple views. Views are XSL files, which are used to generate HTML with special InfoPath annotations. The annotations refer to native InfoPath controls. InfoPath supports about 25 common controls, including text fields, buttons, list boxes, and date pickers—to name just a few. You can also use ActiveX controls in your templates and edit the XSL outside of the InfoPath designer for additional customization.
- **Schema (.xsd)** The schema describes the structure of your form's data. InfoPath supports W3C XML Schema definition (.xsd files), and the designer comes with a simple schema creation tool called Data Source.
- **Data (.xml)** Data files are used to prepopulate data on the form and as lookup tables. InfoPath supports XML. This is also the format of the InfoPath forms.
- **Manifest (.xsf)** InfoPath comes with its own template format. The template contains everything that makes up the form—from definitions to file references. The manifest contains references to all of the other files that make up the template, as well as settings of the template that are not stored in the other files. Examples of what you find in the template include rules, data connections, validation, business logic, resource files, and user roles.

- **Business logic (.js, .vbs, .dll)** InfoPath lets you extend your form with custom business logic written using script or the Microsoft .NET Framework. The script file or compiled assembly is stored as part of the template.
- **Custom task pane (.htm, .html)** InfoPath lets you create a custom task pane, using HTML hosted in the task pane window. This HTML can access the InfoPath object model to work with the form data and code, and code can access the task pane HTML object model too, subject to certain security rules.
- **Resource files** InfoPath templates can also contain other resource files, such as images used when displaying the form, debug symbols for development versions of forms, and XSL files used for custom merge.

InfoPath is an office worker productivity application, but it is also a platform that provides form templates, editing services, business logic, data interoperability, and developer support.

XML Standards and Data Interoperability

By just looking at the format of the document that InfoPath creates, you can quickly see that InfoPath supports XML standards. The XML for InfoPath forms is defined using an XML Schema .xsd file. With the exception of the processing instructions (which follow XML standards), InfoPath stores no application-specific information in the form data. When you open an InfoPath XML form, InfoPath loads a form template. This form template includes a manifest that is defined in XML and described in a publicly accessible XML Schema. InfoPath uses another standard to display the form views. It stores view information in .xsl files formatted using Extensible Stylesheet Language Transformations (XSLT). You can define rules and filters using XML Path Language (XPath). InfoPath connects to Web services and databases using standard protocols:

- WSDL (Web Services Description Language)
- SOAP (Simple Object Access Protocol)
- UDDI (Universal Description, Discovery, and Integration)
- ADO (ActiveX Data Objects)
- WebDAV (Web Distributed Authoring and Versioning)

Figure I-2 shows where these standards exist within the InfoPath platform.

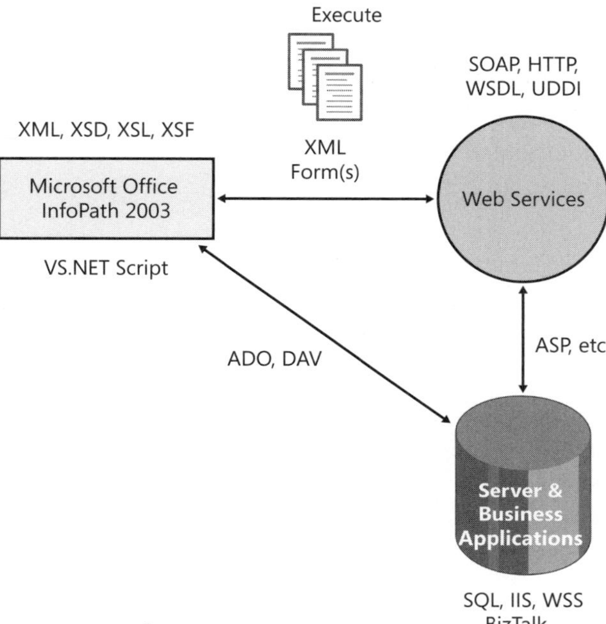

Figure I-2 InfoPath forms achieve data interoperability via XML standards.

A Rich Office Client

InfoPath provides an information technology (IT) platform for your XML forms, but it is also a rich client for existing IT infrastructures. As a rich client running on your desktop, InfoPath can provide features that you won't find on most Web pages:

- **Offline support** InfoPath runs on your computer, not on a server. Losing connectivity is not a problem. InfoPath lets you work on your form when you are offline.
- **Rich text and formatting** You don't have to remember HTML codes to get boldface, italics, underlining, lists, tables, hyperlinks, and images. InfoPath comes with a rich text control that gives you all that and more. You also get spell checking and AutoCorrect.
- **Validation** Validation is one of the most important features of InfoPath. In addition to enforcing data types and restrictions defined in your form's XML schema, InfoPath also lets you define conditional validation using a declarative syntax. You can also add custom business logic.
- **Undo and redo** InfoPath keeps an edit history so you can use undo and redo.

- **Document recovery** If your computer crashes or you lose power, InfoPath can recover documents.
- **Automatic upgrades** If a more recent version of the form exists, InfoPath downloads it automatically. If you're offline and open a form saved with a more recent version, InfoPath attempts to use your local version.
- **Microsoft Office toolbars and dialog boxes** InfoPath is a member of the Microsoft Office family. If you are an Office user, the toolbars and dialog boxes will be familiar.

Word vs. InfoPath

InfoPath is a rich client, but it is not a rich content editor like Word. The main difference between Word and InfoPath is the editing environment and the resulting document format. Word's canvas gives you free reign—you can click and type anywhere and format any run of text. InfoPath supports rich text fields, but the intent is not to create an entire form with one. Rather, InfoPath is a structured data tool: forms have many fields that restrict input and formatting depending on data type and other validation parameters.

Word has XML support—you can attach an XML Schema and bind a range of text to an XML node in it, and Word even saves the resulting data in an XML format. However, the XML binding tags are placed in the document stream, and unless you use document protection, there is little to prevent the user from cutting and pasting the range of text (including the tags) to create a document that is not valid. Word keeps track of schema validation problems, but it doesn't actively intervene to correct the data on entry. Adding protection and validation support to your Word document is one solution, but this requires a lot of work and means that you lose all the benefits of a rich editing environment.

Conversely, creating an InfoPath form out of one big rich text field means that you lose all of the benefits of structured data. Rich text fields are encoded in Extensible Hypertext Markup Language (XHTML), and that means you can't reliably extract data from it. Why is that? If you have an XPath expression in your form's business logic that is always looking for a node in your rich text field, by definition the expression is assuming a structure. However, the control doesn't enforce any structure, and nothing prevents the user from changing it. In essence, this is the same limitation as in Word. Structured data and rich text editing are often at odds with one another.

Here are a few general guidelines for when to use InfoPath vs. Word:

Use InfoPath for paper forms:

- Quick form creation
- Lots of controls
- Validation
- Structured data
- Data interoperability

Use Word for documents:

- Two-dimensional layout (vs. InfoPath's layout table approach)
- Extensive formatting and printing support
- Grammar checking and other advanced features
- Change tracking
- Lots of other rich document features

As a member in the Microsoft Office family, InfoPath works well with other Office applications. InfoPath comes with the following features:

- **Send as e-mail** You can send your form using Outlook. InfoPath supports Outlook envelopes.
- **Export as MHTML** MIME-encapsulated HTML (MHTML) files allow viewing by users who do not have InfoPath. You can export your forms as .mht files to your Web site or another location.
- **Export to Excel** Excel allows you to manipulate your form data in a spreadsheet so you can quickly perform data analysis with data from one or multiple forms.
- **Connect to Access** InfoPath comes with native support for databases, including Access databases.
- **Submit to Windows SharePoint Services** InfoPath works well with Windows SharePoint Services. When you use your InfoPath forms in SharePoint form libraries, you gain access to SharePoint list features such as sorting and filtering of data across multiple forms.

An Enterprise Business Client

InfoPath's native support for Web services, databases, SharePoint, and BizTalk make it a natural front end for enterprise business solutions. In fact, InfoPath was designed with the enterprise in mind. In addition to support for XML standards and data interoperability, InfoPath also comes with the following features for the enterprise:

- **SQL** InfoPath comes with native support for databases, including SQL server.
- **Secondary data sources** InfoPath connects to external data sources or configuration files in your solution. Secondary data sources are great for dynamically prepopulating drop-down lists, guidelines, and other content on your form that is not part of your form data.
- **Query and submit adapters** InfoPath comes with query and submit adapters, which enable easy integration with Web services, databases, and SharePoint.
- **Master-detail tables and sections** The master-detail control is a native InfoPath control that clarifies the display of repeating results from Web service and database queries.

- **User roles** InfoPath supports Active Directory. You can assign roles to users based on their credentials and use them to control the form display and business logic.
- **Digital signatures** You can sign all or part of your form using digital certificates.
- **Tablet PC** InfoPath understands ink images and lets you input forms using ink.
- **Human Workflow Services** InfoPath comes with native support for BizTalk's Human Workflow Services. You can build a workflow by defining actions in InfoPath and integrating with a BizTalk orchestration.

A .NET Programming Tool

InfoPath is a rich office client and a natural client for enterprise business processes, but with programming support for Microsoft Visual Studio .NET it's also a .NET development tool.

Nowadays, developers use XML in all kinds of ways, but configuration files are a common contingency. Applications everywhere use XML to store configuration information. InfoPath can be a natural editing tool for these configuration files.

If you have a Web service, database, or XML Schema, you can quickly create an InfoPath form to query and submit data. InfoPath understands XML Schemas, and using the designer you can rapidly design a form. Simply design a form from the Web service, database query, XML Schema (.xsd), or XML file. The designer will create a data source based on the respective WSDL document, SQL query, .xsd file, or XML file. Once you have a data source, you can drag and drop fields and controls into the view. InfoPath creates sections and controls based on the underlying schema. In fact, this support for *sniffing schemas* was the original inspiration behind XDocs, the code name for the precursor to InfoPath.

InfoPath, .NET Forms, and SharePoint Web Parts

The main advantage of using InfoPath as a tool to create forms is that it allows you to rapidly create a form and has native support for validation. The main disadvantage is availability. Each user must have InfoPath installed to fill out forms.

The same availability limitation will likely be the biggest barrier to the adoption of InfoPath in place of other forms technologies. In some scenarios, .NET forms (Windows Forms and Web forms) and SharePoint Web parts will still make more sense. The following list provides some comparisons:

Use InfoPath for rich client forms:

- Offline support
- Office user interface, interoperability

- Validation
- Spell checking
- Repeating sections
- Automatic update and version upgrade
- Secure sandbox for restricted-mode e-mail deployment

Use Windows Forms when you don't have InfoPath:

- Offline support
- Rapid prototyping environment
- Easier full trust deployment

Use Web forms for server-based solutions:

- Server-based deployment and security model

Use SharePoint Web parts for SharePoint solutions:

- Native support for SharePoint user interface
- Seamless integration with SharePoint site
- Hard to deploy, no sandbox

The Goals of This Book

The purpose of this book is to explain how to develop solutions using InfoPath. The programming projects involve various challenges, and the best solution will rely on various factors. This book presents multiple solutions for many of the programming tasks you will encounter, and it discusses the pros and cons of various solutions. The goal is to give you an understanding of when to use a particular solution for a particular problem.

InfoPath is a powerful platform with many components. Like any complex system, it has numerous undocumented gotchas. A secondary goal of this book is to present tips and tricks for some of the more obscure aspects of InfoPath. The Developer Nugget sidebars throughout the book highlight handy tips and tricks that are hard to find documented.

While we assume that you are a programmer, the examples in this book assume no prior programming knowledge. The examples target the Office developer and appear in Microsoft Visual Basic .NET or, when extending the included solutions, script. For the purposes of clarity, the code examples in the book do not contain robust error handling.

How This Book Is Organized

In Part I, we spend two chapters taking a whirlwind tour of InfoPath. Chapter 1 shows how to create a solution using the sample forms that ship with InfoPath. Chapter 2 shows how to build your first solution from scratch and add workflow and data connectors to make it ready for the enterprise.

Part II focuses on forms design. Chapter 3 shows how to create smart forms that dynamically interact with the user to reduce layout noise. Chapter 4 shows how to design rich forms to take advantage of the many powerful editing features in InfoPath. Chapter 5 explains how to leverage advanced controls for your form and extend your form with custom controls.

Part III focuses on the enterprise. Chapter 6 starts off by looking at database integration. In Chapter 7, you'll see how to hook up your forms to Web services. Chapter 8 details the trust and security model and how to deploy InfoPath forms. Chapter 9 covers SharePoint integration. Chapter 10 shows how to implement forms-based workflow using an end-to-end solution. Chapter 11 summarizes support for Microsoft BizTalk Server 2004.

Programming Prerequisites

Here's a list of what you need to program InfoPath. These are also the programming prerequisites for this book.

Windows Components

- **Windows XP Professional or Windows Server 2003** You can use InfoPath on Windows 2000 with Service Pack 3, but you need Windows XP Professional or Windows Server 2003 to develop solutions for it.
- **InfoPath** Office Professional Enterprise Edition 2003 includes InfoPath. You can also buy InfoPath 2003 by itself. Once you have InfoPath, be sure to update it to SP1. SP1 contains numerous feature enhancements for InfoPath and, more important, this book assumes that you have SP1.
- **Office 2003 Service Pack 1** Microsoft released the Office 2003 Service Pack 1 (SP1) on July 28, 2004, and this book assumes that you have it. If you haven't updated to SP1, visit the Microsoft Office Web site for more information: *http://office.microsoft.com/*. You do not need the entire Office suite to install the service pack; the service pack will automatically update InfoPath and other Office components you have installed.
- **Outlook** The e-mail workflow examples in Chapter 2 and Chapter 9 require Outlook 2003. InfoPath uses Outlook to send forms via e-mail.
- **Excel** The Export To Excel feature described in Chapter 2 and Chapter 9 requires Excel 2003.

- **Visual Studio .NET** The book includes programming samples created with Visual Studio .NET 2003. You can also use the standalone Visual Basic .NET 2003 or Visual C# .NET 2003 to create InfoPath templates with the .NET Framework. You will also need the .NET Framework 1.1. Form users need to have the .NET Framework installed for solutions which use .NET assemblies, but they do not need to install Visual Studio.
- **InfoPath 2003 Toolkit for Visual Studio .NET** This is a plug-in that works with Visual Studio .NET to help you create and manage InfoPath 2003 projects. You can download the tools from the following URL: *http://www.microsoft.com/downloads/details.aspx?familyid=7E9EBC57-E115-4CAC-9986-A712E22879BB&displaylang=en*.
- **Internet Information Services (IIS)** The Web services in Chapter 7 require IIS.

Other Server Software

InfoPath is an ideal enterprise business client. Enterprise business processes include middle-tier services and back-end servers. To get the most out of this book, you need access to servers running the following software:

- **SQL Server** Chapter 6 assumes that you have access to an installation of Microsoft SQL Server.
- **Windows SharePoint Services** InfoPath is designed to work well with SharePoint. Many chapters in this book include examples that involve SharePoint form libraries. Chapter 9 focuses on SharePoint integration.
- **BizTalk 2004** Chapter 11 requires an installation of BizTalk 2004.

Online Companion Content

The complete code for all of the examples in this book is available online, along with additional content including C# versions of some examples. You can download the companion content from the Web site at *http://www.microsoft.com/learning/books/7128*.

Share Your Experience

We have spent countless hours making sure that this book presents the most accurate and up-to-date information available, and we have strived to make this book easy to read. Of course, we have also tested our code! Nevertheless, as programmers we know that there will always be bugs. We would greatly appreciate any feedback you have on this book, the examples, and the code. Please send comments and bug reports to *book@infopathdev.com*.

Support

Microsoft Learning provides corrections for books through the World Wide Web at the following URL: *http://www.microsoft.com/learning/support/*.

If you have a question regarding this book, you can connect directly to the Microsoft Learning Knowledge Base and query to see if an answer exists. Go to *http://www.microsoft.com/learning/support/search.asp*.

You can also send comments, questions, or ideas regarding this book to Microsoft Learning:

Postal mail:

Microsoft Learning
Attn: *Developing Solutions with Microsoft InfoPath* Editor
One Microsoft Way
Redmond, WA 98052-6399

E-mail:

mspinput@microsoft.com

Please note that product support is not offered through these addresses. For support regarding Office 2003, Visual Studio .NET, or the .NET Framework, please visit the Microsoft Product Standard Support Web site at *http://support.microsoft.com/*.

Part I
Getting Started

Chapter 1

Customizing Sample Forms

In this first chapter, you'll learn how to use the sample forms that ship with InfoPath to build your first InfoPath solution. The goal of this chapter is to introduce you to the InfoPath forms technology. We'll create a form from the Meeting Agenda sample to help users organize and summarize meetings. The form captures meeting minutes and action items. We'll add controls to the form to make it useful in a common engineering scenario—the specification review meeting. You will publish your new InfoPath form to a file server. (Or you can publish it to SharePoint.) Publishing your sample form and then sending a notification e-mail to your teammates are the first steps in familiarizing yourself and your team with the InfoPath forms technology.

Choosing Among 25 Sample Forms

InfoPath ships with 25 sample forms that are designed to work "out of the box." You can easily deploy these sample forms as they are and start using InfoPath in your workplace. The sample forms are also good starting points for new solutions; for example, they are a good source for sample code snippets. The forms also illustrate general development techniques for schema design and form layout.

The InfoPath sample forms also come in the Office 2003 add-in: Web Parts and Components. If you install the add-in, you can create a form library based on one of these samples directly from the SharePoint user interface. Without the add-in, you can't create a form library from the SharePoint create page, but you can still do so from InfoPath by simply publishing a form.

Note In this book, a *form* can be either an InfoPath form template or the XML data file created using the form template, depending on the context. The form template describes the form and is encoded in a file package ending in the .xsn extension. The XML data file is a text file containing XML data.

The samples originally shipped with the initial release of InfoPath 2003. The InfoPath 2003 Service Pack, released in the summer of 2004 and available as a standalone retail product or bundled in Microsoft Office Professional Enterprise Edition, doesn't update the samples to include any of the new InfoPath features found in the Service Pack (for example, ActiveX controls, master-detail repeating tables, recursive sections, and file attachments). However, the fact that the samples are still based on the initial InfoPath 2003 release doesn't prevent you from customizing the forms to include Service Pack features, and in any case, the samples are still a great reference for how to build good InfoPath forms.

The InfoPath team developed the sample forms with two primary goals in mind: to appeal to a broad set of users and to cover important enterprise areas. As you can see in the following lists, the team succeeded in these two goals. The 25 forms cover familiar scenarios spread out over six enterprise categories.

Human Resources

- Absence Request
- Applicant Rating
- Performance Review
- Resume
- Status Report
- Timecard (Detailed)
- Timecard (Simple)

Finance and Accounting

- Asset Tracking
- Expense Report (Domestic)
- Expense Report (International)
- Sales Invoice (Multiple Tax Rates)
- Sales Invoice (Single Tax Rate)
- Vendor Information

Orders and Inventory

- Change Order
- Invoice Request
- Purchase Order
- Purchase Request
- Service Request

Meetings and Project

- Issue Tracking (Detailed)
- Issue Tracking (Simple)
- Meeting Agenda
- Project Plan

Travel and Maps

- Travel Itinerary
- Travel Request

Marketing

- Sales Report

Customizing a Sample Form

To see how easy it is to use the sample forms, let's quickly step through customizing and deploying a form. For this example, we'll target a topic close to our hearts: the ubiquitous specification review process. As you probably know, the formal process of developing quality software includes a design and specification phase, and the "spec" is the documented result of that phase. The spec is the set of requirements that code must meet, and software developers and quality assurance engineers care about the spec because it determines the features they will implement and test. Before the coding and testing officially begin, a review meeting typically takes place. The meeting is an opportunity for the stakeholders to raise questions, make comments, and sign off on the project requirements. The spec process is most successful when attendees have read the spec, scribbled their comments and questions on it, and brought the marked-up hard copy to the spec review meeting–so that's our scenario for this example. Which one of the 25 samples should we use?

Spec review meetings generate action items, so let's create a form to capture those action items. We'll derive our form from the Meeting Agenda sample; we'll modify its data source and view, and then deploy the form to a file share and notify our team of the new form. They'll start using InfoPath and thank us for the proactive introduction.

Let's get started. To find the samples, start InfoPath by choosing Start | All Programs | Microsoft Office and selecting the Microsoft Office InfoPath 2003 icon. InfoPath displays the default Fill Out A Form dialog box. This dialog box is the first thing to appear when you start InfoPath. If you haven't installed the service pack (or if you have disabled service pack features via the Advanced Settings tab of the Option dialog box), you'll see the display screen for the initial version of InfoPath 2003, which doesn't automatically greet you with the Fill Out A Form dialog box.

Caution As stated in the Introduction, this book assumes that you have installed the InfoPath Service Pack. If you turned off the service pack features to run in stealth V1 mode, you'll have to clear the Disable check box on the Advanced Settings tab of the Options dialog box. After you do that, don't forget to restart InfoPath.

To customize one of the sample forms, select the Sample Forms category in the Form Categories pane on the left. Then select the Meeting Agenda sample from the Sample Forms list. Finally, move your cursor to the Form Tasks pane, and hover over the Design This Form task. Figure 1-1 shows the dialog box after you prime it to load the Meeting Agenda sample.

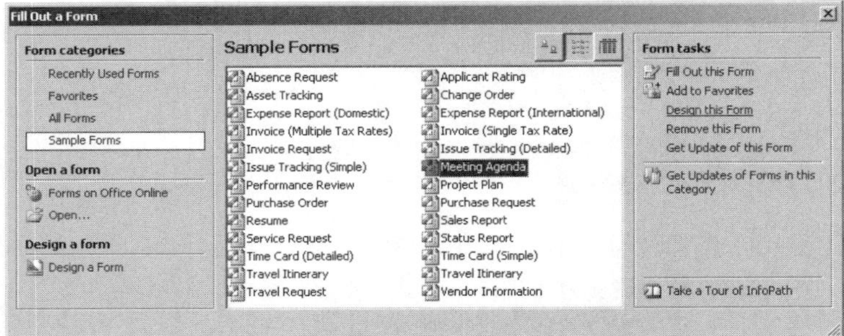

Figure 1-1 You can choose from 25 sample forms in the Fill Out A Form dialog box.

Selecting the Design This Form task causes the InfoPath Designer to open the Meeting Agenda form for customization. Figure 1-2 shows the initial load screen.

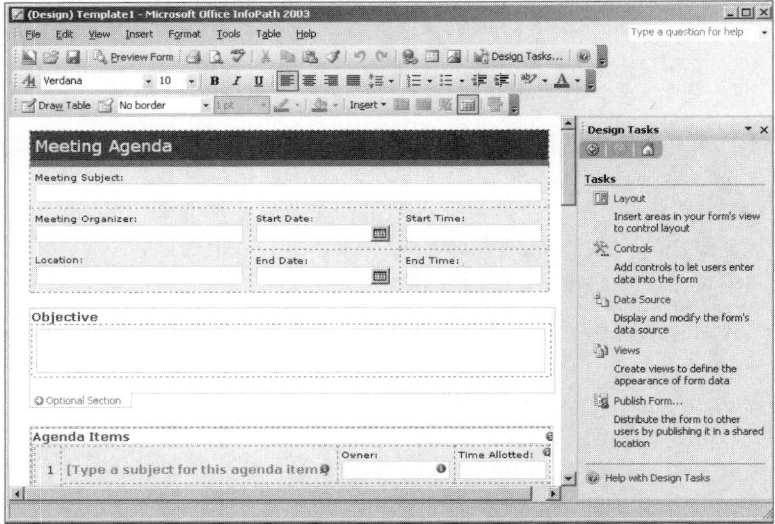

Figure 1-2 The Meeting Agenda form

> **Note** If you just double-click Meeting Agenda without using the Design This Form task, the form opens in editor mode, which lets you use the form but doesn't let you customize it. You can click the Design This Form button to customize it.

Working with Data Sources

Each form will have one main data source and zero or more secondary data sources. The main data source specifies the XML data for the form and corresponds to an XML schema stored in the form package. (See the sidebar "Cracking the Form Package" for more on how to explore the contents of the form package.) The schema specifies the structure and type of the form's data. When you edit and save a form, InfoPath uses the schema to verify and validate the form's contents.

Secondary data sources complement the XML data of your form. Your form can use these to prepopulate list boxes from a SharePoint list or to fill in a detailed section of your form with the results of a database query. The form template's .xsn file stores secondary data sources as resources. Secondary data sources are internal to the form template, but they are external to your form's XML schema. In other words, when you fill out a form, it doesn't include the data from the secondary data sources. Secondary data sources let you leverage existing data for use in your form without requiring that the data live inside the XML of your form. This data can come from a variety of sources.

How does InfoPath support data sources? When InfoPath opens in form design mode, Design Tasks is the default task pane. Click the Data Source link under the Tasks label and the task pane will display the Main data source for the form. Let's take a brief look at modifying the Main data source.

Modifying the Main Data Source

InfoPath allows you to add nodes to extensible schemas via the Add button in the Data Source pane. If this button is disabled, it means that either you haven't selected a node to extend or the schema isn't extensible. All sample forms have extensible schemas—that means they are designed so that you can add your own nodes to them. How is that done? Well, each extensible sequence block ends with an *xsd:any* element with a *namespace="##other"* attribute. Here's an example:

```
<xsd:sequence>
    <xsd:element name="participants" type="xsd:string"/>
    <xsd:element name="item" type="xsd:string"/>
    <xsd:element name="quantity" type="xsd:double" nillable="true"/>
    <xsd:element name="notes" type="mtg:xhtml"/>
    <xsd:element name="required" type="xsd:boolean"/>
    <xsd:any namespace="##other" minOccurs="0"
        maxOccurs="unbounded" processContents="lax"/>
</xsd:sequence>
```

Let's see what happens when the schema is extended. Select the *meetingAgenda* root node, and click the Add button. (If the Add button is disabled, it probably means you haven't selected the *meetingAgenda* node.) The Add Field Or Group dialog box appears, as shown in Figure 1-3.

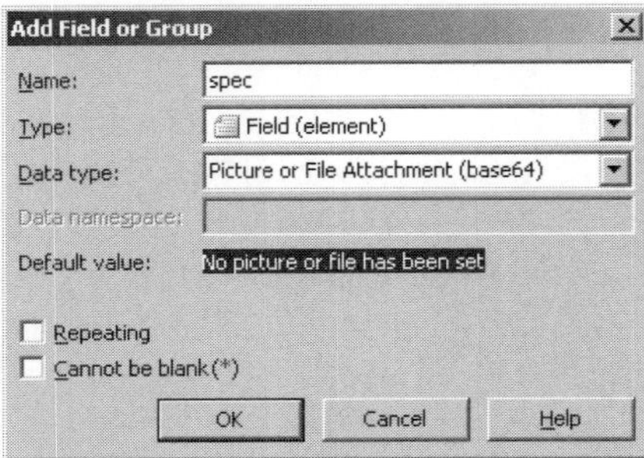

Figure 1-3 The Add Field Or Group dialog box supports extending existing schemas.

Type **spec** in the Name field, and select the Picture Or File Attachment (Base64) value in the Data Type list box. Click OK to accept the other defaults. While we're at it, let's add a node named *project* in the same way. Type **project** in the Name field, and select Text (String) for its Data Type. Congratulations! You just extended the schema with two new nodes–but where did they go? If you examine the data source pane by scrolling to the bottom, you'll see that InfoPath added two nodes–*my:spec* and *my:project*–at the end of the list. Figure 1-4 shows what this should look like.

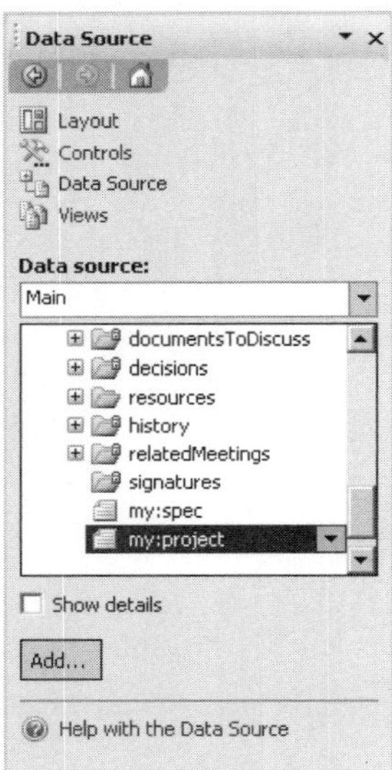

Figure 1-4 When you extend a sample schema, new fields appear at the bottom of the selected data source section.

Notice that the new elements have the *my* namespace prefix. The samples that ship with Info-Path come with predefined namespaces. Customized forms based on the samples don't need to specify a schema. (In Chapter 8, we'll go over methods of deployment in detail.) When you extend the Meeting Agenda sample, InfoPath doesn't change the default schema at *http://schemas.microsoft.com/office/infopath/2003/sample/MeetingAgenda*. On the contrary, it creates a new schema that imports the schema from the sample. So, the namespace for Meeting Agenda remains *http://schemas.microsoft.com/office/infopath/2003/sample/MeetingAgenda*. And the new namespace for the schema in your customized form becomes something like *http://schemas.microsoft.com/office/infopath/2004/myXSD/2004-02-02T22:44:37*. InfoPath generates the namespace based on the current date and time.

When you create a form template from scratch using the form designer—that is, when you drag controls onto a form and create a data source on the fly—InfoPath marks the resulting schema as fully editable. *Fully editable* means that you can extend, delete, or rename any node in the schema. When you make changes to the form's data source, InfoPath updates the schema in place and stores the resulting changes in a single .xsd file without change history.

Fully editable schemas can lead to upgrade problems. Suppose you create and publish a form template but later decide to change or delete fields in its data source. What happens to forms created with the original template? These forms won't open in InfoPath because they will be incompatible with the new data source. If the new form results from a field addition, where the field accepts nil values, you can still open forms created using the original template. In the case of a change or deletion, InfoPath solves the versioning problem by providing a custom version upgrade feature for your forms.

However, if the XML form came from an external process that relied on a specific schema, the upgrade feature might not work because it upgrades only forms edited in InfoPath and won't interoperate with external processes. To handle this scenario, InfoPath doesn't modify the contents of a schema if the form started from an existing external schema. We call form templates created from an existing schema *noneditable*, and form templates created from scratch using the designer, *editable*. The sample forms are noneditable—they use predefined schemas. You can still extend noneditable schemas if they are open and use the XSD *any* element wildcard. In other words, InfoPath supports extending open schema; a schema is open if it contains *xsd:any* elements. InfoPath creates an additional schema file to contain extensions.

You might be wondering where all of these schema files are in the form template. The upcoming Developer Nugget describes how you can extract the files from your form template and examine these settings.

InfoPath has extensive support for XML schemas. You can change the namespace prefix for your schema, and you can import preexisting schemas to use with InfoPath. We'll explore more schema customization topics around deployment in Chapter 8.

Developer Nugget: Cracking the Form Package

InfoPath saves a form in a file with an .xsn file extension (from XML SolutioN). This is a compressed format (.cab) file that packages all the form files together for easier deployment. You can see the contents by simply renaming the extension from .xsn to .cab and double-clicking the file. Another easy way to see the contents is to use the File | Extract Form Files menu option from within the designer.

Form packages contain the following files:

- **Manifest (.xsf) files** A file ending in .xsf (by default named "manifest") describes the entire form. This is an XML file that declares all of the files, views, schemas, sample data, data adapters, editing components, business logic events, data validation, and other optional settings for the form (such as SharePoint form library properties or Merge Form options). Microsoft publishes the schema for this file online at *http://www.microsoft.com/office/xml/default.mspx.*
- **View (.xsl) files** Files ending in .xsl usually correspond to a unique view in the solution. InfoPath auto-generates the first view file and names it View1. Initially, View1 is the default view, but you can change the default view via the right-click menu in the Select A View list. InfoPath names all other views based on the name of the view. For example, if you name your view *foo*, then the view will be foo.xsl. These view files contain the XSL (Extensible Stylesheet Language) that is applied to the data to render the HTML view. An .xsl file also includes references to special controls that only InfoPath supports (for example, date pickers).
- **Business logic files (.js or .vbs for script; .cs or .vb for managed code)** A file ending in .js or .vbs contains script business logic for the form. By default, InfoPath names the first script file script.js, but your form won't have that file unless the form includes logic. You can also add additional files and name them anything, but you will have to manually update the *<xsf:scripts/>* block in the manifest to include the additional files. For example, common.js could be a file that includes the common script shared throughout your forms. You can't mix managed code and script languages, and InfoPath only loads a single scripting engine, which means that you can't support mixed language script either. For forms that use script, InfoPath automatically generates a file named internal.js (or internal.vbs), which contains logic that controls view switching.

  Managed code projects in Visual Studio .NET 2003 include .cs or .vb files in C# or Visual Basic .NET, respectively. Chapter 2 steps through an example InfoPath project using managed code.
- **Schema (.xsd) files** A file ending in .xsd describes the XML schema for the solution. For a form created in the designer from scratch, InfoPath automatically generates a file and names it myschema.xsd. If multiple data sources are included in the solution, there might be more than one .xsd file (depending on the data sources), but by default only one corresponds to the main data source.

- **Sample data (.xml) files** A file ending in .xml describes the default data for the form. By default, there are two data files, sampledata.xml and template.xml. The sampledata.xml file contains sample data for each data source. It isn't valid against the form's underlying schema, and InfoPath uses it only at design time. Don't edit this file outside of InfoPath. The template.xml file describes the seed data for the form when users open it in the editor.
- **Image (.gif, .bmp, etc.) files** A file ending in .gif, .bmp, jpg, or .png includes an image to display in the form's view or in the InfoPath task pane.
- **Task pane (.htm, .xsl, etc.) file** If the form includes a custom task pane, an .htm file will likely describe its presentation, but the form may also include other files—such as .xsl files—to render the task pane.
- **Merge form (.xsl and .xsd) files** Forms that support merging with other forms include additional .xsl and .xsd files. The .xsl files are for transforming the incoming XML form into the XML for the existing form. The .xsd files are schemas used to validate the files prior to merging.
- **Upgrade form (.xsl) files** The form might include a file that describes how to upgrade from previous versions. By default, InfoPath generates a file named upgrade.xsl, which can be manually modified to support custom upgrade scenarios.

Adding a Data Source

You can add a secondary data source to your form by using the Tools menu. Before doing this, type the following code into your favorite Notepad-like editor and save it as projects.xml:

```
<?xml version="1.0" encoding="UTF-8"?>
<Projects xml:lang="en-us">
    <ProjectName>Deploy InfoPath 2003</ProjectName>
    <ProjectName>Create Form Libraries on SharePoint</ProjectName>
    <ProjectName>Install BizTalk 2004 Server</ProjectName>
    <ProjectName>Install SharePoint Adapter for BizTalk</ProjectName>
    <ProjectName>Install InfoPath Pipeline Tool for BizTalk</ProjectName>
</Projects>
```

From the Tools menu, choose Data Connections, and click the Add button to start the Data Connection Wizard. Select Receive Data, and click Next. Since this is an XML file, leave XML Document selected and click the Next button again. Enter the location of the file you created. Finally, click the Finish button. InfoPath asks you if you want to add the file to the form. This is important because if the file isn't part of the form, other people might not have access to it. Click Yes. You have just added a secondary data source. Figure 1-5 displays the result. Click Close to return to the form.

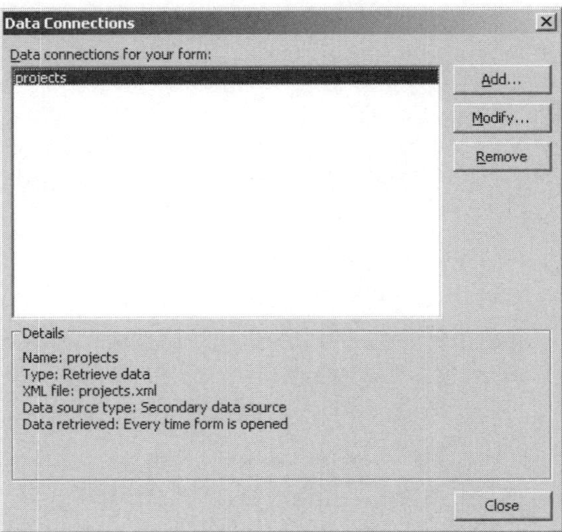

Figure 1-5 Using the Data Connections dialog box to add secondary data sources

Modifying the View

Now that you have added a data source to the form, the next step is to add controls to the view. The controls display the form's data. We'll add the link to the spec at the beginning of the form to make sure attendees don't overlook it.

In fact, let's delete the text box bound to the *subject* node, which appears just after the Meeting Subject label, and add our new *my:spec* element in its place. Click the text box and delete it. Right-click the *my:spec* node in the data source pane, and choose File Attachment. Now edit the existing label text "Meeting Subject:" to read "Please read the following document before the meeting!" Change the color of this label to red to make it stand out to your users.

For the project's secondary data source, insert a Drop-Down List Box control before the Objective section. First position the cursor in the Objective section just above the label of the same name. Go to the Data Source, and select the *my:project* field; then click the down arrow to display a list of controls. Choose Drop-Down List Box from this list. Press Enter afterward to move the Objectives label down to the next line. You have just added a drop-down list box to the view. You can also do this by switching from the Data Source to the Controls task pane and dragging and dropping the appropriate controls directly from the task pane. However, if your schema is editable when you do this, InfoPath will create a new node in your form's Main data source. You can easily change the binding of your control to the desired XML node, but you will be left with an extra node in your form. You can delete this extra node by right-clicking it in the task pane and choosing Delete.

To bind this to the secondary data source, double-click the control to bring up the Drop-Down List Box Properties page. Select the Look Up Values In A Data Connection option. Be sure to select Projects for the Data Connection list box. You'll also see an Add button for adding a data source. If you click it, the same dialog box we saw earlier (via the Tools | Data Connections| Add operation) appears. This button is quite handy to have on the Drop-Down List Box Properties page because you don't have to remember to add the data source in advance. We'll ignore it now, though, because you already added the data source. Click the button to the right of the Entries field, and choose the *ProjectName* node underneath the *Projects* root. Refer to Figure 1-6.

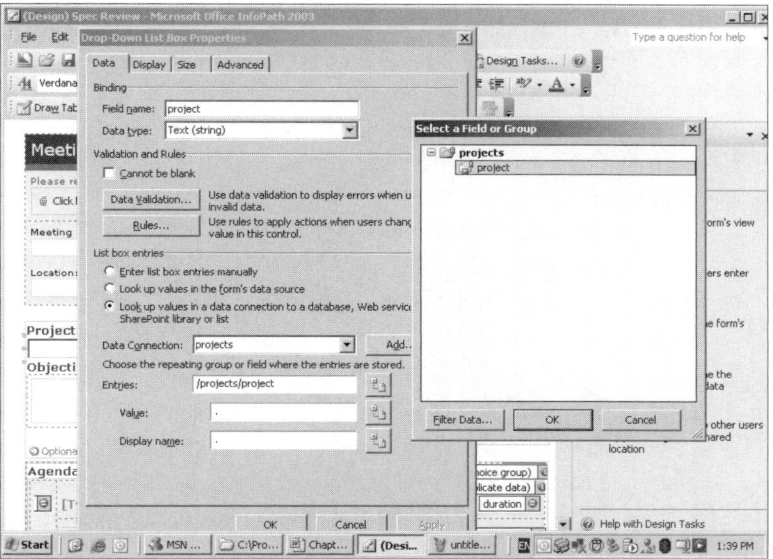

Figure 1-6 Attaching a secondary data source to a drop-down list box

Click OK twice to close the open dialog boxes, and return to the view. Now let's make one final modification and change the title of the form from "Meeting Agenda" to "Spec Review–Meeting Agenda." Remember that you can use Ctrl+Z to undo any overzealous edits. When you're done, the top of your view should look something like that shown in Figure 1-7.

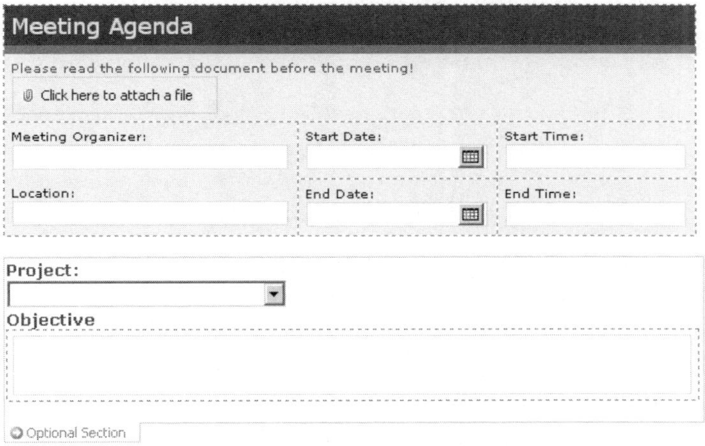

Figure 1-7 A customized sample form

Developer Nugget: Multiple Views

InfoPath forms support multiple views. You can use multiple views in a variety of ways. For example, you can use them to implement simple workflow–each view corresponds to a separate step in the business process. Multiple views can reduce the complexity of the form by creating sections that are filled out in a sequence. The Meeting Agenda sample form contains two views (bonus points if you discovered the second view). We've been modifying only the first one, named Meeting Agenda. If, by chance, you switched to the Meeting Minutes view, the banner will be green. We'll discuss a variety of forms in this book, and many will include multiple views.

Examining the Form

This section introduces three techniques for examining forms. Using the form you just modified, we'll show how to preview the form from within the InfoPath designer; then we'll save the form and fill it out from the InfoPath editor. Finally, we'll use Notepad to examine the XML data that results from filling out a form in the editor.

Previewing the Form

While still in the designer, you can test the form by choosing Preview Form | Default from the File menu or by typing Ctrl+Shift+B (for those of you who enjoy using keyboard accelerators). You can also use the Preview Form button on the toolbar. Don't forget to try the Send Meeting Agenda button at the bottom of the form. This handy button is linked to code that brings up an envelope allowing you to send the form via e-mail.

Previewing the form is a convenient way to test and debug the form while you are still designing it, but the InfoPath designer doesn't support all of the features of the editor. To truly test the form, you have to save the form and open it with the InfoPath editor. Choose Save As from the File menu. A dialog box will appear with two options: Publish and Save. Click Save, and then click the Desktop icon in the left pane. Type **Spec Review** in the Filename field and click Save. After you have saved your form template, close the InfoPath designer.

Editing the Form

Double-clicking the Spec Review .xsn file on your desktop launches the InfoPath editor. The editor supports all form features. In particular, the following features weren't available in preview mode:

- **Export To Web** Export To Web lets you save your form as an .mht file. These files are saved in Microsoft Office HTML format. You can use the .mht files on your Web site for viewers who don't have InfoPath installed.
- **Export To Excel** InfoPath supports exporting your forms to Microsoft Excel. From the File menu, choose Export To | Microsoft Office Excel. We will introduce the Export To Excel feature in Chapter 4.
- **Merge Forms** Merge Forms is also available from the File menu. Export To Excel and Export To Web provide two ways to export forms. Merge Forms supports importing forms. Using Merge Forms, you can aggregate form content–a process commonly referred to as "roll-up." You can also implement simple workflow. Chapter 2 gives a simple example of Merge Forms. We will examine it in depth in Chapter 8.
- **Submit, Send To Mail Recipient** In general, InfoPath disables *submit* data adapters in preview mode. This includes the Submit and Send To Mail Recipient options on the File menu. However, InfoPath does support *retrieve* data adapters in preview mode–for example, you can query a Web service, database, or SharePoint list.
- **Save, and Save As** The Preview feature in the designer supports entering data, but to save it out as XML you have to use the editor. The next section examines the results of saving a form.
- **Open** Open is disabled, but the File | Preview Form | With Data File option on the menu supports previewing your form with a sample .xml file. You can use File | Preview Form | With User Role to test the form for a specific user. The Book Purchase example in Chapter 2 introduces you to user roles.

Note About user roles and view switching: when you preview the form, InfoPath always shows the view that is currently open in the designer. If you have a form with multiple views and a rule to automatically switch to a non-default view on load depending on the user's role, that rule will not be executed when you preview and as a result you won't see the other view. Remember that Preview Form always shows the currently open view. If you want to test user roles, don't forget to choose the menu option Preview Form | With User Role.

Form Contents

InfoPath saves your forms in plain XML. Let's take a look at the contents of a form file. First enter your name in the Meeting Organizer field of the Spec Review form, and save it to your desktop as Form1.xml. Right-click on this file and choose Open With | Notepad. Figure 1-8 shows the file in Notepad. For readability, we've placed each of the processing instructions (PIs) on a separate line.

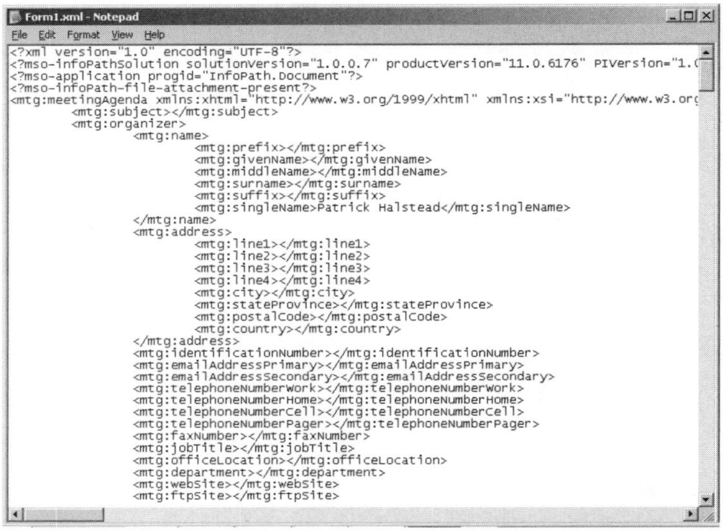

```
Form1.xml - Notepad
File Edit Format View Help
<?xml version="1.0" encoding="UTF-8"?>
<?mso-infoPathSolution solutionVersion="1.0.0.7" productVersion="11.0.6176" PIVersion="1.(
<?mso-application progid="InfoPath.Document"?>
<?mso-infoPath-file-attachment-present?>
<mtg:meetingAgenda xmlns:xhtml="http://www.w3.org/1999/xhtml" xmlns:xsi="http://www.w3.org
        <mtg:subject></mtg:subject>
        <mtg:organizer>
                <mtg:name>
                        <mtg:prefix></mtg:prefix>
                        <mtg:givenName></mtg:givenName>
                        <mtg:middleName></mtg:middleName>
                        <mtg:surname></mtg:surname>
                        <mtg:suffix></mtg:suffix>
                        <mtg:singleName>Patrick Halstead</mtg:singleName>
                </mtg:name>
                <mtg:address>
                        <mtg:line1></mtg:line1>
                        <mtg:line2></mtg:line2>
                        <mtg:line3></mtg:line3>
                        <mtg:line4></mtg:line4>
                        <mtg:city></mtg:city>
                        <mtg:stateProvince></mtg:stateProvince>
                        <mtg:postalCode></mtg:postalCode>
                        <mtg:country></mtg:country>
                </mtg:address>
                <mtg:identificationNumber></mtg:identificationNumber>
                <mtg:emailAddressPrimary></mtg:emailAddressPrimary>
                <mtg:emailAddressSecondary></mtg:emailAddressSecondary>
                <mtg:telephoneNumberWork></mtg:telephoneNumberWork>
                <mtg:telephoneNumberHome></mtg:telephoneNumberHome>
                <mtg:telephoneNumberCell></mtg:telephoneNumberCell>
                <mtg:telephoneNumberPager></mtg:telephoneNumberPager>
                <mtg:faxNumber></mtg:faxNumber>
                <mtg:jobTitle></mtg:jobTitle>
                <mtg:officeLocation></mtg:officeLocation>
                <mtg:department></mtg:department>
                <mtg:webSite></mtg:webSite>
                <mtg:ftpSite></mtg:ftpSite>
```

Figure 1-8 Using Notepad to inspect your form's XML data

This book assumes familiarity with XML, and with the exception of three PIs, InfoPath saves your form in standard XML. The three PIs in question all begin with the *mso* prefix, which stands for Microsoft Office.

Processing Instructions Specific to InfoPath

```
<?mso-infoPathSolution solutionVersion="1.0.0.7" productVersion="11.0.6176"
PIVersion="1.0.0.0" href="file:///C:\work\book\01%20-
%20Customizing%20Sample%20Forms\Spec%20Review.xsn" name="urn:schemas-microsoft-
com:office:infopath:Spec-Review:-sample-MeetingAgenda" ?>
<?mso-application progid="InfoPath.Document"?>
<?mso-infoPath-file-attachment-present?>
```

InfoPath requires only two of these PIs to open the file. The last one, *mso-infoPath-file-attachment-present*, is needed only for forms that include file attachments. The *mso-application* PI is used to start InfoPath. If you change the *progid* attribute from *InfoPath.Document* to *Word.Document*, the form opens as a smart document in Word 2003. Figure 1-9 shows what you see.

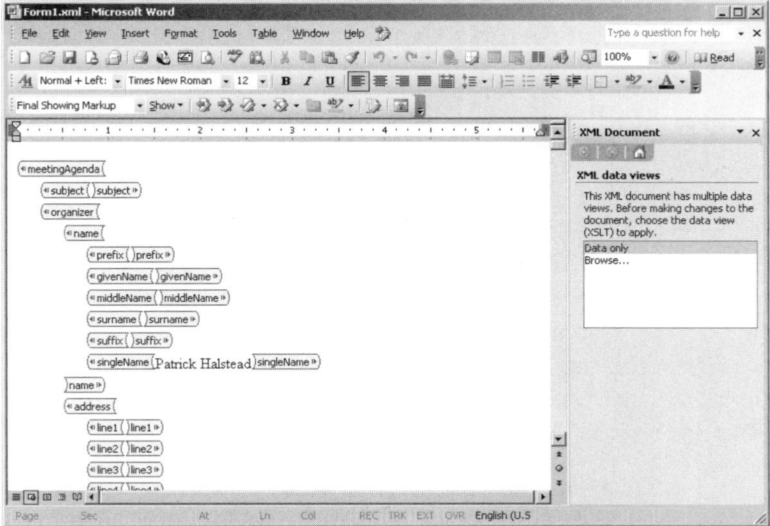

Figure 1-9 Word 2003 opens forms saved from InfoPath as XML smart documents.

InfoPath parses the *mso-infoPathSolution* PI to determine which form template (sometimes called a *solution*) to load. The following five attributes control how InfoPath loads your form. Brief descriptions follow:

- **solutionVersion** This attribute refers to the version of the form template used to save the form. Form templates can be updated and upgraded. Each time a form is saved, the InfoPath designer increments the version number. In our example, the *solutionVersion* is the string value *1.0.0.7*, which implies that the form was updated, or saved, seven times. You can reset or change the version number in the designer via the Tools | Form Options | Advanced property page.
- **productVersion** This attribute refers to the version of InfoPath that was used to create the form template. InfoPath version numbers correspond to Office version numbers. In our example, the *productVersion* is the string value *11.0.6176*, which corresponds to Office build 11 and InfoPath build 6176, dated January 26, 2004.
- **PIVersion** For future extensibility and backward compatibility, the PI itself is versioned. If a sixth attribute is added in the future, InfoPath can use the *PIVersion* attribute to correctly parse the PI.
- **href** The *href* attribute identifies he URL of the form template. You can use this handy attribute to determine where InfoPath saved (or published) the form template.
- **name** The *name* attribute encodes the URN of the form template. If the form template has been sent via e-mail and the recipient doesn't have access to the URL, the URN is used to identify the solution and allow the e-mail recipient to open the form. If the URL becomes accessible in the future, InfoPath can reconcile the form to it. Coupled with the *href* attribute, the *name* attribute is very useful for debugging.

Developer Nugget: Refreshing the Form Template

Recall that we added the projects.xml document as a secondary data source to the form. Suppose you want to add an additional ProjectName to the projects.xml document. It's as easy as editing the file, right? The answer is yes and no.

Assuming that you have your form open in the designer, the first step is to use the Extract Form Files command on the File menu to save the form. This expands the .xsn package and saves the form as separate files. You can then edit the file in place by using your favorite Notepad-like editor. Before you save your edits, you'll need to close the designer to release its write lock on your form files. However, you aren't out of the woods yet–InfoPath caches the forms on your computer, and the caching algorithm doesn't refresh the form unless the manifest.xsf changes. Try it and you'll see that the drop-down list box doesn't display your changes. You can work around this problem in several ways:

- Remove the form template from the Fill Out A Form dialog box. The first dialog box to appear when you start InfoPath is the Fill Out A Form dialog box (which you saw earlier in Figure 1-1). The dialog box has an option to show All Forms registered for you. You can select a form and remove it by clicking Remove This Form in the right pane. Removing the form deletes it from your cache. The next time you open it, InfoPath updates the cache with a fresh version. Deleting the form from the cache via the dialog box is the preferred way to update the cache for it can be used even if you have hand-edited the .xsl view files whereas resaving the form in the designer (next option) may strip out your changes.
- Open the form template in the InfoPath designer and make any edits in the view; for example, you can type a space and then backspace (to delete it). A simple view edit marks the form template for saving. Then save the form template. InfoPath updates the manifest.xsf. This is the easiest solution.
- Remove and then add the resource file. This forces InfoPath to reload it with the new data. This is a good solution for anyone who is familiar with the form but feels uncomfortable editing the view, and it is essential if the XML structure changed in a way that requires InfoPath to create a new schema. InfoPath creates a new schema only the first time it loads a resource.
- Touch the manifest file. You must extract the files first. Open the manifest.xsf file in Notepad and resave it (Ctrl+S).

InfoPath uses the forms cache to enable offline forms usage and to maintain your recently used and favorite form settings. You might be tempted to delete the cache to a clean state for one form, but this is a radical step. It's much easier to simply remove the cached entry for the problematic form using the Fill Out A Form dialog box. Deleting the entire cache will have the unintended effect of removing all of your offline forms as well as your form settings. Manually tweaking the cache can also cause corruption. For those reasons, we recommend that you steer clear of direct interaction with the cache via the file system. In fact, we won't even tell you where the cache lives or how to delete it.

Publishing the Form

InfoPath supports several mechanisms for deploying forms to your team. You can use a Web server, a shared folder, or a full-blown SharePoint server. For collaborators outside of your intranet, you can send the form using e-mail. Chapter 8 describes these deployment mechanisms and shows several real-world scenarios. For this introductory example, let's take a look at two deployment scenarios: using a shared folder and using SharePoint.

Using a Shared Folder

When you're ready to publish your form, choose Publish from the File menu in the designer (File | Save As, and then Publish will also do the trick.) This brings up the Publishing Wizard. After the initial screen, you'll be presented with three options. Select the first option to publish to a shared folder, and then enter a UNC path where you want to publish your form. The UNC path is a publicly accessible path on your computer's domain to the shared folder where you want to publish your form. End the path with the name of your form. You must have write access to this location. Figure 1-10 shows this dialog box. The wizard presents the option of sending out e-mail notifications to your team to announce the newly published form.

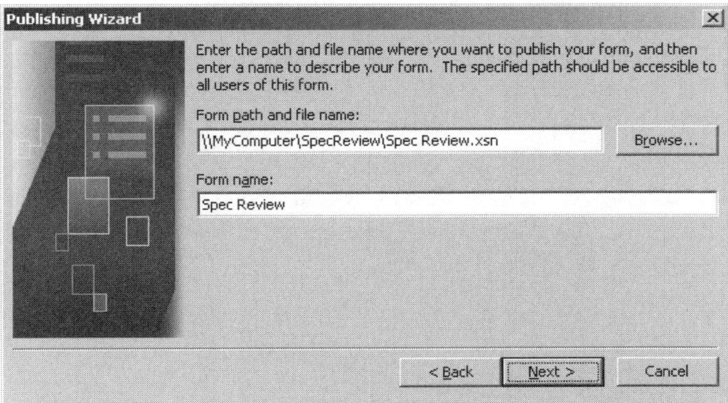

Figure 1-10 The Publishing Wizard simplifies form deployment.

Using SharePoint

Windows SharePoint Services (SharePoint) comes with a new kind of document library, called a form library, which supports XML-based business forms. That means SharePoint works great with InfoPath. It's easy to create a form library and take advantage of SharePoint's new XML support. From a SharePoint Web site, click the Create button at the top of the page. Figure 1-11 shows the result. Notice that Form Library appears at the top of the list, just under Document Library.

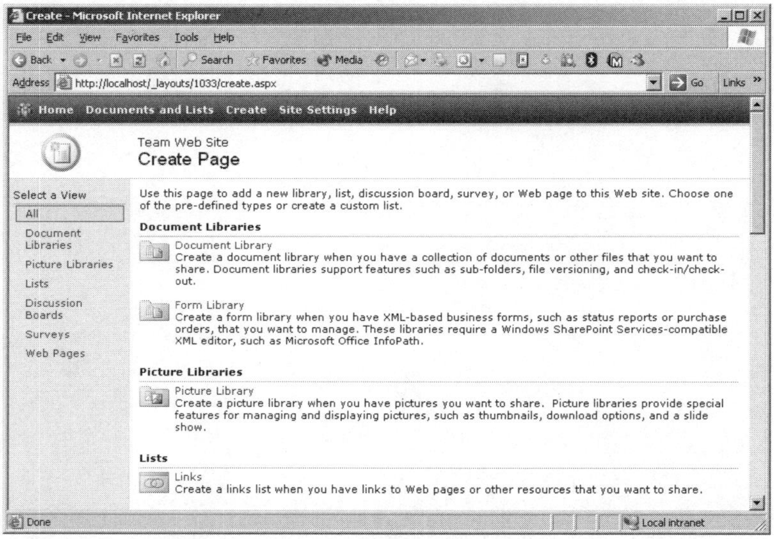

Figure 1-11 Creating InfoPath form libraries from SharePoint

In addition to all of the cool SharePoint collaboration features, form libraries support the following unique features:

- **Promoted fields** SharePoint extracts data from the fields in your form and displays it in the form library columns. SharePoint promotes data from subsequently saved forms automatically. This feature lets you create custom lists of the important data in your forms. You can then use SharePoint's built-in filtering and sorting functionality to quickly take account of the saved forms and determine which ones require your input and action.
- **Aggregation functions** These functions apply to promoted fields. If you have a collection of items in a repeating section or if your promoted field is rich text, you can choose one of the following aggregation functions:
    - First–displays the first item in the collection
    - Last–displays the last item in the collection
    - Count–displays a count of the number of items in the collection
    - Merge–displays a concatenated string of items from a collection
    - Sum–displays sum of items from a numeric collection
    - Average–displays the average of items from a numeric collection
    - Min–displays the smallest item from a numeric collection
    - Max–displays the largest item from a numeric collection
    - PlainText–extracts the plain text portion of the rich text field

> **Note** Unfortunately, form libraries don't support promoting images. If your form includes an image, you can't display it in your SharePoint list. However, you can customize your SharePoint list to promote a thumbnail representation of an image in your form, as we'll discuss in Chapter 9.

- **Merge Forms** This is a custom SharePoint view for form libraries. From this view, you can select multiple forms for merging. Clicking the Merge Forms button loads InfoPath and creates a summary form for the selected forms.
- **Samples** As noted earlier, the Office 2003 add-in: Web Parts and Components comes with the 25 InfoPath samples.

Creating a Form Library from InfoPath

From the File menu, choose Publish to open the Publishing Wizard. In the second step, select the second option to publish your form to a SharePoint form library. The next page asks you to choose between creating a new form library and modifying an existing one. Select the first option, Create A New Form Library. Enter the name of your SharePoint server. The wizard will verify that the SharePoint server exists and then ask you to name the new form library. The final page lets you configure the promoted field data that SharePoint displays in the form library columns upon receiving a form. Figure 1-12 shows what this screen looks like for our Spec Review form.

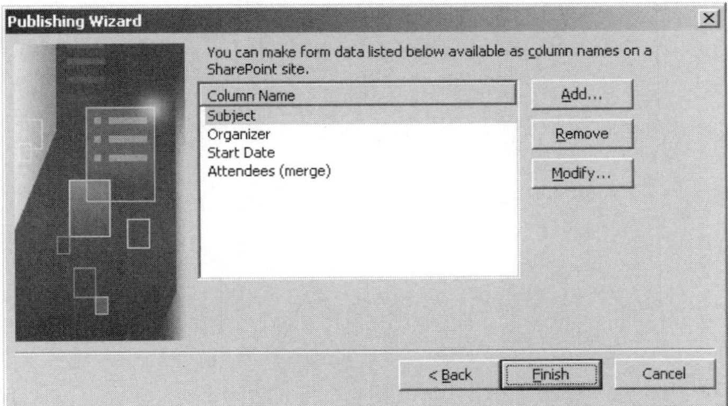

Figure 1-12 You can display data from your InfoPath forms in SharePoint form library columns.

Let's modify the field data that InfoPath promotes to the SharePoint form library columns. Select the Attendees (Merge) column, and click the Modify button. The Select A Field Or Group dialog box appears. This field is a collection, so the bottom of the dialog box displays a drop-down list from which you can select an aggregation function. Change the aggregation from merge to count. Click OK, and then click Finish. Instead of concatenating the attendee names, the logic in the SharePoint form library will now display the total number of attendees.

Summary

This chapter has provided a quick tour of InfoPath. You learned how to customize a sample form by modifying the data source and view. We explored secondary data sources and discussed publishing to SharePoint. In the process, we took a closer look at several developer nuggets. You got a brief overview on the contents of the forms package. And we discussed how caching can affect your InfoPath form.

In the next chapter, we'll dig deeper and discuss extending InfoPath with code, creating workflow between InfoPath forms, and hooking up with Web services.

Chapter 2

Creating and Using Forms

In this chapter, we'll continue our tour of InfoPath features with an introduction to application logic (yes, coding!), simple workflow, and data connections. We'll begin by using the "Hello World" program to illustrate how InfoPath integrates with Microsoft Visual Studio .NET 2003 and Microsoft Visual Basic .NET. Then we'll explore InfoPath programming further by introducing you to InfoPath event handlers. Event handlers are the key entry points to your form's application logic. We'll create a form and add code to the *OnLoad* event handler that populates a field in your form with the logged-in user. You'll see how to do this in both Visual Basic .NET and VBScript.

We'll take a look at enterprise scenarios by examining three ways to easily implement workflow in InfoPath. First you'll see how to use rules and user roles to control the common user actions of opening and submitting forms. The second workflow example shows how to implement roll-up using the Merge Forms feature. The third workflow example shows how to export form data to Microsoft Excel for advanced reporting and analysis.

Our tour of InfoPath features will continue with a section on data connections. We'll show how to prepopulate data and drop-down lists in your form from a database, a Web service, and a SharePoint list. Connecting to data sources and enabling form workflow are important features for enterprise forms, and InfoPath is uniquely positioned to handle enterprise forms for business processes.

Writing Application Logic

You can write application logic to extend your InfoPath forms. Application logic is code that responds to events in the user interface (UI) and data source of the form. For example, when you click a button, InfoPath fires an *OnClick* event. If the button has an *OnClick* event handler defined, it is then processed. By implementing the *OnClick* event handler, you can intercept the event and take some action. You can also implement event handlers that InfoPath calls when the data changes–for example, *OnAfterChange*.

InfoPath 2003 supports writing application logic in VBScript and JScript. The SP1 release of InfoPath added support for managed code–both C# and Visual Basic .NET. SP1 also comes with a Visual Studio .NET 2003 plug-in called Visual Studio Toolkit for InfoPath 2003. If you install this plug-in, you can use Visual Studio's integrated development environment (IDE) to program InfoPath, and that means you get important features such as IntelliSense and native debugging support. If you don't have the full edition of Visual Studio .NET 2003, the plug-in will work with Visual Basic .NET Standard or Visual C# .NET Standard. Managed code is the future of software development for the Microsoft Office system, and most of the examples in this book will use it. This chapter offers a brief introduction to both managed code and script programming support in InfoPath.

Managed Code Support

Let's take a look at InfoPath's support for managed code by using the well-worn introductory Hello World programming example that displays "Hello World" text. For our Hello World program, we'll add a button to our form and use an *OnClick* event handler. When the user clicks the button, we'll display the nirvana-inducing Hello World dialog box. Then, to provide a little extra insight, we'll extend the form. To illustrate how InfoPath's forms technology works, we'll add two common fields to our form, Name and Date. The form will use an *OnAfterChange* event for a check box to show how to automatically fill in the Name field. In addition, we'll use the *today()* function to prepopulate the Date field. As we step through this programming example, we'll use IntelliSense to browse the InfoPath object model and use debugging support to set breakpoints. InfoPath's support for managed code means that you can use the full power of Visual Studio .NET to develop your form applications.

Note To use managed code in InfoPath, you must first have Visual Basic .NET Standard or Visual C# .NET Standard (Visual Studio includes both) and the InfoPath plug-in for it installed on your computer. As mentioned in the Introduction, the InfoPath plug-in is called InfoPath 2003 Toolkit for Visual Studio .NET. It is available on the Microsoft Web site and can be downloaded from the following URL: http://www.microsoft.com/downloads/details.aspx?familyid=7E9EBC57-E115-4CAC-9986-A712E22879BB&displaylang=en.

Start Visual Studio .NET, and choose File | New | Project to open the New Project dialog box (shown in Figure 2-1) . If you have SP1 and the Visual Studio plug-in installed, you will see a new project type called Microsoft Office InfoPath Projects. Two languages are available underneath it–Visual Basic and Visual C#. As shown in the figure, each project corresponds to an InfoPath form template. Name your project **Hello World**, and then click OK to proceed to the next dialog box.

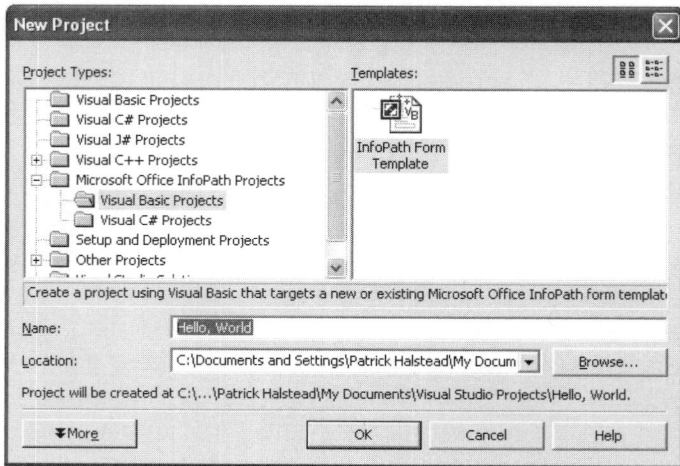

Figure 2-1 Download the InfoPath 2003 Toolkit for Visual Studio .NET from Microsoft's Web site.

You can migrate an existing InfoPath form into a Visual Studio managed project. Figure 2-2 shows the Visual Studio dialog box that lets you associate an existing form template with your new Visual Studio project.

> **Note** InfoPath doesn't support mixed-mode programming—you can't use both unmanaged script and managed code in your form. If your existing InfoPath form contains script, InfoPath disconnects the script from the form when you migrate it to Visual Studio. However, the script file remains in the solution for reference purposes. The converted form no longer binds to script, but to managed code. When you've finished porting the script to managed code, you might want to remove the script file and its associated *xsf:file* reference in the manifest.xsf file from your project.

For now, select the first option, Create A New Form Template. When you click Finish to create your project, you see a flurry of activity as Visual Studio creates a new project and launches InfoPath in Design mode.

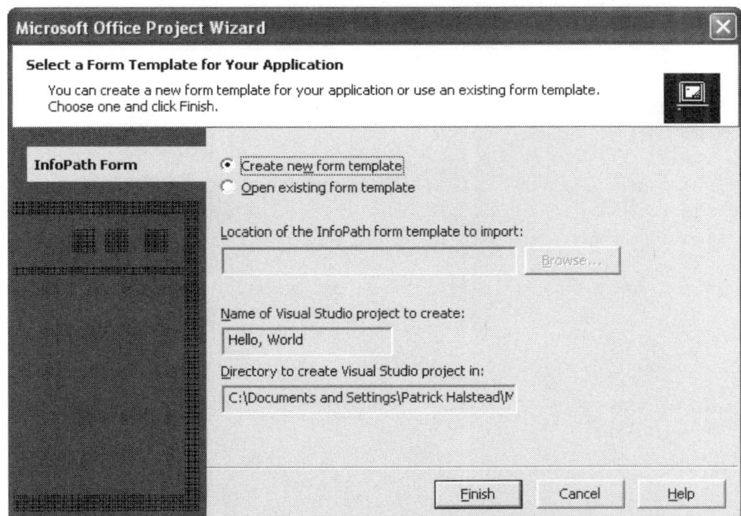

Figure 2-2 The New Project Wizard lets you create a project from an existing InfoPath form template.

After Visual Studio creates your new project, you should see InfoPath in the foreground. Switch back to Visual Studio, and take a look at the project that Visual Studio created. Figure 2-3 depicts your initial Visual Studio project. From Solution Explorer (top right), you can see that your new Hello World project contains the Visual Basic assembly named "Hello World-FormCode" and a list of files: manifest.xsf, sampledata.xml, view1.xsl, myschema.xsd, and template.xml. One important difference between developing your form in InfoPath and developing it in Visual Studio is that InfoPath defaults to save your entire form template as an .xsn file packaged in the CAB format but Visual Studio saves your form template as an .xsn file only as the result of the build process; in the project directory, you will find your form template saved as a set of extracted files alongside the files that compose your managed code assembly. In addition to the standard AssemblyInfo.vb file, your project contains a file named FormCode.vb, where the code for our Hello World form resides. Visual Studio has conveniently opened FormCode.vb and inserted the following boilerplate code:

```
Imports System
Imports Microsoft.Office.Interop.InfoPath.SemiTrust
Imports Microsoft.VisualBasic

' Office integration attribute. Identifies the startup class for the form. Do not
' modify.
<Assembly: System.ComponentModel.DescriptionAttribute("InfoPathStartupClass, Version=1.0,
    Class=Hello_World.Hello_World")>

Namespace Hello_World

    ' The namespace prefixes defined in this attribute must remain synchronized with
    ' those in the form definition file (.xsf).
    <InfoPathNamespace("xmlns:my='http://schemas.microsoft.com/office/infopath/2003/myXSD/
        2004-02-07T05-55-01'")> _
    Public Class Hello_World

        Private thisXDocument As XDocument
        Private thisApplication As Application

        Public Sub _Startup(app As Application, doc As XDocument)
            thisXDocument = doc
            thisApplication = app

            ' You can add additional initialization code here.
        End Sub

        Public Sub _Shutdown()
        End Sub

    End Class

End Namespace
```

The boilerplate code imports the Office interop assembly for InfoPath—*Microsoft.Office.Interop.InfoPath.SemiTrust*—and adds a reference to it. This gives you IntelliSense for the InfoPath object model. The boilerplate code also declares and initializes two private objects, *thisXDocument* and *thisApplication*. These are your access points to the InfoPath object model, and your code will refer to them often. You cannot call the InfoPath object model from within the *_Startup* or *_Shutdown* method, but you can use these methods to initialize and clean up state for your form. When you add a new event handler from the designer, InfoPath inserts a method and switches your focus to the IDE so you can quickly do the coding.

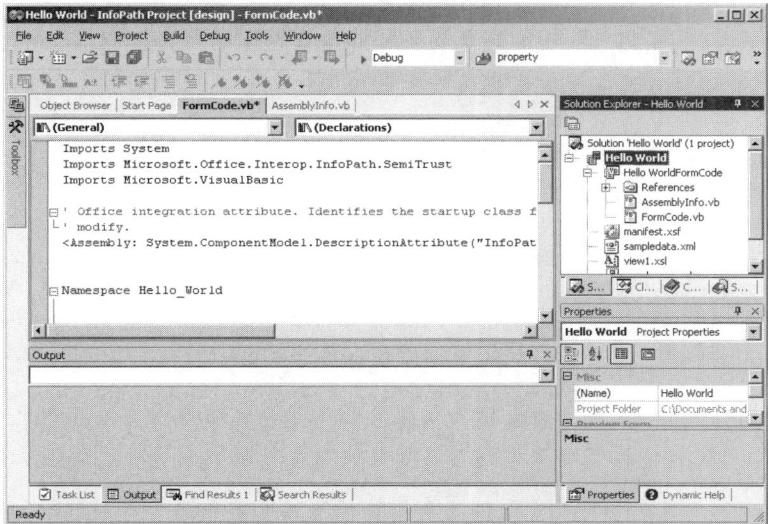

Figure 2-3 The Solution Explorer in Visual Studio .NET 2003 shows a list of all files making up your InfoPath project; for InfoPath forms developed outside of Visual Studio .NET 2003, you can use File | Extract Form Files to see a similar list.

Let's switch back to InfoPath and select the Controls link on the task pane. For our introductory Hello World form, double-click Button to insert a button into the view pane on the left. Then double-click the button in the view pane to change its properties. InfoPath displays the Button Properties dialog box. Change the label to **Hello World** and then click the Edit Form Code button. InfoPath switches back to Visual Studio and inserts a method for your *OnClick* event handler:

```
<InfoPathEventHandler(MatchPath:="CTRL1_5", EventType:=InfoPathEventType.OnClick)> _
Public Sub CTRL1_5_OnClick(ByVal e As DocActionEvent)
    ' Write your code here.
End Sub
```

The *InfoPathEventHandler* class is used as a custom attribute for event handler methods. It contains two parameters. The *MatchPath* parameter specifies the XPath of the event source. For unbound controls, such as buttons, the *MatchPath* parameter holds the control's ID. The *EventType* parameter specifies the type of event. InfoPath inserts attributes that correspond to definitions in the form template's manifest file.

If you change the *InfoPathEventHandler* attribute or its parameters, you break the correspondence between the control and its event handler. The result is that the event handler is never called. This is also true if you change the ID for a button control in the Button Properties dialog box: InfoPath does not automatically update the event handler for you; you have to manually modify it to match the new control ID. A simple solution is to create a new event handler for the control and then copy the code from the old event handler into the new one.

Finally, let's add code to display the "Hello World" message. Type the following code after the *'Write your code here* comment:

```
thisXDocument.UI.Alert("Hello World")
```

As you type, the IntelliSense feature pops up to offer just the right list of type-ahead options for your code. By importing *Microsoft.Office.Interop.InfoPath.SemiTrust*, IntelliSense walks the InfoPath object model. If that doesn't paste a grin on your face, the next feature should. Place the cursor on the new line that you inserted, and insert a breakpoint (press F9 or click in the gray area on the left margin next to the line of code). Then build the solution and start debugging your code. (To build, choose Build | Build Solution; to debug, choose Debug | Start.) Visual Studio launches InfoPath. Click the Hello World button and watch how Visual Studio breaks the code execution and brings you back into the IDE to examine your code. Your screen should resemble Figure 2-4. In a difference from the Microsoft Script Editor (MSE), you no longer need to insert *debugger* statements to halt program execution when you're using the new Visual Studio plug-in. Now *that* is worth rejoicing over.

> **Note** The *debugger* command is one example of how managed code differs from script. If you are migrating an existing form that uses script, don't forget to replace the *debugger* commands with breakpoints.

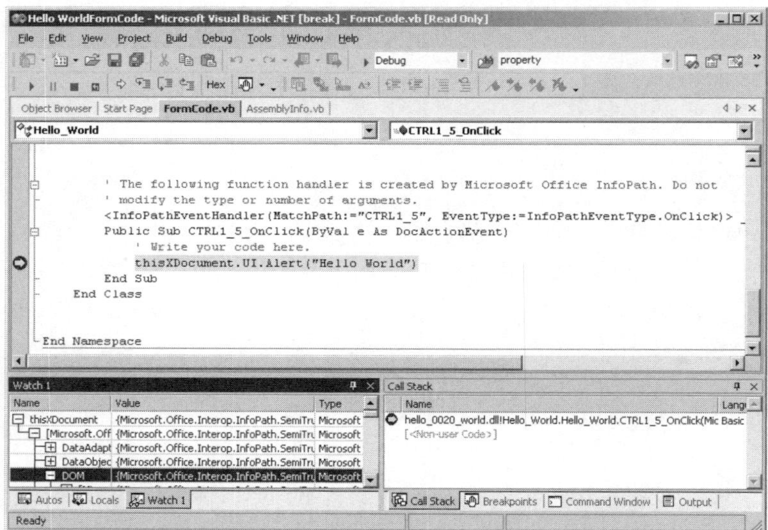

Figure 2-4 Visual Studio .NET 2003 offers much more than the MSE; for starters, how about IntelliSense and full debugger support?

If you continue execution via Debug | Continue or F5, your special "Hello World" message appears in an InfoPath dialog box. You have completed your first InfoPath form that uses managed code. Figure 2-5 displays the result.

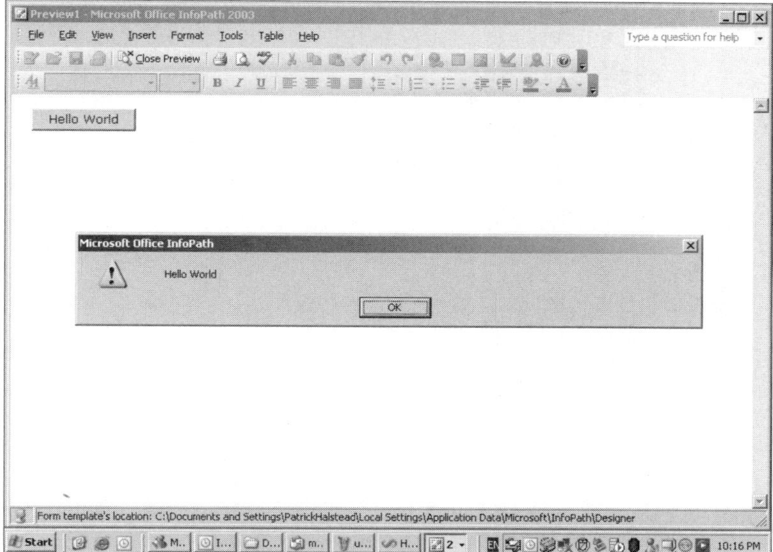

Figure 2-5 Hello World!

Data Source Event Handlers

InfoPath supports XML standards, including XML namespaces, XSL Transformations (XSLT), XML Schema (XSD), and XML Path Language (XPath). InfoPath differs from other Office applications in its adoption of the XML Document Object Model (DOM) to provide access to the form's XML data. (If you don't know what the DOM is, take a quick glance at http://www.w3.org/DOM/.)

The XML data in your form resembles a tree that maps to the structure of the main data source. As you saw in Chapter 1, the main data source represents the collection of fields and groups that define the data for an InfoPath form. You should pay careful attention to the InfoPath event model, which is based on the XML DOM. In this book, we use the term *DOM* to refer to the XML data in your form and the XML DOM interface that accesses it. In your code, you can access the DOM through the *DOM* property of the *XDocument* object. The following code snippet uses the *xml* property of the XML DOM to return all of the form's XML data:

```
Dim strXML As String = thisXDocument.DOM.xml
```

You can extend the functionality in a form by adding application logic. InfoPath executes this application logic using an event model. When something important happens—for example, the data changes—InfoPath fires an event. You can add code to your form that handles these events, and InfoPath will call it with notifications. Here are the predefined event handlers and what they are used for:

DOM Event Handlers

OnAfterChange

Use *OnAfterChange* to change data in your form after other changes have occurred, to perform a calculation, or as an entry point to launch another process.

OnBeforeChange

Use *OnBeforeChange* to validate data or cancel a change.

OnValidate

Use *OnValidate* to handle errors in validation.

Other Form Event Handlers

OnAfterImport

Use *OnAfterImport* to make changes or execute business logic after merging forms.

OnClick

Use *OnClick* to handle a button click event.

OnLoad

Use *OnLoad* to prepare your form after it is loaded but before it is displayed.

OnSubmitRequest

Use *OnSubmitRequest* to prepare for a submit operation.

OnSwitchView

Use *OnSwitchView* to make changes or execute business logic after a switch has occurred but before the view is displayed.

OnVersionUpgrade

Use *OnVersionUpgrade* to customize your form's version upgrade logic.

New SP1 Event Handlers

OnContextChange

Use *OnContextChange* to do something when the context changes—for example, when the user changes fields. InfoPath generates context change events when the user changes the input context of the form. You can do a lot with *OnContextChange*. One common example is displaying contextual help when the input field changes.

OnMergeRequest

Use *OnMergeRequest* to prepare your form before merging.

OnSaveRequest

Use *OnSaveRequest* to prepare for a save operation.

The InfoPath event model is rich and provides many entry points for custom application logic. You should remember several things when writing your event handler:

- InfoPath updates the DOM only after you leave the input field. In other words, even though the text in the field changes when you type in it, you don't get notifications for each key press. InfoPath sends the change notifications after you move out of the field—for example, by pressing Tab or by clicking somewhere else with the mouse.
- Changes to the text value of a node result in two notifications—one for delete and one for insert. InfoPath executes the code in your event handler twice, and this can cause problems if your code changes the state of the document (not to mention the performance penalty of executing everything in duplicate). Changes to the text value of nodes are different from node insertions and deletions. When you input data into a field that was initially blank, you are "inserting" the text node, resulting in only one notification. Subsequent changes to the text value of the field result in updates and the two notifications. The following code filters out events that are not insertions:

  ```
  If ("Insert" <> e.Operation) Then
      Return
  End If
  ```

  For optional sections, you get a single event for an insert or delete of the section, but any fields within that section will double-notify, with the exception of the initial value, which single-notifies.
- Event handlers receive notifications for all of their child nodes. In other words, InfoPath bubbles up events on leaf nodes to the parents in the DOM. Processing the events for all child nodes has performance implications. Consider the worst-case scenario: you attach an event handler to the root node in your DOM. InfoPath will call the event handler for every change to the document. The simplest advice here is: don't attach event handlers to nodes in your tree that have many leaf nodes underneath them, or write code to filter such events and prevent the code from always executing. The following code illustrates the latter approach:

  ```
  If (Not (e.Site Is e.Parent)) Then
      Return
  End If
  ```
- Event handlers will reenter for modifications made to the node on which they are listening or, in the case of a group, for modifications made to any descendant node. In other words, new events will fire as a result of modifications that your handler makes to the DOM. InfoPath prevents infinite recursion in event handlers when the stack reaches a certain depth. But relying on InfoPath to catch this recursion is not only bad practice, it incurs a performance penalty and an error message is displayed to the form user. Currently, InfoPath has no general way to cancel the bubbling up of events, as is possible in HTML DOM scripting. If you have to modify the node on which the change event fired, add code to your event handler to filter out all events happening below the node:

```
If (e.Source.nodeType <> DOMNodeType.NODE_TEXT) Then
    Return
End If
```

Another approach is to filter using the *e.Site* property and *Return* calls for all events where the *Site* does not equal the field that you want to modify.

- InfoPath fires events even when your form is read-only. There are two main scenarios here:

Digital signatures

If you open a form signed with a digital signature, InfoPath protects it by preventing the user from modifying fields. Your DOM event handlers do not receive notifications, and attempts to modify the contents of the DOM fail. The following code checks to see if the form is signed in the *OnLoad* event handler:

```
' Determine whether the form is in a signed state.
If (thisXDocument.IsSigned()) Then
    ' Do special processing for signed forms
End If
' Continue normal processing...
```

Undo and redo operations

InfoPath fires events when you press Undo or Redo. During an undo or redo operation, InfoPath must ensure a clean and atomic update to the DOM—otherwise, the undo and redo operations will be unreliable. To achieve a clean and atomic update, InfoPath locks access to the DOM by making it read-only. If your event handlers make changes to the DOM, they should ignore notifications corresponding to undo or redo operations. The following code demonstrates how to do this:

```
If (e.IsUndoRedo) Then
    ' An undo or redo operation has occurred and the DOM is read-only.
    Return
End If
```

Alternatively, the following code checks for when the DOM is read-only. You can use this property to handle both of the preceding scenarios:

```
' Determine whether the XML DOM is read-only.
If (thisXDocument.IsDOMReadOnly()) Then
    Return
End If
' Continue normal processing...
```

Note that if you want to check whether the user's evaluation version of InfoPath has expired, either *IsReadOnly()* or *IsDomReadOnly()* will work.

Writing an Event Handler for the DOM

In the Hello World example, we created an *OnClick* event handler for the button in our form. The *OnClick* event handler is not associated with DOM changes; it occurs as the result of a button click. Let's apply what you just learned by writing a simple *OnAfterChange* event handler.

For this example, we'll create a simple form that fills in the name of the user using the *System.WindowsIdentity* method in the .NET Framework.

Start Visual Studio .NET 2003, and create a new project named Get Username, just as you did for the earlier Hello World example. Many forms will contain a date and the name of the user, so let's begin by adding these two fields to our data source. In the InfoPath task pane, click Data Source, select *myFields*, and select *Add* to add a *date* field and then a *user* field. The *date* field should be of data type Date (date), and the *user* field should be of type Text (string). Let's also add a check box to the form to control whether the username is automatically populated. Add another field of type True/False (Boolean), and name it *auto* to represent this check box.

Note Controlling your form's UI with a check box is a common technique, but be careful about adding fields to your main data source to store view state. If you want to reuse your form's XML in your business process, you will have to filter out these UI fields later, and they can add needless junk DNA to your data source. Consider binding UI-only controls to a secondary data source. Chapter 10 has an example that shows how to do this.

When you are finished adding these three fields, select the Show Details box to display the data types for the fields. Your data source should look like Figure 2-6.

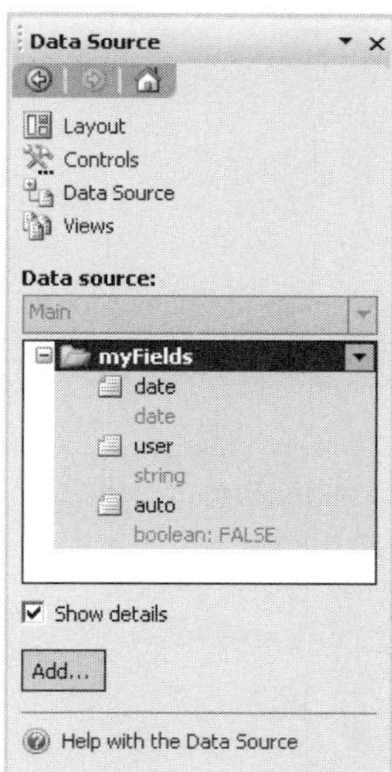

Figure 2-6 Many forms will contain a date and username.

The easiest way to create a form from your newly added data source fields is to simply drag and drop the fields into the view. To do this, right-click and drag *myFields* into the view. When you release the button, InfoPath displays a pop-up menu with a list of options to insert the view controls. (See Figure 2-7.) For this example, select Controls in Layout Table; InfoPath creates a 2×3 table for your controls. Figure 2-8 shows a snapshot of your new InfoPath form.

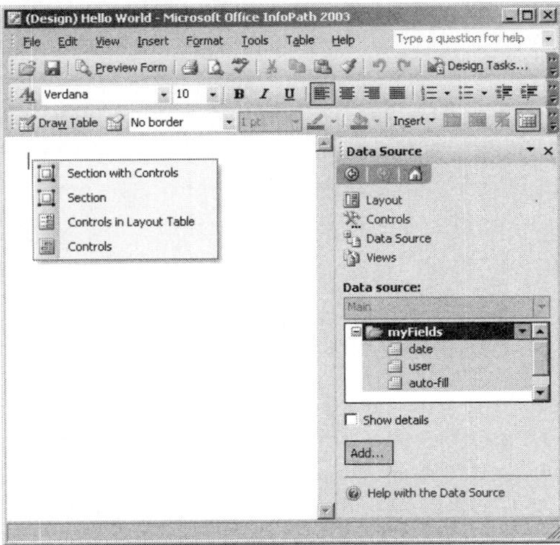

Figure 2-7 Creating forms in InfoPath is easy—you just drag and drop your data onto the view.

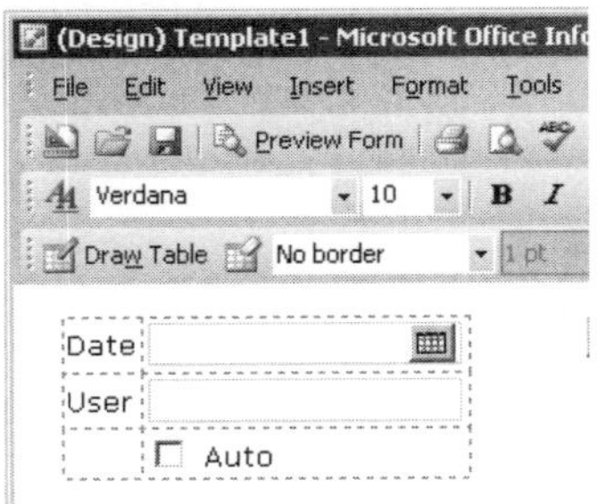

Figure 2-8 InfoPath views use tables and don't support 2-D positioning.

> ## Tables vs. 2-D Positioning
>
> The InfoPath development team chose to use tables instead of 2-D positioning to create the view layout. The main reason tables were chosen was simplicity. Table-centric layout has many implications for your InfoPath solution. You cannot do absolute positioning of elements on the page, and that means you have to create tables and embedded tables to create views that resemble your paper forms.

Now that you have created your view, let's add the *OnAfterChange* event handler. The logic for the form will be to fill in the username field when the check box is selected, so we'll want to add the event handler to the check box. There are two ways to add an *OnAfterChange* event handler to the check box. The first way is to double-click the check box control, and in the Check Box Properties dialog box, click Data Validation. In the Events drop-down list, select

OnAfterChange, and then click Edit. An alternative way is to right-click on the Auto field in the data source and choose Properties. Then in the Field Or Group Properties dialog box, click on the Validation and Event Handlers tab. In the Events drop-down list, select OnAfterChange and then click Edit. Either way you choose, InfoPath switches to Visual Studio and inserts Visual Basic .NET boilerplate code:

```
<InfoPathEventHandler(MatchPath:="/my:myFields/
my:auto", EventType:=InfoPathEventType.OnAfterChange)> _
Public Sub auto_OnAfterChange(ByVal e As DataDOMEvent)
    ' Write code here to restore the global state.

    If (e.IsUndoRedo) then
        ' An undo or redo operation has occurred and the DOM is read-only.
        Return
    End If

    ' A field change has occurred and the DOM is writable. Write code here to respond
    ' to the changes.

End Sub
```

InfoPath has already added an *If* condition to handle read-only states resulting from undo and redo events. The data source for this form is simple, so we don't need to add any special conditions to handle event bubbling. (Check out Chapter 3 for an example of how to filter out events from descendant nodes.) Our task is to fill in the *my:user* field with the current active user. We'll access the *UserName* property of the *Environment* object to do this. Here's the code:

```
' A field change has occurred and the DOM is writable. Write code here to respond
' to the changes.
Dim name As String
name = Environment.UserName
thisXDocument.DOM.selectSingleNode("/my:myFields/my:user").text = name
```

The *selectSingleNode* call takes a string argument corresponding to the XPath of the node to be selected. Specifying the correct XPath here is critical. Notice how the XPath, */my:myFields/my:user*, is an absolute path starting with the *myFields* root node. Wherever possible, you should use absolute XPaths instead of relative XPaths because InfoPath can process them faster. You must also specify the *my* namespace. Recompile and debug your form. Select the check box, and notice how the user field is filled out with the current username.

Warning The .NET security model prevents execution of the *Environment.UserPame* code unless the user has security permissions to view environment settings. If you are an administrator, you have permissions and you won't see a problem. If you are not an administrator, you might see .NET throw a security exception. For details on how to work around this problem, see the section titled "Configuring Security Permissions" in Chapter 8.

Writing an Event Handler in VBScript

If you don't have Visual Studio .NET 2003, or if you're more comfortable writing script, you can still use InfoPath to develop forms that are just as powerful as in managed code. InfoPath comes with full support for JScript and VBScript. Let's take a look at an event handler in VBScript.

To create a form that uses script, start by launching the InfoPath application and selecting the Design A Form option located at the bottom of the left pane. In the Design A New Form task pane, click New Blank Form. Go ahead and add a text field named **user** to your view.

For this example, we'll add an *OnLoad* event handler. First we need to select the programming language that we want InfoPath to use. By default, InfoPath uses JScript. On the Advanced tab of the Form Options dialog box, accessible from the Tools menu, select VBScript from the drop-down list in the Programming Language section. Note that you must do this before adding any code to your form. Once you add code, InfoPath no longer lets you change the language and the Programming Language drop-down list is disabled. After you select VBScript and then click OK to close the Form Options dialog box, go back to the Tools menu and choose Programming | On Load Event. InfoPath starts the MSE and inserts VBScript boilerplate code.

Here's the code you should see:

```
'=======
' The following function handler is created by Microsoft Office InfoPath.
' Do not modify the name of the function, or the name and number of arguments.
' This function is associated with the following field or group (XPath): /my:myFields/
     my:user
' Note: Information in this comment is not updated after the function handler is created.
'=======
Sub XDocument_OnLoad(eventObj)
' Write your code here
End Sub
```

InfoPath calls this event handler when it loads the form. You cannot change view properties in the *OnLoad* event handler because no view is active at the time of loading. InfoPath doesn't actually create the view until after the *OnLoad* event handler has exited, but the DOM is ready and we can add code to initialize it. Insert the following code into your *OnLoad* event handler:

```
'Create a WScript.Network object, which provides access to the user data
Dim WshNetwork
Set WshNetwork = CreateObject("WScript.Network")

'Retrieve the UserName and write it into the my:user field
Dim objUserName
Set objUserName = XDocument.DOM.selectSingleNode("/my:myFields/my:user")
objUserName.text = WshNetwork.UserName
```

This code instantiates an ActiveX object for *WScript.Network* and uses it to set the *user* field to the current user's name. Save the script.vbs file by pressing Ctrl+S, and switch back to InfoPath. Remember that you can preview the form from the File menu, via the Preview Form toolbar button, or by using Ctrl+Shift+B. When you do this, InfoPath might prompt you with an Internet Explorer security dialog box, as shown in Figure 2-9. InfoPath shows this warning dialog box for forms that use untrusted ActiveX controls. Untrusted ActiveX controls are those that don't implement *IObjectSafety* or report that they're unsafe for scripting. You can change the security setting for your form to Full Trust to prevent this dialog box from appearing–see Chapter 8 for details. For now, click Yes to let the *WScript.Network* object run.

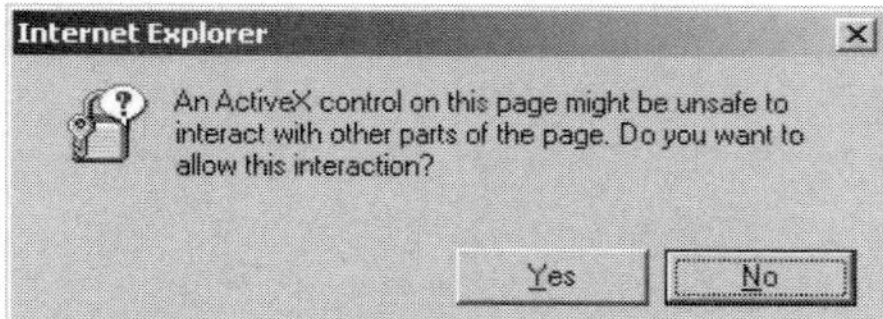

Figure 2-9 Internet Explorer security dialog box for forms using untrusted ActiveX controls.

Unlike managed code in Visual Studio, the MSE does not have support for easy debugging. The easiest way to break in your code is to add a *Stop* statement if you are using VBScript or a *debugger* statement if you are using JScript.

Implementing Workflow

Workflow is a trendy topic in enterprise business circles. Companies are increasing productivity by further automating their business processes using Web services and databases. InfoPath forms are a natural fit to do data entry on the front end of these business processes because they are easy to create, they provide validation and data proofing, and they support XML standards. In fact, InfoPath provides an ideal client for business processes that use Microsoft BizTalk Server. Some people at Microsoft even say that "InfoPath is to BizTalk what Outlook is to Exchange." Chapter 11 explores various ways of implementing workflow with InfoPath and BizTalk 2004 Server.

You don't need BizTalk to implement forms-based workflow, and InfoPath provides several features that you can use to create simple forms-based workflow. For example, using InfoPath rules and user roles, you can control who opens the form, what they see, and how they submit the forms. By creating a form with multiple views and multiple data connections, you can leverage rules and roles to create a simple approval process. For example, a corporate book purchase may involve a book buyer who submits the request and a manager who receives and approves it. The view and the supporting application logic that the form presents depends on the user role. For the purchaser, we want to implement a submit button to execute application logic to send the form by e-mail to the manager. For the manager, we want to have two buttons–one for approve and one for reject. In the next sample, we show how to control access to each view and application logic actions using rules and roles.

Rules and user roles are new in InfoPath SP1, but the Merge Forms feature has been around since the initial version of InfoPath 2003. This feature enables aggregation of form data. It is relatively obscure and underappreciated as a workflow feature largely due to lack of user familiarity and lack of support in the InfoPath designer. In the designer, the General tab of the Options dialog box has an Enable Form Merging check box, but this provides default support only for forms that come from the same form template, i.e., the roll-up scenario. This is the most common scenario. The roll-up process takes several forms of the same underlying schema and rolls them up into one form that includes all of the instances. Roll-up is an important process, but what many InfoPath users don't know is that they can also import forms from different schemas. We'll refer to this powerful workflow feature as Custom Merge.

Custom Merge is powerful because you can use it to create a workflow process that chains forms together. Form A can include application logic that submits the form to a Web site and opens Form B, which then imports the data from Form A and processes it using application logic. Implementing Custom Merge requires manually editing the manifest.xsf file to add custom file-importing rules. In addition, for each type of form to import (each different schema), you must create a corresponding XSL file to map the data from the imported form to the base form—that is, the form from which you are doing the merging. The InfoPath designer does not support defining these custom XSL files, nor does it support specifying the import rules for them. You must manually edit the manifest.xsf and use other programming tools to develop and debug the custom XSL files. This section takes a brief look at how the Meeting Agenda sample form implements Custom Merge to import Issue Tracking forms.

Finally, for simple reporting and analysis, InfoPath supports exporting a list of forms to Excel. You can use the many analytical functions in Excel to get a better handle on the data entered via InfoPath. We'll briefly explore this feature.

Brace yourself! We are about to begin several step-by-step exercises. These won't take much time, but there are quite a few steps that you must execute in sequence. The first exercise, on rules and user roles, is the longest, but it shouldn't take more than 10 minutes. Rapid prototyping prowess is one of InfoPath's key features.

Rules and User Roles

In this section, we'll create a simple book purchase approval form. This form will include two roles—requester and approver. Each role will have a separate view and customized submit methods. We will use rules and user roles to enable a simple approval workflow, as depicted in Figure 2-10. The Merge Forms feature detailed in the next section will describe how to create the Report and Analyze view depicted in Figure 2-10.

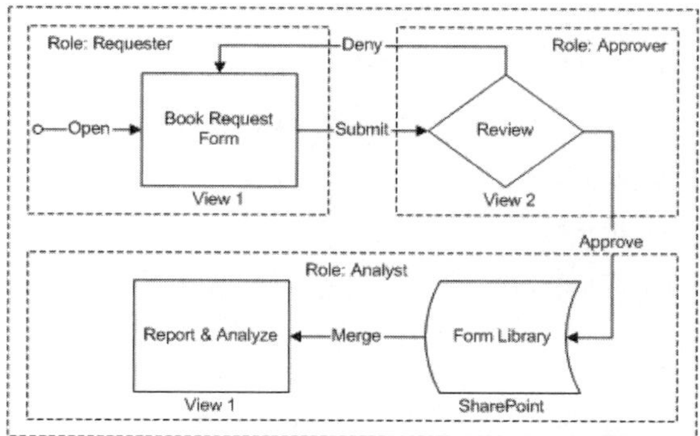

Figure 2-10 InfoPath rules and user roles can enable simple workflow processes.

Create a Book Purchase Approval Form

The following steps describe how to create the sample from scratch. This will take a few minutes, but the steps contain a wealth of information.

Create the Request View

1. Create a new InfoPath Visual Basic .NET project in Visual Studio called **BookPurchase**.
2. After Visual Studio launches InfoPath, choose Color Schemes from the Format menu, and then select Blue in the Color Schemes task pane.

> **Tip** InfoPath uses the current color scheme when creating new views, so it's important to set it for the default view before adding other views.

3. Navigate to the Views link by clicking on Color Scheme link at the top of the task pane and selecting Views.
4. Double-click View 1, and change the name from View 1 to **Request**.
5. Under Actions in the same task pane, click the Add A New View link and name this new view **Approve**.
6. Double-click your new Approve view and clear the Show On The View Menu check box.
7. Add a third view named **Report**, and clear the Show On The View Menu check box.
8. Select the Request view, and then click the Data Source link.
9. Right-click *myFields*, and add a repeating group named **Requests**. Don't forget to select the Repeating check box.
10. Right-click *Requests*, and add a date field named **Date**, a text field named **EmailAddress**, a text field named **BookTitle**, a Rich Text field named **BookLink**, a decimal field named **BookPrice**, a text field named **Purpose**, and a True/False field named **Approved**.

11. Click Layout, select Table With Title under the Insert Layout Tables section in the task pane, and then select One-Column Table.
12. Replace the Click To Add Title text with **Book Purchase Request Form**.
13. Replace the Click To Add Form Content text with **Fill out this form and submit your new requests for new book purchases**.
14. Navigate to Data Source in the task pane, drag the Requests field into the one-column table, and select Repeating Section With Controls.
15. Double-click on the Repeating Section tab, and clear the Allow Users To Insert And Delete The Sections check box in the Repeating Section Properties dialog box.
16. Edit the view by clicking on items in it and using the keyboard and mouse: increase the width of the *EmailAddress* field, reduce the height of the *BookLink* field to one line, expand the *Purpose* field to make it accommodate more text, delete the *Approved* check box and label, and delete the blank space after the *Purpose* field.
17. Double-click *Date* in the Data Source tree.
18. In the Default Value section, click *f*x to bring up the Insert Formula dialog box.
19. Select Insert Function, and select the *today* function listed under the Date And Time category, and then click OK three times to close the dialog boxes.
20. Double-click *BookLink* in the Data Source tree, and type *http://www.microsoft.com/learning/books* in the Value field in the Default Value section.
21. Double-click the *BookPrice* field in the view, click Format, and then choose *Currency*.
22. Double-click the *Purpose* field in the view, and select the Cannot Be Blank check box in the Validation And Rules section.
23. Click in the view at the bottom of the form to set the insertion point.
24. Navigate to the Controls task pane, and then click the Button control to insert a button into the view.
25. To add an E-Mail Message data connection to your form to send the request, choose Tools | Data Connections and then click Add.
26. In the Data Connection Wizard, choose Submit Data and then click Next.
27. Choose As An Email Message and then click Next.
28. In the To field, type your e-mail address (for example, **name@domain.com**).
29. Click the formula button (*fx*) next to the Subject field and type in the following:

```
concat("Book Request -", my:Requests/my:BookTitle)
```

30. Click Next, and name this data connector **Send Request**, then click Finish to close the wizard.

31. Close the Data Connections dialog box, and then double-click the button in the view and change the label to **Submit**.
32. Select Submit in the Action drop-down list.
33. In the Submitting Forms dialog box, click Enable Submit Commands And Buttons, and make sure E-mail is selected in the Submit To drop-down list.
34. Click Submit Options, and then select the Close The Form.
35. Click OK three times to close these dialog boxes.
36. Preview your form.

Your form should look like that shown in Figure 2-11.

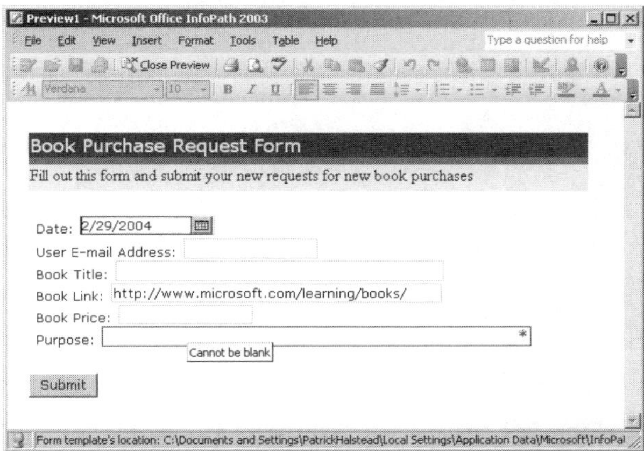

Figure 2-11 The Request view for the Book Purchase form

In your form preview, you can test the submit functionality. Click the Submit button to view the e-mail message data. You can't edit the data in this dialog box, but you can cancel it. Click Send, and notice that InfoPath closes the preview form. The new submit options support in SP1 is extremely convenient.

You might be wondering whether InfoPath sent you the preview form via e-mail. But before you check that, let's return to the designer and create the Approve view.

Create the Approve View

1. You can get a head start on the contents of the Approve view by copying the contents from the Request view into it. Place your cursor in the Request view, and press Ctrl+A to select the entire view. Press Ctrl+C to copy the contents.
2. Navigate to the Approve view by clicking on Views in the task pane and then clicking Approve in the Select A View section. InfoPath presents the blank view.
3. Press Ctrl+V to paste the contents of the Request view into the Approve view.

4. Change the title from Book Purchase Request Form to Book Purchase Approve Form, and replace the text underneath the title with **Please review the following book purchase and click Approve or Reject**.
5. Make the date field read-only by double-clicking the date field and selecting Conditional Formatting on the Display tab. Add a condition for *Date* by selecting *Date* in the first drop-down list and Is Not Blank in the second drop-down list; select the Read-Only check box, and then click OK.
6. Make the other fields read-only by double-clicking each field, selecting the Display tab of the Properties dialog box, and selecting the Read-Only check box.
7. Add a Deny button by clicking on Controls in the task pane and dragging a Button control onto the view next to the Submit button. Position your cursor in between the buttons, and insert a couple of spaces. Double-click the new button, and change the label to **Deny**.
8. Change the Submit button to Approve by double-clicking Submit and changing the label to **Approve**.
9. Preview the view.

Your form should look like that shown in Figure 2-12.

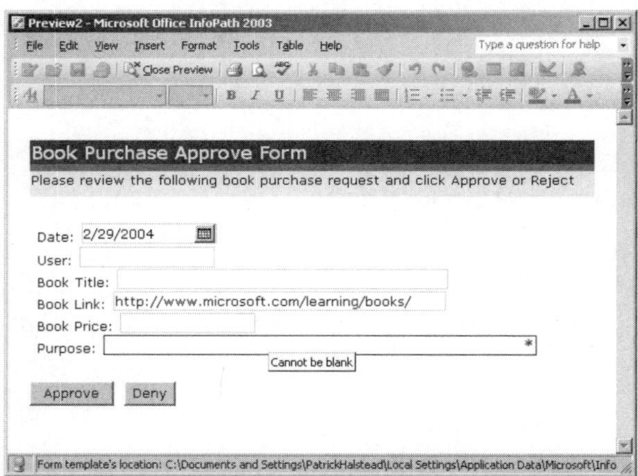

Figure 2-12 The Approve view for the Book Purchase form

The next set of steps adds the user roles. You will need to add user roles before defining the rules that reference them.

Add User Roles

1. From the Tools menu, choose User Roles.
2. Add the Requester user role by clicking Add and entering Requester for the name. To create it as the default user role, select the Set As Initiator box. Leave the Assign Users Or Groups To This Role section blank.

3. Add the Approver user role by clicking Add again and selecting the first check box under the Assign Users Or Groups To This Role section. Click on the single person button to the right of this field, and type your username in the form of DOMAIN_NAME\username. (For this example, you will be the Approver.)

> **Tip** If you don't have Active Directory, or if it is unavailable, InfoPath displays an error message when you click the buttons in the Assign Users Or Groups To This Role section. The error message reads as follows: "The program cannot open the required dialog box because no locations can be found. Close this message and try again." You can type the COMPUTER_NAME\username into the text field to work around Active Directory.

The Manage User Roles dialog box should look like that shown in Figure 2-13.

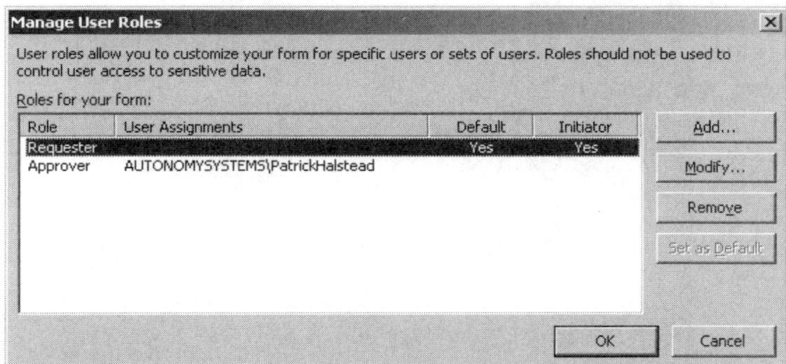

Figure 2-13 Managing user roles is one key to unlocking forms-based workflow for your InfoPath SP1 forms.

We're almost done. We have only two more tasks to complete: defining the data connections and setting up the workflow rules. The simple workflow requires e-mail data connectors to send the request and respond with approval or denial. For the approval step, we'll also need a data connector to save the form to SharePoint or to your local file system.

Define the Data Connections

1. Create data connectors for sending approval and denial. Send these to the *EmailAddress* in the form. Instead of hardcoding the To field, click *fx*, click Insert Field Or Group, and then select *EmailAddress* from the DOM tree to use the value of the form's field to send the e-mail. For simplicity, this form won't send the data back to the requester, so delete the Attachment Name. Finally, add Approved or Denied to the Subject formula. For example, the formula for Send Approval is as follows:

   ```
   concat("Book Request Approved -", my:Requests/my:BookTitle)
   ```

2. Name these data connectors Send Approval and Send Denial.

3. If you have a SharePoint site, create a fourth data connection named **Save Approved Form** to submit to it. You will need to save the form template to the SharePoint library first before creating the data connection. Close the data connector dialog box, and then publish your form to SharePoint. After creating the form library, add the data connector. You'll want to use a unique filename. Here's an example:

```
concat(my:Requests/my:EmailAddress, " - ", my:Requests/my:BookTitle, " - ", my:Requests/
my:Date)
```

4. If you do not have a SharePoint site, continue with the three e-mail adapters. In the next section, we will make a change to force saving of the form.

The Data Connections dialog box should look like that shown in Figure 2-14.

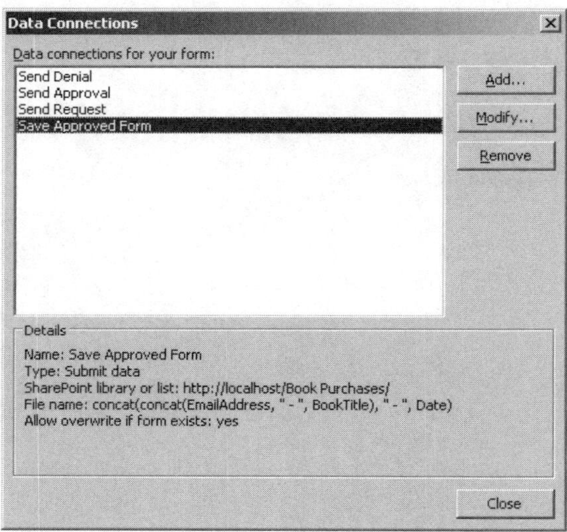

Figure 2-14 With multiple data connections, you can submit data via e-mail and SharePoint and define rules that use both.

Each arrow in Figure 2-10 depicts a rule. The first rule is for opening the form. The second rule is for sending the request. We also need sets of rules for approval and denial.

Define Open Rules

1. Define the open form rule by choosing Form Options from the Tools menu, selecting the Open And Save tab, and then clicking the Rules button under the Open Behavior section.
2. Next you define an open rule for the approver. Because the default view is the requester view, you only need to add a rule for the other views. Add a rule named **Approver** with a condition that the user's role be equal to "Approver" and that the Purpose not be blank. (Any field that cannot be blank will substitute equally well for Purpose.) After defining the condition, add an action to switch to the Approve view.
3. Define an open rule for reporting. Condition this rule on Approved equaling TRUE and the user's role equaling "Approver." Set the action to switch to the Report view.

For simple submit scenarios, you can enable submit through the Submitting Forms dialog box (reachable via the Tools menu). For views that have more than one submit option, you have to use custom rules. The InfoPath designer doesn't support controlling submit on a per-view basis. If we enable submit for the first view, we can still define custom rules for the Approve and Deny buttons on the second view, but the Submit command will still be available on the File menu and it will likely not work for this view. The remedy is to disable submitting forms and use custom rules or write custom code for the *OnSubmitRequest* event.

Define Custom Submit Rules

1. In the Request view, double-click the Submit button. Select Rules And Custom Code in the Action drop-down list.

> **Warning** When you select Rules And Custom Code, InfoPath changes the label for your button. This is a known issue with InfoPath SP1. You will have to change the Label text back to **Submit**.

2. Click the Rules button and add two rules–one to submit the request using the Send Request data connection and another to close the form without asking to save. The order of the rules matters because closing the form first will cause the second rule to fail. Both rules have no condition defined.
3. Switch to the Approve view.
4. Double-click the Approve button, select Rules And Custom Code from the drop-down list, fix up the label text and then click Rules to add the following four rules: **Send Approval**, **Set Approved**, **Save Approved Form**, and **Close Form**. Once again, the order matters. Use the Send Approval data connection for the first rule and the Save Approved Form data connection for the third. If you don't have a SharePoint site, you can remove the Save Approved Form action and have InfoPath prompt the user to save the form on close. Figure 2-15 shows the Close The Form action and the check box that controls user save prompting. For the second rule, you need to set the value of the Approved field to *TRUE*. Entering TRUE in the Value field will not work because InfoPath will treat it as a text string. Use the *true()* function instead.
5. Double-click the Deny button, and add two rules: **Send Denial** and **Close Form**. Use the Send Denial data connector for the Send Denial rule.

Rules and Actions

Which is better, four rules each containing one action or one rule with four actions? You can do it both ways. For the example in this section, we define four rules, each containing one action. This lets you see each step from the Rules dialog box. If you were to use four actions for one rule, you would have to drill one level deeper and first open the rule to see the actions.

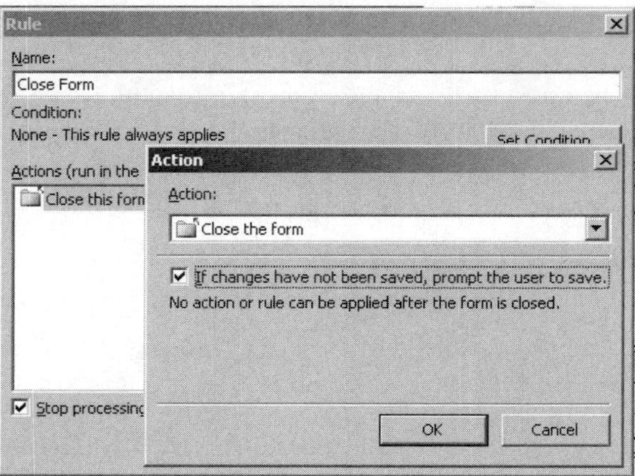

Figure 2-15 You can enable user save prompting as an alternative to SharePoint submit.

Using the Book Purchase Form

After saving or publishing your form, you are ready to test it out. InfoPath will not show the form in the dashboard until after the first runtime usage. Designing, previewing and publishing don't count. You have to open the form in the editor. To work around this problem, you will have to click Fill Out This Form from your SharePoint site, or if you are not using SharePoint, you can double-click the Book Purchases.xsn file from the published location. Fill out the form and submit it. InfoPath displays the e-mail message dialog box shown in Figure 2-16. Click the Send button.

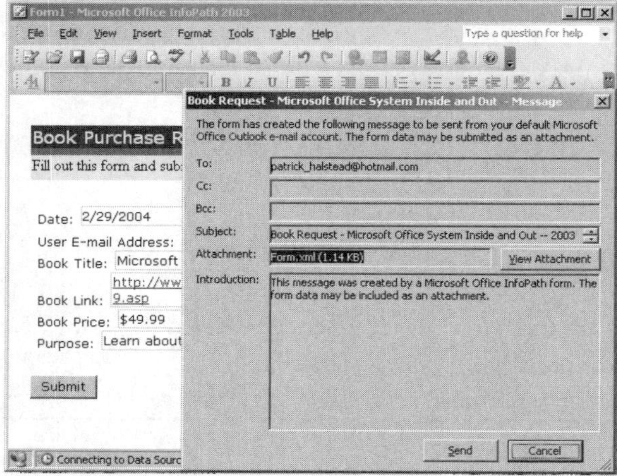

Figure 2-16 For security purposes, InfoPath prompts the user before sending e-mail messages.

InfoPath supports sending forms via e-mail but you must have Outlook 2003 or later installed to do so. InfoPath will not work with other e-mail clients. Assuming you have Outlook installed, you will receive an e-mail message with the form attached. Clicking the attached form opens it in the Approval view. If you click Approve on this view and send the e-mail, the form will be saved to your SharePoint site.

For the next section, we'll need three to four sample Book Purchases forms filled out. Take a moment and create three more forms. If you're not using SharePoint, be sure to save the forms in the same location.

Implementing Roll-Up

This section describes how to use the Merge Forms feature to implement simple roll-up. We'll use the Report view that you created earlier and enable Merge Forms.

Create the Report View

1. Open the Book Purchase form in the designer. Select Views in the task pane, and switch to the Report view by clicking it.
2. Switch to Data Source by clicking the Data Source link above the Views link in the task pane.
3. Drag the Requests node to the view, and select it to add it as a Repeating Table.
4. Delete the Book Link, Purpose, and Approved columns and resize the remaining columns to improve readability.

Now you can open a saved approved form, and it will switch to the Report view. Figure 2-17 shows an example of this. You can merge forms into the Report view by using the Merge Forms command on the File menu.

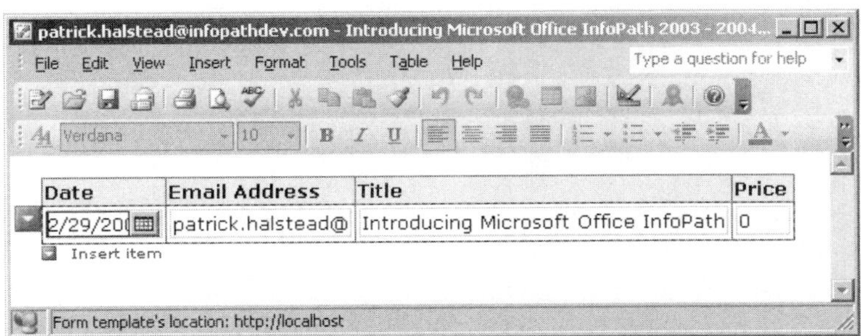

Figure 2-17 Creating a Report view to roll up forms

Merging Forms

InfoPath enables form merging by default. To disable form merging, clear the Enable Form Merging check box on the General tab of the Form Options dialog box.

The Open rule that we defined earlier switches to the Report view only if the state of the form is approved. If you use the Merge Forms view from SharePoint, InfoPath will merge the forms but will add a blank request to them. Because this blank form has not been approved, the Open rule will fail and InfoPath will not switch to the Report view. SharePoint adds this extra blank form to the view when merging so that all forms are merged in the same way. If it didn't do this, and it instead opened the first form in the list before merging the others into it, the merge behavior could vary, depending on which form was first in the list. That would be bad. This extra blank form is a bit of a nuisance, but we can work around the problem for now by adding the following code:

```
<InfoPathEventHandler(EventType:=InfoPathEventType.OnAfterImport)> _
Public Sub OnAfterImport(ByVal e As DocEvent)
    thisXDocument.View.SwitchView("Report")
End Sub
```

The *OnAfterImport* even handler shown here switches to the Report view. Recompile and republish your form from Visual Studio. Don't forget to publish the form back to the same location that you used above.

Caution When you create a form project from Visual Studio, it stores your form files in an extracted state. When you build a solution, Visual Studio creates a form package (.xsn file) out of the form files and the managed code assembly.

InfoPath lets you publish a form from its Visual Studio project (you can also right-click on the project in Visual Studio's Solution Explorer and choose Publish), but after publishing, InfoPath prompts the user to close the form template. You should always choose Yes. Not closing the form template can cause synchronization problems between the InfoPath designer and Visual Studio. In fact, we recommend that you close both InfoPath and Visual Studio after publishing InfoPath forms.

You cannot resave a Visual Studio form to the publish location from InfoPath because it might have to be recompiled, and InfoPath doesn't instruct Visual Studio to recompile.

You also cannot modify the managed code for a form that is published to SharePoint by clicking the Modify Settings and Columns view and Edit Template link on the SharePoint site. If you try to do so, InfoPath will display an error message.

If you used SharePoint to store your forms, navigate to the site and then click Merge Forms. Otherwise, open the form in InfoPath and choose Merge Forms from the File menu. Notice that the view is switched after import completes. Figure 2-18 shows what a successful merge from SharePoint looks like.

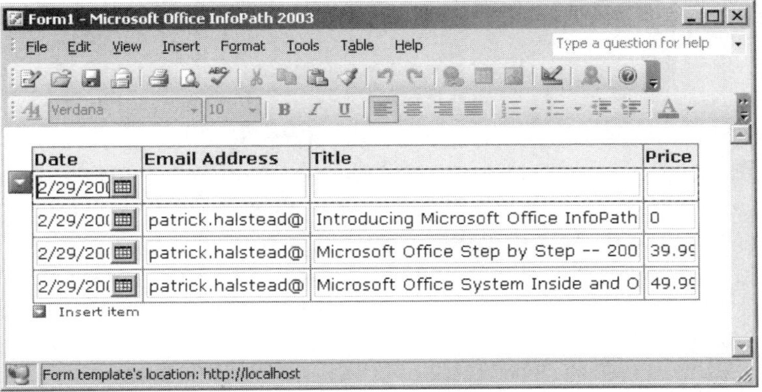

Figure 2-18 SharePoint uses a blank form as a base when merging forms.

Developer Nugget: Deploying a Form Package via E-Mail

InfoPath SP1 supports e-mailing published forms. Deploying forms in e-mail is an effective workflow technique because users can download the forms via e-mail and work on them offline. This is a win for business travelers as well as those on extranets who might not have access to an intranet SharePoint site. But sending a form in e-mail has security implications. Specifically, if the form uses managed code, it must be fully trusted. In addition, controls marked unsafe require fully trusted forms. (See Chapter 8 for more on full trust and other InfoPath trust models.)

Sending a Published Form

If you need to share a form with a colleague and you don't have access to a Web server, you can send the .xsn file as an e-mail attachment. From the designer, choose Send Form As Attachment from the File menu. If the form uses managed code or unsafe controls, you will need to trust the form.

Warning InfoPath disables the Send Form As Attachment option from the File menu if you don't have Outlook installed on your machine.

Trusting the Form

The easiest way to trust the form is to sign it. SP1 simplifies the signing process with a Form Signing section in the Security tab of the Form Options dialog box. Just click Sign This Form and select a certificate. Of course, this requires a trusted certificate. Another way to install a form as fully trusted is to create a Microsoft Installer .msi file.

Creating an MSI File

InfoPath ships a tool in the SDK called RegForm that allows you to create a fully trusted form. You can then send this file in e-mail without signing. Because it is an MSI file, Windows runs special code in the MSI package to register and install it on your machine. (See the InfoPath SDK for more information on this technique. You can download the InfoPath SDK from http://www.microsoft.com/downloads/details.aspx?familyid=351f0616-93aa-4fe8-9238-d702f1bfbab4&displaylang=en.)

Trusting the Domain of a Form

If you have access to the form location via your browser but receive a security error when loading the form, the error is probably due to domain security. You must trust the site where the target form resides. In Internet Explorer, from the Tools | Internet Options dialog box, select the Security tab. Select Trusted Sites and then click Sites to view the Trusted Sites dialog box and add the target domain to the list of trusted sites. For Web sites starting with *http:* you will need to clear the Require Server Verification check box on this dialog box.

Saving the Form Locally

If you receive the .xsn file for a form template in e-mail and it isn't signed, you can open it in the designer and resave the form template to your local hard disk. Right-click on the .xsn file and choose Design. Then save the form template locally or to a file share where you have domain access. Resaving the form template can change its identity, but now that SP1 supports dual-mode URL/URN form templates, fixing up the form is no longer necessary.

URL and URN Form Templates

Before SP1, when the location (URL) of a form template changed, the only way to open a form created using the old version was to fix up the *href* attribute to point to the new location. You might recall that *href* is an attribute on the *?mso-infoPathSolution* processing instruction in the form's .xml file. SP1 has significantly improved this situation by doing away with the distinction between URL and URN form templates. URL forms were identified by location; URN forms were identified by name. By default, InfoPath now attaches a URN to each form template. When you open a form for the first time, it caches a copy of the form template on your local machine. If the form's location moves or becomes inaccessible (for example, if you go offline), your forms will still open because the form template exists in your cache.

Custom Merge

You can customize the Merge Forms feature to enable forms-to-forms workflow. Custom Merge is not supported in the InfoPath designer, but it is described in detail in the SDK. To use Custom Merge, you have to create an XSLT file that maps fields in a source form to fields in a destination form. This XSLT file is then added as a resource to the destination form template and manually referenced in the form's manifest.xsf file. Using the XSLT map, you can create a form of schema type A that imports a form of schema type B or schema type C, or both. In fact, there is no limit on the number of forms you can import. The Custom Merge feature creates some powerful chaining possibilities between forms.

Next we'll walk through a custom merge exercise using two sample forms. The form you will use as the merge destination is the Meeting Agenda sample we explored in Chapter 1. The merge source form is from another sample, Issue Tracking. We'll fill out the Issue Tracking form to create several issue forms. Then you'll see how Meeting Agenda supports merging these forms even though they conform to a different schema.

Create Source Forms

1. Open the Issues Tracking form by starting InfoPath, selecting Sample Forms, and double-clicking Issue Tracking (Detailed).
2. Fill in the fields of the Action Items section, and save your issue form. Repeat to create a second form with different Action Items. Use the filenames Issue1.xml and Issue2.xml. Scroll down in the view until you find this section, and fill it out.
3. Save these forms as separate files in the same folder. See Issue1.xml and Issue2.xml for examples.

Figure 2-19 shows the Action Items section of the Issue Tracking form that Meeting Agenda imports. If you don't fill out this section, the result of the custom merge won't be interesting because the Custom Merge feature for Meeting Agenda ignores the other data.

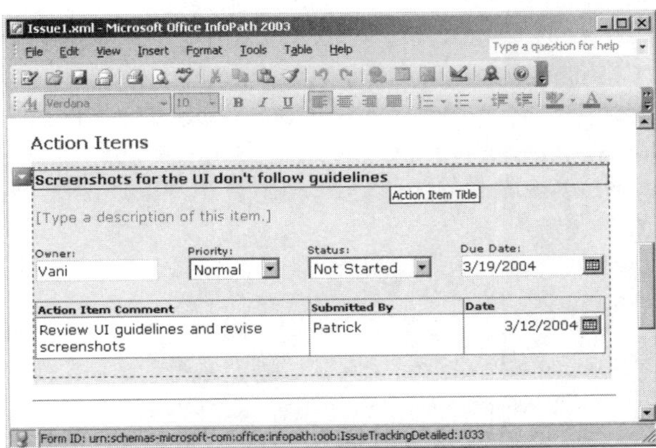

Figure 2-19 Meeting Agenda implements custom merge logic to import action items from Issue Tracking forms.

Create Destination Form for Merge

1. Open the Meeting Agenda form by starting InfoPath, selecting Sample Forms, and double-clicking Meeting Agenda.

2. From the File menu, choose Merge Forms.
3. Select both of the files you created earlier, and then click Merge.
4. Scroll down to the Action Items section.

Figure 2-20 shows the result of merging two Issue Tracking forms into Meeting Agenda. The Meeting Agenda form imported the Action Items from the Issue Tracking forms data. Figure 2-20 actually contains three action items, but only two were imported. The third action item is blank and shows up as the first row in the table. This is an artifact from the blank Meeting Agenda form and can be deleted.

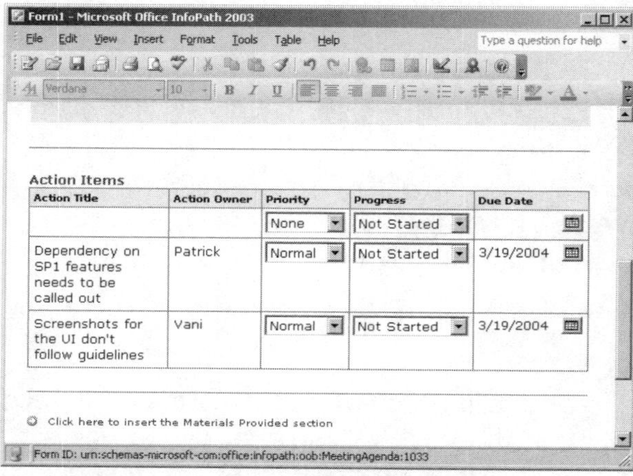

Figure 2-20 Meeting Agenda's custom merge aggregates all of the action items from the imported Issue Tracking forms.

We'll return to custom merge in Chapter 10 and discuss an example using two SharePoint form libraries. The InfoPath SDK is a great resource for Custom Merge. Not only does it contain a more extensive Custom Merge sample form, but the feature is very well documented. In the SDK documentation, search on *importParameters* or explore Merge Forms under the Developer Sample Forms section.

Exporting to Excel

For reporting and business intelligence metrics, your InfoPath data will benefit from a richer set of data analysis. With comprehensive support for numerical functions, Excel is a great tool for data analysis. To get your data into Excel, you can use InfoPath's built-in support for exporting data to Excel. From Excel, you can then create reports and do more in-depth data analysis.

Let's take a look at the Book Purchase example we created earlier in this chapter. The following steps walk through an example of exporting InfoPath data to Excel.

1. Using the Merge Form feature, create a merged form that contains several sample book purchases.
2. InfoPath should automatically switch to the Report view. From here, you can choose Export To | Microsoft Office Excel from the File menu.

Note Figure 2-21 shows the second page of the wizard. The Export To Excel feature supports two modes of exporting: Form Fields Only and Form Fields And Table. The first option exports all of the leaf nodes that are not part of repeating sections. You can think of this as the single-occurrence data in your form. The second option includes the single-occurrence data but adds one table of repeating information. InfoPath creates a separate column in Excel for each form field. For tables, InfoPath creates separate rows for the repeating data.

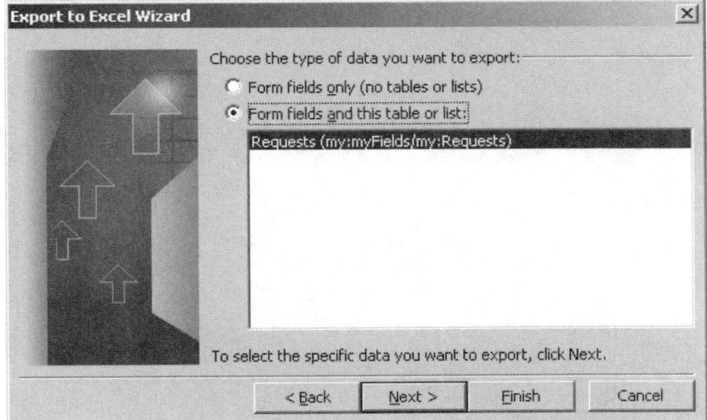

Figure 2-21 InfoPath supports exporting form fields and tables to Excel.

Important InfoPath limits what you can export to the data that exists in the current view. For forms with large schemas, exporting all data is not practical because of the number of columns that InfoPath would need to create to hold the data. Exporting only what appears in the view is also more intuitive: what you see is what you get. If you want to export the data, make sure it appears in the view.

Note In Chapter 1, you learned how to promote fields to SharePoint form libraries as columns. Exporting form fields to Excel is similar. The main difference is that Export To Excel supports tables, whereas SharePoint does not. SharePoint supports nine inline aggregation functions to assist in rolling up values from tables; Export To Excel doesn't have to support any aggregation functions because once you have the data in Excel, you have the entire armada of Excel functions at your disposal.

3. Select the second option, Form Fields And This Title Or List.
4. The Report view contains only the Requests table. Select that and continue.
5. On the next page, you select the data to export for your table. By default, everything is selected. Continue to the final page, which lets you select additional forms to export.

> **Note** If we hadn't merged the forms, we could use this page to select multiple forms. InfoPath exports the data in each additional form as a separate set of rows. The ability to export multiple forms is a key element because it enables the Export To Excel feature to function as a separate form of roll-up. Unlike Merge Forms, Export To Excel requires no modifications to the form to support multiple forms.

6. Click the Finish button. InfoPath will launch Excel and have it load the exported data into a spreadsheet.

Figure 2-22 shows the results of the export. The columns contain both the label and the XPath of the exported field.

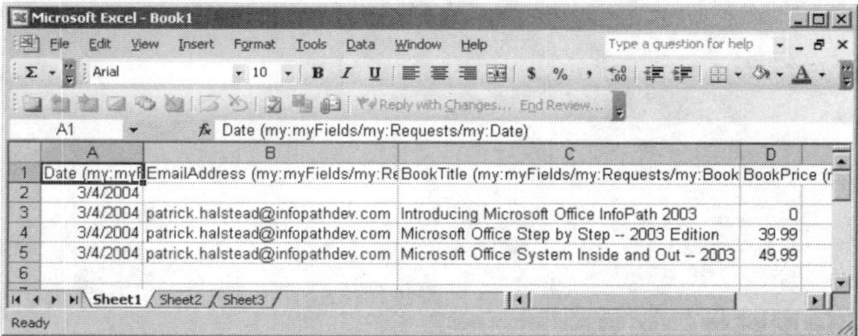

Figure 2-22 Excel displays column names and XPath expressions in a header row above the exported data.

Excel 2003 supports binding to XML Schemas, which means you can map a cell in your Excel spreadsheet to a node in an XML file. You can then have Excel import your form, validate it against the specified schema, and load the mapped node values into the cells of your spreadsheet. InfoPath is an XML standard bearer, and the intent was to have XML Schema interoperate with Excel. The InfoPath developers pursued this goal but unfortunately had to disable it–Excel could not support schemas with *xsd:any* because of the complexity of mapping and validating ad hoc data types. InfoPath implements rich text fields (XHTML) using *xsd:any*.

For more advanced integration with Excel, you can add code to your application logic to start Excel and manipulate it via the VBA object model.

Using Data Connections

InfoPath supports data connections for both receiving and submitting data. Each data connection corresponds to a data adapter. InfoPath supports a variety of data adapters, depending on the data source and the type of the connection (receive or submit):

Main data source

- Database (ADO)–retrieve and submit data
- Web Service–retrieve data

Secondary data source—retrieve data

- XML file
- Database (ADO)
- SharePoint list
- Web service

Secondary data source—submit data

- E-mail
- SharePoint services (DAV)
- Human Workflow Services (HWS)
- Web service

In the Book Purchase example, you learned how to create data adapters that submit data to e-mail and SharePoint. Chapter 1 showed how to retrieve data from an XML document to populate a list box. Next we'll take a brief look at the three remaining retrieve data adapters–database, Web service, and SharePoint list.

Connecting to a Database

InfoPath provides two ways to connect to a database–using the main data source or a secondary data source. If you create a form from scratch by specifying a database connection, you can use the main data source to retrieve and submit data to a single database. You can also retrieve data from one or more databases using secondary data sources. We'll create a database adapter for the main data source. This form is defined to retrieve and submit data to a single database, but to simplify the example we will only query the database and display the results. If you want to add database connections to an existing form (for example, to populate data for a drop-down list), you can do this using a secondary data source. In other words, you don't have to specify a database when you create a form. Here's an overview of the features you get for both types of database adapters:

Main data source

- Pro: Supports submitting data to a database. The data source of the form is the database.
- Con: Form depends on database schema. You have to create it from scratch using the database.

Secondary Data Source

- Pro: Easy to add to existing forms.
- Con: Doesn't support submit.

You can add database adapters as secondary data sources to forms where the main data source is already connected to a database table.

The database connection example assumes that you have a copy of the Northwind database and Microsoft SQL Server 2000 installed. If you don't have Northwind installed, you can skip this section. To verify that you have Northwind installed open SQL Server Enterprise Manager from the Start menu by choosing All Programs | Microsoft SQL Server. The management console loads the SQL Server Enterprise Manager component. Expand the node for Microsoft SQL Servers, SQL Server Group, and then for SQL Server Link, which is named (LOCAL) (Windows NT) if you are running the SQL server locally. Expand the Databases folder and look for Northwind.

The following steps describe how to create a simple query form using a database as a source. This simple introduction shows how to integrate InfoPath with the Northwind SQL database.

Create a Blank Form

1. Start InfoPath and choose Design A Form.
2. In the Design A New Form section of the task pane, select New From Data Connection.

Add a Database Data Connection

1. Select Database, and then click Next.
2. Click Select Database, and then double-click Connect To New Data Source.
3. Select Microsoft SQL Server in the Select Data Source dialog box, and then click Next. Note that InfoPath supports OLAP, ODBC DSN, Oracle, and Other/Advanced data sources.
4. The Connect To Database Server page appears. Type the name of your database server–(LOCAL) if SQL is running on your development machine. Specify logon credentials. For (LOCAL) servers, this is usually Windows Authentication. Click Next.
5. The next page lets you select the database to use. Select Northwind from the drop-down list. The fourth table in the list will be Customer And Suppliers By City. This is actually

a view. Select it and then click Next. Click Finish to create your new .odc file. You can use this .odc file to specify another database receive connection in the future. Click Next and then Finish to open your new data connection form.

6. The Data Source Structure is displayed. This dialog box lets you add or remove tables and edit the SQL statement used to query and submit to SQL. We'll explore this more in Chapter 11; for now, accept the defaults by clicking Next.
7. You can name the data connection. Because we are designing this form from a database connection, the name will default to Main Connection, which is fine for now. Click Finish.

Create the View

1. InfoPath creates a view to query the database and display data resulting from the query, but it doesn't add any specific fields.
2. Drag the *queryFields* node from the Data Source task pane to the section in the view that displays the text "Drag Query Fields Here." Choose to add a Section With Controls when prompted. Delete all of the fields except *City*.
3. Drag the *dataFields* node from the Data Source task pane to the section in the view marked with the "Drag Data Fields Here" placeholder text. Choose to add a Section With Controls when prompted. InfoPath will add a section containing a repeating table. Remove the column for City from the table, and adjust the width of the other columns to fill the space.
4. Replace the "Click To Add A Title" placeholder text with **Sample Northwind Database Form**.
5. Replace the "Click To Add Form Content" placeholder text with **Get Customers By City Query**.
6. Remove extra white space from the form. White space refers to areas where there are spaces or extra blank lines. You can use the Delete or Backspace keys to remove it.
7. Remove the New Record button.

Preview the Form

1. Save the form to your desktop.
2. Preview the form using Ctrl+Shift+B.
3. Type the name of a city in the *City* field. For this example, type **London**, and then click Run Query.
4. Now type **Seattle** in the *City* field and then click Run Query.

You have just created an InfoPath form that queries a database. Figure 2-23 displays the result. This rather simple example shows an easy integration scenario that does not require any code. We'll explore database integration in more depth in Chapter 8.

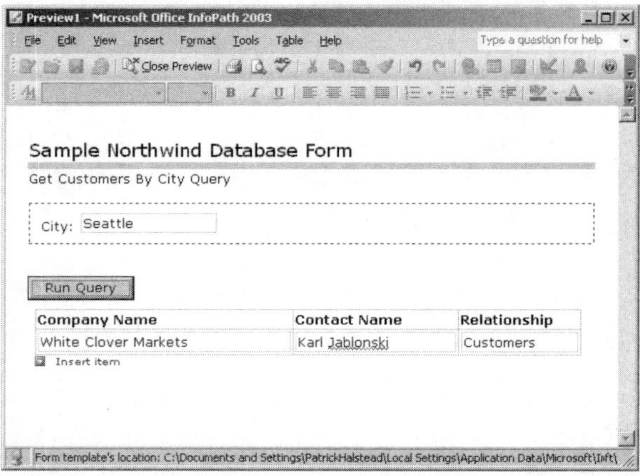

Figure 2-23 Setting up a form to query a database

Connecting to a Web Service

InfoPath provides three ways to connect to Web services. Using a secondary data source, you can retrieve data from a Web service. You can also use a secondary data source to submit data to a Web service. Finally, you can create a form from scratch and specify a Web service for the main data source that can both receive and submit data. This section presents an example of using a main data source to connect to a Web service, but we will look only at the retrieve data side of things.

The following example uses a Web service created by Roger Jennings for his book titled *Introducing Microsoft Office InfoPath 2003* (Microsoft Learning), which is an excellent introduction to InfoPath. The Web service home page is available at http://www.oakleaf.ws/InfoPath/nworders.aspx.

The following steps create a form that queries the NwOrders Web service and displays the results.

Create a Blank Form

1. Start InfoPath, and choose Design A Form.
2. In the Design A New Form section of the task pane, select New From Data Connection.

Add a Web Service Data Connection

1. Select Web Service, and then click Next.
2. Select Receive Data, and then click Next.
3. Enter the location of the Web service: http://www.oakleaf.ws/nwordersws/nwordersws.asmx?wsdl and then click Next.
4. Select the *GetProductsDetailed* operation, and then click Next.
5. Click Finish.

Create the View

InfoPath creates a view to query the Web service and display data resulting from the query. To see the results, we must add fields to the view.

1. Expand the nodes under the *dataFields* node in the Data Source task pane until you see the *productDtl* node. Drag this node into the section with the "Drag data fields here" placeholder text. Choose to add it as a repeating table.
2. Delete the query section (marked with the "Drag query fields here" placeholder text).
3. Replace the "Click To Add A Title" placeholder text with **Sample Northwind Web Service Form**.
4. Replace the "Click To Add Form Content" placeholder text with **Get Products Detail**.
5. Remove extra white space from the form.

Preview the Form

1. Save the form to your desktop.
2. Preview your form by pressing Ctrl+Shift+B.
3. Click Run Query.

You have just created an InfoPath form that queries a Web service. Figure 2-24 displays the result. Like the earlier database example, this simple example is an easy integration scenario that does not require any coding. In general, InfoPath supports many integration scenarios without requiring any coding, but real-world scenarios will require more extensive coding. We'll explore Web service integration in more depth in Chapter 7.

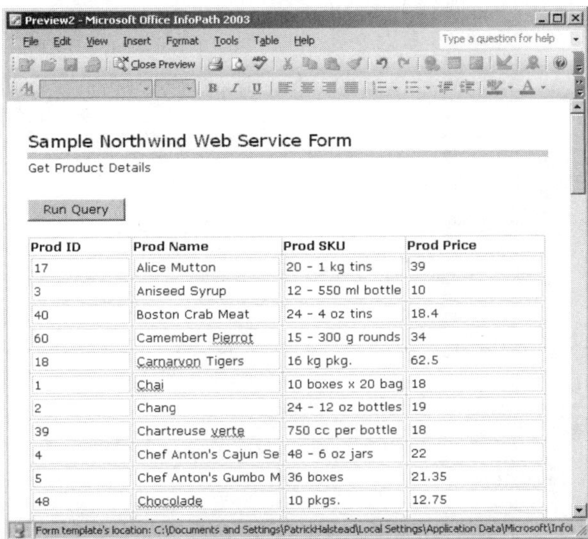

Prod ID	Prod Name	Prod SKU	Prod Price
17	Alice Mutton	20 - 1 kg tins	39
3	Aniseed Syrup	12 - 550 ml bottle	10
40	Boston Crab Meat	24 - 4 oz tins	18.4
60	Camembert Pierrot	15 - 300 g rounds	34
18	Carnarvon Tigers	16 kg pkg.	62.5
1	Chai	10 boxes x 20 bag	18
2	Chang	24 - 12 oz bottles	19
39	Chartreuse verte	750 cc per bottle	18
4	Chef Anton's Cajun Se	48 - 6 oz jars	22
5	Chef Anton's Gumbo M	36 boxes	21.35
48	Chocolade	10 pkgs.	12.75

Figure 2-24 Setting up a form to query a Web service

Connecting to a SharePoint List

A common form scenario is to prepopulate a drop-down list when the form loads. You can query a database or a Web service to do this, but only if you already have the data. Adding data to a database may require a separate form and possibly a Web service operation to map the XML data into your database tables. If you have a SharePoint site, you can easily define a data connection to a library or a list and use it to populate your form.

For this example, we'll create a simple form that populates a drop-down list from a predefined SharePoint list. You must have access to a SharePoint site and permission to create a list.

Create a SharePoint List

1. Navigate to your SharePoint site in Internet Explorer.
2. The default SharePoint site will display a menu at the top of the page. This menu will include Home, Documents And Lists, Create, Site Settings, and Help. Click Documents And Lists.
3. Scroll down to the Lists section, and then click Contacts.
4. If your site contains no contacts, click New Item and add a few contacts.

Create a Blank Form with a List Box

1. Start InfoPath, and choose Design A Form.
2. Select New Blank Form.
3. Click Layout, and then insert the layout table, Table With Title.
4. Replace the "Click To Add A Title" placeholder text with **Sample SharePoint List Form**.
5. Replace the "Click To Add Form Content" placeholder text with **Get Users**.
6. Click in the view beneath the title table, and add a blank line by pressing Enter.
7. In the task pane, click Controls and then Drop-Down List Box.

Connect to the SharePoint List

1. Double-click the Drop-Down List Box control that you added to the view.
2. In the Drop-Down List Box Properties dialog box, select Look Up Values In A Data Connection.
3. Click Add to create the data connection.
4. Select SharePoint Library Or List, and then click Next.
5. Enter the location of your SharePoint site and then click Next. InfoPath queries the site and presents a list of libraries and lists that it finds there.
6. Select Contacts, and then click Next.
7. Select the *Last_Name* field, and deselect all other fields. Click Next and then click Finish.

8. Click the button next to Entries, and press the asterisk key (*) to expand the tree.
9. Select the repeating Contacts node and then click OK twice to close the dialog box.

Preview the Form

1. Save the form to your desktop.
2. Preview your form by pressing Ctrl+Shift+B.
3. Click on the drop-down list to see the values.

You have just created an InfoPath form that queries a SharePoint list. Figure 2-25 displays the result. Like the earlier examples, this SharePoint list example is meant to show an easy integration scenario that does not require any code. In general, most SharePoint list examples won't require much code. However, you can get creative with SharePoint lists. For example, to create a form that loads an XML fragment from a form library based on the value of a drop-down list, you would define an *OnAfterChange* event handler that loads a file corresponding to the selected entry and injects the XML into your form. We'll explore this and other examples in Chapter 9 when we dig into SharePoint collaboration scenarios.

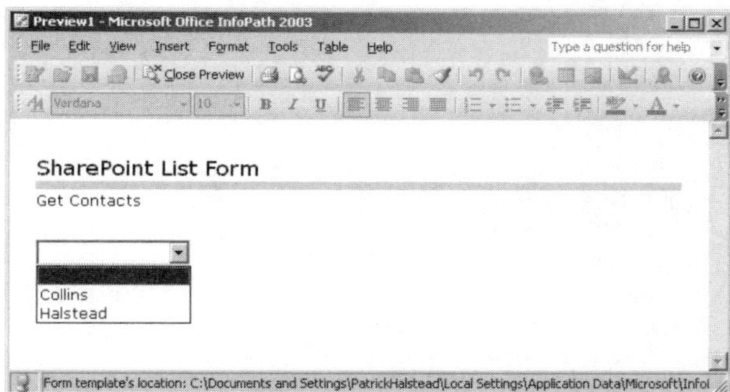

Figure 2-25 Setting up a form to query a SharePoint list

Summary

This chapter, which completes Part I, introduced you to InfoPath programming, event handlers, simple workflow, and data connections. In the process, you learned how to create InfoPath forms that use managed code. You created several sample forms from scratch in the designer and learned about some key enterprise features–workflow and data connections.

Part II
Form Design Patterns

Chapter 3

Creating Smart Forms

This chapter introduces several techniques for creating "smart" InfoPath forms. InfoPath forms are highly customizable and extensible. With some up-front planning, you can create forms that are easy to maintain and that the user can fill out in the most efficient way. We will cover four main topics—conditional visibility, data validation, autopopulation, and master/detail controls for repeating data—and use example forms to demonstrate techniques. Some of the techniques accomplish overlapping goals—for example, the goals of dynamic filtering for conditional visibility are closely related to the goals of master/detail controls for repeating data. The examples will give you a clear idea of how and why you should use a specific technique in a given scenario.

Using Conditional Visibility

One of the big drawbacks of paper forms—other than the obvious workflow nightmare—is that they are often crammed with input fields to accommodate various types of users with different input profiles. A good user interface for a form, on the other hand, maximizes input by minimizing controls and options so the form is not cluttered and the user does not get lost. InfoPath allows you to clean up views of your form and to focus users on data that is specific to their needs by using the conditional visibility design pattern.

Why Use Conditional Visibility?

Conditional visibility means showing or hiding fields in a form depending on input context. This results in a better experience for the user because data that is invalid or irrelevant to the form instance is eliminated. Conditional visibility techniques in InfoPath include conditional formatting, data filtering, and rules. It is also possible to implement on-demand, show-and-hide behavior of form input fields by using dynamic controls such as optional or repeating sections, multiple views, and views based on user roles, but we'll first talk about conditional visibility.

By hiding a control in the form, you are not eliminating the data in your form's instance or in the XML. Most of the examples in this chapter implement conditional visibility in typical ways—for example, hiding controls to disallow user input and show filtered data based on values in the form. You can also restrict controls within the view or views by adding only the controls that you require in that view. We'll take a closer look at that topic when we talk about multiple views in Chapter 6.

Parking Registration Form Example

Many of us have been late to an offsite meeting because we did not anticipate the parking registration process at the building reception desk. In this scenario, we'll encourage greater punctuality by creating an InfoPath parking registration form.

We won't show you how to create this form from scratch because by now you should have a fairly good idea of how to get started with InfoPath. You can find the forms for the examples in this chapter in the companion content on the Web site for this book. Take a look at the data source for the form (ParkingRegistration.xsn) we'll use. (See the Introduction of this book for the URL for the Web site.) Right-click it, and choose Design. If you receive a warning dialog box telling you that the form has been moved since it was published, click OK. Open the Data Source task pane to see the data source for the parking registration form. This data source was created from a blank new form in InfoPath by using the functionality provided in the Controls and Data Source task panes.

Note Chapter 1 introduced the Data Source task pane. If you are an InfoPath newbie and need more information on basic design tasks, see the InfoPath Help topics. Remember to browse InfoPath Help in an online, connected state to get the latest Help content. To read InfoPath Help content for using the data source pane, follow these steps:

1. Press F1 to open the Help task pane in InfoPath.
2. Click the Table Of Contents link to open the list of Help topics.
3. Click the Working With The Data Source link.

Conditional Formatting

The conditional formatting feature can be used to for conditional visibility, a technique that has proved to be very useful in InfoPath form templates. We recommend conditional formatting when you want to show and hide controls based on simple conditions–that is, when the conditions are independent of the data you want to show and hide. For example, we can use this technique in our parking registration form to show the Additional Permits section only if the user explicitly asks for additional permits. Here's how to use this technique:

1. Open C:\Microsoft Learning\Developing Solutions with InfoPath\Chapter03\Samples\ParkingRegistration.xsn in InfoPath design mode by right-clicking it and choosing Design. Figure 3-1 shows the design view for this form.

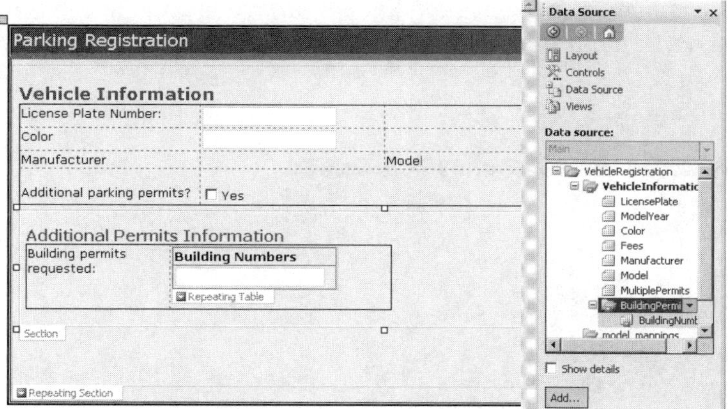

Figure 3-1 The Parking Registration Form

2. Double-click the Section label that appears below the Additional Permits Information section.
3. In the Section Properties dialog box, click the Display tab, and then click Conditional Formatting.
4. In the Conditional Formatting dialog box, click Add.
5. In the Conditional Format dialog box, select Select A Field Or Group in the first drop-down list.
6. In the Select A Field Or Group dialog box, select the *MultiplePermits* field and then click OK.
7. In the third drop-down list, select FALSE.
8. Select the Hide This Control check box to complete the condition and then click OK three times to all of the open dialog boxes.
9. Save, and then preview the form.
10. Toggle the value of the Additional Parking Permits check box to see the Additional Permits Information section show or hide.
11. Close the preview.
12. Open the form at C:\Microsoft Learning\Developing Solutions With InfoPath\Chapter03\Samples\ParkingRegistrationCF.xsn to compare its behavior with what you just implemented.

You might notice from Figure 3-2 that conditional formatting actually "formats" the control on which it is defined. Conditional visibility is only one of the patterns you can implement using this feature. Behind the scenes, a condition is added to your view's style sheet using an *<xsl:if>* or *<xsl:choose>* construct.

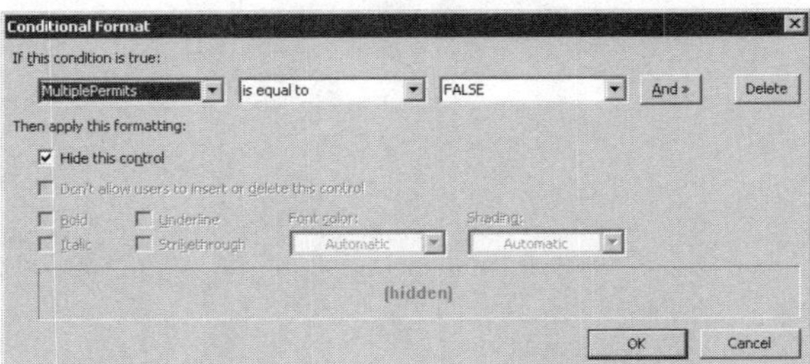

Figure 3-2 The Conditional Format dialog box

Figure 3-3 shows what the conditionally visible section we just created looks like when the Additional Parking Permits check box is both selected and cleared.

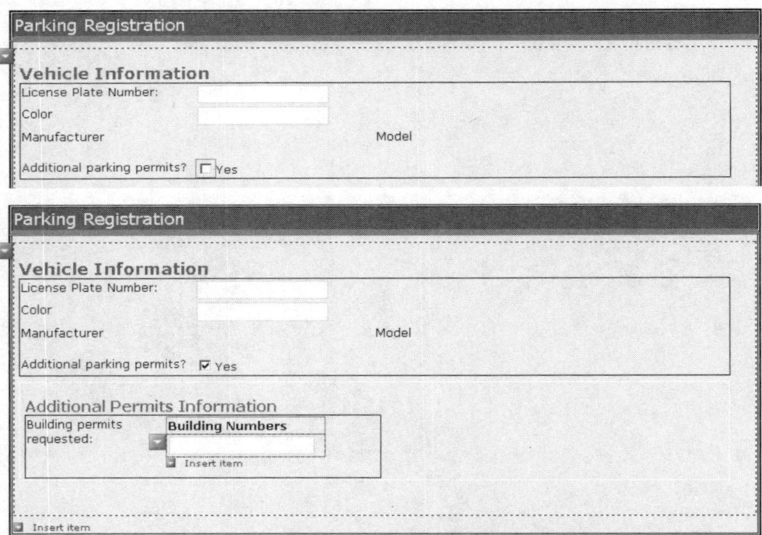

Figure 3-3 Showing or hiding a section based on user input

Conditional formatting is commonly used in a shipping/billing scenario. You insert a check box labeled "Check here if shipping address is different from billing address" and then show the shipping address section only if the user checks this box.

Dynamic Data Filtering

Let's move on to some more complex examples of data filtering. You can filter information in repeating data controls based on both static and dynamic conditions. When you use data filters on static conditions, the conditions are determined at design time. Data filtering on dynamic conditions is based on run-time conditions.

Designing conditional visibility by using data filtering is more involved and, of course, more fun than implementing conditional formatting. To study data filtering in its simplest form, we'll insert a repeating table in an InfoPath form.

1. Design a new blank form, and then insert a Repeating Table from the Controls task pane.
2. Double-click the Repeating Table label that appears below the Building Numbers table to open the Properties dialog box. You can also right-click on the table header or near the text "Repeating Table" and then choose Repeating Table Properties.
3. In the Repeating Table Properties dialog box, click on the Display tab, click Filter Data, and then click Add.
4. In the Specify Filter Conditions dialog box, play with implementing different conditions to filter data in the repeating table. For example, select field1 in the first drop-down list, select Is Equal To in the second drop-down list, select Type A Number in the third drop-down list, and then type **1**.
5. Click OK three times to close all open dialog boxes.
6. Preview the form, and add a few rows to the repeating table.
7. Type **1** in the first column of some of the table rows.
8. Click on the arrow at the left edge of the table to open the shortcut menu, and choose Refresh Filter. Notice that only the rows with value 1 in the first column are displayed in the repeating table.

Dynamic data filtering uses the rules functionality that the InfoPath design mode provides. We'll take a closer look at design patterns that involve rules in Chapters 5 and 6.

Filtering data using drop-down list box values InfoPath allows filtering data within repeating controls based on conditions that you specify when you create the controls. The filtered values can then be displayed using a list box or a drop-down list box control. For example, to show the parking registration entries by building, you can use a filter to display all the vehicles that are parked at a certain building. You can use a drop-down control that displays all the buildings or locations for parking. When the user makes a selection, all the vehicles registered for that location are displayed in a separate list box control. Here's how to filter vehicle data based on parking location:

1. Open ParkingRegistration.xsn in design mode. (You can build on the form you created in the previous exercise, or you can use the form C:\Microsoft Learning\Developing Solutions With InfoPath\Chapter03\Samples\ParkingRegistrationCF.xsn.)
2. Open the Data Source task pane, and click the root node *VehicleRegistration*.
3. Add a Group node called VehiclesByBuilding.
4. Add two Text Field child nodes into this group called Building and LicenseNumber.
5. Right-click and drag *VehiclesByBuilding\Building* in the view just below the repeating section, and then select Drop-Down List Box from the context menu.
6. Right-click and drag *VehiclesByBuilding\LicenseNumber* in the view below Building, and then select List Box from the context menu.
7. Right-click on the drop-down list for Building, and choose Drop-Down List Box Properties. You can also open the Properties dialog box for the drop-down list box or for any other control by double-clicking the control.
8. In the Drop-Down List Box Properties dialog box, click Add.
9. In the Add Choice dialog box, type **1** in the Value text box and then click OK.
10. Repeat the previous two steps to add the numbers 2, 3, 4, 5, and 6. The Properties dialog box will look like that shown in Figure 3-4.

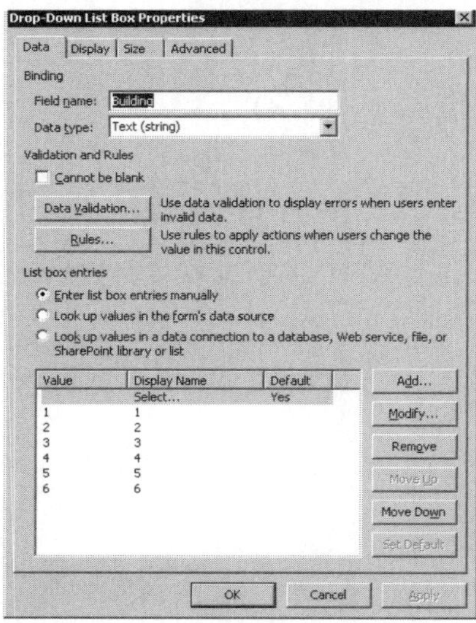

Figure 3-4 The Drop-Down List Box Properties dialog box for the Building field

11. Click OK to close the Drop-Down List Box Properties dialog box.
12. Right-click on the License Number list box, and then choose List Box Properties.
13. Select the Look Up Values In The Form's Data Source option, and then click the Select XPath button next to Entries.
14. In the Select A Field Or Group dialog box, select the *VehicleRegistration/VehicleInformation/LicensePlate* node.
15. Click Filter Data, and then click Add.
16. In the first drop-down list, select Select A Field Or Group.
17. Select *VehiclesByBuilding\Building*, and then click OK.
18. In the third drop-down list, select Select A Field Or Group.
19. Select *BuildingPermits\BuildingNumbers*, and then click OK twice. The Filter Data dialog box will look like that shown in Figure 3-5.
20. Cick OK three times to close all the open dialog boxes.
21. Preview the form.
22. Type the license plate number **123ABC**.
23. Select the Additional Parking Permits check box.
24. In the Building Numbers table, add rows for buildings numbered 1 through 6.

    Click Insert Item at the bottom of the Vehicle Information section.

    Add a few more parking registration entries with multiple building permits.
25. Select a building from the drop-down list. The license plates for this building appear in the list box.
26. Close the preview, save the form, and then close InfoPath.
27. Open the form ParkingRegistrationbyBuildings.xsn from the Samples folder to compare its behavior with what you just implemented.

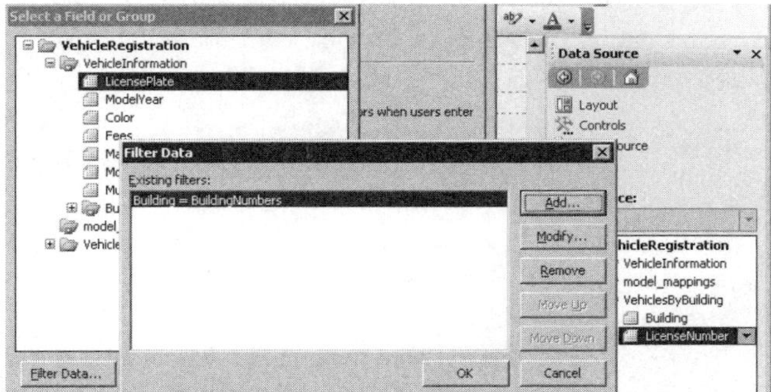

Figure 3-5 Filtering data for License Plate field

Figure 3-6 shows what the filtered values look like. You can use this filter pattern when you want to show summary data based on values entered previously in the form. You can also extend this technique to create cascading drop-down lists with values based on previously entered values, as described next.

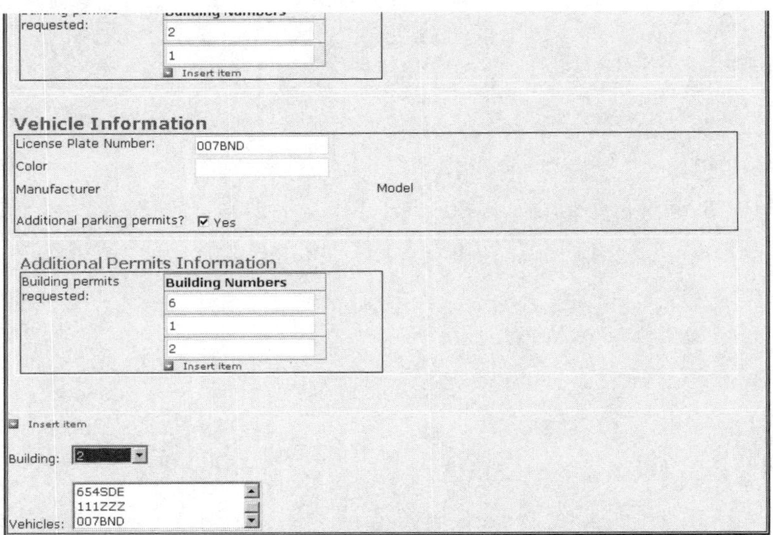

Figure 3-6 Vehicle license numbers filtered on building numbers

> **Developer Nugget: Dynamic Drop-Down Lists and Unique Entries**
>
> Our parking registration example reveals data based on a list of buildings. But what if we don't have this list when we design the form? It can be tedious to create filter conditions from static data in the form. What if we want to read the list of building numbers based on user input? Or what if we want to read a list of U.S. cities? InfoPath makes it easy to create such dynamic filters by allowing you to use a secondary data source for the filter.

Instead of adding the building numbers 1 through 6 in the Building drop-down list box , you can select Look Up Values In The Form's Data Source in the Properties dialog box. (This would be similar to what you did earlier in step 13 when you looked up values for the License Number list box control by using the forms data source.) You can click the Select XPath button next to Entries and select BuildingPermits\BuildingNumbers in the Select A Field Or Group dialog box. Click OK to dismiss all dialog boxes. This causes the Building drop-down list box to read the building numbers directly from the form input; you don't have to worry about populating the list when you design the form.

However, something is very wrong with the form. Did you notice? The Building drop-down list has duplicate entries for building locations–one entry for each time a building number is used. We need to add a filter to enforce uniqueness of the entries. In the Select A Field Or

Group dialog box where you selected BuildingPermits/BuildingNumbers, click the Filter Data button, then click Add. The first and second drop-down lists in the Filter Data dialog box will have as their default values BuildingNumbers and Is Equal To. In the third drop-down list box select Use A Formula. Type the following formula:

```
not(.= preceding::BuildingNumbers)
```

Select the Edit XPath check box in this dialog box. Add the *my* namespace prefix to Building-Numbers so the condition becomes

```
not(.= preceding::my:BuildingNumbers)
```

The complete condition implemented can be seen in the Entries XPath of the Drop-Down List Box Properties dialog box:

```
/my:VehicleRegistration/my:VehicleInformation/my:BuildingPermits/
my:BuildingNumbers[(. = not(. = preceding::my:BuildingNumbers))]
```

It might look daunting, but we have written only a small part of this XPath. The XPath filter uses a predicate *[...]* that eliminates duplicates *(. = not(...))* through a preceding axis that returns all nodes that occur before the context node *BuildingNumbers*. Open the form ParkingRegistrationUniqueBuilding.xsn from the Samples folder to compare its behavior to what you just implemented.

To learn more about XPath, you can refer to XPath Help from the MSXML Help file that comes with your InfoPath installation. The file is at C:\Program Files\Microsoft Office\OFFICE11\1033\XMLSDK5.CHM. You can also get help on numerous topics related to developing InfoPath forms, including the InfoPath OM, the InfoPath XSF, MSXML, scripting, and many others, through the MSE10.CHM file from the same location. For the detailed specification of the standard, refer to the XPath document at http://www.w3.org/TR/xpath.

Filtering data using cascading drop-down lists In many Web forms, you fill in a field that populates subsequent input choices. Many of these forms have multiple levels of such "cascades." Let's extend the dynamic filtering technique shown in the previous section to enable such cascading input controls.

We'll extend our parking registration form so that when the user selects a car manufacturer from a drop-down list, the list populates a second drop-down list with that manufacturer's models. For this, we will create the form using an XML file as a secondary data source with manufacturer and model information for cars. We will add some filtering to remove any anomalies with the cascading drop-down lists. Finally, we will delve into a bit of schema design for the secondary data source itself to make optimal use of it. Following are the steps to create the cascading drop-down lists:

1. Open ParkingRegistration.xsn in design mode.
2. Click Data Source in the task pane, and then expand the *VehicleInfomation* group.

3. Insert *Manufacturer* as a Drop-Down List Box into the table cell just right of the Manufacturer label, and then delete the label that InfoPath inserted with the control.

4. Open its Properties dialog box, select Look Up Values In A Data Connection, as shown in Figure 3-7, and then click Add.

5. In the Data Connection Wizard, select XML Document as shown in Figure 3-8.

6. Click Resource Files, click Add, locate the VehicleMappings.xml file, and then click OK. Figure 3-9 shows the file added as a resource file.

7. Click OK, click Next, and then click Finish.

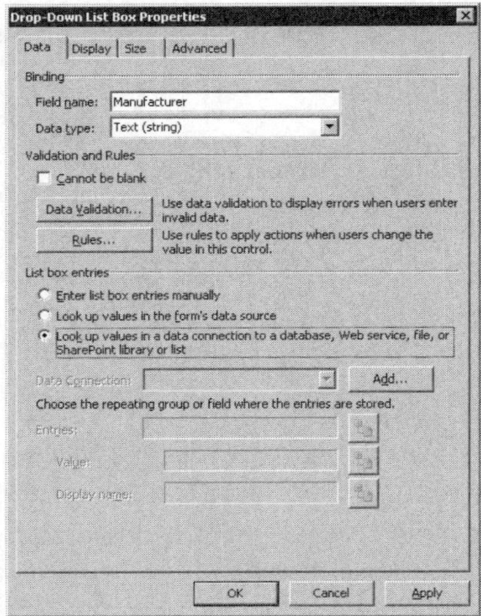

Figure 3-7 The Look Up Values in a Data Connection option

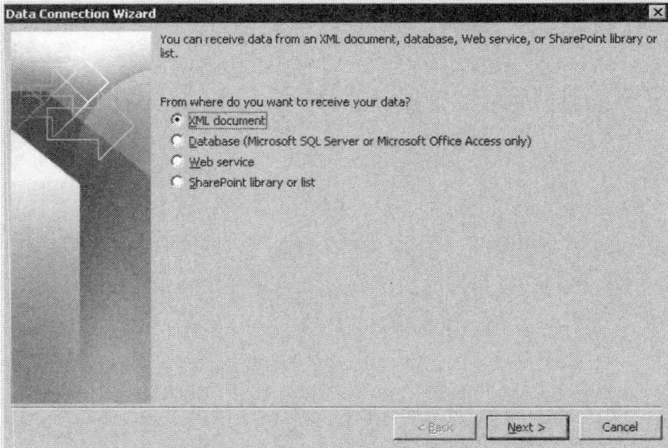

Figure 3-8 The Data Connection Wizard dialog box

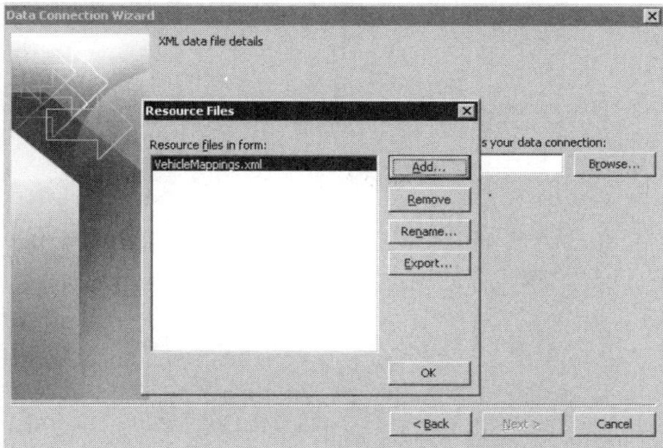

Figure 3-9 Add Data Connection XML file as a Resource file

8. This file has the following XML:

```
<?xml version="1.0" encoding="UTF-8"?>
<model_mappings>
    <car>
        <manufacturer>Volkswagen</manufacturer>
        <model>Beetle</model>
    </car><car>
        <manufacturer>Volkswagen</manufacturer>
        <model>Jetta</model>
    </car><car>
        <manufacturer>Volkswagen</manufacturer>
        <model>Passat</model>
    </car><car>
        <manufacturer>Volkswagen</manufacturer>
        <model>Cabrio</model>
    </car><car>
        <manufacturer>Volkswagen</manufacturer>
        <model>Rabbit</model>
    </car><car>
        <manufacturer>Volkswagen</manufacturer>
        <model>Fox</model>
    </car><car>
        <manufacturer>Chrysler</manufacturer>
        <model>LeBaron</model>
    </car><car>
        <manufacturer>Chrysler</manufacturer>
        <model>Sebring</model>
    </car><car>
        <manufacturer>Chrysler</manufacturer>
        <model>Concorde</model>
    </car><car>
        <manufacturer>Chrysler</manufacturer>
        <model>Town and Country</model>
    </car><car>
        <manufacturer>Chrysler</manufacturer>
        <model>Crossfire</model>
    </car>
</model_mappings>
```

9. In the Drop-Down List Box Properties dialog box, click the Select XPath button next to the Entries text box.
10. In the Select A Field Or Group dialog box, select *manufacturer*, as shown in Figure 3-10, and then click Filter Data.
11. Add a filter condition using the default values *Manufacturer* and *Is Equal To* for the first two drop-down lists and *Use A Formula* for the third drop-down list.
12. In the Insert Formula dialog box, **type not(. = preceding::manufacturer**) This will eliminate duplicate manufacturers.

Note If the secondary data source element manufacturer had a namespace prefix, you would have to click the Edit XPath check box, and add the namespace prefix for manufacturer. If the namespace for the data source collided with some namespace in the main DOM, for example "my", then you would have to use the new namespace prefix that InfoPath assigned to the elements with the conflicting namespace. This would follow a patter preceded by "ns" and followed by a number. This namespace would show up under Entries in the Drop-Down List Box Properties dialog box. You can also find it in the .xsf file. The edited XPath would then be something like *not(. = preceding::ns1:manufacturer)* as shown in Figure 3-11.

13. Click OK five times to close all the open dialog boxes.
14. Insert *Model* as a Drop-Down List Box into the table cell just right of the Model label, and then delete the label that InfoPath inserted with the control.
15. Open its Properties dialog box, select Look Up Values In A Data Connection, verify that VehicleMappings is selected in the Data Connection drop-down list, and then click the Select XPath button next to the Entries text box.
16. In the Select A Field Or Group dialog box, select *model*, click Filter Data, and then click Add.
17. In the Specify Filter Conditions dialog box, select Select a Field or Group in the first drop-down list.
18. In the Select A Field Or Group dialog, select Main from the Data Source drop-down list, select *Manufacturer*, and then click OK.
19. In the third drop-down list select Select a Field or Group, select *manufacturer*, and then click OK.
20. You have successfully implemented the filter to show only those vehicles whose *Manufacturer* (main data source) is equal to *manufacturer* (VehicleMappings secondary data source). The filter appears as "Manufacturer is equal to manufacturer."

21. Click OK four times to close all open dialog boxes.
22. Preview the form.
23. Select a manufacturer from the drop-down list.
24. Click the Models drop-down list and—voilà!—you see only vehicle models for that manufacturer.
25. Open the form \Samples\ParkingRegistrationCascadingDropdowns.xsn to compare its behavior with what you just implemented.

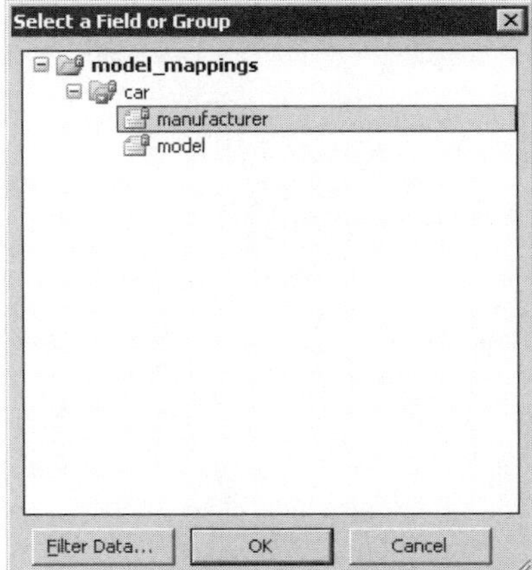

Figure 3-10 The Select A Field Or Group dialog box

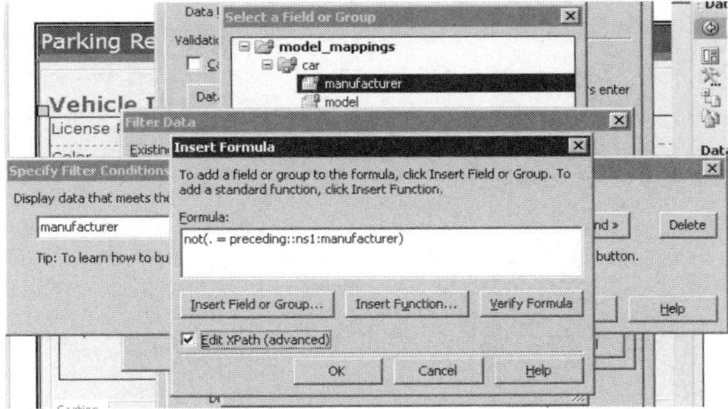

Figure 3-11 The Insert Formula dialog box

Using the technique just described, you can insert multiple drop-down lists based on conditions determined during run time by user input in previous controls.

Developer Nugget: Resetting a Cascading Drop-Down List Value

To make sure the cascading drop-down lists you just implemented do not store incorrect or mismatched values, you should test them by selecting values in the first drop-down list and making sure you get the required value in the second drop-down list. Did you find a bug? There is one! The second drop-down list is not reset when the first drop-down list is changed. You need to make one more change to get that working. Follow these easy steps:

1. Double-click the Manufacturer drop-down list box to open its Properties dialog box.
2. Click Rules, and then click Add.
3. Name the Rule Reset.
4. We will not set a condition so that this rule is applied every time the value of the Manufacturer drop-down list changes.
5. Click Add Action, and then select Set A Field's Value in the Action drop-down list.
6. Click the button to the right of the Field text box.
7. In the Select A Field Or Group dialog box, select *Model*, and then click OK.
8. Leave the Value text box blank so that the value of the *Model* node will be set to blank.
9. Click OK four times to dismiss all the dialog boxes, and you're all set.

Now if you preview the form and select a value in the Manufacturer drop-down list, any old value in the Model drop-down list will get cleared as expected.

Let's look at a simple example of schema design based on the above procedure. The condition *not (. = preceding::ns1:manufacturer)* was implemented.

As in the building numbers example, this XPath eliminates duplicate manufacturer entries from the list. The absence of this condition would result in N identical manufacturer A entries for each model, 1 through N, manufactured by A. However, you can avoid this problem. Read on!

As in the preceding example, the secondary data source, VehicleMappings.xml, has the following structure:

```
<car>
    <manufacturer>Volkswagen</manufacturer>
    <model>Beetle</model>
</car>
```

Instead of being a child element of *<car>*, if the manufacturer is an attribute of *<car>*, you do not have to remove the duplicate *<manufacturer>* values, and you thus eliminate the need for the XPath condition in the filter. If you do this, you have to look up Manufacturer using the element parent of the attribute and use Value and Display Name in the Properties dialog box to display the manufacturer values.

Better still, you can define the manufacturer as a nonrepeating child element:

```
<car>
    <manufacturer>
    <name>Volkswagen</name>
        <models>
            <model>Beetle</model>
            <model>Jetta</model>
            . . .
        </models>
    <manufacturer>
</car>
```

The lesson here is that you should use secondary data sources wisely. If you do not have permission to modify the secondary data source, you don't have much choice. However, if you end up implementing your own secondary data sources, give some thought to the schema, just as you do when you plan the schema for the main data source.

Figure 3-12 shows the cascading effect of the manufacturer/model Drop-Down List Box controls that we created.

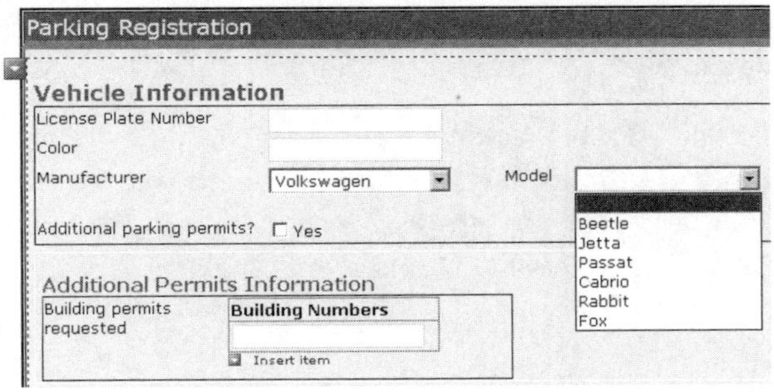

Figure 3-12 Vehicle models for selected manufacturer

We have covered a few examples of conditional visibility patterns that you can use in your form templates. In general, you can use this technique in the following scenarios:

- Hiding a section or sections in the form based on a Boolean value. For example:
    - A hospital registration form where you can display conditional visibility fields based on whether the patient is male or female.
    - A check box or other Boolean control outside a section that makes the section conditionally visible.

- Sorting information on input by adding entries to separate sections of the form that filter based on specified criteria. For example:
    - Sorting the employees in different filtered repeating tables based on the city they work in.
- Using different data sources to store the data that you use for cascading drop-down lists:
    - In our example, we used an XML document as a secondary data source to get vehicle mappings. Instead, you can add this data to the main data source of your form template. You typically do this when you do not expect to maintain or update this data too much after it has been initially defined.
    - InfoPath allows you to create a data connection to an Access or SQL database as you will see in Chapter 6 on database integration. You can use a connection to a Vehicle inventory database to populate the drop-down lists.
    - It is common to have databases exposed as Web services. If you have access to a Web service that returns a list of vehicle models based on the manufacturer, you can use this Web service. You can also write your own Web service and use that in your form.

Implementing conditional visibility in your forms allows for a streamlined user experience. This approach is not new for forms built using ASP and DHTML-like technologies, but InfoPath makes it easy to implement this approach. You might sometimes be required to manually edit the XPath expression, as seen in the previous procedures—especially if your secondary data sources are cumbersome to work with or if the filtering provided by the formulas and conditions through InfoPath user interface is insufficient. Fortunately, XPath is a powerful language, and you can use it to implement even very complex filters.

Another useful example of additional XPath tweaking in cascading drop-down filters is when you use the *current* function at the beginning of an XPath to refer to the current row in a repeating structure. If *model* and *manufacturer* are drop-downs lists in a repeating control, you would use *current()/ns1:manufacturer* to access the manufacturer for the current row.

Using Event Handling

If neither conditional formatting nor dynamic data filtering meets your conditional visibility needs, you can use InfoPath's event model and write code that responds to any change in the value of data required for conditional visibility. For example, in an extended parking registration scenario, you can write code to add an entry to the renewal list depending on certain parameters. This would be part of an *OnAfterChange* event handler for the vehicle node. We will describe the *OnAfterChange* event handler and the InfoPath event model in more detail when we talk about validation and rules in the next section. However, you should use code to implement conditional visibility only if the conditions are not easy to implement using the InfoPath UI.

Using Data Validation

As the term implies, data validation is simply a property of data that makes it "valid." The validity of the data is determined not only by the schema but also by conditions that you can specify through the InfoPath design interface.

InfoPath supports two kinds of data validation at run time–schema validation and custom validation. Schema validation means that InfoPath enforces the defined XML Schema when a user enters data in the form. In other words, InfoPath marks with errors or rejects data that violates the rules defined in the .xsd file included in the form template. Custom validation means specifying validation conditions through the InfoPath design-time UI. You can also customize the user experience when errors occur as a result of these conditions at run time.

Schema Validation

InfoPath always enforces schema validation. The two main types of schema validation are data-type validation and structural validation. Data-type errors are errors that you see–for example, when you add string input to a field that has been defined with the integer data type. Structural errors result from structural limits set using XSD *minOccurs* and *maxOccurs* on repeating fields, groups, or attributes. For example, if you want to prevent users from adding more than 50 rows to a repeating table, you can enforce that in the schema by using *maxOccurs=50* on the repeating element. Structural validation can also include validating against the defined schema structure for the group of data being inserted/deleted/replaced in the form. Schema-invalid data in the form results in error indicators such as a red dashed border around the control that the data is bound to for data-type errors, red asterisks for blank controls that require data, and error dialog boxes for invalid structural edits. The only XSD constructs that InfoPath does not validate when the user enters data in the form are *key/keyref*, *id/idref*, and *unique*. These schema constructs are validated when the form is first loaded, but not for DOM changes as a result of editing actions.

To learn more about XSD, you can refer to the following resources:
XML Schema specification from http://www.w3.org/XML/Schema
http://www.w3schools.com/schema/default.asp
http://msdn.microsoft.com/library/default.asp?url=/library/en-us/xmlsdk/html/xmconXMLSchemas.asp

Custom Validation

Schema validation might not always meet your form's data validation needs. You need sufficient knowledge of the XSD standard/language to implement restrictions in your XSD schema file. For example, compound conditions are not easy to implement using XSD. If you don't plan ahead, you have to go back and modify the schema and sometimes redesign the controls associated with the new restrictions. The InfoPath design mode supports the ability to build the schema incrementally as you go or replace it in your form, but you can leverage the InfoPath schema design features only if you have control over the schema. It is strongly recommended that you plan your schema so that you get it right before you start building your form. Redesigning the schema after your form is built can be quite a painful task. You can use two approaches to implementing custom validation: using the InfoPath UI and using the InfoPath object model through business logic code.

Validating Data Using the InfoPath UI

The InfoPath UI has functionality to add validation conditions to the form. Because you do not have to add business logic code to implement validation conditions using the UI, this technique is also referred to as "declarative validation."

> **Note** In the context of designing within the InfoPath view, we sometimes use the term *field* to refer to a control that is bound to the data source.

We will implement data validation in the Expense Report sample form that you worked with in Chapter 1. We'll customize the form, which has an Expense Code field that takes any string as valid input. Most organizations that use an expense report form use expense codes that follow a specific alphanumeric pattern. While we are at it, we can also enforce a maximum amount for the Expense field and a cost limit. To summarize, we will implement the following data validation conditions in the Expense Report sample:

- Inline validation with a dialog box to enforce a valid pattern for the Expense Code.
- Inline validation without a dialog box to enforce a maximum amount for an Itemized Expense.

Implementing dialog-based validation Error dialog boxes notify a user of a validation error and include an OK button. For the sake of brevity, we will refer to this feature as "dialog-based validation." We'll show an example of dialog-based validation to enforce a pattern for the Expense Code field in the Expense Report form. Let's enforce the pattern of two digits followed by a hyphen followed by three letters.

The Data Entry Pattern

The Data Entry in InfoPath supports a list of common patterns, such as Phone Number, Social Security Number, Zip Code, and Zip Code + 4. It also supports Custom Pattern, which can consume regular expressions that are made using combinations of zero or one, zero plus, or one plus alphabets, digits, characters, hyphens, commas, periods, or parentheses.

All these elements show up in the Data Entry Pattern dialog box. If the regular expression you need cannot be created using the characters and patterns provided by the Data Entry Pattern dialog box, you are free to add valid regular expressions of your own—these will work too. For example, you might want to add a regular expression that validates that the string is an e-mail address from a certain domain. If you add custom regular expressions, just be sure to test your form with patterns that might not be valid but are allowed because of a bug in the expression.

Implement the following steps to enforce the pattern 00-AAA in the Expense Code field:

1. Launch InfoPath.
2. In the Fill Out A Form dialog, select Sample Forms, click Expense Report (International), and then click Design This Form.
3. Right-click on the Expense Code field, and then choose Text Box Properties.
4. In the Text Box Properties dialog box, click Data Validation, and then click Add.
5. In the second drop-down list, select Does Not Match Pattern.
6. In the third drop-down list, select Select A Pattern.
7. In the Data Entry Pattern dialog box, select Custom Pattern from the Standard Patterns list.
8. In the Insert Special Character drop-down list, select Any Digit.
9. Finish with the pattern by selecting Any Digit, Hyphen, Any Letter, Any Letter, Any Letter. Figure 3-13 shows what the dialog box looks like.
10. Click OK to return to the Data Validation (expenseCode) dialog box.
11. In the Error Alert Type drop-down list, select Dialog Box Alert (Immediately Show Message).
12. Type Expense Code pattern should be 00-AAA for the ScreenTip.
13. Type **Please correct the Expense Code**. The pattern should conform to 00-AAA for the Message.
14. Click OK three times to close all the open dialog boxes.
15. Preview the form.
16. In the *Expense Code* field, type an invalid pattern: **123-XY**.
17. Press Tab or click outside the field to allow the data to bind. You will see the Validation Error dialog box.

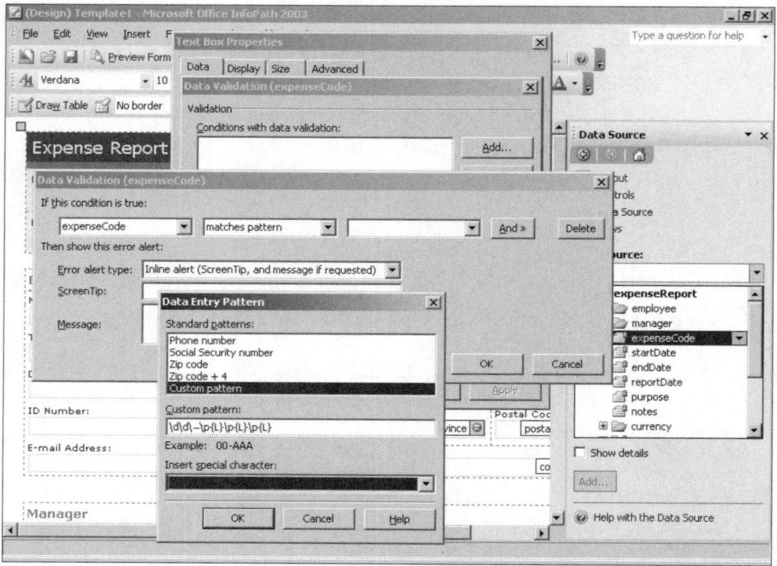

Figure 3-13 The Data Entry Pattern dialog box

Open C:\MS Learning\Developing Solutions With InfoPath\Chapter03\Samples\Expense-ReportErrorDialog.xsn to see the sample implemented using this procedure.

You should use a dialog box for validation errors if the error is serious enough that the user shouldn't proceed without knowing about it. It also goes without saying that too many error dialog boxes will result in an annoying user experience.

Implementing inline errors Inline errors add a red dashed border to the field that has the incorrect data in it. The border is similar to the error notification in the field that you saw in the previous section. The only difference is that you do not see the error dialog box as soon as you tab out of the field. This is a good way to use validation errors without interrupting the user who is filling out the form. You can use inline errors in two ways: with or without a dialog box that has more details regarding the error.

Inline error with details Let's take a look at how to add an inline error with details to the Total field in the Itemized Expenses. We'll implement an inline error based on the validation condition that the total for any single item not exceed 1500:

1. Launch InfoPath.
2. In the Fill Out This Form dialog box, select Sample Forms, click Expense Report (International), and then click Design This Form.

3. Right-click on the *totalAmount* field in the repeating table for Itemized Expenses, and then choose Text Box Properties.
4. In the Text Box Properties dialog box, click Data Validation, and then click Add.
5. In the second drop-down list, select Is Greater Than Or Equal To.
6. In the third drop-down list, select Type A Number, and then type **1500**.
7. Type **Maximum amount allowed is 1500** for the ScreenTip.
8. Type **Amount for any single item cannot exceed 1500** for the Message.
9. Click OK twice to return to the Text Box Properties dialog box.
10. Click on the Advanced tab.
11. Delete the existing ScreenTip. It is important to note here that if a ScreenTip exists, it will take precedence over your data validation ScreenTip.
12. Preview the form.
13. Type **100** in the Cost field and **20** in the Rate field.
14. Click away for the data to bind. The invalid data results in a red dashed border around the field.
15. Hover over the field with your mouse and notice the ScreenTip.
16. Right-click in the field and choose Full Error Description. You should see the message you entered in a warning dialog box. Figure 3-14 shows the invalid field and the context menu with the short error message and Full Error Description item.

Open C:\MS Learning\Developing Solutions using InfoPath\Chapter03\Samples\Expense-ReportInlineError.xsn to see the sample implemented using this procedure.

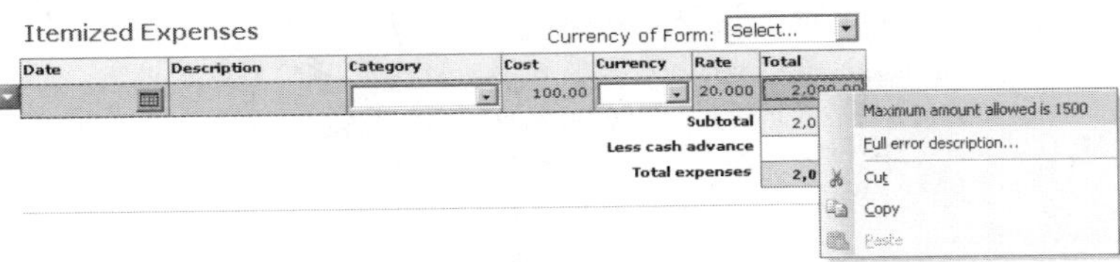

Figure 3-14 Invalid data in the totalAmount field for Itemized Expenses

Inline error without details If you need to implement an inline error without the detailed error, simply omit step 9 from the above procedure. The context menu will not show the Full Error Description button. The validation error message that you specify for the ScreenTip will continue to appear as the topmost item on the shortcut menu, as with the "inline error with details" scenario.

Validating Data Through Code

Even though the Data Validation dialog box lets you specify a wide range of conditions as shown in Figure 3-15, you might still need specialized conditions. No worries–InfoPath provides object model functionality to implement validation in your form through code. Using code, you can also interact with the errors caused by invalid data. We'll look at the guts of how data validation through code works in InfoPath.

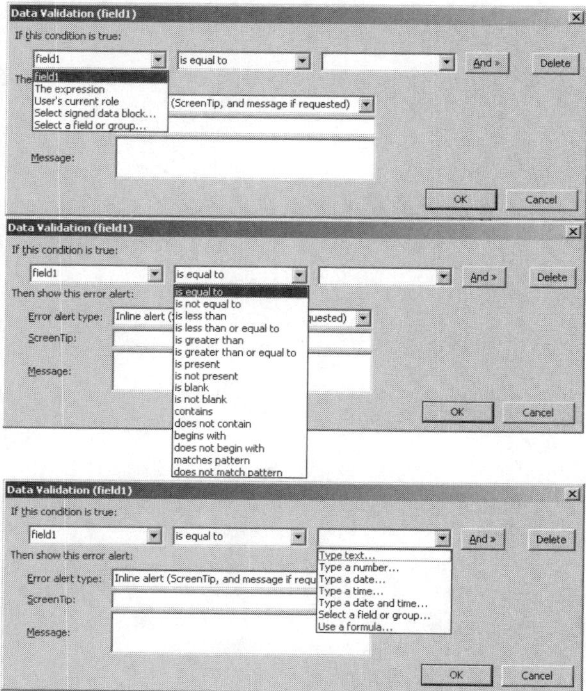

Figure 3-15 Options available on the Data Validation condition builder

Using the DataDOMEvent object We talked about the InfoPath DOM and event handling in Chapter 2. When you edit a field bound to a node, the DOM fires an insert, delete, or both, depending on the kind of edit made to that field. You can use the *DataDOMEvent* object to write code that responds to these events. Using this event handling mechanism, you can "listen" to a node in the DOM and write code that responds to changes in its value.

Let's get further acquainted with event handling and use it to implement data validation techniques. Three event handlers are useful for data validation: *OnBeforeChange*, *OnAfterChange*, and *OnValidate*. They make it possible to "listen" and "respond" to events that InfoPath fires when an edit is made in the view.

OnBeforeChange event handler The *OnBeforeChange* event handler executes before the DOM accepts the change that the user makes via an edit the field. As mentioned in Chapter 2, the DOM is read-only during an *OnBeforeChange* event. The attempted change to the value of a node is actually rejected when *OnBeforeChange* returns a failure value. Imagine that all individuals who have ID numbers beginning with 7 or the letter Z need to use a different form. Let's implement an *OnBeforeChange* event handler that rejects such IDs. You learned how to create an InfoPath project that uses Visual Basic .NET code in Chapter 2. Using the same steps to get started with the project, we'll implement data validation in the *OnBeforeChange* event handler:

1. In Visual Studio .NET 2003, choose New | Project from the File menu.
2. In the New Project dialog box, click on Microsoft Office InfoPath Projects/Visual Basic Projects and select the InfoPath Form Template icon.
3. Type **ExpenseReport** for the project name, and then click OK.
4. In the Microsoft Office Project Wizard, click on Open Existing Form Template.
5. Click Browse.
6. Navigate to C:\Program Files\Microsoft Office\OFFICE11\INFFORMS\1033, select the file EXPRPTI.XSN, and then click Open.
7. Click Finish, and then click OK to close the Microsoft Development Environment dialog informing you that you will be working with a copy of the original form template.
8. In InfoPath, right-click on *ID Number* and choose Text Box Properties.
9. In the Text Box Properties dialog box, click Data Validation.
10. In the Events drop-down list, select OnBeforeChange, and then click Edit.
11. Add the following code snippet to the event handler:

```
Dim idNumber As String = e.Site.text
If (idNumber.StartsWith("Z") Or idNumber.StartsWith("z") Or idNumber.StartsWith("7"))
    Then
    e.ReturnMessage = "Invalid ID Number - you need to use a different form"
    e.ReturnStatus = False
End If
```

12. In InfoPath, close the Data Validation and Text Box Properties dialog boxes.
13. Preview the form using Alt+Shift+F or Ctrl+F5 from Visual Studio or Ctrl+Shift+B in InfoPath. Alternately, you can press F5 and test the form in Visual Studio debug mode.
14. Type **z8** for the identification number. The *OnBeforeChange* event will result in an error. Figure 3-16 shows the error.
15. Click OK to close the error dialog box. Notice that the input value you just typed is rejected from the ID Number field. The field reverts to its previous value–blank in this example.
16. Publish the form as expreport1.xsn.

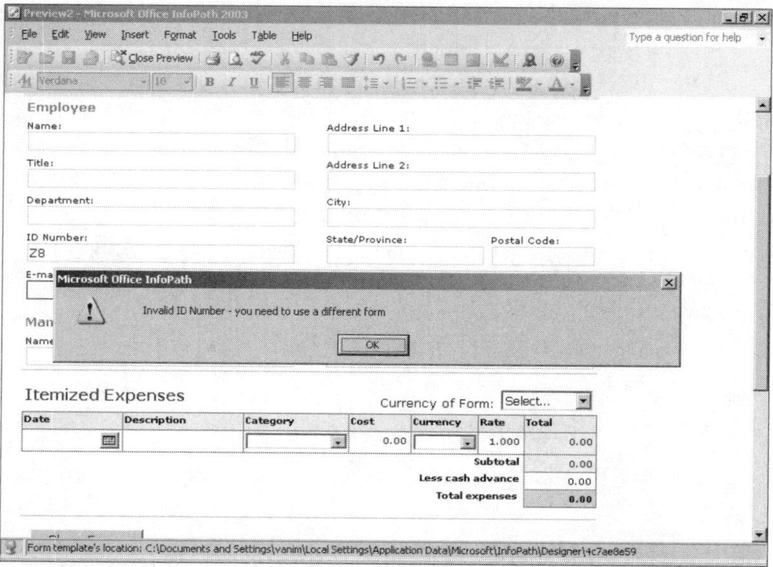

Figure 3-16 A modal error dialog box displayed by the *OnBeforeChange* event handler, as specified by ReturnMessage

The *OnBeforeChange* event handler fixes the error by reverting the change that the user made, so it is sometimes referred to as "modal" validation.

The error object InfoPath stores errors in the *error board*—an *Errors* object consisting of a collection of individual *Error* items. You can use code to manipulate InfoPath's validation errors through this object. The errors collection for the form instance contains a separate *Error* item for each error. The remainder of this section covers some examples of how to manipulate, add, and remove errors. For detailed documentation about the *Errors* collection and *Error* object, see the InfoPath SDK or the InfoPath Developer's Reference within the InfoPath Help.

Let's design some error conditions in the Expense Report form template, write some code to access those errors, and then test the code by previewing the form. We already added a couple of errors when we discussed using error dialog boxes and using inline errors. We will reuse the form template we created by implementing dialog-based validation and inline error-based validation.

It is easy to introduce errors when filling out a form—for example, a user might introduce an error by typing something other than a date in the Report Date field. Let's get acquainted with the *Error* object by implementing the following procedure:

1. In Visual Studio .NET 2003, choose New Project from the File menu.
2. In the New Project dialog box, click on Microsoft Office InfoPath Projects/Visual Basic Projects and then select the InfoPath Form Template icon.
3. Type **ExpenseReportOnBeforeChange** for the project name, and then click OK.

4. In the Microsoft Office Project Wizard, click on Open Existing Form Template.
5. Click Browse, locate the expreport1.xsn form saved previously, and then click Open.
6. Click Finish, click Finish, and then click OK to close the Microsoft Development Environment dialog informing you that you will be working with a copy of the original form template.
7. From the Controls task pane, add a button anywhere in the view.
8. Right-click on the button and choose Button Properties.
9. Change the label to Show Errors and change the ID to show_errors.
10. Click Edit Form Code. The focus moves to the *OnClick* event handler for the button in the FormCode.vb file.
11. Add the following code snippet to the event handler:

```
Dim i As Integer
'Display the node and short error message for each invalid node
For i = 0 To thisXDocument.Errors.Count - 1
    thisXDocument.UI.Alert("Incorrect value in the " + e.XDocument.Errors.Item(i)
        .Node.nodeName + " node - " + e.XDocument.Errors.Item(i).ShortErrorMessage)
        Next i
'Display the count of errors
thisXDocument.UI.Alert("There are " + thisXDocument.Errors.Count.ToString + " errors
    in the form")
```

12. Preview the form, and then add some invalid data–for example, **xyz** for the *Expense Code* and **abc** for the *date.*
13. Click Show Errors. You will see alerts showing the invalid XML node values and the short error messages for them.

Note that you don't really have to show the values of the errors in the error collection through alerts. You can show errors using the above example in specific examples, for example when Submit fails because of errors. You can also verify the Errors count in the form when the validation code results in errors that may not be exposed through controls in the form view. We included this exercise for demonstration purposes to give you some practice using the *Errors* collection through InfoPath business logic.

OnValidate event handler The *OnValidate* event is fired after *OnBeforeChange* but before *OnAfterChange*. The DOM is read-only during *OnValidate*–the same as *OnBeforeChange*. *OnValidate* is the event that InfoPath provides to perform validation through code. Let's reimplement the *OnBeforeChange* example using *OnValidate*. You can either delete the *OnBeforeChange* handler from the previous example or create a new example by taking the following steps:

1. In Visual Studio .NET 2003, choose New Project from the File menu.
2. In the New Project dialog box, click on Microsoft Office InfoPath Projects/Visual Basic Projects and then select the InfoPath Form Template icon.

3. Type **ExpenseReportOnValidate** as the name of the project.
4. In the Microsoft Office Project Wizard, click on Open Existing Form Template.
5. Click Browse, and navigate to C:\Program Files\Microsoft Office\OFFICE11\INF-FORMS\1033, select the EXPRPTI.XSN file, and then click Open.
6. Click Finish, and then click OK to dismiss the Microsoft Development Environment dialog informing you that you will be working with a copy of the original form template.
7. In InfoPath, right-click on *ID Number* and choose Text Box Properties.
8. In the Text Box Properties dialog box, click Data Validation.
9. Select OnValidate in the Events drop-down list, and then click Edit.
10. Add the following code snippet to the event handler:

```
Dim idNumber As String = e.Site.text
' Report an error if the ID number is invalid
If (idNumber.StartsWith("Z") Or idNumber.StartsWith("z") Or idNumber.StartsWith("7"))
    Then
    ' Report a site dependent modeless error with an error code "100"
    e.ReportError(e.Site, "Invalid ID Numer", False, "", 100, "modeless")
End If
```

11. In InfoPath, close the Data Validation and Text Box Properties dialog boxes.
12. Preview the form using Alt+Shift+F or Ctrl+F5 in Visual Studio or Ctrl+Shift+B in InfoPath.
13. Type **z8** for identification number. The *OnValidate* event will result in an error.
14. Right click on the field and click Full Error Description to view the error message.
15. Click OK to close the Error dialog box.
16. Change the *ID Number* field to a valid value, **a123**. Click away, and the error is gone!

You should use the *OnValidate* event and the *ReportError* method to validate fields that require more complex validation than is supported by the InfoPath designer. *ReportError* is convenient because it clears the error after the data is corrected.

OnLoad Validation The form data is validated when a document is first loaded. As a part of this validation, any *OnValidate* event handlers that are defined in the code are also run.

For example, say you have an *OnValidate* event handler defined on *nodeA*. This handler has code to report an error if the value of *nodeA* equals *foo*. The *OnValidate* event handler code for *nodeA* is executed when the form is first loaded. If the default or last saved value of *nodeA* is *foo*, the *OnValidate* event handler returns a failure and the field is marked with an error in the view.

It is important to implement validation using the *OnValidate* event handler if you are expecting incorrect or invalid saved values in your form at the time of load.

Developer Nugget: Overriding MSXML Error Messages

Schema validation errors caused by restrictions in the XSD schema file result in error messages that come directly from MSXML. These error messages are quite technical. If your form will be filled out by someone who doesn't care about XSD, much less about MSXML, it might be worthwhile to craft clear and friendly error messages. For example, in the Expense Report form, enter the text **One Hundred** in the *Cost* field. Click away for the data to persist to the DOM. You will see the red dashed border around the field indicating an error in the field. Right-click in the field and choose Full Error Description. The error message you see is "Only numbers between -1.79769313486231E308 and 1.79769313486231E308 allowed (double-precision)." If you did not try it for yourself, you can see the error in Figure 3-17. Now imagine you are a user filling out this Expense Report form. Won't this error message confuse you?

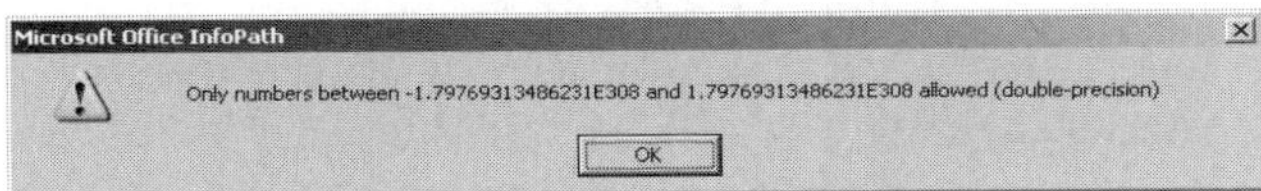

Figure 3-17 An MSXML error message for noninteger input in a field with the data type double

Overriding MSXML error messages through the InfoPath user interface is possible but not supported, and you need to edit the manifest.xsf file directly. The XSF construct that makes it possible to override default error messages is *xsf:xDocumentClass* | *xsf:schemaErrorMessages* | *xsf:override*.

Here's how to use *xsf:override* to override error messages:

1. Open the manifest.xsf file.
2. You can insert *<xsf:schemaErrorMessages>* anywhere as an immediate child of *xsf:xDocumentClass*. For clarity, we'll insert the following section at the end of the manifest.xsf file just above the closing tag *</xsf:xDocumentClass>*:

```
<xsf:schemaErrorMessages>
    <xsf:override match="/exp:expenseReport/exp:items/exp:item/exp:amount">
        <xsf:errorMessage shortMessage="Invalid Cost value">The Cost should be
        an integer value with no symbols or alphabets</xsf:errorMessage>
    </xsf:override>
</xsf:schemaErrorMessages>
```

3. Save the manifest.xsf file, and then preview the form.
4. Type the value **$100** for *Cost*.
5. Right-click on the invalid field to see the new short message in the context menu.
6. Click Full Error Description to see the new and improved error message in the dialog

You must insert a new *xsf:errorMessage* snippet for each error you want to override. The *match* attribute of *xsf:override* is the XPath of the node whose MSXML error you want to override. This technique is useful for overriding data-type errors like the one we just did.

***OnAfterChange* event handler** The *OnAfterChange* event handler code runs after the DOM accepts a change made to the node that the event handler is defined on. Even though you can write code in the *OnAfterChange* event handler to populate the error board based on validation conditions, the *OnAfterChange* event handler is designed more to handle side effects than for data validation. If you end up using the *OnAfterChange* event handler instead of the *OnValidate* event handler for data validation, you can use the *Add* method of the *Errors* collection to add errors. You must then use the *Delete* method to clear the error manually.

To learn more about event notification and handling, study the business logic script in the Calculations sample in the InfoPath SDK. You can download the InfoPath SDK from http://msdn.microsoft.com/library/default.asp?url=/downloads/list/infopath.asp.

Data Validation on Save and Submit

The InfoPath submit functionality prevents you from submitting a form that has invalid data. However, if you try to save that form, you get a warning that allows you to cancel the save and fix your errors. Figure 3-18 shows the dialog box that InfoPath displays when you try to submit a form that has validation errors. You will see several submit examples later in this book..

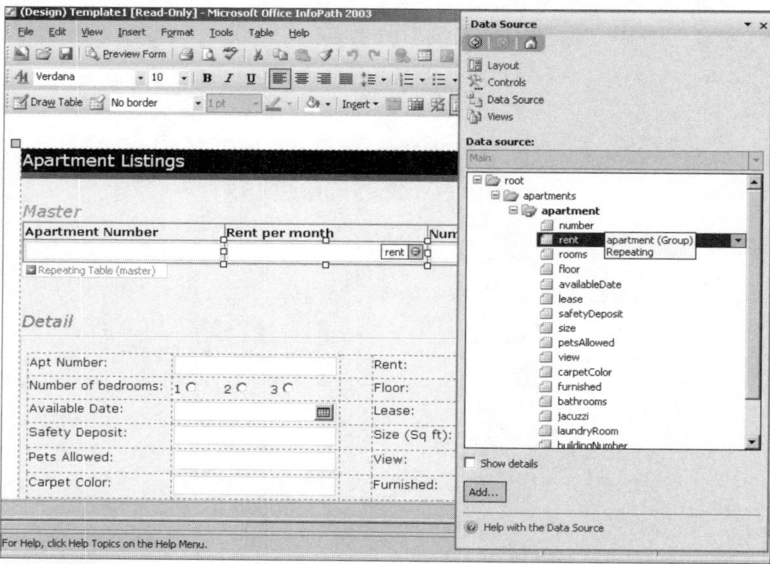

Figure 3-18 The error dialog box that appears when the user tries to submit a form with invalid data

The three errors that the user can get in this situation are

- **Errors in the current view** The user can easily find these errors by choosing Go To Next Error from the Tools menu. You can then fix the errors and resubmit the form.

- **Errors in a different view** The user must manually switch views to find the errors in each view. You cannot successfully resubmit until you have fixed all the errors.
- **Errors not in any view** If errors in your form are not exposed in any of the views, it means there is at least one error in some DOM node that is not displayed in the view. Fixing this problem is not trivial. This is one reason why you should not go validation-happy while adding error conditions through code. You also want to be careful with any schema-level validation and designer UI-enabled validation, as these can be automatically handled with proper conditions. If you are implementing errors through code, remember to clear those errors when the data is valid. This is especially important when adding errors using the *Add* method of the *Errors* collection. You should always test your form to make sure the errors can be found and fixed after the form is filled out. Another way to prevent errors is to be careful when manipulating node values through script.

Developer Nugget: Handling Nillable Content

Many XSD data types consider blank values invalid. To fix this, InfoPath makes these fields nillable in the schema using the *nillable="true"* attribute and value, and also adds a *nil* attribute to the XML node if it does not have any default data. To see this in its simplest form, add a node with the integer data type to your form. Edit the myschema.xsd file and notice the *nillable* attribute on this element:

```
<xsd:element name="field1" nillable="true" type="xsd:integer"/>
```

Edit the template.xml file, and notice the *xsi:nil* attribute on the XML node:

```
<my:field1 xsi:nil="true"></my:field1>
```

This attribute should be present on the node only when its value is blank. You should clear it when you add a value to this node through code. You'll see the error *#PCDATA' is in nil content* if you don't remove he *xsi:nil* attribute. You should also put it back when you clear the value of this node through code. For your reference, the VB.Net code for changing the value of a nillable node from blank or nil value is the following:

```
'Need to assign valueNode to intNode
If (Not (valueNode.text Is String.Empty)) Then
    'Check if myNode has an "xsi:nil" attribute
    If (Not (myNode.getAttribute("xsi:nil").GetType Is "DBNull")) Then
        'Remove the "xsi:nil"
        myNode.removeAttribute("xsi:nil")
        'Assign the value of valueNode to myNode
        myNode.nodeTypedValue = valueNode.nodeTypedValue
    End If
End If
```

The code for adding back the *nil* attribute to the XML after clearing the value of the field is the following:

```
'Need to clear the value of myNode
'Create a node of type attribute for the nil
Dim xmlNil As IXMLDOMNode = myNode.ownerDocument.createNode(2, "xsi:nil", "http://
    www.w3.org/2001/XMLSchema-instance")
xmlNil.text = "true"
'Clear the value of the node
myNode.text = ""
'Add the nil attribute to the node to avoid red asterisk required field error
myNode.setAttributeNode(xmlNil)
```

If you clear a nillable node without adding the *nil* attribute, a red asterisk will appear in the the view on the empty field to indicate that the blank value is invalid. Figure 3-19 shows an example of a form with invalid fields as a result of blank values. When you create required fields, InfoPath does not add the *nil* attribute to the XML for the field. Hence, you also see the same red asterisk error in a control that you designate as required using Cannot Be Blank in the Properties dialog box.

Name: *
Manager Name: *
E-mail Address: *
Billing Code: *
Project: *
Department: *

Figure 3-19 Form with red asterisks in controls indicating several required field errors

Adding a Warning Dialog Box Using Rules

You can use a rule to add a warning dialog box instead of an error to notify the user about unwanted data in the field. Remember that this will not add an error to the error board–it notifies the user only when data is first entered in the field–so this is not data validation. You should use rules instead of data validation when the condition is based on a recommendation rather than a validity constraint.

Let's see a quick example of how to implement a warning dialog box using rules. Suppose you want to discourage employees from submitting expenses over $500 for a single item. Implement the following procedure to add a rule that shows a warning dialog box for costs over 500 USD:

1. In the Expense Report template, double-click on the *Cost* field.
2. In the Text Box Properties dialog box, click Rules, and then click Add.
3. Name the rule **Dollar Validate**.

4. Click Set Condition.
5. Select Currency in the first drop-down list and Is Equal To in the second drop-down list.
6. In the third drop-down list, select Type Text, and then type **USD**.
7. Click And to create a second condition.
8. Set Amount, Is Greater Than Or Equal To, and 500 in the drop-down lists.
9. Click OK to dismiss the Condition dialog box.
10. Click Add Action, select Show A Dialog Box Message from the Action drop-down list, and then type **You are about to submit an expensive item** for the Message.
11. Clicking OK four times to close the open dialog boxes.
12. Preview the form.
13. Select USD from the drop-down list box.
14. Type **700** in the *cost* field.
15. Click away from the data to see the dialog box implemented using the preceding rule.

Autopopulating Data

Next we will take a brief look at how to autopopulate data in your InfoPath form. You have seen several techniques related to automatically showing or hiding input controls in your form earlier in this chapter. Conditional visibility involves input controls, whereas autopopulation involves the actual XML data in your form. With autopopulation, InfoPath populates data in the form at run time based on the input values of other fields or conditions that are specified when you design the form.

Declarative Default Data

The simplest autopopulation technique is to use default data for your input controls when you design your form. You can define the default data for your form through the InfoPath UI when you design your form. This does not require any business logic code, so it is a declarative method of using autopopulation. If you design form fields using this technique, when the user creates or opens the form, the specified fields will be populated with data. Examples of common data fields that can be autopopulated with default data are date fields and user name or author name fields. Your form can also have more specific default data that you can determine at design time and that InfoPath will fill as soon as the user creates or opens a form.

Autopopulating the Last Modified Date

You saw an example of populating the current date in a form in Chapter 2, where we included a date picker control in the form and set its value to today's date. Setting a default value works great for a new form. But what if you want to update the value of this date for a saved form?

Also, wouldn't it be great to keep track of when the form was last modified in InfoPath? We'll break up this task into two procedures:

1. Insert a date picker control that is autopopulated with the date when the form is created or when a saved copy is opened.
2. Insert a second field that shows the date and time when the form was last saved.

Take the following steps for the first procedure–adding a date picker to the form to always show the current date.

1. In Visual Studio, choose New | Project from the File menu.
2. In the New Project dialog box, click on Microsoft Office InfoPath Projects/Visual Basic Projects and then select the InfoPath Form Template icon.
3. Name the project **ModifiedDateSample**, and then click OK.
4. In the Microsoft Office Project Wizard, click on Create New Form Template, and then click Finish.
5. From the Controls task pane, insert a Date Picker control in your view.
6. In the Data Source task pane, rename the node to **timeStamp**.
7. Choose Form Options from the Tools menu.
8. In the Form Options dialog box, click on the Open And Save tab, and then click Rules.
9. In the Rules For Opening Forms dialog box, click Add.
10. Name the Rule **DateRule**, and then click Add Action.
11. In the Action drop-down list, select Set A Field's Value.
12. Click Select A Field, select *timeStamp*, and then click OK.
13. Click the *fx* button to open the Insert Formula dialog box.
14. Click Insert Function.
15. In the Categories list, select Date And Time, and then in the Functions list, select Today.
16. Click OK six times to close all the open dialog boxes.
17. Preview the form.

    The date field will show today's date. Note that you could have reached this result in a new form by using the *today* function in the default data for the *timeStamp* node through the Date Picker Properties dialog of the control. But implementing the rule using the Open And Save rules is necessary when you want the date and time value to be updated even for a saved instance of the form.

18. Create a new instance of the form by double-clicking on the .xsn file in the \bin\debug folder in your InfoPath project folder. Alternately, you can publish the form and open it from its published location.
19. Change the date to some date other than today's date.
20. Save the form as Sample1.xml and close it.
21. Reopen Sample1.xml and notice that the date value is updated to show the current date.

We will now take a look at the second procedure–keeping track of the last modified date for the form. InfoPath provides an *OnSaveRequest* event handler that you can use to run custom code when the user saves the form. We will use this to update the last modified date for the form. We have to check whether the form is dirty, meaning there have been changes to at least one value of the form fields, because the user might save the form without making any changes to it. To check for dirtiness, we use the *XDocument* object's *IsDirty* property. Note that the *OnSaveRequest* event handler requires the form to be fully trusted on the machine that you open the form on.

The following procedure builds on the form from the previous procedure. If you have not implemented the previous procedure, start by creating a new InfoPath Visual Basic .NET project using the existing form C:\Microsoft Learning\Developing Solutions with InfoPath\Chapter03\Samples\ModifiedDateSample.xsn. Figure 3-20 shows this form.

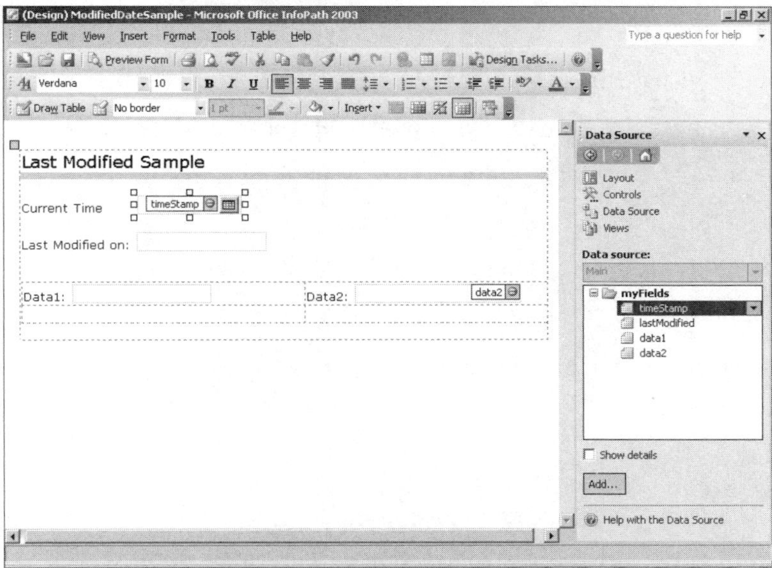

Figure 3-20 The form for the modified date example

Take the following steps to autopopulate the last modified date in the form:

1. Insert a Text Box control in the view.
2. In the Data Source task pane, rename the text box field to **lastModified**.
3. Insert two additional Text Box controls in the view to use as data fields.
4. In the Tools menu, choose Form Options.
5. In the Form Options dialog box, click on the Open And Save tab.
6. In the Save Behavior section, select the Save Using Custom Code check box, and then click Edit. The focus will move to the location in the FormCode.vb file where InfoPath created the *OnSaveRequest* event handler for you.
7. Just below the line *' Write the code to be run before saving here,* write the following code:

```
' Check if the form is dirty
If (e.XDocument.IsDirty) Then
    ' Get the timestamp and lastModified nodes from the DOM
    Dim timeStampNode As IXMLDOMNode = thisXDocument.DOM.selectSingleNode("my:myFields
        /my:timeStamp")
    Dim lastModifiedNode As IXMLDOMNode = thisXDocument.DOM.selectSingleNode
        ("my:myFields/my:lastModified")
    ' Assign the timestamp value to the last modified date field
    lastModifiedNode.nodeTypedValue = timeStampNode.nodeTypedValue
End  If
```

8. Switch to InfoPath and then click OK to dismiss the Form Options dialog.
9. Switch back to Visual Studio, and then press Ctrl+Shift+B to build the solution.
10. Open the form from the \bin\debug folder in your InfoPath project folder.
11. Save the form as MyForm.xml on your machine, and then close the form.
12. Reopen MyForm.xml.
13. Make a change in the form by typing data in one of the data fields.
14. Save the form. Notice that the last modified field gets updated.

You can also open the form at C:\Microsoft Learning\Developing Solutions with Info-Path\Chapter03\ModifiedDateSample.xsn to compare the behavior of the form to what you just implemented.

In the procedure to autopopulate the last modified date using the OnSaveRequest event, we opened the .xsn file from the \bin\debug folder at the project location instead of testing the solution in InfoPath Preview mode. The OnSaveRequest event cannot be tested in Preview mode because the Save commands are disabled there.

The limitation of not being able to test events in Preview mode also applies to the OnMergeRequest and OnSign events. We will talk some more about the OnSign event in Chapter 4.

Data Based on Primary Fields

You can add default data to your form based on the value of a primary field. We use the term *primary field* to refer to a form field that the user must fill out. You can use the value of this field to autopopulate other fields in your form. If you use a database as the main or a secondary data source in your InfoPath form, this primary field maps to the primary key of your database.

Earlier you saw how to add values to input controls, such as cascading drop-down lists, based on values supplied in certain fields. We can extend that technique to add data to the form based on the values of primary fields. For example, the vehicle registration example can be extended to become a service request for a vehicle in which the primary fields, manufacturer and model, are used to autopopulate other vehicle specifications, such as engine type, fuel efficiency, and transmission life. Recall that the choices in the cascading drop-down list were populated from a secondary .xml file. You also saw an example of populating data from a secondary .xml file in Chapter 1.

Autopopulating data in the form using secondary data sources is a common use of data connections. Many forms require repetitive information in fields that can be determined only at run time based on values in primary fields. You can use secondary data sources to add this data after the form user fills in the primary fields in the form. Let's move on to an example that autopopulates data in the form based on a secondary data source.

Programmatic Autopopulation

In this example, we will use InfoPath business logic code to autopopulate information about an individual based on the Social Security number (SSN) field. We will first use a dummy .xml file containing Person records as our secondary data source. We will then write code behind the form to populate fields in the form based on the SSN value the user enters. If the SSN does not have any records in the secondary .xml file, the autopopulation will not take place and the user must manually fill in all the information fields.

Autopopulating Person information based on SSN To create a form that populates information about a person based on SSN, implement the following procedure:

1. In the Tools menu, choose Data Connections.
2. Create a new InfoPath Visual Basic .NET project from the existing PersonIdentification.xsn form with the book's companion content. This is a straightforward sample form that has fields for Person information, as shown in Figure 3-21.

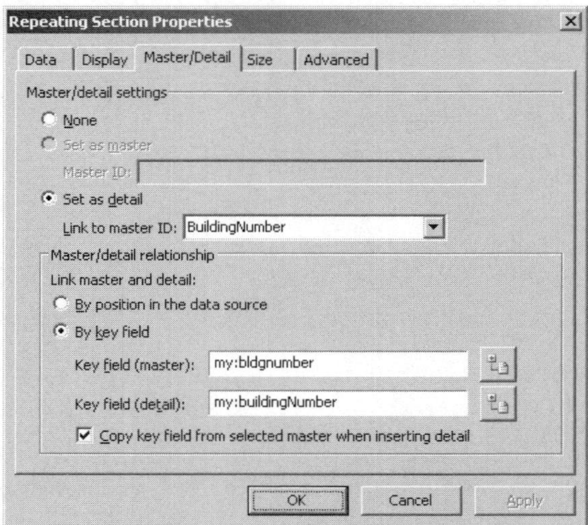

Figure 3-21 Sample form fields for the person identification section of an InfoPath form

3. Add a new data connection which will receive XML from the file C:\Microsoft Learning\Developing Solutions with InfoPath\Chapter03\Samples\People.xml. As stated earlier, this .xml file is a sample data file with People information. This .xml file has been prepopulated with five records, which will suffice for this example.

4. Double-click on Social Security in the form, and click Data Validation. Notice that we already added a condition to validate the Social Security pattern for the field.

5. From the Events drop-down list, choose *OnAfterChange* event and then click Edit to go to the location in FormCode.vs where InfoPath created the code stub for the SSN *OnAfterChange* event handler.

6. Insert the following code just below the line *'A field change has occurred and the DOM is writable. Write code here to respond to the changes.* Figure 3-22 shows this code in the InfoPath project for the form.

```
'Reject spurious notifications - nodeType value for DOMNodeType.NODE_TEXT is "3"
If ((e.Operation = "Delete") And (e.Source.nodeType = 3)) Then
    Return
End If
'Get nodes from the main DOM
Dim fNameNode As IXMLDOMNode = thisXDocument.DOM.selectSingleNode("/my:myFields/
    my:PersonInfo/my:firstName")
Dim lNameNode As IXMLDOMNode = thisXDocument.DOM.selectSingleNode("/my:myFields/
    my:PersonInfo/my:lastName")
Dim dobNode As IXMLDOMNode = thisXDocument.DOM.selectSingleNode("/my:myFields/
    my:PersonInfo/my:DOB")
Dim photoNode As IXMLDOMElement = thisXDocument.DOM.selectSingleNode("/my:myFields/
    my:PersonInfo/my:picture")

'DataObject for the secondary XML data source
Dim peopleXML As DataObject = CType(thisXDocument.DataObjects(0), DataObject)
Dim peopleList As IXMLDOMNodeList = peopleXML.DOM.selectNodes("/people/person")
Dim ssnNode As IXMLDOMNode
Dim personNode As IXMLDOMNode
```

```
For Each personNode In peopleList
    'If the SSN matches a value in the secondary XML personNode, then populate values
    If personNode.selectSingleNode(“ssn").nodeTypedValue = e.Site.nodeTypedValue Then
        fNameNode.nodeTypedValue = personNode.selectSingleNode("fname").nodeTypedValue
        lNameNode.nodeTypedValue = personNode.selectSingleNode("lname").nodeTypedValue
        dobNode.nodeTypedValue = personNode.selectSingleNode("dob").nodeTypedValue
        'Remove the "xsi:nil" for photoNode before setting its value
        If (Not (photoNode.getAttribute("xsi:nil").GetType Is "DBNull")) Then
            photoNode.removeAttribute("xsi:nil")
            photoNode.nodeTypedValue = personNode.selectSingleNode("photo").node
                TypedValue
        End If
    Return
    End If
    fNameNode.nodeTypedValue = ""
    lNameNode.nodeTypedValue = ""
    dobNode.nodeTypedValue = ""
    'Add back the xsi:nil before clearing value to avoid required field error
    Dim xmlNil As IXMLDOMNode = photoNode.ownerDocument.createNode(2, "xsi:nil",
        "http://www.w3.org/2001/XMLSchema-instance")
    xmlNil.text = "true"
    photoNode.text = ""
    photoNode.setAttributeNode(xmlNil)
Next
```

7. In InfoPath, close all opened dialog boxes.
8. In Visual Studio, preview the form using Alt+Shift+F.
9. Type any of the SSN values from the People.xml file in the SSN field—for example, 333-333-3333. All the Person information fields of the form are populated according to the code you just wrote.

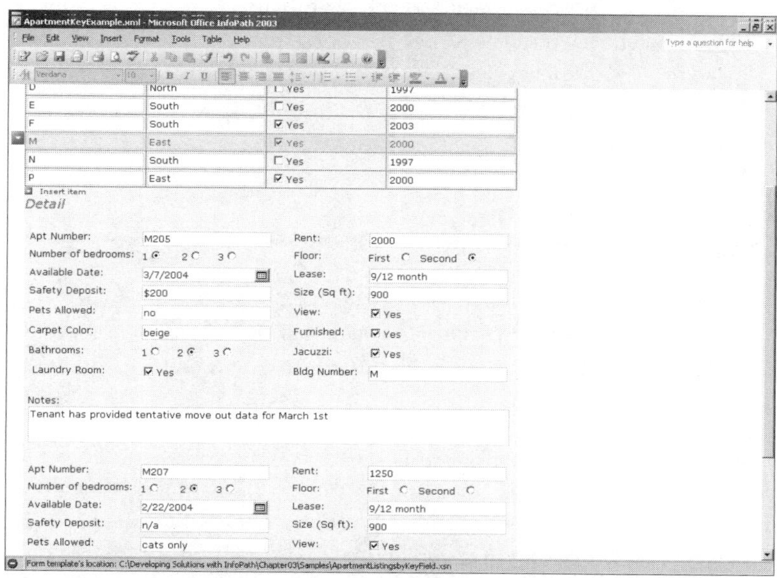

Figure 3-22 The *OnAfterChange* code for autopopulating form fields

Developer Nugget: Avoid Multiple Notifications in Data DOM Event Handlers

The term *multiple notifications* refers to Data DOM event handlers that execute more than once for a DOM change. Two factors lead to multiple notifications: leaf node updates and event bubbling.

Leaf Node Updates

Updating a leaf node in the form will fire an Insert and Delete event pair on the text node associated with the leaf node, resulting in two notifications. To avoid the multiple notifications caused by updates to leaf node values through Insert and Delete events, you can implement the following condition at the beginning of your event handler:

```
If ((( Not("Insert" = e.Operation)) And (3 = e.Source.nodeType)) Then
    Return
End If
```

Notice that we used the above condition in the autopopulation *OnAfterChange* event handler in the previous example.

Event Bubbling

When a DOM node changes, the event "bubbles up" the tree along the ancestors to the root node. For example, imagine that *nodeB* (leaf) and *nodeC* are children of *nodeA*, and *nodeD* (leaf) and *nodeE* (leaf) are children of *nodeC*. A Data DOM event handler for *nodeA*–for example, an *OnAfterChange* event handler–is executed for an event that occurred in the grandchild *nodeD*. As a result, the Data DOM event handler for *nodeA* is executed not only for changes to leaf node *nodeB* but also for changes to *nodeD and nodeE*. You can add a condition using the *Site* property of the *DataDOM* event object to prevent the event handler from executing when changes occur to child nodes. This condition should be defined at the beginning of your event handler and should be as follows:

```
If (Not (e.Site Is e.Parent)) Then
Return
End If
```

You can use the above code with appropriate modifications if your form design requires programmatic autopopulation of fields. Earlier you saw a Developer Nugget on clearing and setting nillable fields. Notice that we used the code for removing and adding the *nil* attribute for the *photo* node in the preceding example.

You could create the same example using default values combined with rules through the InfoPath user interface. To do this, you would have to set the default value on each of the fields to read from the secondary data source. You would then use rules to add an action to the SSN field to set the values for the other fields. The Insert Field Or Group dialog box is quite simple to use; you saw similar examples that used this dialog box earlier in this chapter. If you set these rules on the SSN field thorugh the Open and Save dialog as well, the form fields whose default values are set to be read from the secondary data source would be conveniently filled out when the form is loaded.

In general for complex autopopulation scenarios that involve multiple conditions or repeating groups, rules can be used but might not be intuitive. You should write code as shown in the above example. We leave it as an exercise to implement the functionality of the above code sample on load of the form through the *OnLoad* event handler.

Autopopulating Data from a SQL Database

Using a secondary .xml file to store metadata is a better technique than storing all the data within the main data source in your form. Your main data source should always have only fields that are relevant to the form instance. Adding a data connection to your form design is feasible only when form users actually have access to that data source. You must be aware of security concerns in such cases. For example, it might be okay to create a form that gives an admitting nurse at a hospital access to data connections that autopopulate person information from a database based on Social Security numbers. But if the end user of the forms is a hospital patient, this would be a security breach.

The advantage of using a data connection to an .xml file or a data connection to an Access .mdb file is that you can include the secondary data source as a resource in your form template. However, for performance reasons, it is not a good idea to include large secondary .xml data sources in your form design. This is also true with cascading lists with more than three to five levels. If you decide to not include the secondary .xml file in your form as a resource, you must make sure that your users always have access to the location of your .xml file. If you package the .xml data file with your form, it might bloat your .xsn file. It will also be cached along with the form template at run time, which may have security issues. It is best to use data connections to SQL databases or Web services if you need to access large amounts of data for your form. Another good reason to use a database or a Web service instead of a secondary .xml file is that the InfoPath XML data adapters do not inherently support the submit function. They are designed more to be used as data sources for querying data that should be kept separate from the main data source. You can, however, submit to a database or a Web service.

Using Master Detail Controls

You have seen several examples of techniques for designing dynamic forms that minimize invalid user input. Here, we will look at how to create dynamic and concise controls for repeating data using the Master/Detail control. This control allows you to pivot your data based on key fields so you can use the Master table as a dynamic dashboard for repeating data in the form. Using Master/Details controls is a useful technique for organizing your form views for large amounts of data that you are displaying from a database or a Web service.

Overview of Repeating Controls

InfoPath allows you to insert controls in the view for repeating data—that is, data that has a *maxOccurs > 1* in the XML Schema. InfoPath's built-in controls that you can insert from the Controls task pane includes several controls for repeating data. The simplest repeating controls are Repeating Section and Repeating Table. Both support similar schema structures and differ only in how they appear in the view.

Repeating Table

A default Repeating Table control is created with at least one element contained within the group. In a new blank form, insert a repeating table from the Controls task pane. It displays a spin box for the number of columns, with the default value of 3; you can modify the value to insert anywhere from 1 through 63 columns. It is probably unwise to create a repeating table with 63 columns. In fact, adding more than 15 or 20 columns might result in performance issues with rendering the view. The schema snippet for a three-column repeating table is similar to the following:

```
<xsd:element name="Persons">
    <xsd:complexType>
        <xsd:sequence>
            <xsd:element ref="Person" minOccurs="0" maxOccurs="unbounded"/>
        </xsd:sequence>
    </xsd:complexType>
</xsd:element>
<xsd:element name="Person">
    <xsd:complexType>
        <xsd:sequence>
            <xsd:element ref="Name" minOccurs="0"/>
            <xsd:element ref="PhoneNumber" minOccurs="0"/>
            <xsd:element ref="Age" minOccurs="0"/>
        </xsd:sequence>
    </xsd:complexType>
</xsd:element>
  . . .
```

Repeating Section

Schema-wise, a default Repeating Section is similar to the Repeating Table, but with two differences. A Repeating Table is created in the XSL within an HTML *<table>*, while a Repeating Section is in an HTML *<div>* element. The second difference is that a Repeating Section does not contain any elements by default. The schema construct for a default Repeating Section inserted in the form looks like the following:

```
<xsd:element name="PersonsRoot">
    <xsd:complexType>
        <xsd:sequence>
            <xsd:element ref="Persons" minOccurs="0" maxOccurs="unbounded"/>
        </xsd:sequence>
```

```
    </xsd:complexType>
</xsd:element>
<xsd:element name="Persons">
    <xsd:complexType>
        <xsd:sequence />
    </xsd:complexType>
</xsd:element>
```

You can then insert additional controls within the section that add elements within the *<xsd:sequence>* created for the Repeating Section. If you create a Repeating Section from an existing schema by inserting it into the view from the Data Source pane, you can opt to create it with controls, in which case the elements in the group are inserted as controls within the *<div>* for the Repeating Section in the view.

Repeating Recursive Group

Repeating Recursive Group is a more advanced control for repeating data that supports recursive elements in the schema. For example, the *comment* element in the following XSD snippet is a recursive element whose schema representation is as follows:

```
<xsd:element name="Comments">
    <xsd:complexType>
       <xsd:sequence>
          <xsd:element ref="Comment" minOccurs="0" maxOccurs="unbounded"/>
       </xsd:sequence>
    </xsd:complexType>
</xsd:element>
<xsd:element name="Comment">
   <xsd:complexType>
       <xsd:sequence>
            <xsd:element ref="Comment" minOccurs="0" maxOccurs="unbounded"/>
        </xsd:sequence>
    </xsd:complexType>
</xsd:element>
```

Repeating Choice Group

Repeating Choice Group supports choice elements that can have multiple occurrences. In a blank form, you would use this control if a repeating group has a choice between subgroups—for example, a shopping/gift list for a family. The schema snippet is as follows:

```
<xsd:element name="shoppingList">
    <xsd:complexType>
        <xsd:choice minOccurs="0" maxOccurs="unbounded">
            <xsd:element ref="mother" minOccurs="0"/>
            <xsd:element ref="father" minOccurs="0"/>
            <xsd:element ref="child" minOccurs="0"/>
        </xsd:choice>
    </xsd:complexType>
</xsd:element>
```

Master/Detail Repeating Control

Master/Detail is the only control that InfoPath provides exclusively for view optimization. It is used with repeating data so you can display the more important, or "master," data in a section of the view that is separate from the less important, or "detailed," data. InfoPath displays all the rows of the Master table. When the form user focuses on a specific row in the Master table, the details for that row are displayed in the Details section.

To see the simplest example of a Master/Detail control, insert a default Master/Detail control from the Controls task pane in your view. InfoPath inserts the Master as a three-column repeating table. (Note that Repeating Table is the only control that InfoPath supports for the Master.) The default Details control appears as a repeating section with four text boxes. You can change it to a repeating table if you like, but typically the Details control will look neater in a section because it will have more fields that might look crammed in a table row. Normally, the InfoPath design view displays a blue information icon in the upper-right corner of controls, with the ScreenTip "Control store duplicate data," if more than one control in the view is bound to the same node. However, in the case of the Master/Detail control, this icon does not appear even though the Master and Detail are bound to the same group. InfoPath supports two kinds of Master/Detail techniques. Link By Row Position supports a one-to-one master-detail relationship and Link By Key Field supports a one-to-many master-detail relationship. We will look at scenarios for each of these techniques. In general, we recommend that you use Master/Detail controls for the following kinds of repeating data:

- Data that has too many fields or repeating table columns
- Data that has too many records or repeating table rows

We will create an example for each of these scenarios. We will first look at a scenario where the repeating data has a large number of fields. For example, consider a form that displays available apartment listings in a particular apartment complex. The Master table will have some of the key data fields, such as number of rooms and rental cost. The Details section will have all the other detail fields that you would care to store for an apartment.

Link Detail by Row Position

Link By Row Position is the simpler of the two Master/Detail techniques. It means that the detail displayed is linked to the master row position. The Apartment Listing form that you are about to create uses this technique.

Apartment listing using Master/Detail control To create a form to display a list of apartments that are available for rent in an apartment complex, implement the following procedure:

1. Start InfoPath with a new blank form.
2. From the Controls task pane, insert a Master/Detail control specifying **17** for the Number Of Fields In Details.
3. Double-click each field in the Data Source task pane, and change its name to correspond to the data source that you would want to see in an apartment form. Change the data type of the fields as needed. Figure 3-23 shows a sample data source for an apartment.

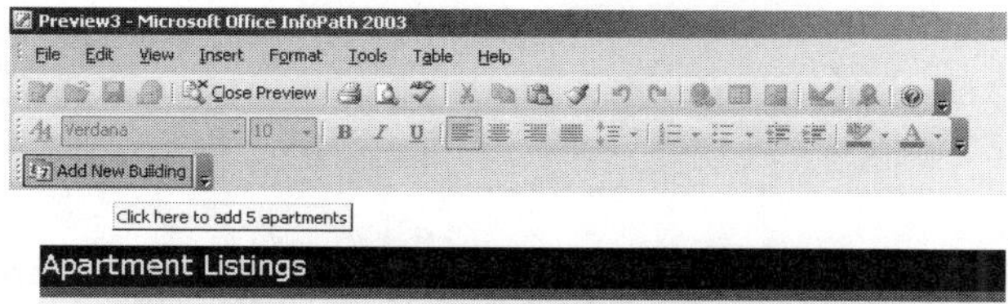

Figure 3-23 Sample data source for an apartment listing form

4. Insert a layout table to the Details section.
5. Move all of the controls to fit nicely in the layout table, adding more rows to your layout table and using Table Properties to fix up the widths of the column as needed.
6. Save and then preview the form. Add some information to the Master table row. Notice that the Details section reflects the values that you add to the Master table. Add values to all the fields that are present in the Details section to complete information for that entry.
7. Insert a new row and add some more data. Repeat this until you have a few records in the form.
8. Click on various rows in the Master table. Notice that the Details section changes as you select different rows in the Master table. Even though the Master and Detail control are each bound to the same set of nodes, they are both editable unless the fields in one have been set to read-only or changed to be expression boxes. Also, the Master row that corresponds to the Details section in the view has a gray selection on it. This selection, which is sometimes called the "master indicator," always appears in the Master table row whether or not you are editing that portion of the form. Figure 3-24 shows what the apartment listing form looks like after the user has filled it out.

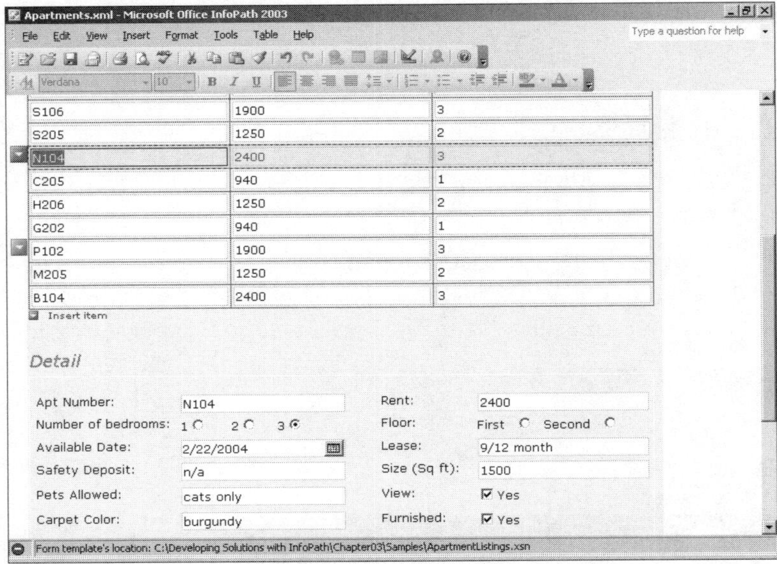

Figure 3-24 Apartment listing form with a Master/Detail control

9. Close the Preview and double-click the Repeating Section (detail) label that appears below the Detail section to open its Properties dialog box.
10. On the Master/Detail tab, note the value of the Link To Master ID drop-down list, and then close the dialog box.
11. Open the Properties dialog box for the Master table.
12. On the Master/Detail tab, notice the value of the Master ID text box. It is the same as the Link To Master ID value that we noted in the Details section. The Master ID is what InfoPath uses to map the Details section to the Master table.

Scrollable region Even though the Master/Detail control is a great way to compact your view for a large amount of repeating data, you may still end up with a large inefficient view if you have too many rows in the Master table. With one simple addition, we can extend our example to prevent displaying all the rows in the Master table at the same time. To do this, insert a Scrollable Region control in the view above the Master table. Move the Master table into the scrollable region by cutting it and pasting it into the scrollable region. The scrollable region will prevent the Master table from bloating the view when the form user inserts several rows in the Master section. Figure 3-25 shows an example of the Apartment Listings form with the Master table in a scrollable region. Doesn't this look neater compared with the Master/Detail view from Figure 3-24?

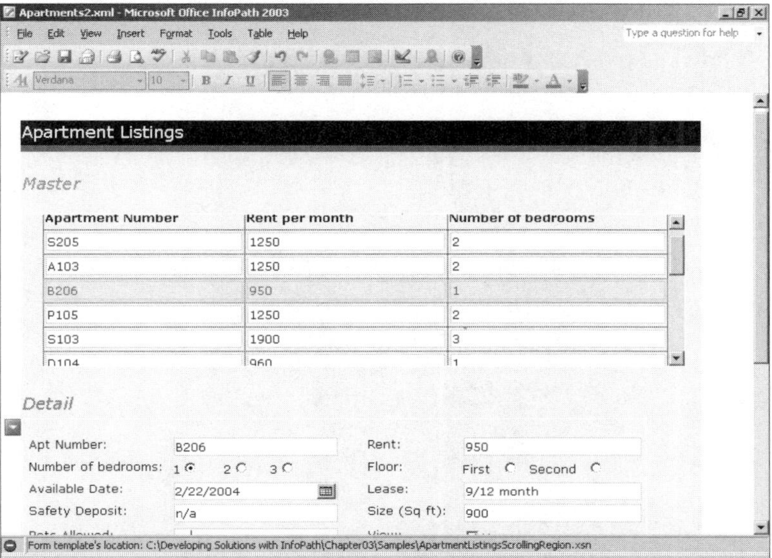

Figure 3-25 Apartment Listings form with the Master table in a scrollable region

Link Detail by Key

The Link By Key Field technique displays detailed data based on a key field in the master table. In other words, it is an advanced filtering technique that can display data in a repeating group (detail) based on a key field on a separate repeating group (master). It is a powerful technique for the Master/Detail control because it supports one-to-many relationships between the master and the detail.

For example, consider a repeating table with information about all the buildings in the apartment complex, with the building number as a primary key. Using Link By Key Field, you can display all the apartments available for rent in a specific building. This technique is more useful for displaying existing data than for adding new data. To see an implementation for the available apartments by key building number, take the following steps:

1. In design mode, open the form from the previous example or open the form C:\Microsoft Learning\Developing Solutions with InfoPath\Chapter03\Samples\ApartmentListingsScrollingRegion.xsn.
2. Delete the scrolling region and the Master repeating table.
3. Insert a new four-column repeating table in the view.
4. Using the Data Source pane, change the names of the fields to **bldgNumber**, **propertyLocation**, **handicappedAccessible**, and **yearBuilt**. While you are at it, change the data type for *handicappedAccessible* to Boolean. Change the table column header labels to match the fields.

5. In the Repeating Table Properties dialog box, click on the Master/Detail tab.
6. Select Set As Master and type **BuildingNumber** as the Master ID, and then click OK.
7. Open the Repeating Section Properties dialog box for what used to be the Repeating Section (detail), and then click on the Master/Detail tab.
8. Select Set As Detail, and then choose BuildingNumber from the Link To Master ID drop-down list.
9. Select By Key Field, and then select bldgNumber for Key Field (Master) and buildingNumber for Key Field (Detail). Figure 3-26 shows what the dialog box should look like.
10. Click OK to apply your changes and close the dialog box.

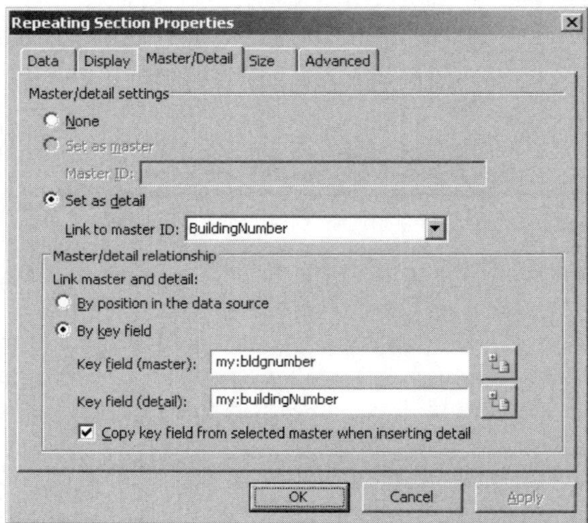

Figure 3-26 The Repeating Section Properties dialog box for the Details section using Link By Key Field

11. Open the form at C:\Microsoft Learning\Developing Solutions with InfoPath\Chapter03\Samples\ApartmentKeyExample.xml to see what a filled-out form looks like for our example. Figure 3-27 shows the form with all the available apartments in building M.

Note Notice that Copy Key Field From Selected Master When Inserting Detail is selected automatically. If you clear this check box, it will be hard to add new data to the Details section unless the primary key has at least one record in the repeating group for the details. The only way to do this is to use a group with a key value that already exists in the Master table, insert a new item, and then change the value of the key for the inserted item.

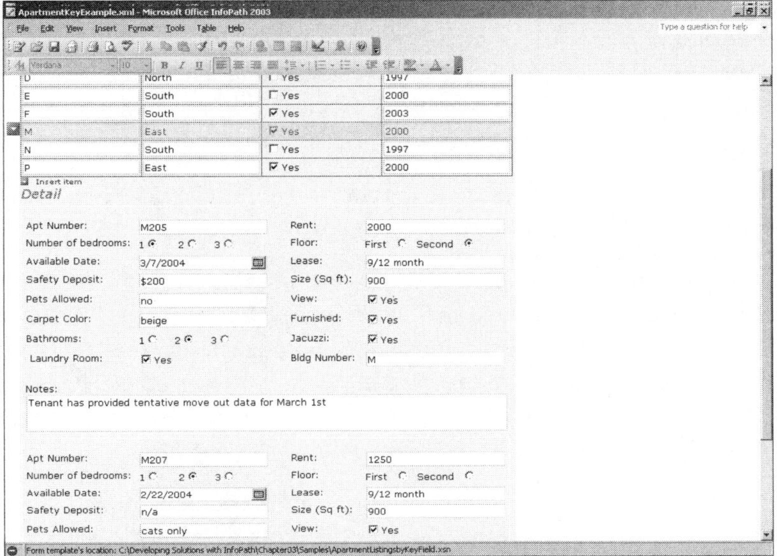

Figure 3-27 Available apartments displayed in the Details Section keyed on building number from the Master table

InfoPath implements data filtering through the XSL. Master/Detail is implemented by enclosing the Detail section in an *<xsl:if>* and adding a condition to display the details for the key field. The XSL snippet for the above example is as follows:

```
<xsl:apply-templates select="my:apartments/my:apartment [ (my:buildingNumber = ../../
my:buildings/my:building[position() = $masterPosCTRL5]/my:bldgnumber) ] " mode="_2"/>
```

The variable *$masterPosCTRL5* used for *position()* is defined in the XSL based on the master ID. Filters are case sensitive because they use XPath and XSL. For example, an A building will not show up in the Details section if the Master building number has the value *a*. As an exercise, use your InfoPath data validation design skills to prevent input that has a different case in the Master than in the Detail.

Adding Repeating Data Programmatically

The InfoPath object model supports adding repeating data through business logic code. It supports this through the *ExecuteAction* method of the *View* object. As such, the object model supports only actions that you can otherwise achieve through the user interface for any of the repeating controls. For example, you might need to programmatically add a new building with five available apartments to the Master/Detail repeating groups. Let's take a quick look at how to add five rows of a new building to the available apartments using a toolbar button.

InfoPath allows you to add toobars, menus, and cascading menus to your form. The InfoPath design mode allows you to add a single toolbar to the form where you can add buttons related to dynamic controls with insert/delete actions on them. You can do this by clicking on the Customize Commands button on the Properties dialog of a control—for example, a Repeating Section—and selecting the Form Toolbar check box.

You can then save the form template to a folder using the Extract Form Files command and look for the xsf:toolbar tag in the manifest.xsf file.

You can manually modify the manifest.xsf file to create cascading or nested menus on custom toolbars or the built-in menus such as the File or View menus. For example, notice the Section submenu that gets added to the Insert menu when you insert a dynamic control in your form. It is written in an xsf:menu section in the manifest.xsf file. You can create nested structures through combinations of the toolbar, menu, menuArea, and button elements in the manifest.xsf file. We will see another example of this in Chapter 4.

1. Create a new InfoPath project from the existing form in the book's companion content.
2. Close InfoPath, and then open the manifest.xsf file through the Solution Explorer in Visual Studio.
3. Insert the following code just below the *</xsf:editing>* tag to add a new toolbar to the form:

```
<xsf:toolbar name="apartmentToolbar" caption="Building">
    <xsf:button name="AddApartments" icon="125" caption="Add New Building"
        tooltip="Click here to add 5 apartments"></xsf:button>
</xsf:toolbar>
```

   You can also add a .gif or .bmp file icon to the button. You must also add the icon file as a resource to your InfoPath form through Tools | Resource Files.

4. Insert the following code in the FormCode.vb file within the Project class:

```
<InfoPathEventHandler(MatchPath:="AddApartments", EventType:=InfoPathEventType.
    OnClick)> _
Public Sub AddApartments_OnClick(ByVal e As DocActionEvent)
    'Disabling the autoupdate feature prevents view flashing and speeds up insertions
    thisXDocument.View.DisableAutoUpdate()
    'Add 5 new apartments
    For I As Integer = 0 To 4
        'Obtain the xmltoEdit name group2_2 from the Properties dialog of the
            repeating item
        thisXDocument.View.ExecuteAction("xCollection::insert", "group2_2")
    Next
    thisXDocument.View.EnableAutoUpdate()
End Sub
```

5. Preview the form.
6. Click on our Add New Building button in the toolbar. This action adds five new rows to the available apartment table. Figure 3-28 shows the toolbar button for the form.

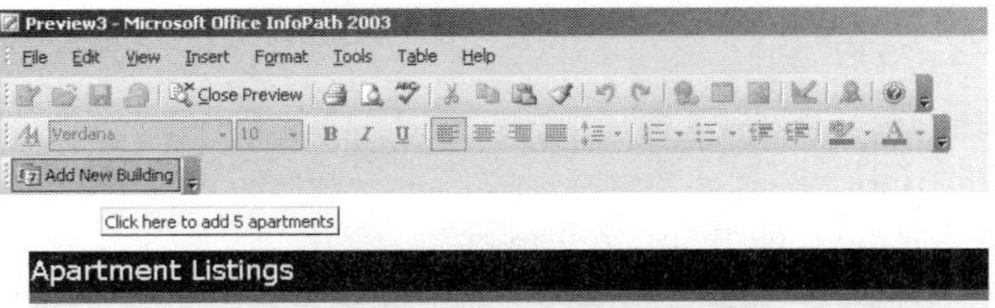

Figure 3-28 A custom toolbar button to add five new apartments for a building using the InfoPath object model

Important The xmlToEdit name that we used in the preceding example is available in most controls in the Properties dialog box for the control, as shown in Figure 3-29. In controls where the xmlToEdit value is not available in the dialog box you can get it from the *name* attribute for that control in the manifest.xsf file. For example, the XSF text for the *apartment* control appears as follows:

<xsf:xmlToEdit name="group2_2" item="/my:root/my:apartments/my:apartment" container="/my:root" viewContext="CTRL5">

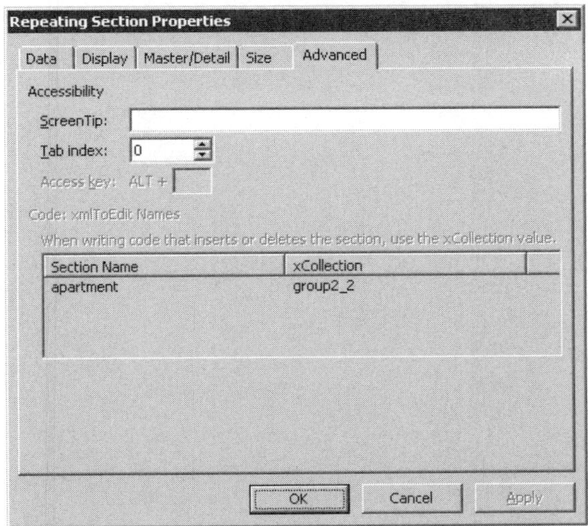

Figure 3-29 Advanced tab of the Repeating Section Properties dialog box showing the xmlToEdit value

If the Master table in your form has only the key field column—only the building number in our example—you can implement the master/detail technique using a drop-down list box control for the master data. In that case, you need not use a Master/Detail control—you can use a simple repeating group filtered on the current value of a drop-down list box. Of course, it is inconvenient for the user if the drop-down list is too long, so avoid using a drop-down if your master table has more than 10 to 15 records. Also, the master data is not editable if you use a drop-down list box instead of a repeating table. You must edit the Detail table instead.

Summary

The user experience in filling out a form is an important metric for determining the quality of a form. By implementing conditional visibility, dynamic controls, and automatically populated fields in your form, you help to optimize and enhance the form-filling experience for the user. Efficient processing of forms requires that all the information in the form data is not only valid but also that no data is redundant or unnecessary. You can minimize the risk of bad or invalid data by using data-filtering and validation techniques. This reduces processing cost when parsing the forms for useful information, as you will have eliminated useless information up front.

In this chapter, you learned a few design patterns and techniques for creating smart forms. We covered four main topics—conditional visibility, data validation, autopopulation, and master/detail controls for repeating data—and we implemented several examples. We also dabbled with InfoPath business logic code to implement programmatic actions in the form.

Chapter 4
Creating Rich Forms

In the previous chapter, you learned how to implement some "smart" techniques for providing a dynamic editing experience in InfoPath forms. Even though the main InfoPath scenarios relate to forms, InfoPath is not merely a Microsoft Office version of a forms builder application. The ability to build forms based on XML technology makes InfoPath as powerful as a forms application. In addition, InfoPath's form controls interface fully supports the structured nature of XML, along with formatted and rich text. You can design InfoPath forms with rich fields, structured and dynamic sections, multiple views, and calculations. You can also use InfoPath's powerful CLR-based object model to implement a variety of complex functionality. And you can add back-end database and Web service integration to provide a feature-rich, workflow-enabled editing experience.

In this chapter, we will focus on some core InfoPath features that make possible a rich and dynamic experience for the form user–including functionality never before seen in traditional electronic forms (much less in paper forms). We will also look in depth at several object model members and XSF elements or attributes related to the features covered in the chapter.

InfoPath form users can format text and spell check it, just like in Microsoft Word. They can also insert tables, inline images, and hyperlinks. When combined with other features such as dynamic views and autocomplete, rich text support differentiates InfoPath from existing form technologies. You can build InfoPath forms around document-centric or form-centric scenarios by combining rich document functionality with plain text functionality. InfoPath stores rich text in XML, encoded as XHTML. We will examine this in more detail later in the chapter.

InfoPath vs. Smart Documents

Word 2003 allows you to save data in XML format through the smart documents feature. When combined with other Word features such as change tracking and Information Rights Management, this XML integration is a powerful asset to the already ubiquitous Word documents. But Word is not meant to be an XML forms package–it is a documents package that has the ability to save documents as XML. We will not cover smart documents functionality in this chapter, but we will talk about some differences between Word smart documents and InfoPath forms to highlight the usefulness of InfoPath for certain scenarios.

For more information about smart documents, refer to the Smart Document SDK at MSDN: http://msdn.microsoft.com/library/default.asp?url=/library/en-us/sdsdk/html/sdcondevelopingsolutionsintroduction.asp.

User Interface

Smart documents do not provide the wide variety of controls for data entry that InfoPath forms provide. Smart documents also do not have a separate design and edit mode. The user interface for a smart document is very basic. You saw some InfoPath structural editing controls in Chapter 3. We will look at some more of these controls in this chapter.

Data and Presentation

Word, unlike InfoPath, does not store data separately from the visual presentation of the data. WordML, Word's native XML format, is represented as an XML tree with two intertwined parts—presentation nodes defined using Word's schema namespace and the XML nodes defined under the customer's schema namespace. The XML data and Word presentation tags coexist in the XML file. This makes it more difficult to extract only XML data that is needed for workflow, unless you use Save As to extract the XML data for the document. Word allows you to save the document only as XML—it does not create any schema (XSD) or transformation (XSLT) files for this XML.

Schema Support and Validation

Word support for schemas is not as powerful as InfoPath's. And unlike InfoPath, Word allows only flat schemas and cannot build documents based on recursive, optional, or choice structures in schemas. The Word Clipboard makes it easy to cut and paste the XML content, resulting in invalid XML. Unlike InfoPath form editing, which always takes the form from one valid state to another, Word is more tolerant of invalid data. You must design the smart document with a lot of validation code so the user will not inadvertently change the XML structure of the document.

Business Logic and Deployment

Word does not have any declarative support for data connections. Smart document scenarios seem to be directed toward developers, not information workers. In general, you must write business logic code to create end-to-end solutions that talk to a database or a Microsoft SharePoint form library. Word's complex object model does not expose the MSXML *DOMDocument* object, like InfoPath does. The easiest way that developers can deploy a Word smart document is by attaching an XML Expansion Pack to a Word document. The document author needs to digitally sign the XML Expansion Pack for a smart document. The user can install the smart document after trusting the signature on the smart document on his machine. This is akin to installing fully trusted InfoPath forms. An InfoPath form needs the full trust security model only for a subset of forms—for example, forms that call into security level-three object model methods. For more on InfoPath's trust model, refer to Chapter 8. For now, suffice it to say that InfoPath forms can be deployed in Restricted and Domain trust mode and do not always need to be fully trusted on the end user's machine.

InfoPath's Rich Features

As promised, we'll now look at some InfoPath features that enable you to create rich forms. By "rich" we are referring not only to rich text but also to the feature-intensive controls that the InfoPath design interface provides.

Rich Text

The InfoPath design area is a rich canvas where you can use layouts and color schemes to create an appealing layout for your form. In working with InfoPath so far, you might have already noticed or used the various layouts and controls that the InfoPath design interface provides.

Developer Nugget: Modifying the XSL Outside InfoPath

InfoPath creates some default-view XSL files, such as view1.xsl and upgrade.xsl, as part of the form template. The views that you create in InfoPath design mode are saved to these XSL files. You can fine-tune the appearance of a view by changing the XSL in its .xsl file. In general, you should do this only if you want to implement some sophisticated styles, layout, or logic for your form view that is not otherwise possible through the InfoPath design interface. You must also be familiar with XSLT to modify the XSL that InfoPath creates for your form template view. InfoPath does not guarantee that you can keep any modifications you make to the view XSL outside InfoPath. That is, if you make changes in the XSL file after creating the form template, you are not guaranteed that the changes will persist if you make subsequent modifications in the view through InfoPath.

InfoPath does, however, provide a way to protect custom edits made to the XSL files. If you write custom XSL in your form template that you do not want InfoPath to touch, you can define it within a Preserve Code Block—an *xsl:template* where you can add any custom XSL that you want the InfoPath designer to overwrite. The *mode* attribute of the template must have a value of *xd:preserve*. The following XSL snippet demonstrates the use of this attribute:

```
<xsl:template match="my:foo" mode="xd:preserve">
    ...
</xsl:template>
```

You must also update the *mode* attribute on the *xsl:apply-templates* associated with the preceding template:

```
<xsl:apply-templates select="my:foo" mode="xd:preserve" />
```

The InfoPath designer shows the preceding section of the view in an outlined red box with the label *Preserve Code Block*, which cannot be modified in the designer. We recommend that you use this technique for sophisticated cosmetic changes or complex XSLT code that you want to use in InfoPath views. You should thus not need to use Preserve Code Blocks for typical forms because InfoPath's design interface is adequate for simple form presentation needs.

For rich text form data, InfoPath provides a Rich Text Box control. Rich text in InfoPath is saved in the XML as XHTML. You can insert rich controls in the view for any element in the data source that is defined in the XHTML namespace.

XML Schema Definition (XSD) for Rich Text

You can enable rich text for an element in the form schema by adding an *xsd:any* element whose namespace attribute points to the URI reference for the XHTML standard. In addition, you should add the *mixed="true"* attribute to the *complexType* element for the rich text. Here is the XSD snippet for a rich text field named *comment*:

```
<xsd:element name="comment">
    <xsd:complexType mixed="true">
        <xsd:sequence>
            <xsd:any minOccurs="0" maxOccurs="unbounded"
                namespace="http://www.w3.org/1999/xhtml" processContents="lax"/>
        </xsd:sequence>
    </xsd:complexType>
</xsd:element>
```

Types of Rich Text

The InfoPath Rich Text Box control has three formatting features (as shown in Figure 4-1): paragraph breaks, character formatting, and full rich text support.

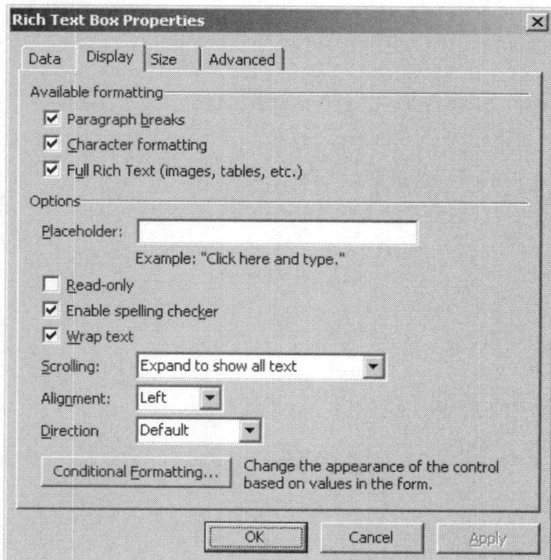

Figure 4-1 InfoPath Rich Text Box Properties dialog box allows you to set various types of rich text formatting options.

Character formatting Character formatting enables rich text input for InfoPath controls. If the input does not need character formatting, do not use a Rich Text Box control. Use a Text

Box control instead. The editing component for a text box in the XSF file is an *xField*. The XSF snippet for a rich text box with only character formatting enabled looks like this:

```
<xsf:xmlToEdit name="field1_1" item="/my:myFields/my:field1">
    <xsf:editWith component="xField" type="formatted"> </xsf:editWith>
</xsf:xmlToEdit>
```

Corresponding XML will look something like this:

```
<my:field1>The <font color="#ff0000" xmlns="http://www.w3.org/1999/
xhtml"><strong>quick brown fox </strong></font>jumped over <em xmlns="http://www.w3.org/
1999/xhtml"><font color="#3366ff"><strong>the lazy dog</strong></font></em></my:field1>
```

Paragraph breaks Paragraph breaks allow you to add new line characters within your rich text data. The XSF snippet for a rich text box with paragraph breaks enabled looks like this:

```
<xsf:xmlToEdit name="field1_1" item="/my:myFields/my:field1">
    <xsf:editWith component="xField" type="plainMultiline"></xsf:editWith>
</xsf:xmlToEdit>
```

Corresponding XML will look something like this:

```
<my:field2><div xmlns="http://www.w3.org/1999/xhtml">The quick brown fox</div>
<div xmlns="http://www.w3.org/1999/xhtml">jumped over</div>
<div xmlns="http://www.w3.org/1999/xhtml">the lazy dog</div>
<div xmlns="http://www.w3.org/1999/xhtml"> </div></my:field2>
```

If you enable character formatting in addition to paragraph breaks, the value of the *xField* attribute in the above snippet is *formattedMultiline* instead of *plainMultiline*.

Full rich text support, including images and tables Full rich text support allows you to add images, tables, and more inside a rich text field. You cannot disable character formatting for this type of rich field. The XSF snippet for a rich text box with full rich text enabled looks like this:

```
<xsf:xmlToEdit name="field1_1" item="/my:myFields/my:field1">
    <xsf:editWith component="xField" type="rich"></xsf:editWith>
</xsf:xmlToEdit>
```

Corresponding XML will look something like this:

```
<my:field3>
    <div xmlns="http://www.w3.org/1999/xhtml"> </div>
    <div xmlns="http://www.w3.org/1999/xhtml">
        <table class="msoUcTable" style="BORDER-RIGHT: medium none; TABLE-
LAYOUT: fixed; BORDER-TOP: medium none; BORDER-LEFT: medium none; WIDTH: 384px; BORDER-
BOTTOM: medium none; BORDER-COLLAPSE: collapse; WORD-WRAP: break-word" tabIndex="-1"
borderColor="buttontext" border="1">
            <colgroup>
                <col style="WIDTH: 192px"/>
                <col style="WIDTH: 192px"/>
            </colgroup>
```

```
                <tbody vAlign="top">
                    <tr>
                        <td><div><font face="Verdana" size="2">The </font></div></td>
                        <td><div><font face="Verdana" size="2">
                            <font color="#ff0000"><strong>quick brown fox</strong>
                            </font></font></div></td>
                    </tr>
                    <tr>
                        <td><div><font face="Verdana" size="2">jumped over </font></div></td>
                        <td><div><font face="Verdana" color="#3366ff" size="2">
                            <strong><em>the lazy dog</em></strong>
                            </font></div></td>
                    </tr>
                </tbody>
            </table>
        </div>
        <div xmlns="http://www.w3.org/1999/xhtml"> </div>
</my:field3>
```

Figure 4-2 shows the InfoPath form with the these rich text controls. To summarize the preceding examples, the five types of *xField* components are *plain, plainMultiline, formatted, formattedMultiline*, and *rich*.

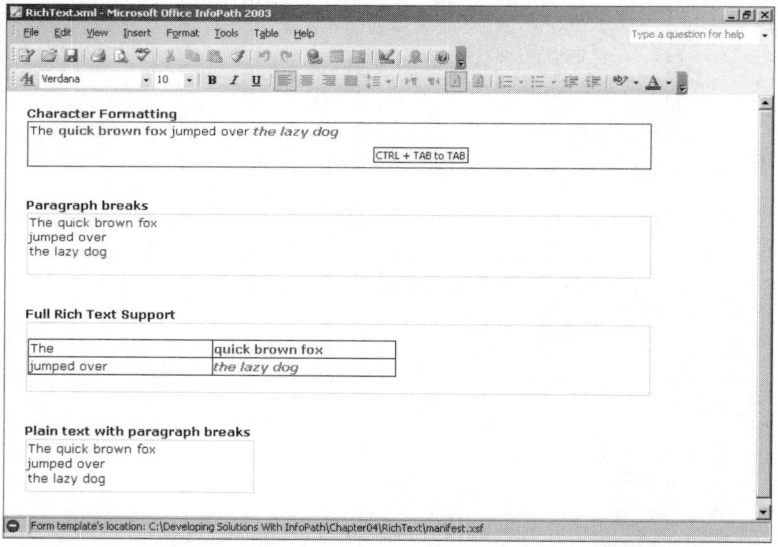

Figure 4-2 InfoPath controls for various degrees of rich text support

As you can see, formatted or rich text can add a lot of clutter to the values of the XML nodes. The actual data value in the above example is a single sentence. To reduce this clutter, we recommend that you select the appropriate formatting options that are just enough to suit the purpose of your rich text field. For example, if you need only character formatting with line breaks in your rich input control, you should avoid using full rich text support. Also, you should not use rich text fields with paragraph breaks if you do not care about character formatting. An example of this is *field2* above; it has each new line in a *div* element. You are better off using plain text fields with paragraph breaks enabled. The rich text sample described in the above section can be found at C:\Developing Solutions With InfoPath\Chapter04\RichText\RichText.xml.

The InfoPath run time allows you to navigate between fields using the Tab key. Consequently, the form user cannot use the Tab key to add Tab characters within the rich text field—it will simply navigate to the next field. The correct way to insert Tab characters in rich text is to use the Ctrl+Tab key combination. If your InfoPath form includes a lot of rich text controls, we recommend that you add this key combination in a ScreenTip for your rich text field. We did this for field1 in the preceding example.

Let's now look at an example form template that uses rich text extensively. We created a partial News Report form that you can open from Chapter04\Report.xml in the book's companion content. Figure 4-3 shows what this form looks like. The form is created using the form template NewsReport.xsn, which you can open from Chapter04\NewsReport.xsn in the book's companion content.

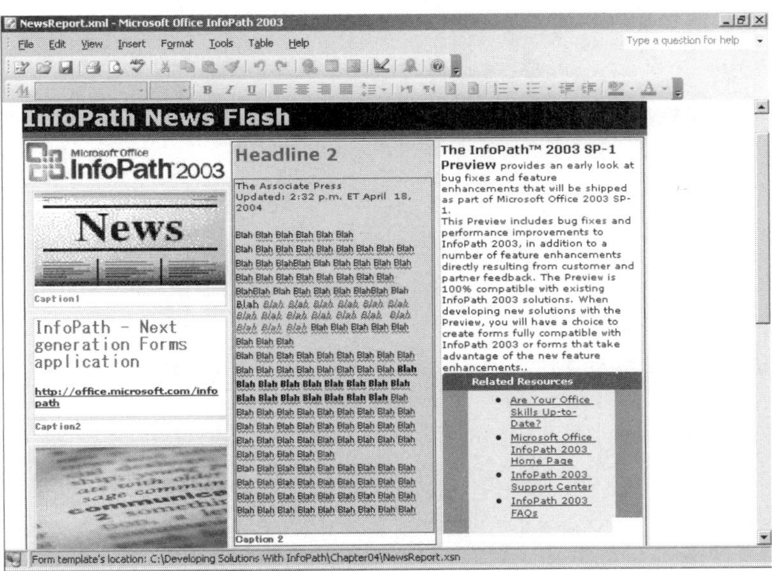

Figure 4-3 The News Report form, created using InfoPath rich text controls

Programmatic rich text values The Autopopulation section of Chapter 3 covered how to assign default values to controls–through the template.xml file or through code. Now suppose you need to populate rich text in your News Report form from a data source such as a Web service or a SQL server. The rich text data exists as XHTML nodes in the XML node that the rich control is bound to. The XHTML data consists of actual nodes from the XHTML namespace. Hence, adding rich text data to a field involves more than adding text values to the node that the field is bound to. You cannot programmatically write XHTML values in rich text controls as simply as you can write text values to plain text controls. You must append XHTML nodes and their values as XML children to the rich text node.

Here's how to populate a rich text field with XHTML data:

1. In Visual Studio .NET 2003, choose New | Project from the File menu.
2. In the New Project dialog box, click on Microsoft Office InfoPath Projects/Visual Basic Projects and select the InfoPath Form Template icon.
3. Type **StatusReportProject** for the project name, and then click OK.
4. In the Microsoft Office Project Wizard, click on Open Existing Form Template.
5. Click Browse.
6. Navigate to C:\Program Files\Microsoft Office\OFFICE11\INFFORMS\1033, select the file STATRPT.XSN, and then click Open.
7. Click Finish, and then click OK to close the Microsoft Development Environment dialog box, which informs you that you will be working with a copy of the original form template.
8. In InfoPath, click Controls in the task pane.
9. Insert a button in the view below the *Project* field and above the horizontal rule.
10. Right-click on the button, and then choose Button Properties.
11. Change the Label to **Auto Summary**, and then change the ID to **auto_summary**.
12. Click Edit Form Code. The focus switches to Visual Studio.
13. In the Solution Explorer tree, right-click on the References node and then choose Add Reference.
14. In the Add Reference dialog box, click on the COM tab, choose Microsoft XML v5.0, click Select, and then click OK.
15. Add an *Imports* statement for this assembly to the top of your FormCode.vb file. Qualify the namespace to avoid ambiguous references to XML OM members from the *Microsoft.Office.Interop.InfoPath.SemiTrust* namespace, as shown here:

    ```
    Imports msxml = MSXML2
    ```

16. In the *auto_summary_OnClick* event handler, write code to create a temporary DOM with some rich text XML from the *xhtml* namespace, and then append it to the *sr:summary* node in the Status Report DOM. Your *OnClick* event handler code should look like the following:

    ```
    'Get the issues node list
    Dim activeIssues As IXMLDOMNodeList = thisXDocument.DOM.selectNodes
        ("/sr:statusReport/sr:issues/sr:item")

    'Get the date from this form
    Dim thisDate As IXMLDOMNode = thisXDocument.DOM.selectSingleNode
        ("/sr:statusReport/sr:date")

    'Get the rich text Summary node
    Dim summaryNode As IXMLDOMNode = thisXDocument.DOM.selectSingleNode
        ("/sr:statusReport/sr:summary")
    ```

```
'Write some rich text to add to the summary using issues count and form date
Dim strXML As String = "<div xmlns='http://www.w3.org/1999/xhtml
'>There are <strong><font color='red'>" & activeIssues.length.ToString() & "
    active </font></strong>issues on " & thisDate.text & "</div>"

'Create a temporary MSXML DOM Document
'You also need to add a reference to MSXML 5.0
Dim tempDoc As New MSXML2.DOMDocument50

'Load the above string into the DOM. For larger rich data, consider using
    createNode et al
tempDoc.loadXML(strXML)
Dim richNode As IXMLDOMNode = tempDoc.documentElement.cloneNode(True)

'Add the XHTML nodes to the Summary node
summaryNode.appendChild(richNode)
```

17. In InfoPath, double-click the *Date* field to open its Properties dialog box.
18. Click the *fx* button, type **today()**, and then click OK twice.
19. Preview the form.
20. Add four or five issues to the Issues list, located toward the bottom of the form.
21. Click Auto Summary to see the rich text summary you just added in the preceding code. Figure 4-4 shows the Status Report view with the autopopulated rich text in the summary field based on the number of issues and date in the form.
22. Close the preview and then publish the form template on your hard drive as **MyStatusReport.xsn.**
23. Close InfoPath.

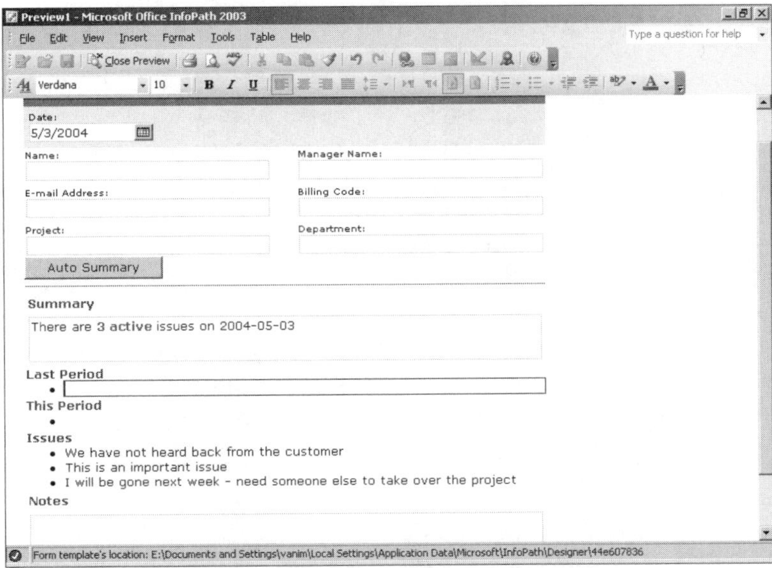

Figure 4-4 A Status Report form with automatically populated rich text summary information

XML Lists

InfoPath supports list controls in which every item in the list is saved as a separate XML item. From a data perspective, an XML list is the same as a single-column repeating table. It is just an additional control for list-like data entry. The three main controls that are provided for XML lists in the Controls task pane are in the Repeating And Optional section. They are Bulleted List, Numbered List, and Plain List. As the names suggest, the Bulleted List and the Numbered List have bullets or numbers preceding the XML list item in the view, respectively, while the Plain List has neither.

One common use of InfoPath list controls is for presentation purposes when you do not care about tabulating items from repeating groups of data. For example, you can use a list control for issues or item lists. The obvious advantage when selecting an XML list control over a regular XHTML list in a Rich Text Box control is that you can process each list item in the XML data a lot easier. Besides, the InfoPath Merge feature only merges data from repeating controls like the list controls.

Merging Lists Across Forms

InfoPath allows you to merge data from any repeating controls across forms based on the same schema. Form merging is enabled by default. You can turn off this feature for a form template by choosing Form Options from the Tools menu and then deselecting the Enable Form Merging check box. If you want to merge forms across different schemas or override the default merge functionality, you can write a custom merge XSLT file and include it in the form template. The InfoPath SDK includes the Merge Forms Developer Sample form which demonstrates this technique.

Spell Checking and Autocomplete

InfoPath supports spell checking for data in all editable fields. This feature is similar to Word's spelling checker–a misspelled word, according to the spell checker dictionary, is underlined with a red squiggle. You can change some spelling options or toggle the feature by choosing Tools | Options and clicking on the Spelling tab. However, toggling the spell checker from this location changes spell checking for the InfoPath application, not the form. Spell checking is "on" by default for all fields. You need to turn it off per field in design mode if you want to turn off spell checking in the form for all users. All of InfoPath's text input controls have a corresponding component associated with them. The component is declared in an attribute in the manifest.xsf file within an *xmlToEdit* element. For example, you saw the *xField* component attribute in the rich text code snippets above. When you turn on spell checking for a particular editable field, a *proofing="yes"* attribute is added to that field's *xmlToEdit* node in the manifest.xsf file.

InfoPath also has autocomplete functionality that uses the autocomplete behavior in Microsoft Internet Explorer. For the autocomplete feature to work in InfoPath, it must be turned on in Internet Explorer. It is on by default. To modify the autocomplete settings, launch Internet Explorer, choose Internet Options from the Tools menu, click on the Content tab, click AutoComplete, and then make any changes you want. Similar to spell checking, this is an application-level setting. If you want to turn off autocompletion for a specific field in the form template for all users, you should do it in design mode. You can toggle autocomplete for a particular field through the Properties dialog box for the control. The autocomplete feature is declared in the *autocomplete="yes | no"* attribute of the *xmlToEdit* node for a particular field in the manifest.xsf file.

Multiple Views

InfoPath allows you to create multiple views of the data in your form template at design time. You can do this using the Views task pane. For example, the Resume solution in the sample forms included with InfoPath has several views in the form. To open the Resume solution, choose Design A Form from the File menu. In the Design A Form task pane, click Customize A Sample. In the Customize A Sample dialog box select Resume from the list of forms. A typical scenario for multiple views is a form with multiple categories of data where you can separate detailed information from summary information. Multiple views can also be used in forms designed for workflow—completing a workflow step, like submitting data in one view, takes you to a separate view denoting the next step in the workflow. You should design each view by grouping related sections of your data and controls in the same view (such as summary/details or role-based groups such as employee/manager). One important advantage of the multiple-views feature is the ability to create a separate print view for your form. You can create a separate print view for each data entry view of your form using the Create Print Version For This View link at the bottom of the Views task pane.

Warning By default, each view in a form appears on the View menu when you fill out the form. This menu allows the user to switch the view. It is not always desirable to allow the form user access to every view. For example, you would not want a standard employee to access a confidential manager view. You can prevent a view from showing up on this menu by selecting the view in the Views task pane, clicking View Properties, and then, in the View Properties dialog box, clearing the Show On The View Menu When Filling Out The Form check box. If you use code to switch or access views and you subsequently change the name of a view, your code will be broken until you update it to reference the new name for the view. InfoPath does not do this automatically.

If you have a large number of views in your form, you should provide some contextual direction to users to switch from one view to another. You can do this by using the Rules feature—you add a rule to switch from one view to another based on a condition. For programmatic view switching, you can call the *SwitchView* method of the *View* object. You cannot, however, call this method from within the *OnLoad* event handler because the view does not exist until after the *OnLoad* event handler exits. Instead, in the *OnLoad* event handler you should programmatically change the default view that is created first by calling *thisXdocument.ViewInfos("View Name").IsDefault = true.*

Task Pane

You can add a custom HTML task pane to your Info Path form–for example, to show additional user interface form commands. The samples CD_EDIT.XSN and UIBASICS.XSN at C:\Program Files\Microsoft Office\OFFICE11\SAMPLES\INFOPATH are good examples of task panes that drive user input. Another common use for a task pane is to show contextual help for your form by using the *OnContextChange* event handler.

Custom User Interface

In Chapter 3, you saw how to add a custom user interface component to an InfoPath form template. InfoPath allows you to create toolbars and menus in your form template. You can add custom UI for controls in the Repeating And Optional group of the Controls task pane by clicking Customize Commands in the Properties dialog box for that control. This dialog box allows you to create buttons on a toolbar named Form Toolbar. If you need to create buttons on additional toolbars or you want a complex custom UI such as one with cascading and drop-down menus, you must edit the manifest.xsf file and add the respective *xsf:menu* elements with *xsf:button* elements within them. You can also edit the manifest.xsf file to add a *tooltip*, *caption*, and *icon* to the *xsf:button*. You can also add the ToolTip by clicking Customize Commands in the Properties dialog box. It will be listed as a ScreenTip in that dialog box. For example, you might want to add additional help items, specific to your form, to the Help menu. InfoPath also supports the Office object model's *CommandBars* collection if you need to access the built-in user interface. However, this interface works only with fully trusted InfoPath forms.

Let's look at an example of some UI manipulation. We'll add a submenu to the File menu with a command for sending e-mail to a manager or a department. (In the Developer Nugget that follows, we'll use the *CommandBars* collection object to move the built-in generic Send To Mail Recipient command to this submenu.

Note For some more information on using the CommandBars OM with managed code, refer to the Knowledge Base article at http://support.microsoft.com/default.aspx?scid=kb;en-us;867442.

First we use simple declarative syntax to add the command to the menu. The next step requires code and also requires the user to fully trust the InfoPath form template. You typically use the *CommandBars* collection, with the additional full trust security requirement, for more compelling scenarios such as adding or removing built-in commands to and from the InfoPath menus.

1. In Visual Studio .NET 2003, choose New | Project from the File menu.

2. In the New Project dialog box, click on Microsoft Office InfoPath Projects/Visual Basic Projects and select the InfoPath Form Template icon.
3. Type **CustomStatusReport** for the project name, and then click OK.
4. In the Microsoft Office Project Wizard, click on Open Existing Form Template.
5. Click Browse.
6. Navigate to the previously saved MyStatusReport.xsn or to C:\Program Files\Microsoft Office\OFFICE11\INFFORMS\1033, select the file STATRPT.XSN, and then click Open.
7. Click Finish, and then click OK to close the Microsoft Development Environment dialog box, which informs you that you will be working with a copy of the original form template.
8. Close InfoPath.
9. In Visual Studio, open the manifest.xsf file by double-clicking on the filename in Solution Explorer.
10. Add the following XSF snippet under the *<xsf:view name="View 1" caption="View 1">* node:

```
<xsf:menuArea name="msoFileMenu">
    <xsf:menu caption="Send Status &amp;Report">
        <xsf:button name="manager" icon="233" caption="To Ma&amp;nager" />
        <xsf:button name="department" icon="235" caption="To De&amp;partment"/>
    <xsf:menu>
</xsf:menuArea>
```

11. Add event handlers for the above two buttons within the project class just before the *End Class* line in the FormCode.vb file:

```
<InfoPathEventHandler(MatchPath:="manager", EventType:=InfoPathEventType.OnClick)> _
Public Sub manager_OnClick(ByVal e As DocActionEvent)
    thisXDocument.UI.Alert("Sending Status report to manager..")
    'Write code to send to manager using email adapter
End Sub

<InfoPathEventHandler(MatchPath:="department", EventType:=InfoPathEventType.OnClick)>
_
Public Sub dept_OnClick(ByVal e As DocActionEvent)
    thisXDocument.UI.Alert("Sending Status report to department..")
    ' Write code to send to department using email adapter
End Sub
```

12. Preview the form in Visual Studio using Alt+Shift+F or Ctrl+F5, or from InfoPath using Ctrl+Shift+B.

13. Click on the File menu, and use the newly created Send Status Report submenus. Figure 4-5 shows what these menus look like on the InfoPath form.

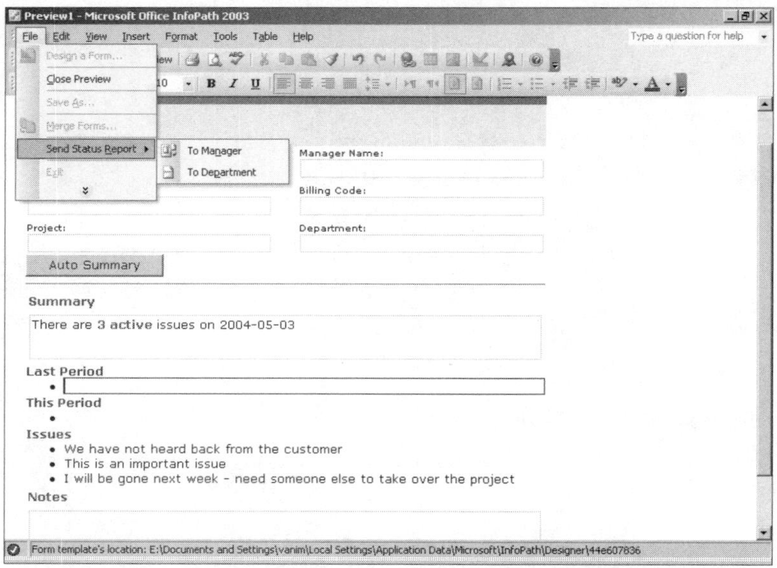

Figure 4-5 The menus added to the File menu for the Status Report form template

Developer Nugget: Using CommandBars with Managed Code

In the example you just saw, we were able to create our own buttons and menus in InfoPath. But what if you need to manipulate the built-in commands that InfoPath provides? You can do so using the CommandBars OM that you might have used with other Office applications. Remember, however, that the CommandBars OM is actually level three security–it can be used only in fully trusted InfoPath form templates. Using the CommandBars OM through managed code is somewhat tricky because of the implementation of the CommandBars collection object for use in managed code. Let's look at an example that deletes the built-in Send To Mail Recipient menu item in the Status Report solution. This will force the form user to use one of the extensible menus that we just provided.

1. Open the solution that you created in the preceding example in Visual Studio. Alternately, you can start a new project from the Status Report form template.
2. Add an *OnLoad* event handler by choosing Programming | OnLoad Event from the Tools menu.
3. Type the following code in the *OnLoad* event handler:

```
Dim commandBars As ObjectWrapper = thisApplication.ActiveWindow.CommandBars
'Set the expected values for flags for the InvokeMember calls
Dim flags As BindingFlags = BindingFlags.GetProperty Or BindingFlags.DeclaredOnly
 Or BindingFlags.Public Or BindingFlags.Instance Or BindingFlags.InvokeMethod
```

```
'Set arguments for InvokeMember calls
'Name of the toolbar (commandbar) that this button will be found on
Dim args As Object() = New Object() {"Standard"}
'Name of the button
Dim mailArgs As Object() = New Object() {"Send to Mail Recipient"}
'Remove the button for this InfoPath instance only
Dim boolArgs As Object() = New Object() {False}

'Get required commandbar
Dim commandBarItem As Object = commandBars.InvokeByName("Item", flags, args,
    Nothing)

Dim mailControl As Object
'Get button control for mail button
Try
    mailControl = commandBarItem.GetType().InvokeMember("controls", flags,
        Nothing, commandBarItem, mailArgs)
Catch ex As Exception
    'Return if the button does not exist or already deleted
    Return
End Try

'Alert the user that the button will be deleted (remove the following two lines
    if you do not think this is necessary)
Dim strCaption As String = mailControl.GetType().InvokeMember("caption", flags,
    Nothing, mailControl, Nothing)
thisXDocument.UI.Alert("Deleting the " + strCaption + "button from toolbar..")

'Delete the button control for mail button
mailControl.GetType().InvokeMember("Delete", flags, Nothing, mailControl,
    boolArgs)
```

4. Add an Imports statement for *System.Reflection* to your form code at the top of the FormCode.vb file:

```
Imports System.Reflection
```

5. Publish the form template.
6. Make the form template fully trusted by signing it or registering it using the InfoPath SDK tool, RegForm.

Note During the development phase, you can register the solution for previewing from within Visual Studio or InfoPath by using external automation to call the *RegisterSolution* method on the manifest.xsf file at the project location. The InfoPath SDK includes a tool that makes this easier. Before you do this, you must remove the *publishURL* attribute from manifest.xsf and add *requireFullTrust="yes"*. (For more details on any of these methods or for more information on working with full trust forms, see Chapter 8.)

7. Open the form template by double-clicking on the XSN. Click OK in the dialog box that appears, asking about deleting the control. Open the File menu and notice that the Send To Mail Recipient button is gone! The completed project for this exercise is at Chapter04\CustomStatusReport in the book's companion content.

Digital Signatures

InfoPath supports XML digital signatures on forms to enable secure workflow scenarios. A digital signature on an InfoPath form is cryptographic evidence that the content has not changed from the time the form user signed it. In other words, a digital signature prevents tampering with the InfoPath form at a physical level. Digital signatures are also supported in other Office applications, including Word, Excel, and Outlook. When a user adds a digital signature to a form, she must use a digital certificate issued by a trusted root authority.

For more information about digital signatures, you can refer to the following articles on MSDN: "Understanding XML Digital Signature" at http://msdn.microsoft.com/library/default.asp?url=/library/en-us/dnwebsrv/html/underxmldigsig.asp and "Introduction to Code Signing" at http://msdn.microsoft.com/library/default.asp?url=/workshop/security/authcode/intro_authenticode.asp.

Signature Metadata

In addition to the signature itself, a digital signature also consists of metadata such as

- A comment field for describing the reason for signing the form
- Machine, operating system, and InfoPath information
- A snapshot image of the form at the time it was signed (in .png format)
- A fingerprint that includes information about the form template that was used to create the signed form

When you set a signature policy for the form template through the InfoPath design user interface, you enable digital signatures in your form template and also define the relationship between the signature and different parts of the form.

Schema Impact

Enabling digital signatures is an explicit schema operation where a *Signatures* node is added to the data source of the form template. If you designed your form template from an existing data source that already had a node in your schema based on the digital signatures namespace, you can select this node to store the digital signature. It is important to remember the specific requirements of this node—that it needs to be an empty group node with a minimum occurrence of 1, and it must be defined with the digital signature namespace *http://www.w3.org/2000/09/xmldsig#*.

For example, if you are creating or extending your form template schema outside of InfoPath, the following is the schema snippet you must add for a digital signature node:

```
<xsd:element name="signatures">
    <xsd:complexType>
        <xsd:sequence>
        <xsd:element ref="my:signature"/>
    </xsd:sequence>
```

```
    </xsd:complexType>
</xsd:element>
<xsd:element name="signature">
    <xsd:complexType>
        <xsd:sequence>
            <xsd:any minOccurs="0" maxOccurs="unbounded" namespace="http://www.w3.org/2000/
                09/xmldsig#" processContents="lax"/>
        </xsd:sequence>
    </xsd:complexType>
</xsd:element>
```

The easiest way to enable digital signing for your form template is via the Digital Signatures tab on the Form Options dialog box. You can choose to enable signing for the entire form or for individual sections of the form. A separate child *Signature* node is added to the *Signatures* node for each signable section of your form template.

Dependent Signing

Each signature that you enable can be dependent or not, depending on whether you allow cosigning or countersigning. For example, you might have an Expense Report scenario, where the Expenses section needs to be signed by the user and then the accountant before it is submitted. In this scenario, you will enable countersigning on the Expenses section of the form template. As a consequence, the user signature cannot be removed unless the accountant signature is removed first. If you try to remove the user signature by mangling the data in the form XML outside InfoPath, the form will become invalid. In a way, when a section has countersigning enabled on it, each signature signs the preceding signature on that section. Figure 4-6 shows the Set Of Signable Data dialog box, which allows you to set these options.

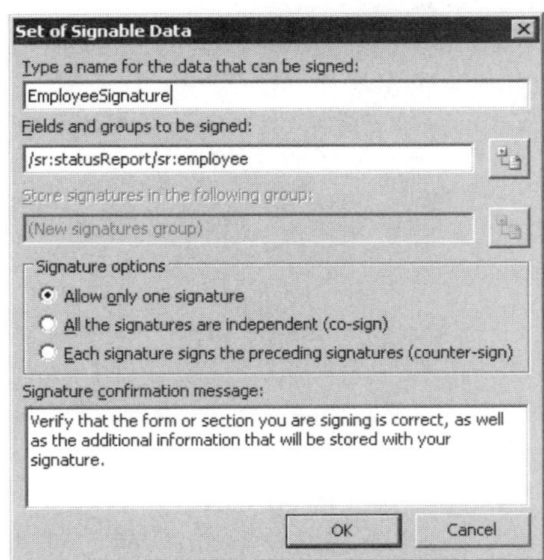

Figure 4-6 The Set Of Signable Data dialog box

Programmatic Support

InfoPath's digital signature support is fully extensible through the object model. The InfoPath OM provides support to access the collection of signatures and the collection of signable sections for the form. It also gives programmatic access to the certificate that was used to sign the form. In addition, an *OnSign* event handler can be used to customize the user experience whenever the sign action is invoked in the form.

Let us add some code to the Status Report form template to thwart a user who tries to send the status report form to the department without signing it first. We'll use the *IsSigned* property on the *XDocument* object. Add the following code snippet to the beginning of the event handler *dept_OnClick* in the preceding example:

```
If (Not (thisXDocument.IsSigned)) Then
    thisXDocument.UI.Alert("Please sign the form before sending it")
    Return
End If
```

Dynamic Structures

In Chapter 3, you saw some examples of repeating structures that InfoPath supports. Take a moment to look at all of the controls that are available in the Repeating And Optional and Advanced sections of the Controls task pane. InfoPath supports several additional dynamic controls that neatly map to corresponding XSD constructs. These dynamic controls are what make InfoPath form controls powerful compared with other form editors.

The power of dynamic structures is in the ability to display only what the user needs, in addition to supporting a variety of design structures. Dynamic editing includes optional, repeating, recursive, and choice sections that allow for heterogeneous repeating data. These sections change the look of the form based on the data entered. When combined with rich text controls, dynamic editing enables a powerful set of patterns for the forms designer.

Dynamic structures are an easy way to keep the form clean and uncluttered and display only what's relevant. It is easy to create large standardized templates with a limited number of views. In the next few sections we'll look at some dynamic structures that InfoPath supports.

Optional Sections

As the name implies, an optional section allows the form user to insert the section at run time. (We briefly mentioned optional sections in Chapter 3.) Optional sections are more efficient than conditionally visible sections because the data for an optional section is not present in the XML unless the form user inserts the section. A conditionally hidden section is hidden in the view but is always present in the data. In a blank new form, this means that a conditionally visible section is always present in the template.xml file. You add values to the data at run time when the section is conditionally visible.

A couple of things should be pointed out about optional sections:

- Optional sections can include built-in commands (in the shortcut menu button and in the Insert | Section menu) as well as a custom placeholder UI in the view that allows the user to easily insert the optional section.
- When the form user removes an optional section, the XML nodes are deleted, including any values they held. These values cannot be recovered unless you programmatically copy the values before the deletion happens and restore them on insertion.
- Nodes inside an optional group, when inserted in the view "outside" the associated optional section, are invalid when the optional section has not been inserted. The form user will find these fields to be read-only.
- If you have a calculated field or expression box that uses optional section fields as part of the calculation, when the option section has not been inserted the calculation will fail and result in a NaN value. With some extra work on your part, you can find ways around this, such as by using two expression boxes instead of one, each with a different calculation, and by using conditional visibility to hide one or the other based on the presence of the optional section.

The Status Report form template that we have looked at has three optional sections at the bottom of the form: *Time Report*, *Budget Report*, and *Task List*. In the schema, each of these sections has a *minOccurs="0"*, which is what makes it possible to insert the element as an optional section at design time. If you insert an optional section into the view at design time and name it **optionalSection**, the schema snippet for the section will look like the following:

```
<xsd:element ref="my:optionalSection" minOccurs="0"/>
```

Choice Groups

If you intend to use several optional sections that are part of a choice in your form design, you should insert each section into a choice group rather than use separate optional sections. For example, you would do this in a scenario in which you have optional serial number fields in an inventory tracking form and inserting the serial number for one item would eliminate the need to insert additional numbers.

Choice Sections

We talked about repeating choice groups in Chapter 3. Choice sections are another structural construct that allows for a dynamic form experience. The Choice Section control is enabled for any elements that are enclosed within an *xsd:choice* element in the schema. You can start with empty choice groups and add controls to them to create large sections containing fields that are clearly part of a choice in a form. For example, in a medical form, you can use a choice group with different sets of information, to match the gender of the patient.

Repeating Recursive Sections

InfoPath supports recursive XSD structures–an element that references itself. For example, the *issues* element in the following XSD snippet is recursive:

```
<xsd:element name="issues">
    <xsd:complexType>
        <xsd:sequence>
            <xsd:element ref="issues" minOccurs="0" maxOccurs="unbounded"/>
            <xsd:element ref="issue" minOccurs="0"/>
        </xsd:sequence>
    </xsd:complexType>
</xsd:element>
<xsd:element name="issue" type="xsd:string"/>
```

If you insert the preceding element from the Data Source task pane into your view, it is inserted in a Repeating Recursive Section control. This control is useful for creating nested repeating structures where you do not know the depth of the data tree when you are designing the form.

Hierarchical Numbering Using Repeating Recursion

Using a Repeating Recursive Section, as described above, you can create nested sections of data with appropriate numbering on them, such as Section 1, 1.1, 2, 3.1, 3.1.1, 3.1.1.1, and so on. This technique is useful for creating a form template for a text-intensive form with several sections and subsections. For example, you can use this structure to create a proposed table of contents view in an InfoPath form template for a book or for a thesis proposal.

Let's implement the hierarchical numbering technique within a repeating recursive section. In this example, we will customize the Project Plan sample. We will replace the Project Plan schema with a schema that supports a repeating recursive section, add the recursive section to the view, and use XPath to implement a numbering scheme to number the sections that are inserted by the form user.

Here are the required steps:

1. In Visual Studio .NET 2003, choose New | Project from the File menu.
2. In the New Project dialog box, click on Microsoft Office InfoPath Projects/Visual Basic Projects and select the InfoPath Form Template icon.
3. Type **CustomProject** for the project name, and then click OK.
4. In the Microsoft Office Project Wizard, click on Open Existing Form Template.
5. Click Browse.
6. Navigate to C:\Program Files\Microsoft Office\OFFICE11\INFFORMS\1033, select the file PROJECT.XSN, and then click Open.
7. In InfoPath, choose Convert Main Data Source from the Tools menu.

8. In the Data Source Wizard, click Browse.
9. Navigate to Chapter04\ProjectPlan in the book's companion content, select the ProjectPlanRSchema.xsd file, and then click Open.
10. Click Next, and then click Finish to close the Data Source Wizard.
11. In the Data Source task pane, expand the *details* node until you reach the *section* node.
12. Drag and drop the section node in the view just below the Plan heading.
13. Fix the layout to look like the Project Plan layout by copying and pasting the layout table with the fields Owner, Status, Start Date, End Date, and Title, which has the placeholder text. Type a name for this phase of the plan. You can paste over the text boxes inserted in the section in the previous step.
14. Delete the old section's Repeating Section control.
15. Fix the binding for the owner node by right-clicking on the node, choosing Change Binding, and then selecting the section/owner node.
16. In the Data Source task pane, insert sectionNumber in the view, as an expression box, just left of the title text "Type a name for this phase of the plan."
17. Open the Properties dialog box for the outer Repeating Section.
18. Click Modify, and then click Edit Default Values.
19. Clear the *section* node check box at the bottom of the list, and then click OK twice.
20. Change the hint text to **Insert new section**, and then click OK.
21. Open the Properties dialog box for the inner Repeating Section.
22. Change the default values to not include the *section* node by following the same steps that you did above for the outer Repeating Section, only this time change the hint text to **Insert subsection**.
23. Save the form. If you are presented with dialog boxes, click Yes or OK for each one.
24. Close InfoPath.
25. In Visual Studio, open the manifest.xsf file by double-clicking on it in the Solution Explorer.
26. Add the following XSF snippet just before the *</xsf:xDocumentClass>* closing tag to include an XPath to compute the section and subsection numbers. Alternatively, you can add these expressions with the InfoPath UI via rules using the the Set A Field's Value feature.

```
<xsf:calculations>
    <xsf:calculatedField target="prj:sectionNumber" expression="concat(../../
        prj:sectionNumber, 1 + count(../preceding-sibling::prj:section),
        &quot;.&quot;)" refresh="onChange"></xsf:calculatedField>
</xsf:calculations>
```

27. Save and close the manifest.xsf file.
28. Preview the form in Visual Studio by using Alt+Shift+F or Ctrl+F5.
29. Insert new sections and subsections. Enjoy your new numbering system!

Figure 4-7 shows the sections and subsections with a couple of levels of nesting. In this example, we have skipped over some of the layout-related steps that you might notice in the figure. You can adjust the layout tables and sections in the view for this sample using your mouse or the Table Properties dialog box.

The completed project for this exercise is at Chapter04\ProjectPlan\CustomProjectPlan in the book's companion content.

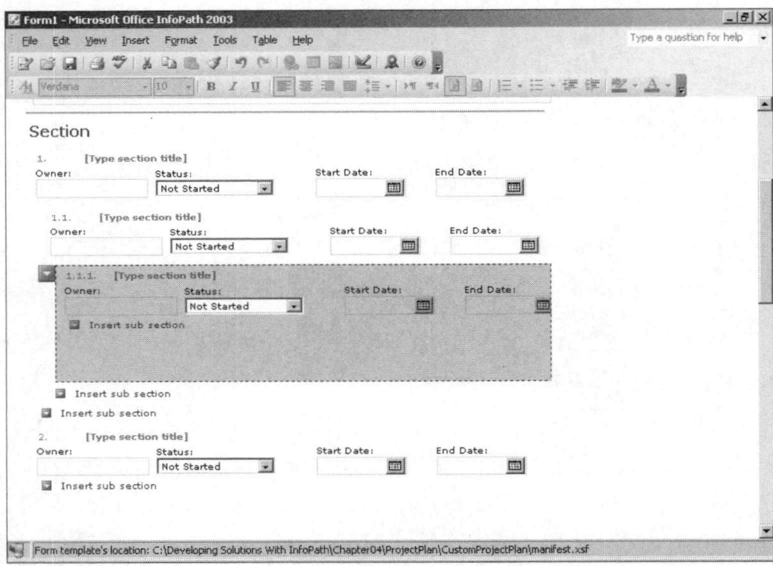

Figure 4-7 Numbered recursive sections in the customized Project Plan form template

In the previous example, we used InfoPath's Convert Data Source feature, which allows you to replace the schema in an existing form, after which you can modify the form design to conform to the new schema. It is useful when you want to modify a part of the form schema without having to re-create the form.

Programmatic Support for Dynamic Sections

You can programmatically manipulate structured sections such as repeating, optional, and choice sections through the InfoPath object model. We used the *executeAction* method of the *View* object earlier to insert a new item in the repeating control. You can generally achieve through the InfoPath object model just about anything that you can achieve through the InfoPath user interface. In addition, the *executeAction* method supports the *xCollection* component for repeating controls, the *xOptional* component for optional controls, and the *xReplace* component for choice controls.

Contextual Editing

InfoPath's form editing model is sensitive to where the user is currently editing in the form. Structural editing works in InfoPath by using the current context in the form. "Context" means where the cursor or current selection is in the view. Contextual editing is what enables custom commands to insert, delete, or replace sections in the form or prevents them from doing so. For example, in the Status Report form, Choose Section from the Insert menu and notice that the commands are enabled depending on the context.

InfoPath's contextual editing behavior is declarative because it is defined by parameters specified for the different controls in the manifest.xsf file. This parametric method of contextual command enabling makes InfoPath form filling efficient. Contextual editing is complex and uses several attribute values defined in an *xsf:xmlToEdit* element for the specific component in the manifest.xsf file. The *showIf* attribute on the *xsf:button* element in the XSF file makes it possible to control the visibility of the commands. You can enable, disable, or hide the button based on context by setting the value of the *showIf* attribute as required. When designing your form template, you must always test the form editing experience for the user by using the form in Preview mode to make sure the context in different parts of the form makes logical sense.

Programmatic Selection and Clipboard Support

InfoPath forms allow two kinds of selection in the view—text selection within a field and XML selection of a dynamic control such as a Repeating Section, XML list item, or Repeating Table. The InfoPath object model includes some methods on the *View* object and one event, *OnContextChange*, for programmatic selection and focus support. The following are a couple of caveats about programmatic selection support in InfoPath:

- The object model members provided by InfoPath for selection provide programmatic access only to operations implemented by InfoPath. For example, the InfoPath object model supports the XML clipboard, not the regular text clipboard. When filling out a form, notice how the selection of a section or repeating table structure in the view is lighter than regular text selection. When you execute clipboard actions on this structural selection, you are using the XML clipboard. You can cut, copy, or paste a structurally selected section in the view by calling the *ExecuteAction* method of the *View* object with the parameters Cut, Copy, and Paste.

> **Note** Managed code business logic in InfoPath does not work kindly with optional parameters in InfoPath object model methods. You need to use *Type.Missing* (Visual Basic .NET) or *Missing.Value* (C#) in place of each optional parameter that you would have been able to omit if you were using the OM method through script. This applies to a many of the selection and dynamic editing operations that use a lot of optional parameters in their function signatures.

- Programmatic support allows only operations that you can achieve through the view in the InfoPath runtime. As a result, you cannot call certain methods from a button in the view—methods such as *View.ExecuteAction* with parameters such as *xCollection::insert After, xReplace::replace*, or *View.GetSelectedNodes*. The workaround is to call these methods from a button on a toolbar, menu, or HTML task pane. In addition, you cannot use these methods to affect collections in a different view. You would have to first switch to a view, using the *SwitchView* method, before calling methods that act on collections in that view.

- The selection methods *View.SelectNodes* and *View.SelectText* take an XML node as a parameter. If there is more than one occurrence of the XML node in the view, you must also pass the *viewContext* as a parameter to the method. Unfortunately, the *viewContext* value is not exposed in the InfoPath design UI. You can obtain this attribute value through the manifest.xsf file. To try this in InfoPath design mode, insert any node *myNode* in the view from the Data Source task pane. Copy and paste the node below itself to create a duplicate bound node—you can verify this by looking at the duplicate binding notification icon that appears at the top-right corner of the control. Close InfoPath and open the view.xsl file for the form template. The *viewContext* is the value of the *xd:CtrlId* attribute that is written in the XSL in the element enclosing the *xsl:value-of* for the node.

```
<span class="xdTextBox" hideFocus="1" title="" xd:binding="my:field1" tabIndex="0"
    xd:xctname="PlainText" xd:CtrlId="CTRL1" style="WIDTH: 130px">
    <xsl:value-of select="myNode"/>
</span>
<span class="xdTextBox" hideFocus="1" title="" xd:binding="my:field1" tabIndex="0"
    xd:xctname="PlainText" xd:CtrlId="CTRL2" style="WIDTH: 130px">
    <xsl:value-of select="my:field1"/>
</span>
```

Summary

In this chapter, we covered a few features that help you create a rich form interface in your InfoPath form templates. So far in the book, we have covered about a third of the InfoPath features that enable you to create compelling InfoPath templates for your form scenarios. The features we have yet to talk about are file attachments, image and ink picture controls, ActiveX controls, and most of the data adapters that allow you to submit and receive data from databases or Web services.

Rich text support in InfoPath is enabled by allowing XHTML nodes in the XML data. If your form template is part of a workflow scenario where the form data will travel extensively over the wire (or wireless), you should avoid using rich text data unless you absolutely need it. Using too much XHTML in your data would defeat the purpose of using XML, in which the data is free from presentation clutter. If your forms require richly formatted views, you can use rich editing in design mode to create rich layouts and labels in the form. This limits the rich text to the XSL rather than leaving it in the hands of the form user to add formatted data to the XML. Even though InfoPath supports rich text data, it is a forms application targeted at efficient data gathering, not rich data entry. It is in your best interest to leverage dynamic controls and the contextual editing capabilities of InfoPath to build dynamic and responsive forms. You can use InfoPath's extensible digital signatures features to turn on security for parts of the form or for the entire form. You can use InfoPath's rich control interface to create an optimal form-filling experience for the user and an efficient postprocessing framework for the data in workflow scenarios.

Chapter 5

Advanced Form Design

We've already covered creating and using forms using the features of InfoPath to make smart forms and smart documents. In this chapter, we will go deeper into some of the features that you can use to complete the functionality of an InfoPath form. We will look at using the advanced built-in controls for file attachments, images, and ink pictures; using and creating custom controls with ActiveX technology; and improving the user experience by using conditional formatting, *Extension*, and *XDocument*.

Advanced Form Controls

InfoPath supports different control types for displaying and editing data. Controls such as the Text Box and Date Picker directly display the bound data, and controls such as the Drop-Down List Box and the Option Button map the bound data to specific UI elements. This section will cover controls that have one more level of abstraction: the File Attachment, Picture, and ActiveX controls.

File Attachment and Picture Controls

You have already seen controls that bind user input directly to the XML data behind the form, such as the Text Box, Rich Text Box, and Date Picker controls. All of these controls bind to text in XML nodes, but binary data is not text. This is where the File Attachment and Picture controls come into play. These controls work with binary data and store the data in the XML using base64 encoding. When you use these controls in the designer and when you fill out a form, the encoding is transparent and works just as you'd expect. If you want to process the saved data in another application, such as a Web service, you have to decode the information.

Let's demonstrate these features by creating a form to track animal sightings.

Designing a New Form Template That Includes a Picture

1. Launch InfoPath.
2. In the Fill Out A Form dialog box, click Design A Form.
3. In the Design A Form task pane, click New Blank Form.
4. Type **Animal Sightings** at the top of the form, and then press Enter.
5. On the Insert menu, choose More Controls to reveal the list of available controls.
6. In the File And Picture section of the Controls task pane, click Picture.

7. In the Insert Picture Control dialog box, select Included In The Form to ensure that the picture is saved when the form is saved, and then click OK to insert the Picture control in the view.
8. Right-click on the newly inserted Picture control and choose Picture Properties.
9. In the Picture Properties dialog box (shown in Figure 5-1), change the Field Name from field1 to **AnimalPicture**. Note two other options that we won't change in this example: specifying a default picture and allowing the user to change the displayed picture.

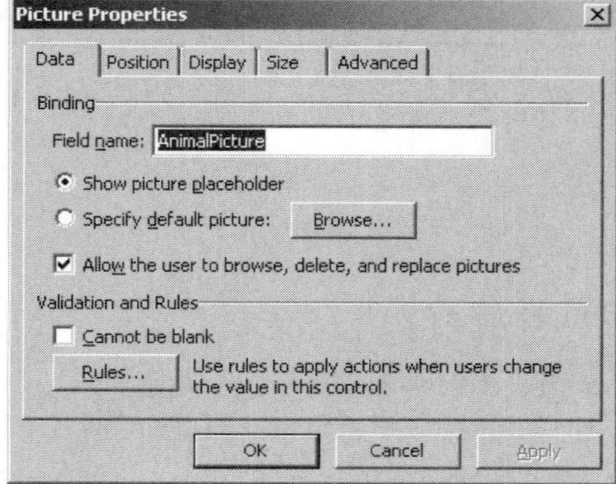

Figure 5-1 The Picture Properties dialog box

10. Click OK to close the dialog box.
11. Click below the Picture control, press Enter to insert a new line, and then type **Animal Name**.
12. Insert a Text Box control.
13. Right-click on the newly inserted text box and choose Text Box Properties.
14. In the Text Box Properties dialog box, change the Field Name from field2 to **Animal-Name**, and then click OK to close the dialog box.
15. Save your form template as **Animal Sightings.xsn**.

Picture Control Options

The Picture control can operate in one of two totally different modes: Included In The Form and As A Link. The former saves the image data in the form and the latter displays an image linked to, but not saved with, the form. You saw the first mode in the previous example; we will continue through the options for the control in this mode before discussing the control in link mode.

You also saw the Picture Properties dialog box. We did not change any of the properties specific to pictures: the default picture and the user's ability to change the picture.

The default picture works in the same way that a default value works for text boxes or other controls: it is stored with the template in the template.xml file used when new forms are created and also in the sampledata.xml file used by the designer. When a user fills out a new form, the default picture is copied into the data for the form and appears wherever that data node is displayed in the view. If the default value for the template later changes, the default image will change for new forms created after the change while forms created before the change will still have the old picture.

The second option is a check box labeled "Allow the user to browse, delete, and replace pictures." This check box applies to the view, not the data. In other words, if you have the same picture displayed twice in your template, you can have one place where users can change the picture and another where they cannot. You can also disable the control through conditional formatting, on the Display tab of the properties dialog box.

Picture Control in Link Mode You can include a reference to a picture on a form by selecting As A Link in the Insert Picture Control dialog box. The reference works much like a hyperlink control: the image displayed on the form is loaded from the URL specified in the bound data node.

Now we will add a File Attachment control to the form so we can compare the two controls.

Adding a File Control to a Form

1. Continue designing the Animal Sightings form.
2. Click below the Animal Name line to put the cursor at the end of the form.
3. Type **Attached Info**.
4. On the Insert menu, choose More Controls.
5. In the File And Picture section of the Controls task pane, click File Attachment.
6. Right-click on the newly inserted File Attachment control, and choose File Attachment Properties.
7. In the File Attachment Properties dialog box (shown in Figure 5-2), change the Field Name from field1 to **AnimalAttachment**, and then click OK.
8. Save and close the form template.

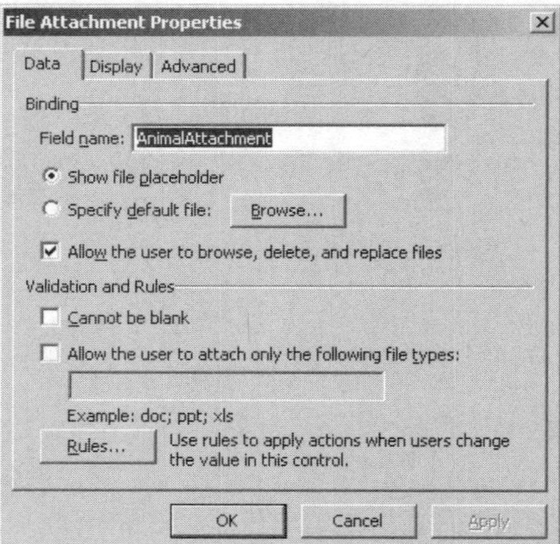

Figure 5-2 The File Attachment Properties dialog box

File Attachment Options

The File Attachment properties are similar to the Picture properties. You can specify a default file, which is added to both the template.xml and sampledata.xml files. By default, InfoPath allows any file type except those marked as unsafe, such as .bat and .exe. InfoPath uses a security model similar to Microsoft Outlook, described in Knowledge Base article 829982 (*http://support.microsoft.com/default.aspx?kbid=829982*). For more information, see the technical article "Microsoft Office InfoPath 2003 SP1 and File Attachments" in the Microsoft Office InfoPath Developer Center (*http://msdn.microsoft.com/office/understanding/infopath/techarticles/default.aspx*).

You can also restrict the allowable file types for a particular control to a specified subset of file types. To do this, right-click on a File Attachment control in the view and choose File Attachment Properties. Select the Allow The User To Attach Only The Following File Types check box, and enter the list of allowed extensions, separated by semicolons. Note that this restriction applies only to the control in the view: if you use the File Attachment control in multiple views, you must set the properties for each instance of the control.

Filling Out a Form That Includes a Picture and a File Attachment

Choose Fill Out A Form from the File menu.

1. In the Fill Out A Form dialog box, click Open.
2. Locate and select the Animal Sightings.xsn template you created earlier, and then click Open.

3. Click on the Picture control in the view labeled Click Here To Insert A Picture.
4. In the Insert Picture dialog box, select a picture from your hard drive, and then click Insert.
5. Click on the File Attachment control labeled Click Here To Attach A File.
6. Select the same file you used in the Picture control, and then click Insert.
7. Type a name for the animal. A completed form is shown in Figure 5-3.
8. Save the form as **My Animal.xml**.
9. Close InfoPath.
10. Open the file My Animal.xml in a text editor. You'll see that the picture has been saved in the XML file using base64 encoding. It will look something like this:

```
<my:AnimalPicture>/9j/4AAQSkZJRgABAQEAYABgAAD ... </my:AnimalPicture>
<my:AnimalName>Kitten</my:AnimalName>
<my:AnimalAttachment>x0lGQRQAAAABAAAAAAAAN5I ... </my:AnimalAttachment>
```

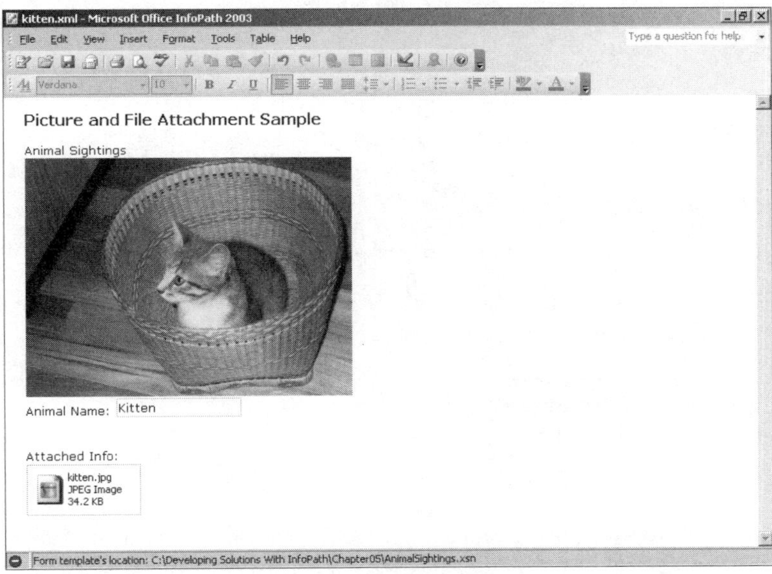

Figure 5-3 A form with Picture and File Attachment controls filled out

Note that *my:AnimalName* is in plain text but *my:AnimalPicture* and *my:AnimalAttachment* are not. The latter two are the encoded picture. Also note that the text in *my:AnimalPicture* is different from that in *my:AnimalAttachment*, even though they are the same file. This happens because the attachment has more information stored in it than the binary bytes of the attached file: it also has the filename and some internal information (described in Table 5-1 later in this chapter). The form user can easily attach a file or an image to the form, but the developer who needs to decode the data outside of InfoPath must understand the format (as discussed later in the chapter).

Controlling the File Attachment Control with Code

You can control the actions of the file attachment control in code with the *ExecuteAction* method, much like you can programmatically add and remove repeating sections (as described in Chapter 3). The supported actions are *xFileAttachment::attach*, *xFileAttachment::saveAs*, and *xFileAttachment::remove*. They open the File Attachment dialog box, open the Save As dialog box, and remove the relevant attachment, respectively. To use these methods, the correct node must be selected in the view and the corresponding *xmlToEdit* value must be used. Use a method such as *SelectNodes* to select the node in the view. Examine the *name* attribute of the *xsf:xmlToEdit* node in manifest.xsf to obtain the *xmlToEdit* value.

The following Visual Basic code-behind function adds a new item in a repeating table or section and then opens the File Attachment dialog box for an attachment in that section. If the user cancels the File Attachment dialog box, the code removes the inserted row.

```
Function AddAttachment(ByVal xmlToEditRepeatingSection, _
    ByVal xmlToEditAttachment, ByVal xpathAttachment)

    Dim nodeInserted As IXMLDOMNode
    Dim nodeAttach As IXMLDOMNode

    ' Add a new item to the group
    thisXDocument.View.ExecuteAction("xCollection::insert", _
        xmlToEditRepeatingSection)

    ' Select the node in the group with the attachment data.
    ' After insert ExecuteAction, the new node will be selected.
    ' The attachment data node must be selected for the next ExecuteAction.
    nodeInserted = thisXDocument.View.GetSelectedNodes().Item(0)
    nodeAttach = nodeInserted.selectSingleNode(xpathAttachment)
    thisXDocument.View.SelectNodes(nodeAttach, Type.Missing, Type.Missing)

    ' Open the Attachment dialog box.
    thisXDocument.View.ExecuteAction("xFileAttachment::attach", _
        xmlToEditAttachment)
```

```
    ' Check to see if an attachment was added.
    If (nodeAttach.text.Length = 0) Then
        ' No attachment added, remove the entire inserted row.
        nodeInserted.parentNode.removeChild(nodeInserted)
    End If
End Function
```

To call the function, insert a button in your view and code it to call the function. If your *xmlToEdit* for your repeating group is *AttachmentGroup_1*, the *xmlToEdit* for the attachment is *AttachmentData_1*, and the name of the attachment node is *my:AttachmentData*, you would call the function like this: *AddAttachment("AttachmentGroup_1", " AttachmentData_1", "my:AttachmentData")*.

Adding an Ink Picture to a Form

Ink pictures work similarly to image attachments. You can add an Ink Picture control, with or without a background image, to a form. A background image is saved as part of the form template, not as part of each filled-out form. The filled-out ink annotations are saved in each form as base64-encoded data. To fill out an Ink Picture control, you need a Tablet PC. (You do not need a Tablet PC to design a form with an ink picture.) A Tablet PC user can also insert an ink picture into a Rich Text field that has the Full Rich Text option enabled.

Using File and Picture Control Data Outside of InfoPath

A file or picture control used entirely within an InfoPath form works transparently to the user. However, if you want to access the data outside of InfoPath, you must decode it. This involves two steps: converting the data from the base64-encoded format into a binary format and determining the name and type of the file. In this section, we will look at a .NET Windows Forms tool that can save images and files attached to an InfoPath-generated XML file. The same techniques can be used in a Web service or any other situation where you need to decode an attachment saved in an InfoPath form.

Using the Attachment Saver Sample Application

1. Locate the InfoPathAttachmentSaver folder included with the companion content.
2. Launch InfoPathAttachmentSaver.exe.
3. Click Browse, select the My Animal.xml file we created earlier, and then click Open.
4. The application fills the namespace of the root node for you.
5. In the XPath field, type **//my:AnimalAttachment**.
6. Click Decode Attachment. You should see the name of the file you saved and the size of the file on the screen (as shown in Figure 5-4).

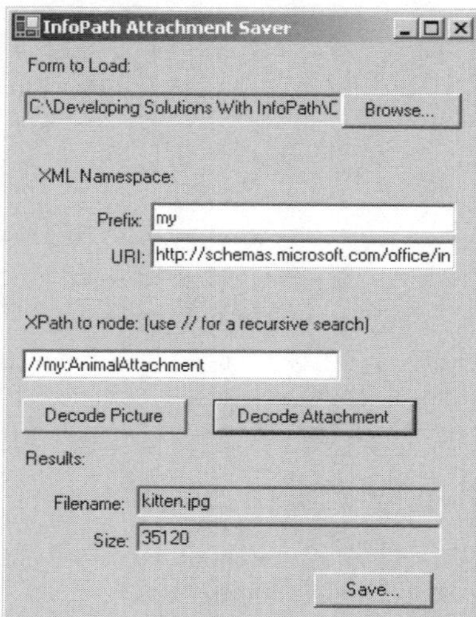

Figure 5-4 Using the Attachment Saver tool to decode an attachment

7. Click Save. Save the file somewhere on your hard drive. Compare the file you just saved to the original file. They should be the same.
8. Click Decode Picture. The application displays an error message stating that the picture is a file attachment and will not continue. If you were to save the decoded data, the InfoPath file attachment header would be on the front of it, and the file would thus be slightly larger than the original file. The resulting binary data would not be usable by other applications.
9. Change the XPath value to **//my:AnimalPicture**.
10. Click Decode Attachment. You should get an error explaining that this is not a valid attachment.
11. Click Decode Picture. The filename becomes an unknown filename, and the size is the size of the picture.
12. Save the file and close InfoPath. Note that the tool always uses the file extension .jpg. The actual type of the file can be determined by sniffing the data in the file. The InfoPath Attachment Saver tool does not have that feature, but most picture display applications sniff the data and correctly display the picture even if it is not truly in JPEG format.

Examining the Code of the Attachment Saver Sample

The Attachment Saver has three classes: *FormInfoPathAttachmentSaver*, which handles the UI and also the loading and saving of XML; *InfoPathImage*, which represents picture data stored in base64-encoded data by InfoPath; and *InfoPathAttachment*, which represents file attachment data stored in base64-encoded data by InfoPath. The *InfoPathImage* and *InfoPathAttachment* classes work in the same way: they have a factory method that takes as input the string of data and returns an instance of the class. The class itself exposes two properties—the filename and the file data.

You must do two things when decoding a picture: read the binary data and check the file type. Here is the function that decodes a picture:

Decoding a Picture

```
Public Shared Function DecodePicture(ByVal InnerTextAttachment As String) As InfopathPicture
    Dim objPicture As InfopathPicture = New InfopathPicture

    objPicture.FileData = Convert.FromBase64String(InnerTextAttachment)

    ' To ensure that the image type is correct, you should sniff here.
    ' Look at the first few bytes or so and look for the signature.
    ' See each image format specification for more info

    ' All we look for now is the InfoPath attachment signature
    If objPicture.CheckInfoPathAttachmentSignature Then
        Throw New Exception("Data represents an attachment, not a picture.")
    End If

    ' Since we have not sniffed the actual file type, we will assume jpg.
    ' There is no stored filename, so use 'UnknownAttachedPicture'.
    objPicture.FileName = "UnknownAttachedPicture.jpg"

    Return objPicture
End Function
```

When decoding a file attachment, you must decode the data into a binary structure. This structure is described in Table 5-1. The .NET Framework *System.Runtime.InteropServices.Marshal* class allows you to convert the entire binary data into a Visual Basic .NET structure all at once.

Table 5-1 File Attachment Binary Structure

Member	Length
Signature	4 bytes
Header size (does not include Signature, Filename, or File Data)	4 bytes (DWORD)
InfoPath version	4 bytes (DWORD)
Reserved	4 bytes (DWORD)
File size	4 bytes (DWORD)
Filename length (characters)	4 bytes (DWORD)
Filename (UTF-16 encoded)	Filename length * 2 bytes
File data	File size bytes

Decoding a File Attachment

```
' Visual Basic .NET representation of the InfoPath File Attachment header.
<StructLayout(LayoutKind.Sequential, Pack:=1)> _
Private Structure AttachmentStructure
    Public Signature As Int32
    Public HeaderSize As Int32
    Public InfopathVersion As Int32
    Public Reserved As Int32
    Public Filesize As Int32
    Public FilenameCharLen As Int32
End Structure


Public Shared Function Base64EncodedLength(ByVal cb As Integer) As Integer
    ' The base64 encoded header will always be 4/3 the size of the
    ' binary version, rounded up to a multiple of 4.
    Return Math.Ceiling(cb / 3) * 4
End Function

Private Shared Function BytesToHeaderStructure( _
    ByVal rg As Byte()) As AttachmentStructure

    Dim cb As Integer
    cb = Marshal.SizeOf(GetType(AttachmentStructure))

    If (rg.Length < cb) Then
        Return Nothing
    End If

    Dim hGlobal As IntPtr
    hGlobal = Marshal.AllocHGlobal(cb)
    Marshal.Copy(rg, 0, hGlobal, cb)

    Dim obj As AttachmentStructure
    obj = Marshal.PtrToStructure(hGlobal, GetType(AttachmentStructure))

    Marshal.FreeHGlobal(hGlobal)

    Return obj
End Function

Public Shared Function DecodeAttachment( _
    ByVal InnerTextAttachment As String) As InfoPathAttachment

    Dim objAttachment As InfoPathAttachment
    objAttachment = New InfoPathAttachment

    ' Decode the header from string to bytes.
    Dim rgHeader As Byte()
    Dim cbHeaderEncoded As Integer
    Dim objHeader As AttachmentStructure

    cbHeaderEncoded = Base64EncodedLength( _
        Marshal.SizeOf(objHeader.GetType))

    If (InnerTextAttachment.Length < cbHeaderEncoded) Then
        Throw New Exception( _
            "Encoded string is not long enough to include header.")
```

```
    End If

    rgHeader = Convert.FromBase64String( _
        InnerTextAttachment.Substring(0, cbHeaderEncoded))

    ' Decode the header from bytes to structure.
    objHeader = BytesToStructure(rgHeader, objHeader.GetType)

    ' Check the signature.
    ' 1095125447 is CIPA, or {199, 73, 70, 65}.
    If Not (objHeader.Signature.Equals(1095125447)) Then
        Throw New Exception( _
            "Signature does not match InfoPath attachment signature.")
    End If

    ' Check the header size.
    ' The size of the header does not include the size of the signature.
    Dim headerSizeRequired As Integer
    headerSizeRequired = Marshal.SizeOf(objHeader.GetType) - 4
    If Not (objHeader.HeaderSize.Equals(headerSizeRequired)) Then
        Throw New Exception("Header size does not match expected size.")
    End If

    ' Decode the rest of the bytes.
    Dim cbBodyEncoded As Integer
    Dim rgBody As Byte()

    cbBodyEncoded = Base64EncodedLength( _
        objHeader.FilenameCharLen * 2 + objHeader.Filesize)

    If (InnerTextAttachment.Length < _
        (cbHeaderEncoded + cbBodyEncoded)) Then
        Throw New Exception( _
            "Encoded string is not long enough to include body.")
    End If

    rgBody = Convert.FromBase64String( _
        InnerTextAttachment.Substring(cbHeaderEncoded, cbBodyEncoded))

    ' Copy out filename.
    objAttachment.FileName = System.Text.Encoding.Unicode.GetString( _
        rgBody, 0, objHeader.FilenameCharLen * 2)

    ' Copy out the rest of the file bytes.
    objAttachment.FileData = Array.CreateInstance( _
        GetType(Byte), objHeader.Filesize)

    rgBody.Copy(rgBody, objHeader.FilenameCharLen * 2, _
        objAttachment.FileData, 0, objHeader.Filesize)

    Return objAttachment
End Function
```

To encode a file attachment, you reverse the process. You must also make sure that any generated XML file with an attachment has this *<?mso-infoPath-file-attachment-present?>* processing instruction at the top of the file. If the processing instruction is not present, the file attachment feature will be disabled for that particular instance of the form.

Using a Picture as a Button

InfoPath forms are based on HTML, but for security reasons they support only a subset of HTML. The only built-in InfoPath control that can trigger scripts directly is a button. What if you want your button to have something other than the default button formatting? You can change some style properties in the designer, and a few more in the XSL. For example, you can add a picture to a button with the following steps:

1. Launch InfoPath.
2. In the Fill Out A Form dialog box, click Design A Form.
3. In the Design A Form task pane, click New Blank Form.
4. In the Design Tasks task pane, click Controls.
5. In the Standard section of the Controls task pane, click Button.
6. Right-click on the newly inserted Button control, and choose Borders And Shading.
7. In the Borders And Shading dialog box, click on the Shading tab, select No Color, and then click OK.
8. Click OK. Right-click the Button control and choose Button Properties.
9. Set the label to a single space so no text is displayed on top of your image, as shown in Figure 5-5.

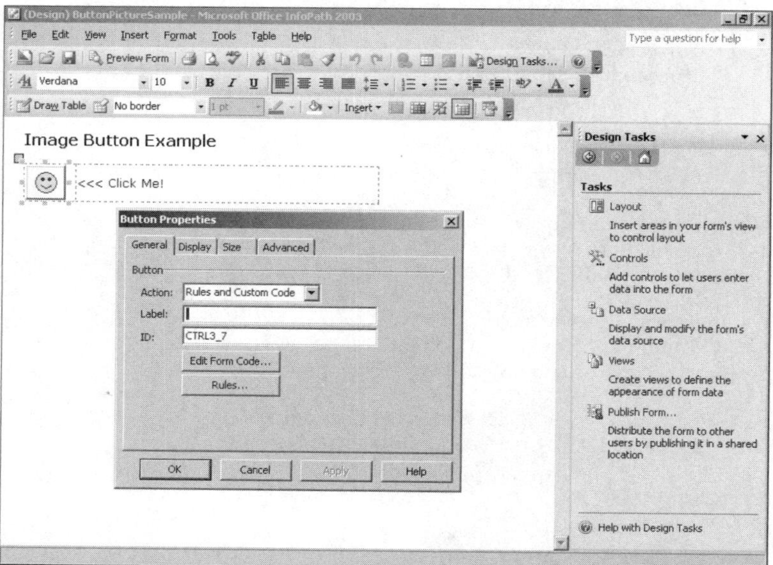

Figure 5-5 Set the button label to a single space to show only the background picture

10. Choose Resource Files from the Tools menu.
11. In the Resource Files dialog box, click Add.
12. Select an image, and then click OK twice.
13. Choose Extract Form File from the File menu, and then extract the files to a folder called **ButtonPictureSample**.
14. Close InfoPath.
15. In the ButtonPictureSample folder, open view1.xsl in a text editor.
16. In view1.xsl, locate the button. It will be an *<input>* tag with a *type="button"* attribute.
17. In the button tag, locate the style attribute. At the beginning of the style attribute, insert the following:

    BACKGROUND-IMAGE: url(*filename-of-the-file-you-added***);** .
18. When you're done, your Input tag should look something like this:

```
<input class="langFont" title="" style="BACKGROUND-
IMAGE: url(ButtonImage.png); BORDER-RIGHT: #000000 1pt;
BORDER-TOP: #000000 1pt; BORDER-LEFT: #0000ff 1pt; WIDTH: 12px;
BORDER-BOTTOM: #000000 1pt; HEIGHT: 12px; BACKGROUND-COLOR: transparent"
type="button" size="12" value=" " xd:CtrlId="CTRL1_5" xd:xctname="Button"
tabIndex="0"/>
```

19. Save view1.xsl and close the text editor.
20. In the ButtonPictureSample folder, right-click on manifest.xsf and choose Design.
21. Adjust the button by changing its size as appropriate and its label (if one is desired), borders, shading, and so on. Note that the image will not appear to depress when the user clicks on the button, although the default borders and label text will appear to depress.

You can also edit other CSS properties in the *style* attribute to control features such as how the image repeats. To prevent the image from repeating, add **BACKGROUND-REPEAT: no-repeat**. To center the image, add **BACKGROUND-POSITION: center center**.

To create a hyperlink using a picture, just add a picture as usual. Then right-click on the picture and choose Hyperlink. You might want to remove the border that will be placed around your picture once it is linked. Hyperlinks launch in the user's Web browser; you cannot use them to create an event in InfoPath.

Custom Controls with ActiveX

InfoPath provides many built-in controls, such as the Rich Text and Date Picker controls that you saw in previous chapters. But what if you want to go beyond the built-in controls? InfoPath lets you use ActiveX controls to display and modify the XML data in your form. You can use an existing ActiveX control or write your own.

Using Existing ActiveX Controls

Many ActiveX controls are out there for you to use. Some are on users' machines, and others can be downloaded and installed as needed. To use a control, you add the control to the list of available controls in the designer and then add it to your form templates.

ActiveX Control Security

ActiveX controls are compiled code that typically has full access to the machine. A safe control is one that has been written so it cannot be repurposed in a malicious manner. A safe control can indicate itself as safe by implementing the *IObjectSafety* interface. InfoPath requires that ActiveX controls be marked as safe for scripting and safe for initialization.

> **Warning** Unfortunately, there are malicious ActiveX controls. Be very careful when choosing a control that it comes from a source that you trust: InfoPath can determine only whether a control identifies itself as safe.

ActiveX controls can also be used in script code without being added to a view. Forms set to the Domain security level use the Internet security settings for the appropriate domain. The two most important settings are *Run ActiveX Controls And Plug-Ins* and, for unsafe controls called from script, *Initialize And Script ActiveX Controls Not Marked As Safe*. Full Trust forms have full access to ActiveX controls.

For more information about security and deployment, see Chapter 8.

Adding a Control to the List of Available Controls

1. Launch InfoPath.
2. In the Fill Out A Form dialog box, click Design A Form.
3. In the Design A Form task pane, click New Blank Form.
4. Choose More Controls from the Insert menu.
5. At the very bottom of the Controls task pane, click Add Or Remove Custom Controls.
6. In the Add Or Remove Custom Controls dialog box, click Add.
7. Select the Microsoft Forms 2.0 SpinButton control and then click Next.

> **Note** The list of available ActiveX controls contains all controls identified in the registry on your machine. This includes controls that are not safe for scripting. For performance reasons, InfoPath will determine whether a control is safe for scripting only after you choose it.

8. The next page offers you the option to include a .cab file with the form template. Click Next to continue without adding a .cab file.

> **Note** If you want to distribute the control along with a form, you can include a signed .cab file while stepping through the Add Custom Control Wizard. The .cab file must be signed, and the form user will be presented with the option to trust the publisher and install the control.

9. On the next page, you select which control property to bind to. You can bind only one property to the form data, unless the control has been designed with InfoPath in mind, as discussed later in this chapter. Select the Value property, as seen in Figure 5-6, and then click Next.

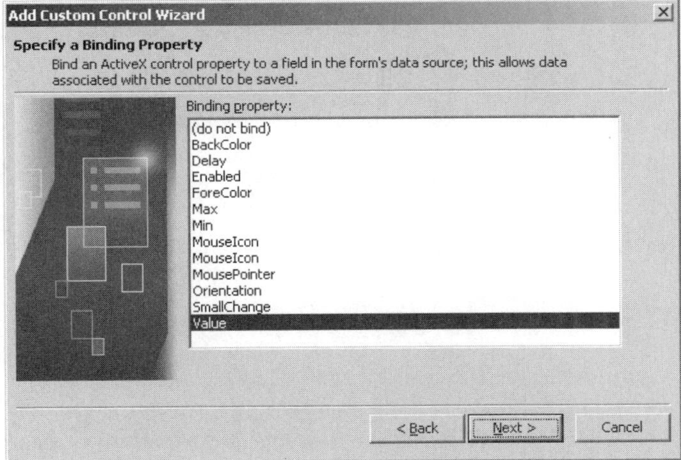

Figure 5-6 Selecting the ActiveX control property to bind to the form data

10. On the next page you select which control property is used to enable or disable the control. This is used along with conditional formatting to disable the control as appropriate. Select the Enabled property, and then click Next.
11. On the next page, you select the data type, as seen in Figure 5-7. In the list of data types, select Text, Whole Number, and Decimal to allow binding to all three of these data types.

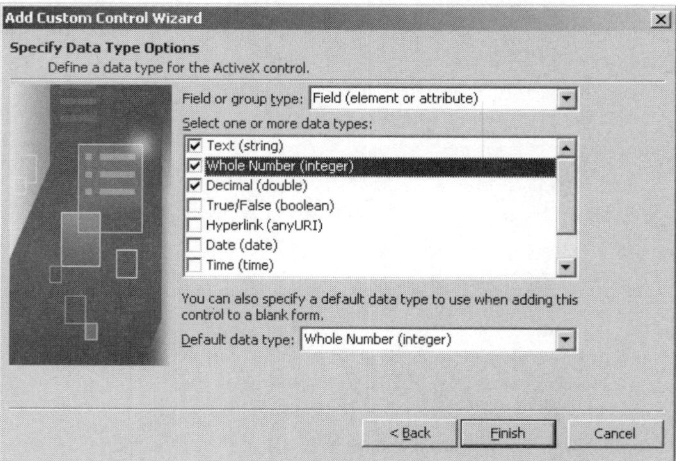

Figure 5-7 Selecting the data type(s) of the ActiveX control bound property

12. Change the Default Data Type to Whole Number. This setting specifies the data type InfoPath will use when creating a new data node from this control.
13. Click Finish. The control now appears in the list of Custom Controls.
14. Click OK to close the Add Or Remove Custom Controls dialog box.

Adding a Custom Control to a Form

1. In the Custom section of the Controls task pane, click Microsoft Forms 2.0 SpinButton. This inserts a SpinButton control in the view.
2. At the top of the Controls task pane, click Data Source.
3. In the Data Source task pane, right-click on field1 and choose Text Box. This text box will be bound to the same data node as the spin button.
4. Preview the form and try out the spin button.

Note You cannot access the instance of the ActiveX control from code running in the form. InfoPath is designed to work on XML data. The view (including the ActiveX control) is frequently regenerated. See the following sections for techniques that a control can use to store and share data with other parts of the form.

You have now seen how to use a basic ActiveX control in your form. Next we will discuss some more advanced ways of working with ActiveX controls, such as sharing control design settings with multiple users or machines, managing the quirks of different controls, and writing your own ActiveX controls.

Sharing Control Design Settings

When you add an ActiveX control to the list of controls available in the InfoPath designer, the settings are only for you on your machine. To use the settings on another machine or to share them with another user, you can copy the settings file. This file is saved in a hidden applications folder under your user profile. To access it, choose Run from the Windows Start menu, type **%USERPROFILE%\Local Settings\Application Data\Microsoft\InfoPath\Controls**, and then click OK. This opens a Windows Explorer window containing .ict files, one per control setting. The filename is the *CLSID* of the control. You can send this file to another InfoPath designer user who has the ActiveX control installed. When the InfoPath designer user adds the .ict file to his Controls folder, he can have access to the control in the designer with the settings specified in the .ict file. Note that you do not need to do this for users who are filling out the form, only for people who are designing the form.

You can use different designer settings for the same control (for example, if you want to bind to *property1* in some situations and *property2* in other situations). To do this, create the first set of settings for the desired control. Then open the Controls folder in the Explorer, as described earlier, and rename the .ict file for your control (e.g., from {DFD181E0-5E2F-11CE-A449-00AA004A803D}.ict to **Alternate{DFD181E0-5E2F-11CE-A449-00AA004A803D}.ict**). Then add the control again from the InfoPath designer. When you add a new control, the filename is always the CLSID of the control, so to add the control twice you must use the renaming technique. The designer displays all controls listed in the Controls folder in the Controls task pane.

Managing the Quirks of Certain ActiveX Controls

One great advantage of using ActiveX controls is the large number of controls that are available. But not all existing controls take advantage of all the features of ActiveX, so you might have to do some work to manage certain features.

Changing properties with XSL Some ActiveX controls implement property pages. If this is the case, you can right-click on the control in the designer and choose Properties. The property pages show up as tabs in a Properties dialog box.

If the ActiveX control does not implement property pages, InfoPath adds the control to the form with default settings and you cannot change the settings from within the designer. To change the settings, extract the form files and look for the object tag in the appropriate .xsl view file. You will find a series of associated *param* tags, which you can change as necessary.

Here is an example of a SpinButton control in which the *SmallChange* parameter has been set to 5. All other settings are the InfoPath designer default. Figure 5-8 shows our form updated with two SpinButton controls, the original one that increments by 1 and our new one that increments by 5.

```
<object class="xdActiveX" hideFocus="1" style="WIDTH: 17px; HEIGHT: 34px"
 classid="clsid:79176fb0-b7f2-11ce-97ef-00aa006d2776" tabIndex="0"
 xd:boundProp="xd:inline" xd:bindingProperty="Value" xd:bindingType="text"
 xd:enabledProperty="Enabled" xd:enabledValue="true" xd:CtrlId="CTRL5"
 xd:xctname="{{79176fb0-b7f2-11ce-97ef-00aa006d2776}}" tabStop="true"
 contentEditable="false" xd:binding="my:field1">
    <xsl:if test="function-available('xdImage:getImageUrl')">
        <xsl:attribute name="src">
            <xsl:value-of select="xdImage:getImageUrl(my:field1)"/>
        </xsl:attribute>
    </xsl:if>
    <param NAME="ForeColor" VALUE="2147483666"/>
    <param NAME="BackColor" VALUE="2147483663"/>
    <param NAME="VariousPropertyBits" VALUE="27"/>
    <param NAME="Size" VALUE="450;900"/>
    <param NAME="Min" VALUE="0"/>
    <param NAME="Max" VALUE="100"/>
    <param NAME="Position" VALUE="0"/>
    <param NAME="PrevEnabled" VALUE="1"/>
    <param NAME="NextEnabled" VALUE="1"/>
    <param NAME="SmallChange" VALUE="5"/>
    <param NAME="Orientation" VALUE="4294967295"/>
    <param NAME="Delay" VALUE="50"/>
    <param NAME="MousePointer" VALUE="0"/>
</object>
```

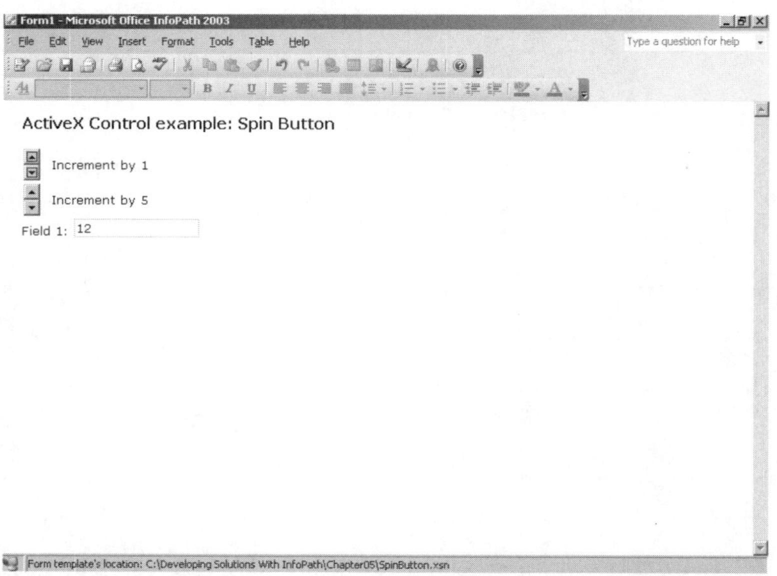

Figure 5-8 A form with two SpinButton controls bound to the same data node

Handling nonupdating properties Some ActiveX controls do not implement property notification. In this case, InfoPath will not know when the value of the control has changed. If the bound data node is not displayed elsewhere on the form, no problems will occur because InfoPath will query the control for the value before saving the form. But if the bound data node is displayed elsewhere, the value will not be updated until rebinding occurs. When an ActiveX control does not implement property notification, rebinding occurs automatically when a form is saved, when the view is switched, and at certain other times. You can force rebinding by calling the *XDocument.View.ForceUpdate* method.

Creating Your Own ActiveX Controls

You can also create your own control. ActiveX controls are COM objects and can be written in many languages, such as Visual Basic and C++. InfoPath does not support .NET user controls, but you can write ActiveX controls using the COM Interop functionality of the .NET Framework. Your control must be safe for scripting (indicated by the *IObjectSafety* interface). Your control should support property event notifications through the *IPropertyNotifySink* interface and connection points.

For more information about ActiveX controls, see http://www.microsoft.com/com/tech/activex.asp. For a discussion of implementing the IObjectSafety interface with zone security in an ActiveX control implemented in C# for use in InfoPath, see http://msdn.microsoft.com/library/en-us/ipsdk/html/ipsdkCreateObject.asp. For a discussion of implementing the IObjectSafety interface in Visual Basic 6.0, see http://support.microsoft.com/default.aspx?scid=kb;EN-US;182598.

When a view containing an ActiveX control is created, InfoPath instantiates the control and binds the data value from the form to the control. Your ActiveX control should update itself whenever its value changes. You can specify the default value of the data node on its property page, just as you would for any other control. When a data node's value changes, InfoPath rebinds the data so the view reflects the most current value. ActiveX controls on the form are destroyed and re-created, possibly more than once. If your control has an additional state beyond the bound value, you can use the *InfoPathControl* interface and named node properties to save the state in the InfoPath object model.

Important Rebinding destroys and re-creates instances of your ActiveX control. You must persist all state in the bound data or use one of the methods described next; you cannot assume that instance data will stay around because the instance itself has a very short life span.

Important It is also important to handle rebinding if your control uses dialog boxes: the form user can modify the form while your dialog box is still active. In this case, the instance of the control your dialog box is connected to will no longer be available in the form. You can watch for the *SaveState* or *Uninit* method of the *InfoPathControl* interface to detect this situation.

Using the *InfoPathControl* and *InfoPathControlSite* interfaces Once you've created an ActiveX control, you can bind one property of your control to a data node using the method described earlier: add your control to the list of available controls and then use it in the form. To bind more than one property or interact with the InfoPath object model, you can implement the *InfoPathControl* interface. This interface is described in the InfoPath developer's reference, and the type information is defined in the type library in infopath.exe.

Tip To include the interfaces in an MSVC++ class, add the following line:

```
#import "C:\Program Files\Microsoft Office\OFFICE11\INFOPATH.EXE" \
no_namespace raw_interfaces_only.
```

Tip You might also want to include msxml2.h.

If your ActiveX control implements the *InfoPathControl* interface, InfoPath calls the *Init* method when the control is instantiated. It passes in an *InfoPathControlSite* interface pointer, which you should cache. ActiveX controls are destroyed and re-created every time the data is rebound. InfoPath calls the *SaveState* method before destroying a control. You can then store any additional view state. InfoPath provides a convenient place to store this type of information with named node properties. These properties allow you to associate temporary data with a node so state information can be restored when the ActiveX control is re-created. A named node property can also be used to share values between code in an ActiveX control and code in a form.

To read and write other fields in the data source, you can get the bound node from the *Node* property of the *InfoPathControlSite* interface. You can then find other nodes using XML DOM methods, such as *selectSingleNode*. A sample control using the *InfoPathControlSite* interface is available as part of the companion content for this book.

Developer Nugget: Named Node Properties

You can use named node properties to associate temporary data with a particular node. The values are stored as long as the form is open in InfoPath, but they are not saved. One use for named node properties is for saving view-related properties of an ActiveX control when the control gets destroyed and re-created as the underlying data is changed. Another possible use is in code-behind or script—for example, to track the number of times a value has changed. The following *OnAfterChange* event handler example does just that:

```
<InfoPathEventHandler(MatchPath:="/my:myFields/my:sampleValue", _
          EventType:=InfoPathEventType.OnAfterChange)> _
Public Sub sampleValue_OnAfterChange(ByVal e As DataDOMEvent)

    If (e.IsUndoRedo Or "Insert" <> e.Operation Or _
        e.OldValue = e.NewValue) Then
```

```
        ' An undo or redo operation has occurred and the DOM is read-only.
        ' Or this is not an insert.
        ' Or the value has not changed.
        Return
    End If

    Dim changeCount
    changeCount = thisXDocument.GetNamedNodeProperty(e.Site, "changeCount", 0)
    changeCount = changeCount + 1
    thisXDocument.SetNamedNodeProperty(e.Site, "changeCount", changeCount)
End Sub
```

The code demonstrates reading and writing the value of a named node property. You can also display the value in the view. Create a new Expression Box control, click the *fx* button, type **GetNamedNodeProperty(**, click Insert Field Or Group, select the relevant node, and then click OK. Type the name of your property in quotes, the default value in quotes, and a closing). Click OK to close the Insert Formula dialog box. The resulting expression will look something like this (as shown in Figure 5-9): *xdXDocument:GetNamedNodeProperty(my:sampleValue, "changeCount", "0")*.

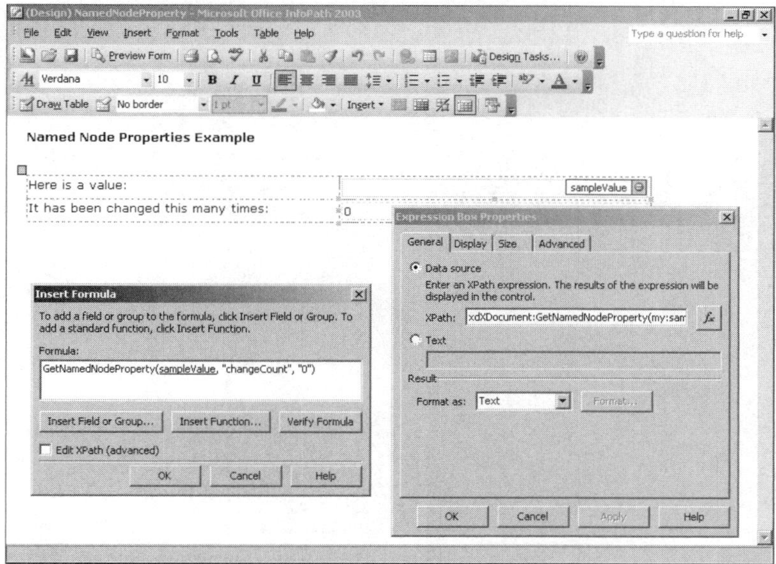

Figure 5-9 Setting an expression box to display a named node property

Note that this technique is similar to using a secondary data connection with an XML DOM to save run-time state information. The difference between a secondary XML DOM and a named node property is that the secondary XML DOM is associated with the entire form, while the named node property is associated with a particular node. Values in a secondary XML DOM can be bound to controls, will fire DOM events, and can use conditional formatting and rules. Values in named node properties cannot be bound directly to controls except for display in an expression box, but they are easier to access with code than values in an XML DOM.

Using stream binding with ActiveX controls Another mechanism for binding multiple nodes is to use stream binding, where the bound property is a stream of serialized XML. This is a useful technique when you are extending existing ActiveX controls that use XML as a data format. To use stream binding, the ActiveX control must define a property that is a string containing namespaced XML. InfoPath reads the property and inserts the value into the form data, and it sends the data to the control on load and during rebinding

> **Important** Stream-bound data is XML. The string passed into the property's *put* method is not guaranteed to use the same namespace prefix as the string returned by the property's *get* method. The control must parse the string as XML to read the values. String matching using the control's preferred prefix will not work.

To add a stream-bound control to the control source, use the Add Custom Control Wizard described earlier in this chapter. On the Specify Data Type Options page, select Field (Element With Custom Data Type) and then type the namespace used by your control, as shown in Figure 5-10. The InfoPath designer will not know about the full structure of the data returned by your control, so you must use custom XSL if you need to bind the data returned by the ActiveX control to another control in the view. Extract the form files.

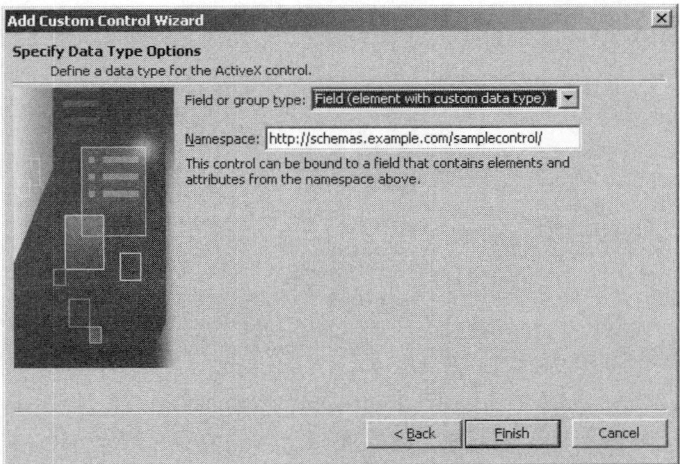

Figure 5-10 Selecting a custom data type for stream binding to an ActiveX control

Using *Extension* and *XDocument* from XSL

Two powerful extensions to XSL that you can use in your views are the *Extension* and *XDocument* objects. The *Extension* object represents the methods and properties defined in your code-behind class or script. It is referenced as *xdExtension* from XSL, as you can see in Figure 5-11. The *XDocument* object represents the document in the object model; this is the same object you have used elsewhere, just accessed directly from the XSL. It is referenced as *xdXDocument* from XSL.

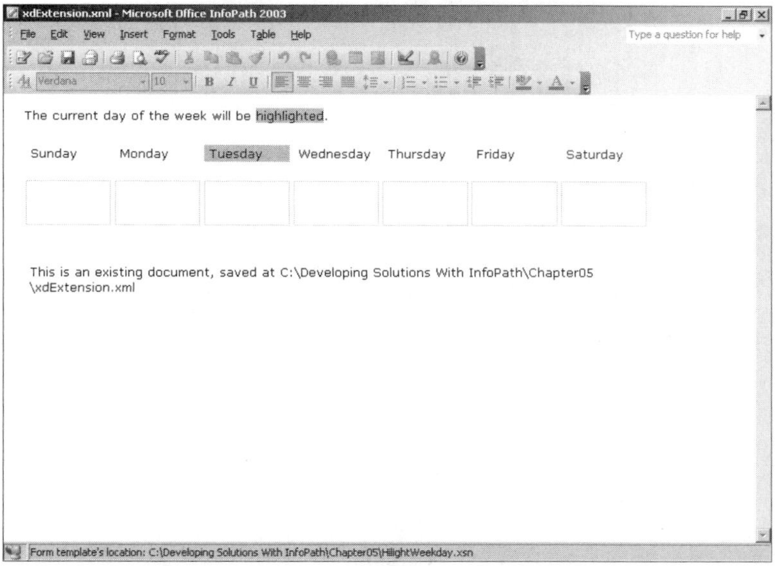

Figure 5-11 A form with a rich UI created using Extension

Extension

The *Extension* object lets you access methods defined in your code-behind class or script. It is frequently used with conditional formatting to extend the rich UI of a form. For example, you can create a calendar week view that automatically highlights the current day of the week. (See the HilightWeekday-xdextension sample.) In the FormCode.vb file, you will find a method that returns the day of the week:

```
Public Function GetWeekday() As Integer
    Return System.DateTime.Now.DayOfWeek
End Function
```

In the view, you will see seven sections, one for each day of the week. (Refer to Figure 5-11.) Right-click on the section containing the word Tuesday, and choose Section Properties. On the Display tab of the Section Properties dialog box, click Conditional Formatting, and then click Modify. You will see the condition, as shown in Figure 5-12: if the expression *xdExtension:GetWeekday()* = 2 is true, the shading of the section is set to a blue highlight color. The sections for the other days of the week have similar expressions—each bound to the value of the appropriate day of the week.

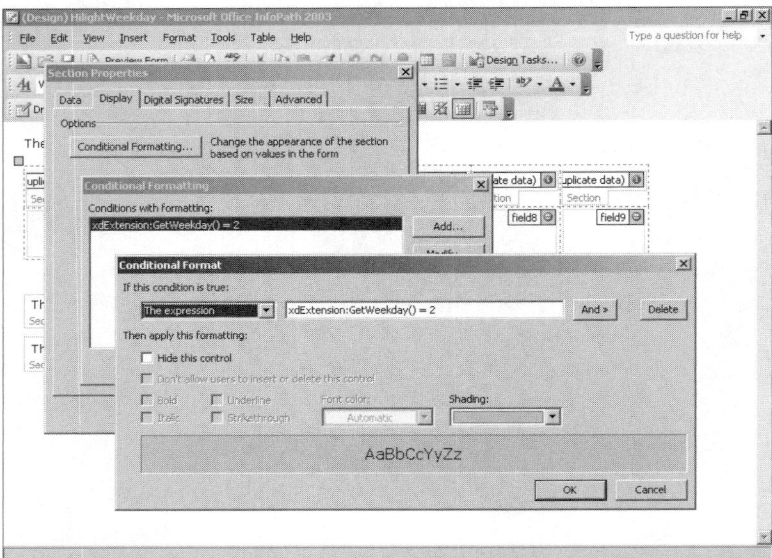

Figure 5-12 Using the Extension object and conditional formatting to highlight the current weekday

In the XSL, the *Extension* object is defined as using the namespace *http://schemas.microsoft.com/office/infopath/2003/xslt/extension*. The InfoPath designer assigns it the prefix *xdExtension*. To call a method in your code from XSL, use *xdExtension:MethodName()*. To display the value of an *Extension* object method in the view, you must modify the XSL outside the InfoPath designer and use an *xd:preserve* block. This is similar to the use of the *XDocument* object to display the URI of the document shown in the upcoming "*XDocument*" section.

The *Extension* object can also be used in other areas. To call it from script for use in a place such as the task pane, you can access the *Extension* property of the *XDocument* object. The following JScript function can be placed in a task pane. It displays the results of the *GetWeekday* function:

```
function ShowWeekday()
{
    var oXDocument = window.external.XDocument;
    alert(oXDocument.Extension.GetWeekday());
}
```

To call the *Extension* object from .NET managed code, you must cast the extension property to the *ObjectWrapper* class and use the method *InvokeByName*. This is available only in fully trusted forms. The following Visual Basic function calls the *GetValue* method in another open document:

```
Public Function GetValueFromOtherDocument() As Object
    ' This only works in trusted forms.
    Dim extension As ObjectWrapper
    Dim result As Object

    ' Get the extension object from another document.
    extension = thisApplication.XDocuments(1).Extension

    result = extension.InvokeByName("GetValue", _
    BindingFlags.InvokeMethod + BindingFlags.DeclaredOnly + _
    BindingFlags.Public + BindingFlags.Instance, _
    New Object() {}, Nothing)

    Return result
End Function
```

XDocument

You can access methods of the *XDocument* object from XSL. The designer uses it to access secondary data sources. You can also use it to access other methods and properties, such as the *IsReadOnly* property. To access a property in the XSL (such as to set conditional formatting), add *get-* in front of the property. The HilightWeekday-xdextension sample has a section with the text "This is a new document." The conditional formatting for this section will hide the control when *not(xdXDocument:get-IsNew())* is true.

In the XSL, the *XDocument* object is defined as using the namespace *http://schemas.microsoft.com/office/infopath/2003/xslt/xDocument*. The InfoPath designer assigns it the prefix *xdXDocument*. To call a method in the *XDocument* object from XSL, use *xdXDocument:MethodName()*. To display the value of an *xdExtension* method in the view, you must modify the XSL outside the InfoPath designer and use an *xd:preserve* block. Here is an example of an XSL template that uses the *XDocument* object to display the current document's URI:

```
<xsl:template match="my:myFields" mode="xd:preserve">
    <xsl:if test="function-available('xdXDocument:get-URI')">
        <xsl:value-of select="xdXDocument:get-URI()"></xsl:value-of>
    </xsl:if>
</xsl:template>
```

To call the preceding template, add *<xsl:apply-templates select="." mode="xd:preserve"/>* in the XSL template.

Summary

This chapter examined the use of advanced controls such as Picture and File Attachments to add even more rich data to a form. It also demonstrated how to use the saved rich data outside of InfoPath. We covered how to use existing ActiveX controls in your form and how to create your own ActiveX controls to create new types of controls. Finally, we looked at using the *Extension* and *Document* objects to increase the richness of a form.

Part III
Deployment Design Patterns

Chapter 6

Database Integration

So far in this book, you have learned how to use InfoPath to build compelling features within your InfoPath form templates. In this next part of the book, starting with this chapter, we will cover the enterprise realm of InfoPath solutions. We will look at InfoPath's database integration features. We will also continue exploring InfoPath's powerful enterprise features in subsequent chapters as we take a look at Web services, SharePoint, and BizTalk integration features.

InfoPath's XML capabilities make it a transparent forms-based environment for integrating a variety of data sources and data providers. Several heterogeneous content providers, such as BizTalk Server, Web services, and database servers, can work together under the hood when you design an InfoPath solution that uses an integrated milieu of such products and services.

This part of the book will also focus on workflow scenarios in which information originates from one type of data source—say, transaction entry in Microsoft SQL Server—and travels across various sources. InfoPath forms work as a front-end application to various back-end data sources to make this workflow process transparent. Back-end data source integration coupled with schema inference and query and submission capability can create powerful dataflow solutions using InfoPath.

InfoPath forms can store and retrieve data from traditional relational databases. InfoPath can also connect to SQL through a Web service that uses Microsoft ADO.NET. We will see more of Web service integration Chapter 7. In this chapter, we will focus on InfoPath's SQL integration through ActiveX Data Objects (ADO). InfoPath's database integration design uses the XML persistence feature available in ADO 2.1 and later. At design time, InfoPath creates an XML schema (.xsd file) from the inline XML-Data Reduced (XDR) schema that ADO creates as part of its recordset through SQLXML.

To learn more about XML data manipulation with ADO, refer to the following article on MSDN: http://msdn.microsoft.com/msdnmag/issues/0800/serving/default.aspx.

InfoPath's extensible database integration features allow you to connect to databases through the InfoPath design UI or through the object model. You can build your InfoPath form using a database as the main data source. Alternately, you can use databases as secondary data sources to perform database lookups.

Integrating with ADO

InfoPath can connect to Microsoft Access and SQL Server databases. We will look at an example for each of the above data sources in this chapter. We will also cover the general concepts around the InfoPath database integration feature. One of the first functionalities we will explore is the way InfoPath infers the schema of the underlying data source. Once the schema is inferred successfully, you can incorporate simple relations and the corresponding attributes to develop the form.

The data connection is transparent to the end user, but it is up to the database designer and the InfoPath form designer to effectively handle the various database constraints to maintain database integrity while integrating with the database. Hence, it is good practice to have a strong understanding of the various relational constraints regarding the particular database being used prior to developing the solution. For effective form design, developers should spend time at the beginning of their projects understanding the database schema and constraints.

After the data source has been defined for an ADO data connection, InfoPath writes the schema as an .xsd file that becomes a part of the InfoPath form template package, or XSN. Most of this integration is transparent to the developer. The ability of InfoPath to store the schema as an .xsd file within the form template package can be viewed as a one-time relational-to-hierarchical mapping for the specific database tables included in the data connection. This allows you to avoid connecting to the data source continually while designing the form. In addition, this provides the functionality of storing the relational-to-XML mapping locally.

Integrating with Access

Let's look at an example using an Access database with an InfoPath form. For the Access database, we will use the Event Management Access template that is available at the Microsoft Office Online Web site at *http://office.microsoft.com/templates*. The Event Management.mdb database is also available as part of the companion content for this book. The template is also available from within Access. We will describe how to design an InfoPath form template with a connection to this database. Let's assume that this database is initially empty. The form we design will be used to submit some records to the database. This will help us understand how to use the InfoPath submit to database feature. Once the database is populated with an initial set of records, we will demonstrate query functionality by using the InfoPath query feature to retrieve some records.

Implement the following steps to create the Event Management form template:

1. Launch InfoPath. From the File menu, choose Design A Form.
2. In the Design A Form task pane, click New From Data Connection.
3. In the Data Connection Wizard, ensure that the Database option is selected, and then click Next.
4. Click Select Database, select the Event Management.mdb database, and then click Open.
5. In the Select Table dialog box, select the Attendees table, and then click OK.

6. Click Edit SQL, and then click Test SQL Statement. You should see a dialog box indicating that the test was successful, as shown in Figure 6-1.
7. Click OK twice to dismiss the Edit SQL dialog box, and then click Next.

   Figure 6-2 shows the final page of the Data Connection Wizard, which contains important information about the data connection. Review it carefully, and retrace the steps of the wizard if you need to change anything. We will revisit this page's nuances in the "Designing for Submit" section later in this chapter.
8. Click Finish. InfoPath infers a schema in .xsd format based on the schema for the underlying database.
9. In InfoPath, open the Data Source task pane to see the data source tree.

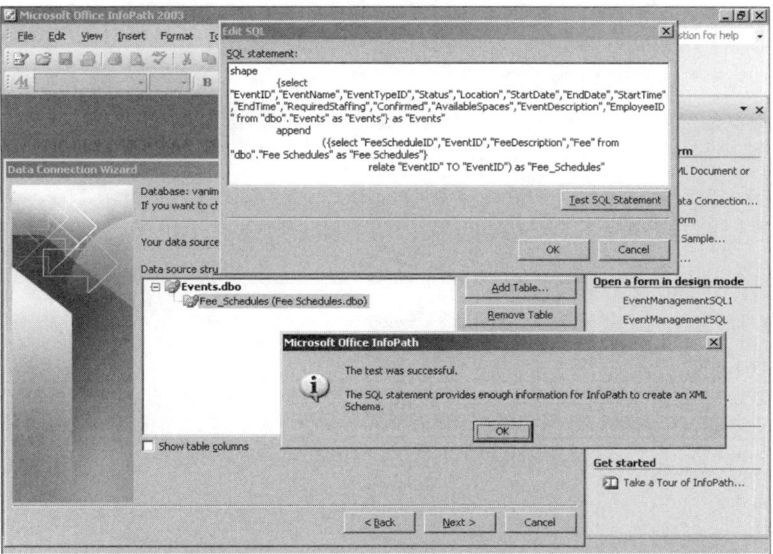

Figure 6-1 Testing a SQL connection string in the Data Connection Wizard

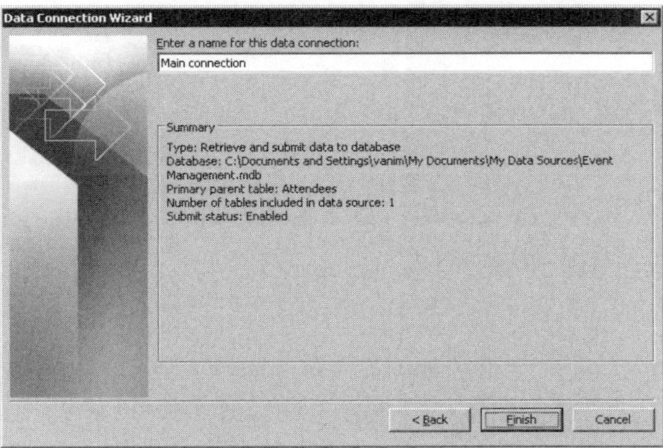

Figure 6-2 The Data Connection Wizard summary page

10. Expand the *queryFields* tree in the Data Source task pane.

11. Drag the *q:Attendees* node and drop it in the view on top of the "Drag Query Fields Here" placeholder text. When the shortcut menu appears, choose Controls In Layout Table.

12. Delete all of the table rows, except those containing Attendee ID, First Name, Last Name, and Company Name, by selecting each row to remove and pressing Delete.

13. In the Data Source task pane, collapse the *queryFields* tree and expand the *dataFields* tree.

14. Drag the *d:Attendees* node and drop it in the view on top of the "Drag Data Fields Here" placeholder text. When the shortcut menu appears, choose Master/Detail. Refer to Chapter 3 for more details on the Master/Detail control.

15. To optimize the view, delete all of the Master table columns, except those containing Attendee ID, First Name, Last Name, and Company Name, by selecting each column to remove and pressing Delete.

16. Resize the Master table columns and then modify the layout of the form as shown in Figure 6-3. Leave all the fields in the Details table as they are.

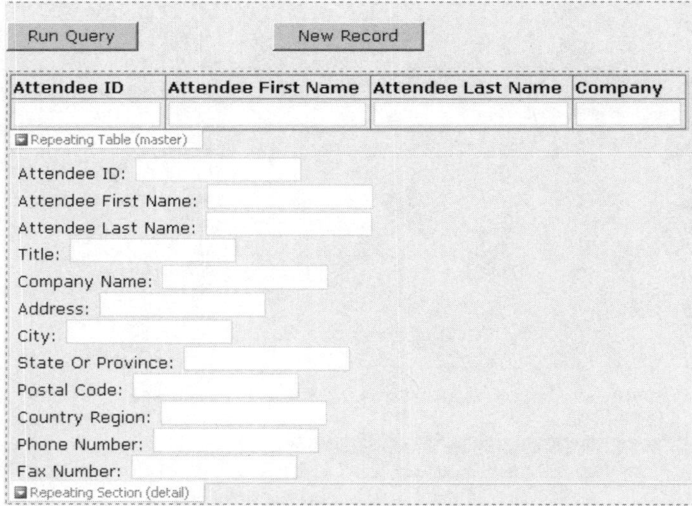

Figure 6-3 The Attendees Master/Detail table is used for query results and data entry.

17. Preview the form.

18. Add several records to the database by filling in the fields and inserting new rows into the Attendees Master/Detail table.

19. After you have entered several records, click Submit on the toolbar. Submit is also available via the File menu.

    This step adds the records to the Event Management database. For the Attendees table, the *AttendeeID* field is set as the primary key and has the data type *AutoNumber*. An auto-incrementing numerical value is automatically assigned to this field. Any value you enter in the *AttendeeID* field will be discarded after the new record has been submitted and will be replaced with the autogenerated number. It is useful to use the *AutoNumber* data type for primary key integer fields in your database.

20. Click Query with no values in any of the query fields to retrieve all of the records in the database. You can also test the query functionality by typing the values in the query fields and then clicking Query.

21. Close the preview, and then save the form on your machine as **EventManagement.xsn**.

Testing and Debugging ADO-Based Forms

InfoPath opens forms on the local machine with local intranet permissions. If you are using a Microsoft Internet Explorer version compatible with Windows XP SP2, you might run into security restrictions due to cross-domain access when you open a form on the local machine that uses a database also on the local machine. You should test your form in preview mode to work around this restriction. Other workarounds are available if you must test your form by opening it from the local machine. The following workarounds apply to InfoPath forms that connect to data connections across domains:

- Register the form using RegForm, an InfoPath SDK tool. You can download the InfoPath SDK by following the link for the SDK from InfoPath's MSDN page at *http://www.msdn.microsoft.com/office/understanding/infopath/default.aspx*. You do not need to change the default security setting of the form before registering it. InfoPath will open the form with local machine privileges instead of intranet privileges once it is registered. Of course, if the form is using level 3 object model calls or needs access to resources that that require it to be fully trusted, you must change the security level to Full Trust before registering the form. Unlike in the cross-domain ADO scenario described above, when you are previewing, the portions of the form that need resources that require Full Trust will fail if the form is not set to Full Trust.
- Change your Internet Explorer security settings. You can do this by choosing Internet Options from the Tools menu in Internet Explorer. On the Security tab, select the Internet Web content zone, and then click Custom Level. Under the Miscellaneous | Access Data Sources Across Domains setting, select Enable or Prompt.

Deploying Access-Based Forms

So far, you have learned how to develop a form that submits and queries data from an Access database. You can deploy the form template to be used as either a standalone or shared database.

Standalone Database

You can deploy the form template to be used as a standalone database by adding the Access .mdb file to the form's resource files. Here are the steps:

1. In the InfoPath designer, choose Resource Files from the Tools menu.
2. In the Resource Files dialog box, click Add.
3. Locate and select the Event Management.mdb database file, and then click OK twice to close all open dialog boxes.
4. Choose Extract Form Files from the File menu, select a folder, and then click OK.
5. Exit InfoPath to release the lock it has on the extracted form files.
6. In the folder containing the extracted form files, edit the manifest.xsf file using a text editor, such as Notepad.
7. In the manifest.xsf file, locate the *connectionString* attribute of the *xsf:adoAdapter* node for the Event Management.mdb database.
8. In the *connectionString* attribute, you will find the statement *Data Source={path}Event Management.mdb*. Remove the path so the statement reads *Data Source=Event Management.mdb*.
9. Save the manifest.xsf file, and close the text editor.

Now the database is included in the XSN. This internal copy will be published as part of the form template and will be used only for forms created from this template.

Shared Database

Consider the scenario where the form needs to be deployed to multiple users who submit to a shared Access database. To enable deployment for such a form, you first need to deploy the database to the shared location. Let's take a quick look at modifying the above example to use shared deployment:

1. Copy the EventManagement.mdb file to a shared location on your server that can host the database.
2. Right-click EventManagement.xsn and choose Design to open the form in the InfoPath designer.
3. Choose Tools | Data Connections, click Modify, and then click Change Database.
4. In the Select Data Source dialog box, click New Source.

5. Select ODBC DSN from the list of data sources, and then click Next.
6. Select MS Access Database from the list of ODBC data sources, and then click Next.
7. In the Select Database dialog box, click Network.
8. Type the path to the shared location in the Database Name field. (Replace the **.mdb* placeholder text with the shared location *yourserver**share* that contains the .mdb file.) Figure 6-4 shows this step of the procedure. Click Finish.
9. Select Event Management.mdb, which now shows up in the Select Database dialog box, and then click OK.
10. Select the Attendees table, and then click Finish.
11. Click Yes if you get a dialog box asking whether you want to replace the existing Event Management Attendees.odc file.
12. In the Select Data Source dialog box, click Open.
13. In the Data Connection Wizard, click Next, and then click Finish.
14. Click Close to close the Data Connections dialog box.
15. Choose Publish from the File menu, and then select a location for your users to open the form from.

    When your users open the file and try to query for data, they will be prompted for credentials to access the database depending on the authentication you provide through Access. If they are not already mapped to the shared location for the database, they will get a prompt to connect to the location for the database.

Figure 6-4 Deploying an Access database to a shared location

Access is not well suited to forms that expect to write to large databases or to form templates that need large-scale deployments. InfoPath's integration with SQL Server databases and Web services is better suited for such scenarios. We will cover InfoPath–SQL Server integration in the next few sections. We will talk about Web service integration in Chapter 8.

Integrating with SQL

In this section, we will take a look at integrating with tables in SQL databases. InfoPath's declarative support does not allow you to create or delete tables, but it allows you to query data from and submit data to existing tables in SQL.

The InfoPath SDK includes a few examples (Data Interop, Data Submit, and Information Lookup) that show the database integration features.

Specifically, we will show how to create InfoPath forms that talk to the *pubs* database available as part of the default SQL Server installation. To work through this section, you need access to a SQL server that has the *pubs* database installed.

Authors Scenario

In the first scenario, we will create an InfoPath form that queries and submits data using the *publishers* table in the *pubs* database.

Creating a Data Connection to SQL

1. Launch InfoPath, and then click Design A Form.
2. In the Design A Form task pane, click New From Data Connection.
3. In the Data Connection Wizard, click Next, and then click Select Database.
4. In the Select Data Source dialog box, select Connect To A New Data Source, and then click Open.
5. Select Microsoft SQL Server, as shown in Figure 6-5, and then click Next.
6. On the Connect To Database Server page, shown in Figure 6-6, type your server name and credentials, and then click Next.

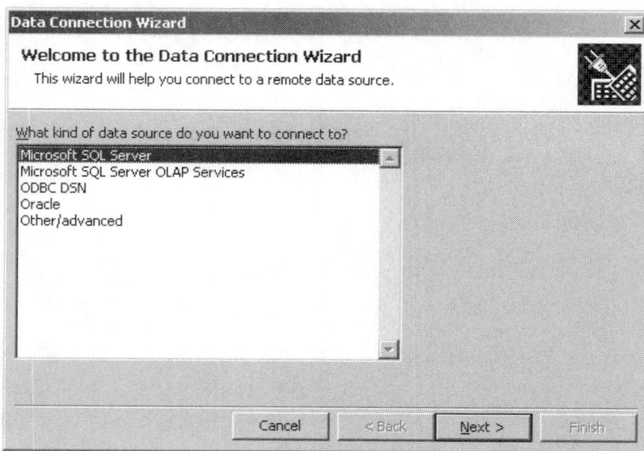

Figure 6-5 Selecting a data source in the Data Connection Wizard

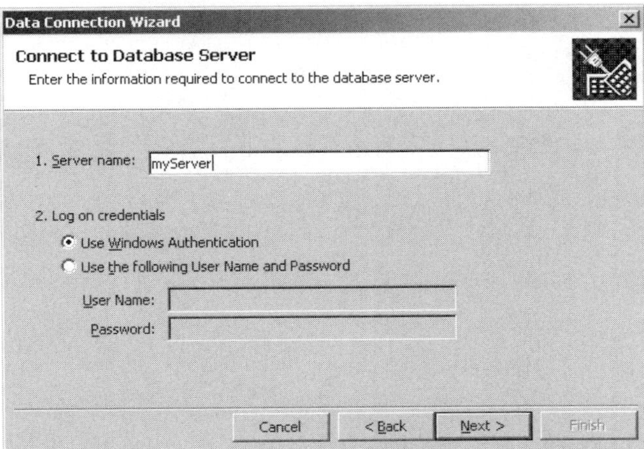

Figure 6-6 Connecting to a database in the Data Connection Wizard

7. On the Select Database And Table page, select *pubs* from the database drop-down list, as shown in Figure 6-7.
8. Select the *publishers* table, as shown in Figure 6-8, and then click Next.

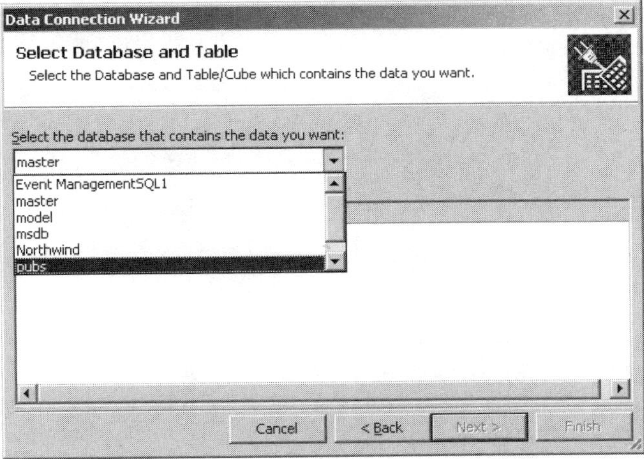

Figure 6-7 Selecting a database in the Data Connection Wizard

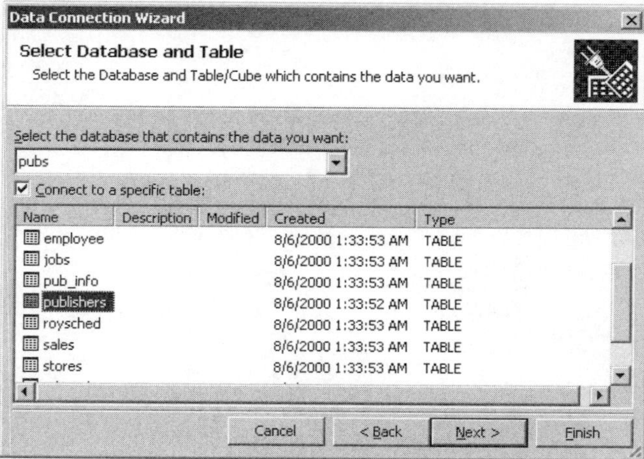

Figure 6-8 Connecting to a specific table in the selected database

9. On the Save Data Connection File And Finish page, type a different filename if desired, type a description for your database, include some search keywords if desired (as shown in Figure 6-9), and then click Finish.

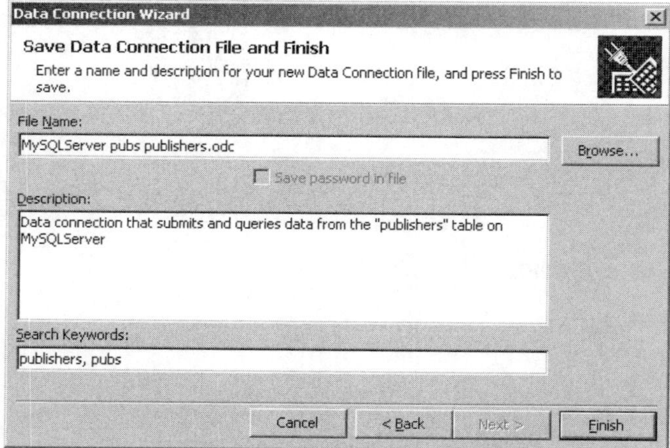

Figure 6-9 The Save Data Connection File And Finish page of the Data Connection Wizard

You are not done yet. The wizard guides you through the data source creation for the table, as shown in Figure 6-10. In this step, you can add more tables and specify relationships for them. We will keep the data source with a single table in this example and play with multiple tables later in this chapter. For now, we'll specify a sort order for the table in the next step.

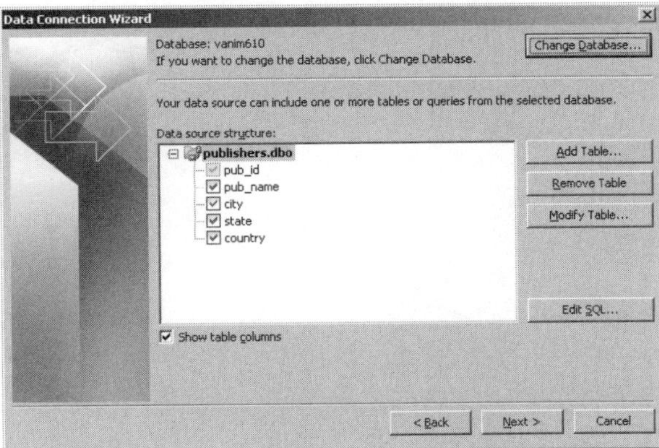

Figure 6-10 The data source structure in the Data Connection Wizard

10. Click Modify Table.
11. In the Sort Order dialog box, select *pub_name* in the first drop-down list, select *state* in the second drop-down list, as shown in Figure 6-11, and then click Finish.
12. Click Next to get to the final page of the wizard (shown in Figure 6-12), and then click Finish.

    InfoPath has created the form based on the *publisher* table in the SQL *pubs* database as the main connection. The data structure for the table is available in the Data Source task pane. The view also has the New Record and Run Query buttons by default.

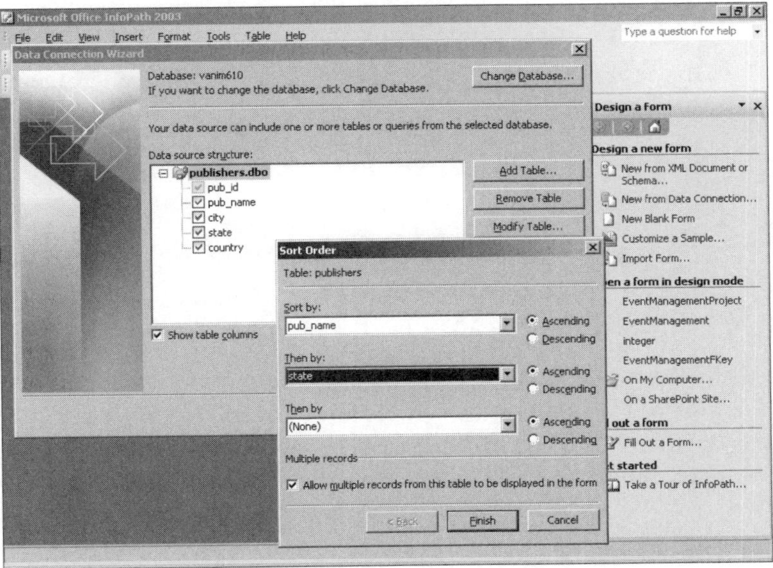

Figure 6-11 Specifying a sort order for columns in the data source

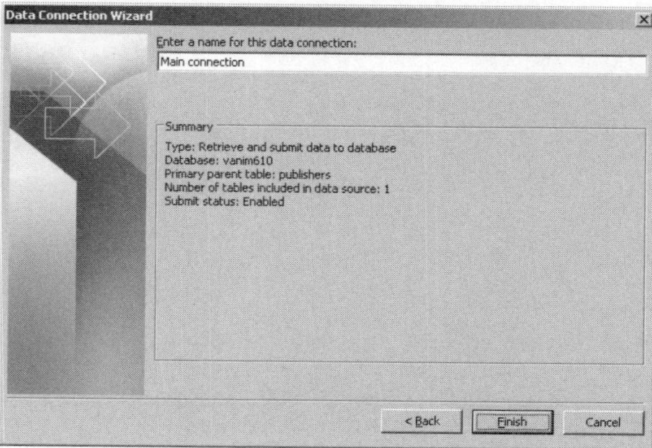

Figure 6-12 Summary for the SQL data connection

Creating the Form View

1. Expand the *queryFields* tree in the Data Source task pane.
2. Drag the *q:publishers* node and drop it in the view on top of the "Drag Query Fields Here" placeholder text. When the shortcut menu appears, select Controls In Layout Table.
3. In the Data Source task pane, collapse the *queryFields* tree, and expand the *dataFields* tree.
4. Drag the *q:publishers* node and drop it in the view on top of the "Drag Data Fields Here" placeholder text. When the shortcut menu appears, select Repeating Table.
5. Click on the "Click To Add A Title" placeholder text and type **Publishers**.
6. Left-click just above the New Record button, and drag down to select all of the view content to the bottom of the view.
7. Drag and drop the selected content on top of the "Click To Add Form Content" placeholder text located under the title you just typed.
8. Choose Color Schemes from the Format menu.
9. In the Color Schemes task pane, select the Blue color scheme.

   Figure 6-13 shows the form view after this has been done. The top half of the view below the New Record button has the fields that you can use for querying the database. The repeating table at the bottom of the view will be populated with the results of the query on the data in the *publishers* table of the database.

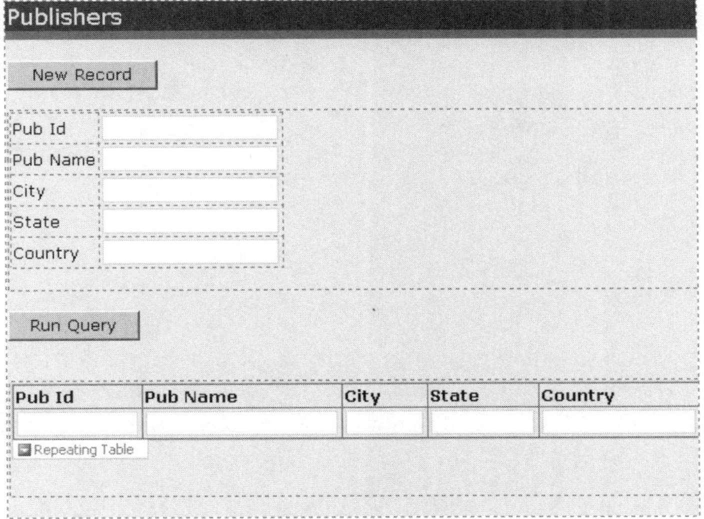

Figure 6-13 The form view for the publishers table

Testing the Form for Query and Submit

Let's preview and test the form the hard way.

1. Preview the form, and then click Run Query. The blank query parameters will result in all the rows of the table being returned, as shown in Figure 6-14. So far, so good!

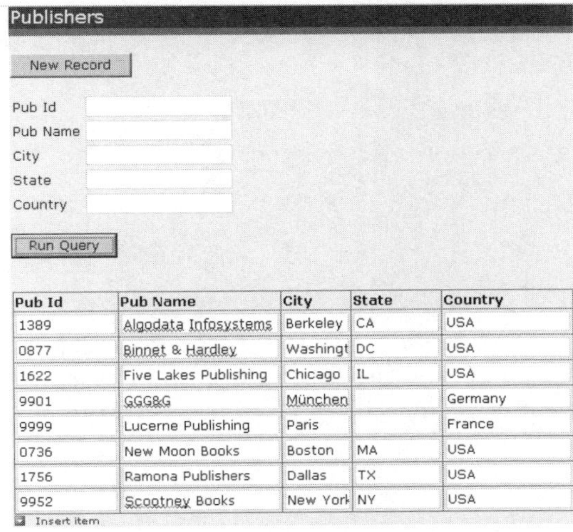

Figure 6-14 A query returning all table rows based on blank query parameters

2. Click New Record, and then type the following values into the specified repeating table columns:
   - *Pub ID:* **1234**
   - *Pub Name:* **Microsoft**
   - *City:* **Redmond**
   - *State:* **WA**
   - *Country:* **USA**
3. Click Submit on the toolbar. You will get a submit error with this message:

   [0x80040E2F][Microsoft OLE DB Provider for SQL Server] INSERT statement conflicted with COLUMN CHECK constraint 'CK__publisher__pub_i__7C8480AE'. The conflict occurred in database 'pubs', table 'publishers', column 'pub_id'. [0x80040E2F][Microsoft OLE DB Provider for SQL Server] The statement has been terminated.

   You will get this error trying to add these values to the SQL table outside InfoPath as well. InfoPath does nothing to interpret SQL errors–it shows them directly to the end user.

Debugging Database Submit Errors

The error string implies that there was a violation of a *CHECK constraint* associated with the *pub_id* column in the database. Let's debug the error above by opening the database using the Microsoft SQL Server Enterprise Manager. You can launch Enterprise Manager by clicking on the Windows Start button and choosing All Programs | Microsoft SQL Server | Enterprise Manager.

1. In Enterprise Manager, expand the *Console Root* tree to select Microsoft SQL Servers | SQL Server Group | (LOCAL) | Databases | pubs | Diagrams.
2. Select New Database Diagram from the Actions menu.
3. In the Create Database Diagram Wizard, click Next.
4. Select the Add Related Tables Automatically check box, double-click *publishers* in the list of available tables, click Next, and then click Finish.
5. From the error message, we need to look for a *pub_id* check constraint. Right-click on the *publishers* table in the diagram, and then click Check Constraints. Sure enough, the *pub_id* value is constrained for this table, as shown in Figure 6-15.

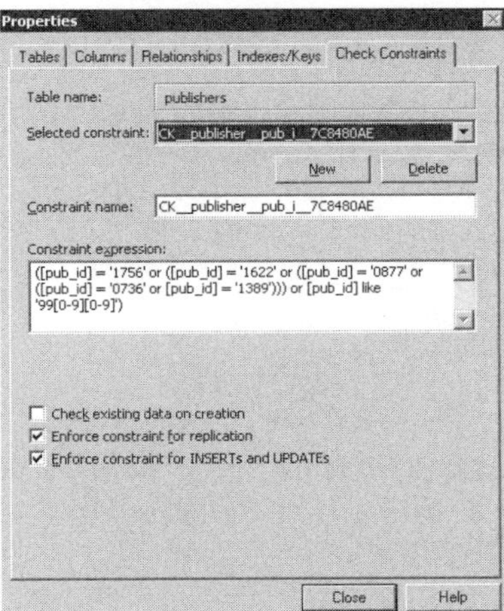

Figure 6-15 *pub_id* constraints in the *publishers* table

Data Validation for SQL Constraints

Close Enterprise Manager, go back to the InfoPath preview window, change the value of the Pub ID field to **9902**, and then submit again–the submit operation will succeed this time, and you will see a dialog box stating that the form was submitted successfully. But it is unlikely that the form user will know anything about the database table's constraints. How can you improve your form design such that the form user will not encounter this error? One way is to add a note in your view above the table explaining the constraint on the field and trust that the form user will read and abide by it. Better still, you can add validation to the specific field that will notify the user of invalid input and how to correct it.

To do this, close the preview, double-click within the *pub_id* field in the repeating table to open its Properties dialog box. Technically, any new records cannot be submitted with *pub_id* values that already exist in the *publishers* table. SQL rejects duplicate primary keys. For example, we cannot submit a new record with the value 9901 or 0877 because these already exist. But we will mirror the SQL constraint in the InfoPath form to avoid bogus validation errors that result from invalid value patterns. Per the constraint, a specific set of static values and values other than 9901 and 9952 that match the 99[0-9][0-9] pattern are valid for this table. We covered validation conditions in detail in Chapter 3, so we will skip the steps for the procedure here and allow you to implement this data validation condition as an exercise. Figure 6-16 shows the validation condition specified for this scenario.

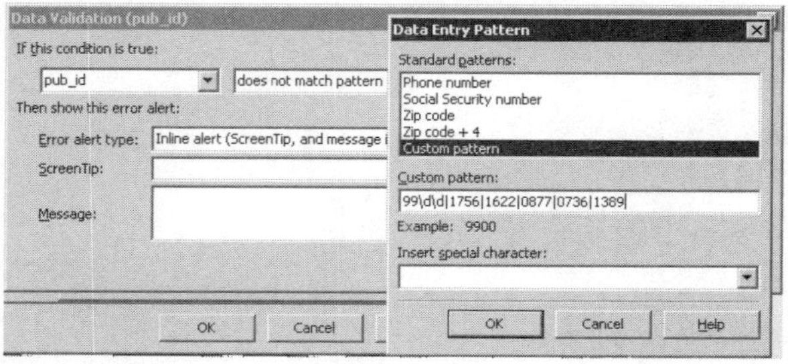

Figure 6-16 Validation condition for *pub_id*

After you have implemented the custom validation, preview the form again, and type the previous values for the table rows. You will notice that a red dashed box appears around the invalid value. Change the value for the *pub_id* field to **9988**, and then click Submit again. The submission succeeds.

Click New Record to clear the repeating table values, and then retrieve the data just submitted by typing **9988** in the *Pub ID* query field and then clicking Run Query. The query returns the *publisher* table values for ID 9988 and populates the repeating table with these values.

Updating Specific Fields

InfoPath populates the results of a query in the same *dataFields* nodes as the ones used to submit data to a database using New Record. You can use these fields to change only specific values of columns in the database. To do this, query for the records you need to update, change the specific values in the returned data, and then submit the form.

Using ADO Connection Through Code

InfoPath provides object model support for database connectivity. You can access the main data connection through the *QueryAdapter* property of the *XDocument* object. You can also access secondary data connections through the *DataObjects* collection.

The following code snippet queries the database with the value of the *pub_id* field after the user types a value in, and exits the field to allow the value to bind to the data source.

```
<InfoPathEventHandler(MatchPath:="/dfs:myFields/dfs:dataFields/d:publishers/@pub_id",
    EventType:=InfoPathEventType.OnAfterChange)> _
Public Sub publishers_pub_id_attr_OnAfterChange(ByVal e As DataDOMEvent)
    ' Write code here to restore the global state.
    If (e.IsUndoRedo) then
        ' An undo or redo operation has occurred and the DOM is read-only.
        Return
    End If
```

```
    ' A field change has occurred and the DOM is writable. Write code here to respond to the
        changes.
    Dim pubIDNode As IXMLDOMNode = e.Site
    Dim pubIDVal As String = pubIDNode.nodeTypedValue
    Dim myADOAdapter As ADOAdapterObject = thisXDocument.DataAdapters.Item(0)
    Dim sCommand As String = "select pub_name from publishers"
    If ("" <> pubIDVal) Then
        sCommand = sCommand + " where publishers.pub_id = " + pubIDVal
    End If
    myADOAdapter.Command = sCommand
    myADOAdapter.Query()
End Sub
```

Developer Nugget: Using InfoPath with SQL Views

You can create a data connection to a view in the SQL database using InfoPath. You can use this feature to leverage InfoPath as a SQL client tool. This is also useful for testing updates to the table when designing your form. The scenario in the following example is to create a sales report form that submits to the *titles* table in the *pubs* database as sales are made. We will create a form based on a SQL view that displays the total sales made by a publisher. We will verify submission to the *titles* table by querying for data returned by this view.

Creating the View in SQL

Let's add a TotalSalesByPublisher view to the *pubs* database through Enterprise Manager, as shown in Figure 6-17.

1. Launch the Microsoft SQL Server Enterprise Manager.
2. In Enterprise Manager, expand the *Console Root* tree to select Microsoft SQL Servers | SQL Server Group | (LOCAL) | Databases | pubs | Views.
3. Select New View from the Actions menu.
4. Replace the "SELECT FROM" text with the following query for the view:

   ```
   SELECT SUM(dbo.titles.ytd_sales) AS TotalSalesByPub_ID, dbo.titles.pub_id,
     dbo.publishers.pub_name, dbo.publishers.state
   FROM dbo.titles INNER JOIN
     dbo.publishers ON dbo.titles.pub_id = dbo.publishers.pub_id
   GROUP BY dbo.titles.pub_id, dbo.publishers.pub_name, dbo.publishers.state
   ```
5. Right-click on the query text you just typed, and choose Run.
6. Press Ctrl+F4 to close the New View window.
7. When asked to save changes, click Yes.
8. In the Save As dialog box, type **TotalSalesByPublisher**, and then click OK.
9. Close Enterprise Manager.

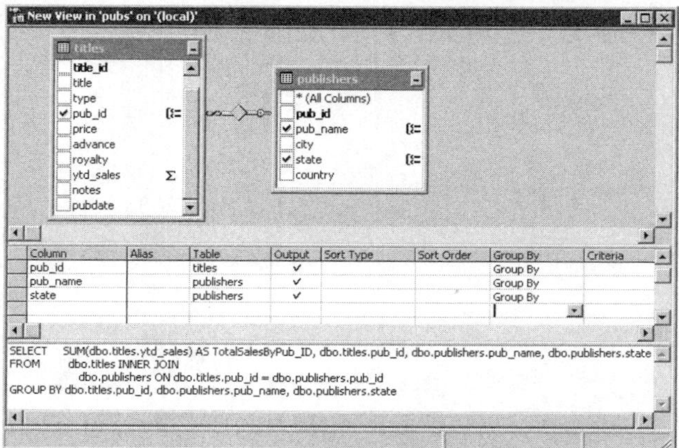

Figure 6-17 Creating the view in SQL

Create the Book Title Sales Report form to submit data to the *titles* table:

10. Follow the steps we previously outlined under the heading "Creating a Data Connection to SQL" to create a form using a SQL Server connection, only this time, on the Select Database And Table page of the Data Connection Wizard, select the *titles* table.
11. Set up the view as we did before so it matches the view snapshot shown in Figure 6-18.
12. Save the form template as **BookTitleSalesReport.xsn**.

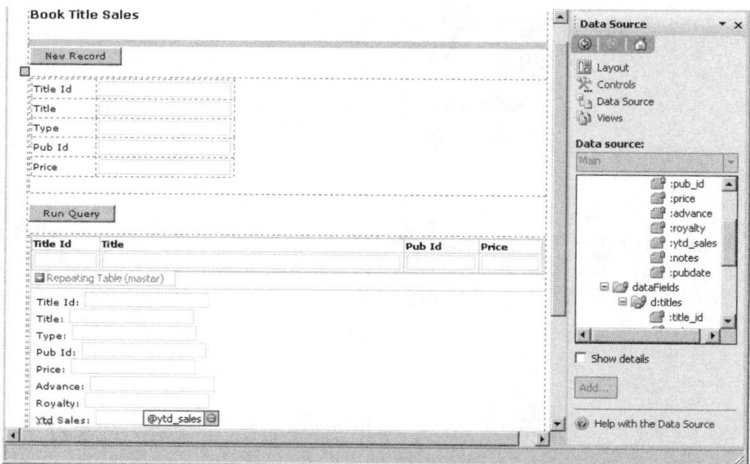

Figure 6-18 The InfoPath form view for the *titles* table

Creating the Data Connection for the View

Create the Total Sales By Publisher form to test the results of changes made in the Book Title Sales Report form we just created:

1. Follow the steps we previously outlined under the heading "Creating a Data Connection to SQL" to create a form using a SQL Server connection, only this time, on the Select Database And Table page of the Data Connection Wizard, select the TotalSalesByPublisher view, as shown in Figure 6-19.

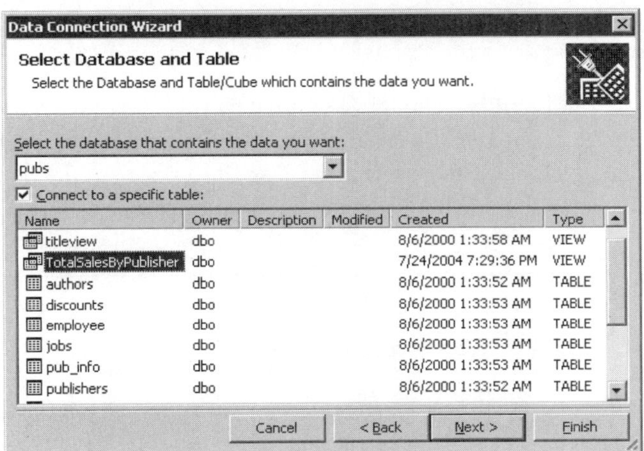

Figure 6-19 Selecting the TotalSalesByPublisher view through the Data Connection Wizard

2. Set up the view as we did before.
3. Save the form template as **TotalSalesByPublisher.xsn**.
4. Preview the form.

Testing Data Submit Based on Database Views

1. Open the BookTitleSalesReport.xsn form, saved earlier. Let's assume that you have to update the database for the book *Silicon Valley Gastronomic Treats* because it just earned an additional $1,000 in sales.
2. Type **Silicon Valley Gastronomic Treats** in the *Title* query field, and then click Run Query. Notice that the query returns a *pub_id* value of 0877 for the book.
3. Switch to the Preview window of the Total Sales By Publisher form.
4. Type the value **0877** for *Pub Id* field, and then click Run Query. The query returns a value of 44,219 as total sales for this publisher.

5. In the Book Title Sales Report form, add $1,000 to the YTD Sales value—changing it from 2,032 to **3,032**, and then click Submit to update this value in the database.
6. In the Total Sales By Publisher Preview window, click Run Query to refresh the total sales. This time the query returns a value of 45,219 as the total sales for this publisher!

This technique is a great way to verify your form updates are being submitted without adding tables, relationships, or secondary data connections for testing purposes. It also demonstrates how you can use InfoPath as a SQL client if the primary need is to insert, update, and view records in the database.

You can query with all blank parameters to return all of the table rows from the main data connection to test whether the database was updated successfully, but for larger tables this would be inefficient and useless because the amount of data returned directly affects the rendering performance of the form, and large query results can make the form unusable.

InfoPath-Related Database Concepts

In this section, we will look at a few additional concepts related to the database integration features in InfoPath

Creating a Secondary Connection to a Database

We created an InfoPath form based on a database as the main data source in the previous example. We have also seen, in previous chapters of the book, examples of using a secondary data connection to populate a drop-down list. The most common example of secondary data connections is for doing lookups on data sources.

You can use a database as a secondary data connection to retrieve data. Let's look at a simple example of retrieving data from a database:

1. In the InfoPath designer, choose Data Connections from the Tools menu, and then click Add.
2. In the Data Connections Wizard, select Receive Data, and then click Next.
3. Select the Database option, and then click Next.

The remaining steps are similar to those in the previous examples for creating the form based on an Access or SQL database. Figure 6-20 shows the last page of the wizard for an Access database added as a secondary connection. Notice that, unlike in Figure 6-12, there is no mention of submit functionality.

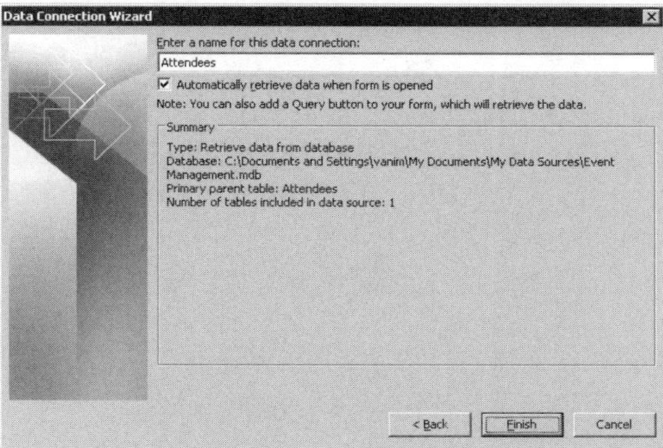

Figure 6-20 Data connection status for a secondary connection to database

In general, you should use secondary data connections if your form design requires you to use the database for querying only. If you create a form based on a data connection as the main data source, you lose the flexibility to extend the form at any time by adding nodes to the data source.

If you use secondary database connections, you can extend nodes in your main data source and populate the main data source with data returned by the secondary data source. The advantage of using secondary data sources is that you do not have to be familiar or experienced with the database schema to be able to define table relationships at design time. Instead, you can create several unrelated data connections and retrieve data from each of them separately, without having to worry about database constraints. However, InfoPath does not support built-in submit functionality for secondary data connections to databases.

Including Required Fields

Data types that do not allow NULL values are required fields in SQL tables. If you design your data connection from a table that has such fields, you can end up with a data connection in which submit always fails because you did not include a required column in your data source.

For example, consider the scenario in which you are designing your InfoPath form from the *sales* table of the *pubs* database. You might not need to keep track of order dates, in which case you can choose to exclude the *ord_date* column in the Data Source Structure step of the Data Connection Wizard. Because the *ord_date* is not present in your data source, it will not be present in your view. Hence, when you submit a new record to the *sales* table, the *ord_date* value for the record will be *NULL*. SQL will reject the update with the error "Cannot insert the value NULL into column 'ord_date', table 'pubs.dbo.sales'; column does not allow nulls. INSERT fails."

Updating a Database Connection

The above situation is by no means fatal. You can easily modify the data connection to include the *ord_date* column in your data source and then add it to the form view from the Data Source task pane. But in general, you should avoid this hassle by not excluding any columns from the data source to begin with, or by verifying in the database schema that NULL values are acceptable in columns that will be excluded. You could also include all table columns in the data source and exclude unwanted ones from the view, but this would not be the cleanest approach.

Data Type Compatibility

InfoPath maintains consistency in data types when inferring the form schema from a data source. In the preceding example, the InfoPath ADO submit functionality cannot submit to binary large objects (BLOBs) supported by ADO, so submit is disabled when data types that can store more than 8 KB of data are present. Access and SQL support several such data types–including *ntext*, *hyperlink*, *image*, *memo*, and *OLE*. The *text* data type is supported for Access but not for SQL.

InfoPath does not explicitly notify the Forms Designer when the database has data types that it does not support. You will see an error on the last page of the Data Connection Wizard indicating that submit functionality was disabled. In the next section, we will talk about the impact of data type incompatibility in your form design.

Query, New Record, and Submit

When you design an InfoPath form based on a database as the main data source, InfoPath sets up query functionality and submit functionality in the form. Unlike the Query and New Record buttons, the Submit button is not present in the view by default. When it is enabled, InfoPath configures the submit functionality of the form to submit to the database. You can then use the Submit button on the Standard toolbar or choose Submit from the File menu to submit data to the database.

You can also add your own Submit button in the view. You do this by inserting a Button control in the view, opening its Properties dialog box, selecting Submit in the Action drop-down list, verifying that Database is selected in the Submit To drop-down list, and then clicking OK twice. The button in the view is renamed to "Submit" and functions the same as the Submit button on the toolbar.

Designing for Submit

In some cases, InfoPath cannot design the form with the submit to database functionality, although this doesn't prevent you from submitting to other adapters such as e-mail or a Web service. For example, the database table might have fields with data types that InfoPath does not support, as described above. The last page of the Data Connections Wizard indicates whether submit to database was enabled. You should review this information carefully because it is the only place in the wizard where you get a notification of whether this functionality was enabled for that data connection. Figure 6-21 shows an example of a data connection where submit to database is not allowed.

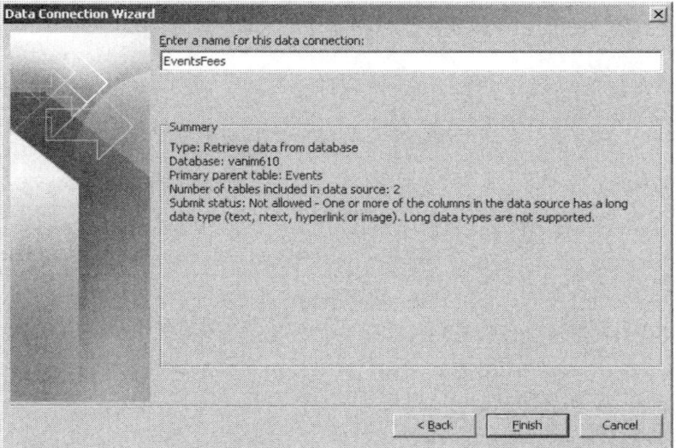

Figure 6-21 A data connection not configured for submit to database functionality

Submit status: Not Allowed ADO data connection types for which InfoPath does not allow submit to database functionality are the tables and views in the categories listed in Table 6-1.

Table 6-1 ADO Submit Not Allowed Errors

Data Source Example	InfoPath Error Message
Single table with no primary key	One or more of the tables in the data source do not have a primary key, unique constraint, or unique index.
Multiple tables where the SELECT statement does not include primary keys from all the parent tables.	One or more of the tables in the data source do not have a primary key, unique constraint, or unique index.
Duplicate tables	A table is being used multiple times.
JOIN operation in table/view statement	A SQL JOIN statement was used.
UNION operation in table/view statement	One or more of the tables in the data source do not have a primary key, unique constraint, or unique index.
GROUP BY in table/view statement	One or more of the tables in the data source do not have a primary key, unique constraint, or unique index.
Unsupported data types	One or more columns in the data source has a long data type (*text*, *ntext*, *hyperlink* or *image*). Long data types are not supported.

The error messages are not always helpful in these cases, but the number of failure cases is limited. With some practice, you will learn how to steer clear of these types of structures. Submit will fail if you try to submit using the object model submit to database functionality through code for all the examples in Table 6-1.

Submit status: Disabled Let's take a quick look at the cases that result in disabled submit to database functionality when the data connection is created. Unlike the examples in Table 6-1, InfoPath does allow you to enable the submit to database command through Tools | Submitting Forms | Database option. In most cases, you have to modify the recordset through the business logic or submit will fail. Submit is disabled in the examples listed in Table 6-2.

Table 6-2 ADO Submit Disabled Errors

Data Source Example	InfoPath Error Message
Multiple tables in which the parent-child relationship is many-to-one	A many-to-one relationship might exist between two tables in the data source.
Repeated columns in a table	A table is being used multiple times.

The easiest way to verify whether submit to database is enabled in your form is to choose Submitting Forms from the Tools menu. If it is enabled for the main data connection, you will see Database listed as a choice in the Submit To drop-down list of the Submitting Forms dialog box. The submit choices available in the Submit To drop-down list map to various data adapters that InfoPath supports submitting to.

If submit to database is enabled, the submit parameters are set in the Submitting Forms dialog box. You can modify the default submit behavior by clicking Submit Options and then making changes in the Submit Options dialog box. For example, you might want to trap the submit errors and display more friendly custom error messages to the form user. In the next exercise, we'll see an example of this.

Defining Table Relationships

All the examples in this chapter have so far used a single table. Let's take a look at a form that uses multiple tables. For this, we will create a new form that uses the *sales* table from the *pubs* database.

Deleting Foreign Key Records

One situation that requires you to design your SQL data connection with multiple tables is when you are deleting records from a table that has a foreign key relationship with another table. For example, consider the *authors* table in the *pubs* database. Figure 6-22 shows the relationship between the *authors* and the *titleauthor* tables in the database.

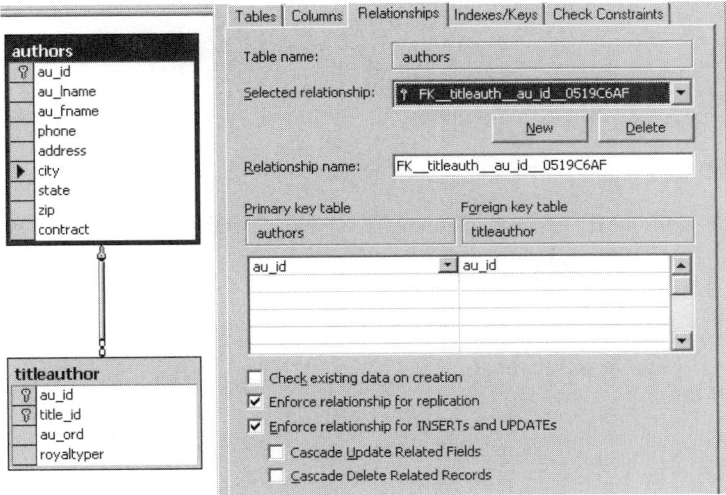

Figure 6-22 Relationship between the *authors* and *titleauthor* tables

Notice that the Delete cascade option for the *authors* table is not enabled. This is usually the case with all foreign key relationships so accidental deletion of related records is avoided. You cannot delete a record from the primary table when there is a foreign key relationship with another table unless you delete the foreign key records from the other table as well. If you do not do this, SQL Server will reject the delete operation and return an error. But how do you delete foreign key records through InfoPath?

Note To see what happens when you delete a record from the *authors* table while ignoring the foreign key relationship, create a form based on a SQL data connection, connecting to the *authors* table. Create the view by dragging the query fields and data fields into the form. Preview the form, type **213-46-8915** in the *au_id* field, and then click Run Query. Select the row returned by the authors table by placing your cursor on the row and pressing Shift+Down Arrow. Press Delete, and then click Submit to attempt to delete the record from the database. You will receive the following error message: "[0x80040E2F][Microsoft OLE DB Provider for SQL Server] DELETE statement conflicted with COLUMN REFERENCE constraint 'FK__titleauth__au_id__1ED998B2'. The conflict occurred in database 'pubs', table 'titleauthor', column 'au_id'. [0x80040E2F]
[Microsoft OLE DB Provider for SQL Server] The statement has been terminated."

To enable error-free deletion by taking into account the foreign key relation for the *authors* table, implement the following procedures:

Creating a Form Based on Additional Tables

1. Create a new form from a SQL data connection using the *pubs* database.
2. On the Select Database Table page of the Data Connection Wizard, select the *authors* table.
3. Click Add Table, and then add the *titleauthor* table.
4. In the Edit Relationship dialog box, notice that a relationship between the *au_id* fields in both tables is created for you, and then click Finish. If you are adding multiple tables with related fields, you should always specify all relationships in the Edit Relationship dialog box of the Data Connection Wizard.
5. Click Next, and then click Finish.

   The hierarchical nature of XML results in InfoPath adding additional related tables only as child groups of the first table. In Figure 6-23, you can see that the query parameters corresponding to the two tables are created using sibling groups under the *queryFields* group but that in the *dataFields* group, the *titleauthor* table is created as a child group of the *authors* table.
6. Drag and drop the *q:authors/au_id* and the *q:titleauthor/au_id* fields from the *queryFields* group into the query area of the form.
7. Drag and drop the *d:authors* group, as a repeating table, into the data area of the form.
8. Select the *titleauthor* repeating table in the last column of the table you just inserted, cut it, and paste it beneath the *authors* repeating table.
9. Adjust column sizes and make other necessary changes so that your view looks like the completed view in Figure 6-24.

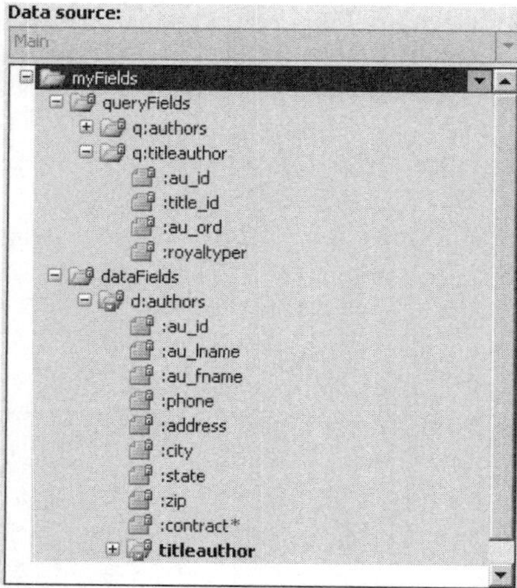

Figure 6-23 A data source for related database tables

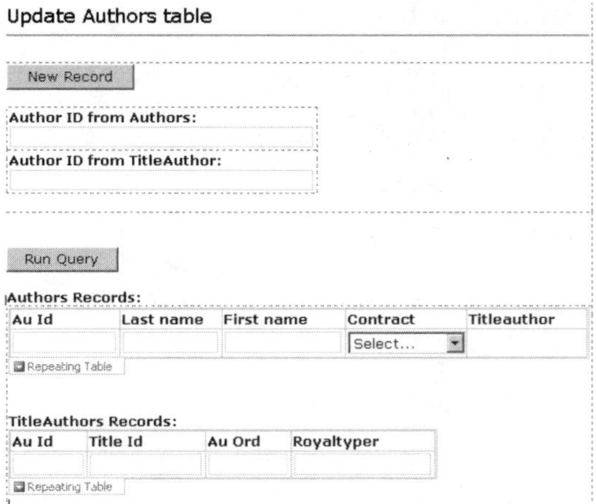

Figure 6-24 The form view for deleting author records

Testing Foreign Key Deletion

1. Preview the form.
2. Type **213-46-8915** in both of the *au_id* query fields, and then click Run Query. The query returns one record in the *authors* table and two records in the *titleauthor* table.
3. Select the two rows in the *titleauthor* table, press Delete, and then click Submit to delete the records from the *titleauthor* table in the database.
4. Select the row from the *authors* table, press Delete, and then click Submit to delete the record from the *authors* table. The *author* table with the ID of 213-46-8915 has been successfully deleted from the database.

It is best to determine foreign key constraints before designing your form. Your ability to do this is determined largely by your experience with the database and your familiarity with the database schema. If you do not have access to the database schema, you might run into failures while designing your form. The *check constraints* error in the earlier procedure is an example of such a failure.

Custom Submit Errors

You have probably noticed that InfoPath does not show friendly errors for invalid ADO operations. Instead, it displays the error that comes from ADO. In addition to the concepts that we have already covered in this chapter, you should always preview and test your form to check for cases where incorrect or invalid user input might make the submit operation fail. You can catch many of these errors before the user submits the form using the *OnSubmitRequest* event handler. In this event handler, you can write custom code to validate the data before submitting and supply the user with more friendly error and success messages.

Executing a SQL Stored Procedure in an InfoPath Form

You can design an InfoPath form to programmatically execute the result of a stored procedure in SQL. You must set the *Command* property of the SQL data adapter to the SQL query for executing the stored procedure. This is useful in cases where InfoPath's native database support falls short in certain data retrieval and update scenarios. For example, if your SQL database tables have columns with image data types, you can have a stored procedure in the database to read the image data. You can then call into that stored procedure using InfoPath's programmatic support for ADO functionality and execute the stored procedure to bring that data to the form.

Detailed steps for executing stored procedures in InfoPath are also outlined in the Knowledge Base article at http://support.microsoft.com/default.aspx?scid=kb;en-us;827007.

Summary

This chapter described InfoPath's database integration features. InfoPath supports SQL Server and Access databases through ADO Recordset functionality. You can use multiple data connections to multiple databases through secondary data connections. In the next chapter, we will look at additional InfoPath data and workflow features through integration with XML Web services built on top of databases.

Chapter 7
Web Services

A Web service is an interface to a software application running on a server across the network. InfoPath can use a Web service as a destination to submit data to, as the source of data for creating a form, and as a data connection to receive supplemental data for use in the UI or business logic of a form. In this chapter, we will cover using Web services to receive and submit data for your forms and then discuss some more advanced techniques for working with Web services that the InfoPath designer cannot support.

InfoPath makes the job of integrating your forms with Web services easy by including support for the core Web service standards: XML, WSDL, UDDI, SOAP, and HTTP. You can connect to a Web service you develop specifically for your InfoPath form, or you can connect to existing Web services within your organization, across organizations, or available on the Internet.

The Web service functions as the middle tier in a three-tier system. In Chapter 6, you learned how to connect an InfoPath form to a database. If you move your database, change the schema, or modify the stored procedures on the server, you have to update the InfoPath form template. InfoPath supports automatic updates if you deploy your form template to a Web server, but if you deploy through e-mail you have to get users to upgrade the form, and that can be costly. An alternative to upgrading your form every time your database changes is to create a Web service. The Web service can then insulate the form by converting the data from the fixed Web service schema to the changed database.

Figure 7-1 shows a simple three-tier architecture for using a Web service to access a database.

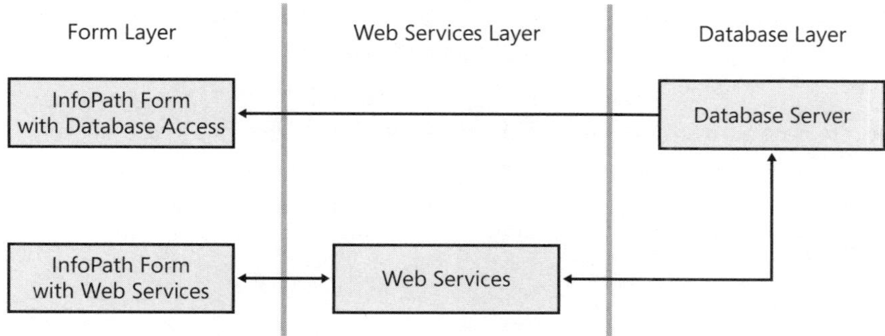

Figure 7-1 Accessing a database through a Web service vs. a direct database connection

Using a Web service to access a database on a server has both pros and cons:

Pros

- Reduced redeployment cost when database changes–make changes in one place
- Supports reuse and extensibility
- Supports validation at the Web service interface

Cons

- More work to design, implement, test, and deploy
- Doesn't work offline unless you implement caching

Middle-tier logic falls into the following buckets:

- **Receive data from database** Database rows are extracted and formatted into XML corresponding to the schema of your InfoPath form.
- **Submit data to database** Transforms the XML form into sets of rows (rowsets) in your database tables.
- **Validate data** Use business rules to validate input. The BizTalk rules engine is a good example of this for workflow.
- **Authorize user** This is a common function to implement in a Web service to control read-write permission to databases and line-of-business applications. Windows Integrated Authentication is used when calling a Web service so you can identify the user.
- **Read data from other applications** Web services can be used as interfaces to existing corporate applications, including Active Directory.
- **Reduce deployment cost** Simplify deployment by moving code from your form to the Web service. If your users do not have The Microsoft .NET Framework, you can move the code to a Web service and do the processing in the middle tier.
- **Integrate data across multiple sources** InfoPath can be used to integrate data across multiple sources, but due to security reasons it is often desirable to grant an InfoPath form domain access and therefore access to only a single Web server. This server can provide a Web service that gathers data from other data sources, including other Web services.

When you implement a Web service, you'll want to consider the following:

- **Error handling** If validation fails, will you prevent submission of the form?
- **Version upgrades** How will you support updates to the schema used on the client?
- **Offline data** Will you cache the data when the user goes offline?
- **Privacy and security** Will you encrypt the message to prevent others from seeing the contents? InfoPath supports HTTPS (HTTP over SSL) for secure connections.

A Brief Overview of Web Service Standards

InfoPath supports XML, HTTP, SOAP, WSDL, and UDDI Web service standards. What do these abbreviations and acronyms stand for?

- XML is Extensible Markup Language, a standard for describing structured data used by InfoPath and many other tools; it is discussed throughout this book.
- HTTP is HyperText Transfer Protocol, which is used to retrieve data from and send data to a Web server. It is the network protocol that InfoPath supports for connecting to Web services. It is also used to load and save templates and forms. You can learn more about how this applies to InfoPath and SharePoint in Chapter 9.
- SOAP is Simple Object Access Protocol, an XML-based protocol for sending and receiving data to and from a Web service. InfoPath communicates with Web services using SOAP. SOAP messages are well-formed XML documents. InfoPath sends the SOAP message to the Web service using HTTP.
- WSDL is Web Services Description Language, an XML format that describes the interface to Web services, including the data formats. InfoPath uses WSDL when creating forms and data sources based on a Web service.
- UDDI is Universal Description, Discovery, and Integration, a standard interface to directories of Web services. InfoPath can connect to a UDDI server to discover available Web services.

To learn more about SOAP and other Web service standards, visit the MSDN Web Services Developer Center specifications Web site at *http://msdn.*microsoft.com/webservices/understanding/specs/default.aspx.

Designer Support

The InfoPath designer can connect Web services in three ways: as the basis for the main data source when creating a form, as a data connection to receive data, and as a data connection to submit data.

Note The InfoPath designer supports only document/literal encoding for Web services. Methods for calling other types of Web services are described later in this chapter.

Creating a Form Based on a Web Service

If you have a Web service that returns the data you want to display and edit in a form, you can design a form directly from the Web service. InfoPath displays the parameters to and the results from the Web service as the main data source for the form. To do this, choose New

From Data Connection on the Design A Form task pane, and then select Web Service. The three options at that point are

- **Receive Data** This creates a form with a data source based on the input and output parameters of the Web service. You can add nodes to the data source, but you cannot change the part of the data schema derived from the Web service (*queryFields* and *dataFields*) except by using the Convert Data Source command on the Tools menu (as described later in this chapter).
- **Submit Data** This creates a form with a data source based on the input parameters of the selected Web service method. You can add nodes to the data source, but you cannot change the part of the data schema derived from the Web service.
- **Receive And Submit Data** This creates a form with a data source based on the input parameters of the selected Web service method. You can add nodes to the data source, but you cannot change the part of the data schema derived from the Web service. InfoPath also creates a submit adapter and enables submit.

Chapter 2 presented a simple example showing how to create an InfoPath form that receives data from a Web service. That example uses the *NWorders* Web service written by Roger Jennings, author of *Introducing Microsoft Office InfoPath 2003 (Microsoft Learning)*.

Using a Web Service as a Data Connection to Receive Data

A Web service data connection can be used as a secondary data source. A common use for this is with a Web service available on your server that has data that can be used for user interface elements such as drop-down lists. You can also use a Web service data connection to receive data, much like a main data source. With InfoPath, you can add controls from a secondary data source to the form just as you can add controls from the main data source, and you can even use them as parameters to a Submit Data Web service data connection. Adding your Web service method as a secondary data source lets you maintain full control over the schema of the main data source. It also lets you add multiple Web service methods to receive data for your template.

To add a data connection to receive data from a Web service, choose Data Connections from the Tools menu, click Add, select Receive Data, click Next, select Web Service, click Next, and then configure the parameters to your Web service. Note that one of the receive data options in the Data Connection Wizard is SharePoint Library Or List. This is a specialized Web service data adapter covered in Chapter 9.

Note Web service data connections are covered by domain security rules. For more information on domain security, see the section titled "Cross-Domain Rules for Calling Web Services" later in this chapter. For more information on security in general, see Chapter 8.

Using Buttons to Query from and Submit to a Data Connection

You can call a Web service method without writing any code by using a data connection and a button. All you do is add a Button control to your form and then change the action in the Button Properties dialog box. There are five actions you can take, and the right one depends on the type of data connection and result you want. The actions are Query, Refresh, Submit, Rules, and Custom Code.

Query

The Query action is available if the main data source of your form is based on a Web service or database data connection. It requeries the main data connection. It does not have any effect on secondary data connections.

Refresh

The Refresh action is available if your form has a secondary receive data connection. You can select which data source to requery, or you can select to refresh all secondary data sources at once.

Submit

The Submit action is available if your form has submit enabled. A form can have only one Submit action. If you choose the Submit action, changing the action parameters changes the form's global *Submit* parameters. If you want multiple buttons, each of which submits to a different data connection, you must use Rules or Custom Code instead. If multiple buttons are all set to submit, each of the buttons will do the same thing.

Rules

If you select the Rules And Custom Code action and then click Rules, you can submit to any data connection. This allows you to have multiple buttons on your form, each one submitting to a different data connection. You can add multiple actions so that a single button can query or submit to one or more data connections. You can also add conditions to the actions to enforce workflow or otherwise control the action.

Custom Code

If you select Rules And Custom Code as the action and then click Edit Form Code, you can have the button call your own method in the form code to modify and call any data connection. If you have both rules and form code, rules run first.

Using UDDI

UDDI is a tool for locating Web services. This is a good way to discover some of the many services available, including bank rate services, weather services, and mapping services. If you do not know the URL of the Web service you wish to use, you can click the Search UDDI button on the Web Service Details page of the Data Connection Wizard. This will open the Search Web Service dialog box, shown in Figure 7-2, where you can search a UDDI server. Once you select a Web service from the Search Web Service dialog box, InfoPath will fill in the location of the Web service in the Data Connection Wizard.

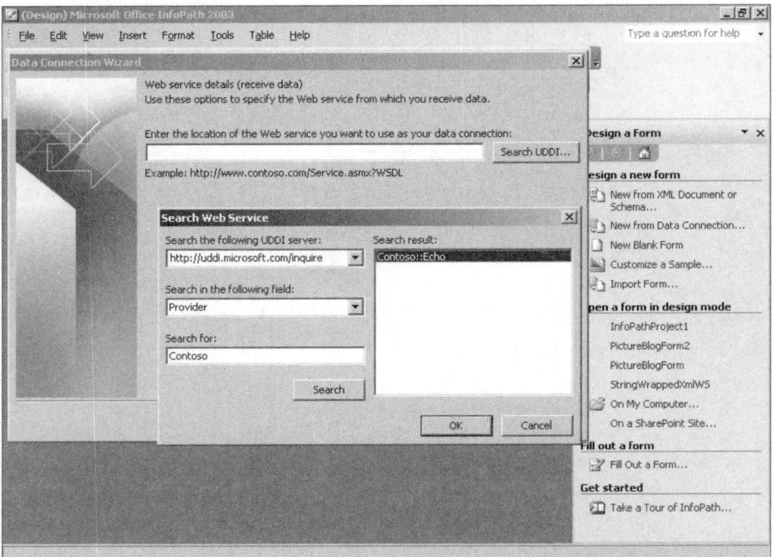

Figure 7-2 Searching for a Web service using UDDI

Using a Web Service as a Data Connection to Submit Data

Using a data connection to submit data to a Web service is a powerful technique. The difference between a submit data connection and a receive data connection is that InfoPath provides automatic mapping between the fields used in your form (both the main data source and other receive data connections) and the parameters sent to the Web service. The next few examples will demonstrate the options for mapping values to a Web service, all combined into a single PictureBlog Web service and InfoPath template.

Note Many of the options for the submit Web service are new in InfoPath SP1. A number of articles online describe ways of achieving this functionality with the original release version of InfoPath, but those techniques are not needed with SP1.

PictureBlog Schema

Mobile road warriors have a plethora of form options—customer visits, interview feedback, property appraisal, insurance claim, medical diagnosis, etc. For the submit Web service examples, we'll use a schema for a mobile weblog, or blog. Imagine you're on vacation and you want to upload some of the pictures you are taking to your database at home—but the Hawaiian hotel you are staying at doesn't have a wireless network that extends to the beach where you are sipping your Mai Tai and taking snapshots of Junior's first surfing lesson. So you load the pictures into your InfoPath form with a few notes, dates, and locations, all to be submitted later, when back in range of the wireless network. Here's the schema for the PictureBlog form:

```
<xs:schema targetNamespace="http://schemas.infopathdev.com/sample/pictureblog"
 xmlns:pb="http://schemas.infopathdev.com/sample/pictureblog"
 xmlns:xs="http://www.w3.org/2001/XMLSchema"
 elementFormDefault="qualified"
 attributeFormDefault="unqualified">
  <xs:element name="PictureBlog">
    <xs:complexType>
      <xs:sequence>
        <xs:element name="Entry" minOccurs="0" maxOccurs="unbounded">
          <xs:complexType>
            <xs:sequence>"
              <xs:element name="Title" type="xs:string" />
              <xs:element name="Date" type="xs:date"/>
              <xs:element name="Time" type="xs:time"/>
              <xs:element name="Location" type="xs:string" />
              <xs:element name="Image" nillable="true"
               type="xs:base64Binary"/>
            </xs:sequence>
          </xs:complexType>
        </xs:element>
      </xs:sequence>
    </xs:complexType>
  </xs:element>
</xs:schema>
```

Save this file as **PictureBlog.xsd** or locate it in the companion content for this book. With this schema file, we'll create an InfoPath form with a Submit button to send the entire form to a Web service.

Creating the PictureBlog Submit Web Service

Launch Visual Studio. Create a new Visual Basic ASP.NET Web Service project. Set the location of the project to **http://localhost/PictureBlogService**. Click the Click Here To Switch To Code View link, and then add the following *Imports* statement and methods:

```
Imports System.Xml ' at the top of the file

' Add one entry and return the entry ID.
<WebMethod()> _
Public Function AddOneEntry(ByVal entryTitle As String, _
    ByVal entryDate As Date, _
    ByVal entryTime As Date, _
    ByVal entryLocation As String, _
    ByVal entryImage As Byte()) As String
```

```
    TraceRequestBody()
    Return AddOneEntryInternal(entryTitle, entryDate, entryTime, _
     entryLocation, entryImage)
End Function

' Add multiple entries.
<WebMethod()> _
Public Sub AddEntriesAsXml(ByVal entryXml As System.Xml.XmlNode)
    Dim nsmgr As XmlNamespaceManager
    Dim entryNodes As XmlNodeList

    TraceRequestBody()

    HttpContext.Current.Trace.Write("Root element in request is " & _
     entryXml.Name)

    nsmgr = New XmlNamespaceManager(entryXml.OwnerDocument.NameTable)
    nsmgr.AddNamespace("pb", _"
     "http://schemas.infopathdev.com/sample/pictureblog")
    ' Use recursive select as input data may have a wrapper node or two.
    entryNodes = entryXml.SelectNodes("//pb:Entry", nsmgr)

    HttpContext.Current.Trace.Write("Adding " & entryNodes.Count & _
     " entries.")

   ' Call the AddOneEntryInternal method for each entry.
    For Each node As XmlNode In entryNodes
        ' Manually break apart each node.
        Dim entryTitle As String
        Dim entryDate As Date
        Dim entryTime As Date
        Dim entryLocation As String
        Dim entryImage As Byte()
        Dim id as String

        entryTitle = node.SelectSingleNode"pb:Title", nsmgr).InnerText
        entryDate = Date.Parse(node.SelectSingleNode( _
         "pb:Date", nsmgr).InnerText)
        entryTime = Date.Parse(node.SelectSingleNode( _
         "pb:Time", nsmgr).InnerText)
        entryLocation = node.SelectSingleNode("pb:Location", nsmgr).InnerText
        entryImage = Convert.FromBase64String( _
         node.SelectSingleNode("pb:Image", nsmgr).InnerText)

        id = AddOneEntryInternal(entryTitle, entryDate, entryTime, _
         entryLocation, entryImage)
        HttpContext.Current.Trace.Write("Entry ID", id)
    Next
End Sub
```

```
' Add multiple entries.
<WebMethod()> _
Public Sub AddEntriesAsXmlString(ByVal entryXmlString As String)
    Dim xmlDoc As XmlDocument

    ' Do processing such as signature validation here.

    xmlDoc = New XmlDocument
    xmlDoc.LoadXml(entryXmlString)
    AddEntriesAsXml(xmlDoc.DocumentElement)
End Sub


' Write HTTP Request body to trace output for debugging.
Private Sub TraceRequestBody()
    HttpContext.Current.Request.InputStream.Seek(0, IO.SeekOrigin.Begin)
    Dim sr As System.IO.StreamReader
    sr = New System.IO.StreamReader(HttpContext.Current.Request.InputStream)
    HttpContext.Current.Trace.Write("Request Body", sr.ReadToEnd())
End Sub

' Fake entry processing: just write values to trace log.
Private Function AddOneEntryInternal(ByVal entryTitle As String, _
    ByVal entryDate As Date, _
    ByVal entryTime As Date, _
    ByVal entryLocation As String, _
    ByVal entryImage As Byte())

    Dim traceContext As System.Web.TraceContext
    traceContext = HttpContext.Current.Trace
    traceContext.Write("Title: " & entryTitle)
    traceContext.Write("Date: " & entryDate)
    traceContext.Write("Time: " & entryTime.TimeOfDay.ToString())
    traceContext.Write("Location: " & entryLocation)
    If (entryImage Is Nothing) Then
        traceContext.Write("Image size (bytes): no image")
    Else
        traceContext.Write("Image size (bytes): " & entryImage.Length)
    End If

   ' return fake entry ID
   Return "1234"
End Function
```

Press F5 to build the Web service and see the URL and documentation.

> **Tip** To install ASP.NET, install the .NET Framework. In certain situations, ASP.NET is not fully installed. If you encounter unexpected problems with an ASP.NET Web service, you can quickly reinstall ASP.NET by running **%WINDIR%\Microsoft.NET\Framework\v1.1.4322\aspnet_regiis.exe –i** in a command prompt.

You now have a Web service with three methods: *AddOneEntry*, which takes all the parameters to create one entry; *AddEntriesAsXml*, which takes any XML node, searches for entries in the XML, and then adds each one it finds; and *AddEntriesAsXmlString*, which takes a string, converts it to an XML node, and calls *AddEntriesAsXml*. All of these methods call *AddEntryInternal*, which uses the ASP.NET trace mechanism to write some debugging information. In a real application, *AddEntryInternal* would do something useful with the data.

The Web service can do any middle-tier task with the data. This can include verifying permissions with Windows Integrated Authentication, running calculations on the data, submitting data to multiple databases, submitting the data to SharePoint using WebDAV or the SharePoint server-side class library, logging events, and sending e-mail.

Creating the PictureBlog Form

Now you will build the InfoPath form to connect to the Web service.

Design a new form, choosing New From XML Document Or Schema. Use the PictureBlog.xsd file that we created earlier. In the Data Source task pane, and drag and drop the *Entry* node into the view, and then choose Repeating Section With Controls from the shortcut menu that appears.

You now have a basic form with the essential elements of the schema. The next step is to connect it to the Web service.

Using the Parameterized Function as a Submit Adapter

1. Choose Data Connections from the Tools menu, and then click Add.
2. In the Data Connection Wizard, select Submit Data, and then click Next.
3. Select To A Web Service, and then click Next.
4. Enter the URL to your new Web service. If you use the name suggested earlier, the URL will be *http://localhost/PictureBlogService/Service1.asmx.*
5. Click Next. A list of methods (operations) in the Web service is displayed.
6. Select AddOneEntry, and then click Next. The parameters for the selected method are displayed. Each parameter must be mapped.
7. Select the *entryTitle* parameter, click the Modify icon to the right of the Field Or Group text box, expand the main data source, select *Title*, and then click OK.

8. Repeat the process for each parameter, mapping *entryTitle* to *Title*, *entryDate* to *Date*, *entryTime* to *Time*, *entryLocation* to *Location*, and *entryImage* to *Image*. Leave the Include drop-down list set to Text And Child Elements Only for each element. The dialog box will look like that shown in Figure 7-3.

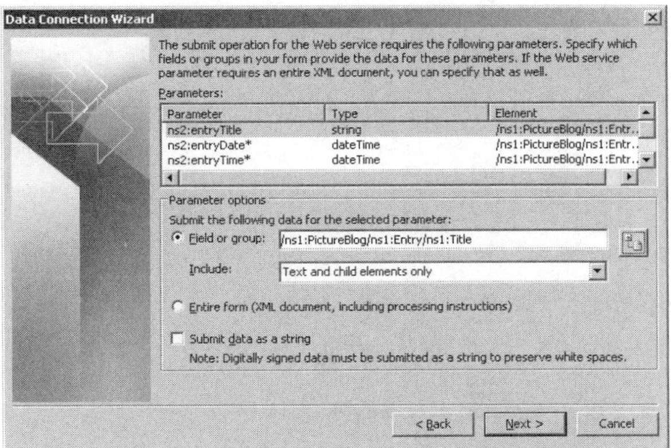

Figure 7-3 Mapping the data for parameters of a submit Web service data adapter

9. Click Next to complete the mapping.
10. Change the name of the data connection to **AddOneEntry**, click Finish, and then click Close.
11. From the Controls task pane, drag and drop a button into the view below the repeating table.
12. Right-click on the button, and then choose Button Properties.
13. In the Button Properties dialog box, change the label to **AddOneEntry**.
14. Click Rules, click Add, and then click Add Action.
15. In the Action drop-down list, select Submit Using A Data Connection.
16. In the Data Connection drop-down list, ensure that AddOneEntry is selected, as shown in Figure 7-4.
17. Click OK four times to close the open dialog boxes.

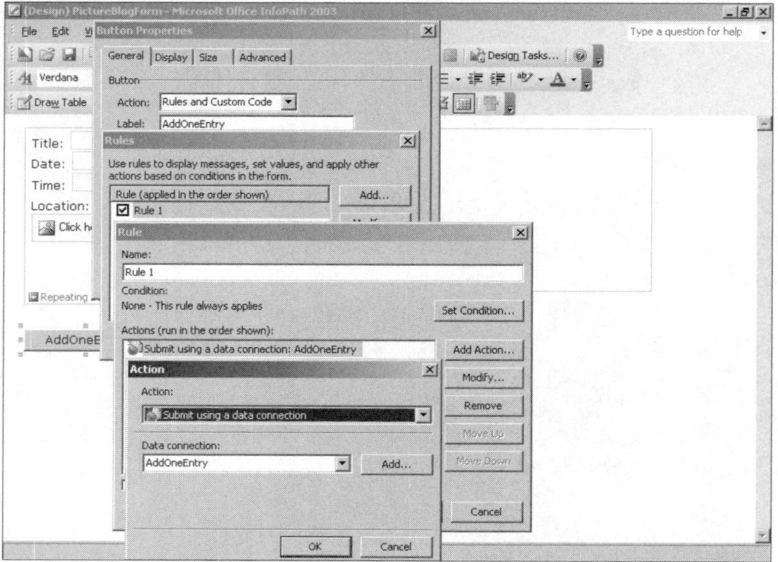

Figure 7-4 Setting the action of a button to submit to the AddOneEntry data connection

You have connected the PictureBlog form to the PictureBlog Web service. Test the data connection by previewing the form, entering data for one entry, and then clicking AddOneEntry. The submission should succeed silently. You can add more rules to the button or use code to add a dialog box message on successful submit.

To view what happened on your Web service, go to trace.axd in the application folder of your Web service (e.g., *http://localhost/PictureBlogService/trace.axd*). Click the View Details link on the most recent trace entry, and then read the trace information. It should contain the title and other values you entered when you submitted the form, as shown in Figure 7-5.

Important The PictureBlog Web service uses the trace mechanism in ASP.NET. To enable tracing, edit the web.config file in the same folder as your Web service (e.g., *C:\Inetpub\wwwroot\ PictureBlogService\Web.config*) and then modify it so there is a *configuration/system.web/trace* node with the *enabled* attribute set to *true*. The default web.config created by Visual Studio will have this node with the *enabled* attribute set to *false*; change it to **true**.

Once you have enabled tracing, you must resubmit your form to create a trace entry. To view the trace results, go to trace.axd in the same folder as your Web service.

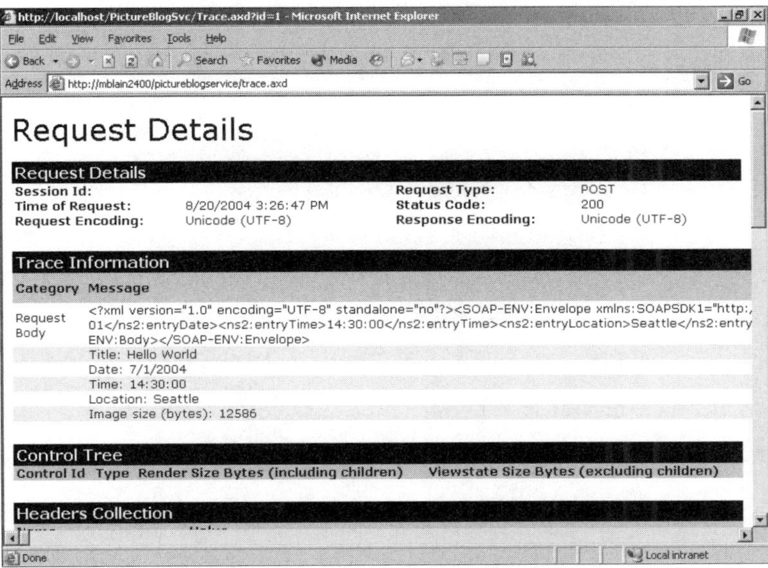

Figure 7-5 Viewing the trace results after calling the AddOneEntry Web service method

Here are the advantages of using a parameterized Web service method:

- Correct type information is propagated across the network.
- Types are deserialized automatically. (Note that the date and binary values are of the correct types.)
- The Web service specifies a strong type relationship for use in multiple clients.
- Loose coupling of InfoPath template schema and Web service.

Here are the disadvantages of using a parameterized Web service method:

- It is time consuming to set up a large mapping relationship.
- You do not have full control over the mapping: the connection we created in this section will fail if you try to submit more than one entry.

> **Note** Serialization is the process of converting a data structure into a "serial" form such as a stream or file of XML. The stream of data can then be saved to disk or transferred across a network. Serialization converts the object into a stream of data, and deserialization converts the stream of data back into an object.

Using the XML-Based Function as a Submit Adapter

Using the XML-based function as a submit adapter is similar to the previous procedure.

1. Open the Data Connections dialog box, and then add a new Submit Data To A Web Service data connection.
2. Enter the URL of your Web service, and then click Next.
3. Select the *AddEntriesAsXml* method, and then click Next.
4. For the *entryXml* parameter, select the *PictureBlog* node, select XML Subtree, Including Selected Element in the Include drop-down list, and then click Next.
5. Name the adapter **AddEntriesAsXml**, click Finish, and then click Close.
6. Add a new button to the view.
7. Change the button label to **AddEntriesAsXml**.
8. Click Rules, click Add, click Add Action, select Submit Using A Data Connection, and then select the AddEntriesAsXml data connection.
9. Click OK four times to close all open dialog boxes.

You now have a data connection that connects to the XML node–based Web service. Test the new data connection by previewing the form, creating an entry, clicking AddEntriesAsXML, and then looking at the results of the ASP.NET trace.

In this example, you selected the root node of the main data source, *PictureBlog*, to submit. You also changed the Include option to XML Subtree, Including Selected Element. This tells InfoPath to send the entire *PictureBlog* node, including the *PictureBlog* tag itself. You can also select to submit the entire form by selecting the Entire Form option. This wraps the entire XML of the form in an *IPDocument* node in the *http://schemas.microsoft.com/office/infopath/2003/dataFormSolution* namespace, including the processing instructions. This sample Web service can handle both forms by doing a recursive search on the submitted XML to look for the desired data. You can write a Web service to explicitly handle one form or the other.

Here are the advantages of using an XML node Web service method:

- Mapping within InfoPath is straightforward.
- A single Web service method can handle multiple XML schemas.

Here are the disadvantages of using an XML node Web service method:

- Strong typing is not enforced.
- Parsing of data must be done in code in the Web service.
- Tight coupling of InfoPath template schema and Web service: if one changes, the other must change too.

One way to combine the best aspects of XML node Web service methods and parameterized Web methods is to use a typed XML node. This is described later in the chapter.

Using the String-Wrapped XML-Based Function as a Submit Adapter

Using the string-wrapped XML-based function as a submit adapter is similar to the previous procedure.

1. Open the Data Connections dialog box, and then add a new Submit Data To A Web Service data connection.
2. Enter the URL of your Web service, and then click Next.
3. Select the *AddEntriesAsXmlString* method, and then click Next.
4. For the *entryXml* parameter, select Entire Form, select the Submit Data As A String check box, and then click Next
5. Name the adapter **AddEntriesAsXmlString**, click Finish, and then click Close.
6. Add a new button to the view.
7. Change the button label to **AddEntriesAsXmlString**.
8. Click Rules, click Add, Click Add Action, select Submit Using A Data Connection, and then select the AddEntriesAsXml data connection.
9. Click OK four times to close all open dialog boxes..

You now have a data connection that connects to the XML node–based Web service. Test the new data connection by previewing the form, creating an entry, clicking AddEntriesAsXml-String, and then looking at the results of the ASP.NET trace.

The sample Web service parses the string as XML and then calls the *AddEntriesAsXml* method. If you want to add additional code that relies on the string, such as code that verifies a digital signature, you can do so with the submitted string.

XML Data vs. Strings

If you are going to pass XML data to your Web service, does it make sense to have the Web service accept it as a string? In general, the answer is "no," for the following reasons:

- The Web service must validate the contents of the string to prevent clients from passing bogus XML—for example, "Hello, World!" and other poorly formed XML strings.
- Passing strings around requires extra steps to load them into XML documents to take advantage of the XML structure.
- InfoPath cannot parse Web services that return strings.

The crux of the problem is that string data is weakly typed. If your Web service is just a gatekeeper responsible for passing data through to a workflow process, weakly typed data (e.g., strings) might be sufficient, but for Web services that will do real work on the data, you'll want to send strongly typed XML data.

Using a Typed, Structured Web Service Method

Another way to work with a Web service is to pass typed XML data across the network. One pattern is to use the same schema in your InfoPath template as in the Web service and pass the entire document in either direction. Let's add this functionality to the PictureBlog Web service. Visual Studio .NET ships with an SDK that includes an xsd.exe tool that creates a class definition based on an XML schema. We will use this tool to create a class that can serialize and deserialize to the same schema the form uses.

Adding a Typed, Structured Web Service Method

1. Launch a Visual Studio .NET command prompt.
2. Change to the directory containing the PictureBlog.xsd file.
3. Run the command **xsd.exe /c /language:VB PictureBlog.xsd**. This generates a file named PictureBlog.vb containing the class definition corresponding to the PictureBlog schema.
4. Add the PictureBlog.vb file to your PictureBlogService Visual Basic project, by choosing Add Existing Item from the Project menu, locating and selecting the PictureBlog.vb file, and then clicking Open.
5. Add the following method to the service1.asmx.vb file just above the *End Class* statement:

```
<WebMethod()> _
Public Sub AddEntriesAsPictureBlog(ByVal entries As PictureBlog)
    TraceRequestBody()

    HttpContext.Current.Trace.Write("Adding " & entries.Entry.Length & _
        " entries.")

    ' Call the AddOneEntryInternal method for each entry.
    For Each entry As PictureBlogEntry In entries.Entry
        AddOneEntryInternal(entry.Title, entry.Date, entry.Time, _
            entry.Location, entry.Image)
        HttpContext.Current.Trace.Write("---")
    Next
End Sub
```

6. Save and recompile your Web service. You now have a new *AddEntriesAsPictureBlog* method that takes typed XML.
7. Design the PictureBlog form.
8. Open the Data Connections dialog box, and then add a new Submit To A Web Service data connection.
9. Enter the URL of your Web service, and then click Next.
10. Select the *AddEntriesAsPictureBlog* method, and then click Next.
11. For the *entries* parameter, select the *PictureBlog* node, leave the Include drop-down list set to Text And Child Elements Only, and then click Next.

> **Caution** It might seem counterintuitive to include text and child elements only and not select XML Subtree, Including The Selected Element. However, the Web service definition for the *AddEntriesAsPictureBlog* operation includes the definition of the root node itself. If you include the selected element, InfoPath will wrap the node twice and the deserialization will fail.

12. Name the adapter **AddEntriesAsPictureBlog**, click Finish, and then click Close.
13. Add a new button to the view.
14. Change the button label to **AddEntriesAsPictureBlog**.
15. Click Rules, click Add, click Add Action, select the Submit Using A Data Connection, and then select the AddEntriesAsPictureBlog data connection.
16. Click OK four times to close all open dialog boxes.

Now you have created a very powerful combination—the form and Web service speak the same "language." The main disadvantage here is the tight coupling between schemas. If the schema of the template changes, you must either change the Web service or write an adapter layer in the InfoPath template or the Web service.

ADO.NET Dataset Integration

InfoPath supports ADO.NET datasets transmitted over a Web service, including support for DiffGrams. (A DiffGram is an XML format that describes an ADO.NET dataset, including updates, insertions, and deletions made to the dataset.) To use this, your Web service should implement a method that returns a dataset, and a method that takes a dataset as an input parameter. You then use those methods for a receive data connection and a submit data connection. The simplest form of these methods is shown here. These methods are in a class with an instance of a data adapter called *MyDataAdapter1* and in a project with a generated dataset class of type *MyDataSet*. The full source code for this example is included as part of the companion content for this book.

```
<WebMethod()> _
Public Function GetDataSet() As MyDataSet
    Dim ds As MyDataSet
    ds = New MyDataSet
    myDataAdapter1.Fill(ds)
    Return ds
End Function

<WebMethod()> _
Public Sub UpdateDataSet(ByVal ds As MyDataSet)
    myDataAdapter1.Update(ds)
End Sub
```

You can use these methods much like any other Web service method. For example, you can create a form to receive and submit data to this Web service. To connect the submit adapter to the Web service, select the group *myFields/dataFields/s0:GetDataSetResponse/GetDataSetResult/ns1:DataSet1*. The default options of including the Text And Child Elements Only is correct.

InfoPath uses the schema information in the dataset to manage relationships, constraints, read-only columns, and auto-increment columns.

You can also create a form based on a submit data connection without a corresponding receive. If the Web service method takes a typed dataset as a parameter, InfoPath creates a template that lets you add new items to the dataset read by the Web service method.

InfoPath does not support displaying more than one dataset at a time. It also does not support *DeleteRule* and *UpdateRule* properties, and copying and pasting nested datasets may generate unexpected relationships.

Using Web Service Data Connections in Code

You can extend the functionality beyond what the InfoPath designer supports for Web services by using code. For example, you can submit to a Web service by setting the parameters in code instead of letting InfoPath map the values. To do this, you create a receive data adapter, update the query parameters by using code, and then call *Query*. Here is an example of using this to call the PictureBlog Web service used earlier in this chapter.

Calling the PictureBlog Web Service from Code in InfoPath

1. Launch Visual Studio. Create a new Visual Basic InfoPath Form Template project named **AddPictureBlogEntry**.
2. Choose Open InfoPath from the Project menu.
3. In InfoPath, choose Data Connections from the Tools menu.
4. Click Add, select Receive Data, and then click Next.
5. Select Web Service, and then click Next.
6. Enter the URL to the PictureBlog Web service (e.g., *http://localhost/PictureBlogService/Service1.asmx*), and then click Next.
7. Select the AddOneEntry operation, and then click Next.
8. Click Next, leaving the parameters values blank.
9. Deselect the Automatically Retrieve Data When Form Is Opened check box, change the name for the data connection to **AddOneEntryReceive**, click Finish, and then click Close.
10. Switch to Visual Studio. A dialog box appears asking if you want to automatically update expressions. Click Yes.

11. Switch to InfoPath.
12. In the Controls task pane, drag and drop a Picture control in the view. When the Insert Picture Control dialog box appears, select Included In The Form and then click OK.
13. Insert a Button in the view.
14. Right-click on the button, and then choose Button Properties.
15. Change the button label to **Create Entry**, and then click Edit Form Code.
16. Add the following method to form code just above the *End Class* statement:

```
' Create a PictureBlog entry with a dummy title, current date and
' time, and picture data from the form.
' Returns the ID of the created entry.
Private Function AddEntry() As String
    Dim dataObj As DataObject
    Dim dataDom As IXMLDOMDocument2
    Dim nodeImage As IXMLDOMNode
    Dim nodeEntry As IXMLDOMNode
    Dim nodeResult As IXMLDOMNode
    Dim dateString As String

    ' Get current date time. Format s = 2000-08-17T23:32:32.
    dateString = DateTime.Now.ToString("s")
    ' Get image from user's entry.
    nodeImage = thisXDocument.DOM.selectSingleNode("//my:field1")

    dataObj = thisXDocument.DataObjects("AddOneEntryReceive")
    ' Cast the DOM to a DOMDocument2 to access setProperty.
    dataDom = dataObj.DOM
    dataDom.setProperty("SelectionLanguage", "XPath")
    dataDom.setProperty("SelectionNamespaces", _
     "xmlns:dfs=""" & _
     "http://schemas.microsoft.com/office/infopath/2003/dataFormSolution" & _
     """ xmlns:s0=""http://tempuri.org/PictureBlogService/Service1""")

    ' Select the query parameters of the Web service.
    nodeEntry = dataObj.DOM.selectSingleNode( _
     "/dfs:myFields/dfs:queryFields/s0:AddOneEntry")
    ' Assign values to each relevant parameter.
    nodeEntry.selectSingleNode("s0:entryTitle").text = "Autogenerated entry"
    nodeEntry.selectSingleNode("s0:entryDate").text = dateString.Split("T")(0)
    nodeEntry.selectSingleNode("s0:entryTime").text = dateString.Split("T")(1)
    nodeEntry.selectSingleNode("s0:entryImage").text = nodeImage.text

    ' Call the Web service method.
    dataObj.Query()

    ' Get the result from the Web service.
    nodeResult = dataObj.DOM.selectSingleNode( _
     "/dfs:myFields/dfs:dataFields/s0:AddOneEntryResponse/" & _
     "s0:AddOneEntryResult")

    Return nodeResult.text
End Function
```

17. If your Web service uses a namespace other than *http://tempuri.org/PictureBlogService/Service1*, be sure to update the definition of the *s0* namespace prefix in the above method. The namespace used here is what Visual Studio and ASP.NET autogenerate if your project is called PictureBlogService and you use the autogenerated service1.asmx file. You can see the namespace required by right-clicking on the node in the Data Source task pane in InfoPath.

18. Add the following code in the button event handler to call the above method:

```
Dim entryId As String
entryId = AddEntry()
thisXDocument.UI.Alert("Created entry " & entryId)
```

19. Save the form code, and press F5 to preview the form.

20. Add a picture, and then click the Create Entry button. You should get a message with the entry ID created, and you can view the trace information from the Web service to verify that you called it correctly.

This example demonstrates how to access the parameters and return values of a Web service adapter through code. Note that you need to set the selection namespace property on the data adapter DOM to correctly select the node. In addition to setting the text values of nodes, you can insert entire XML nodes into the query parameters. You can display the return values from this call directly in your view by binding controls to the *dataFields* nodes in the data source for this data connection.

The Return Value of a Web Service Submit Data Connection

There are two types of Web service data connections: receive and submit. At the beginning of this chapter, you learned how to create a submit data connection through the InfoPath designer UI, letting InfoPath map the values from your primary data source into the parameters of the Web service method. In the previous section, you learned how to use code and a receive data connection to submit and receive data. You can also use code to read the value returned by a submit data connection. The *OutputLocation* property of the *WebServiceAdapter* object contains the XML returned by the Web service wrapped in the same way InfoPath wraps the return value of a receive Web service data connection.

The following function, added to the PictureBlog form, submits using the AddOneEntry data connection and returns the *ID* of the entry created.

```
Public Function AddOneEntryWithSubmitAdapter() As String
    Dim dataObj As WebServiceAdapter2
    Dim domReturn As IXMLDOMDocument2
    Dim nodeReturn As IXMLDOMNode
    Dim nodeResult As IXMLDOMNode

    dataObj = thisXDocument.DataAdapters("AddOneEntry")
    dataObj.Submit()
    nodeReturn = dataObj.OutputLocation
```

```
    ' Set namespace properties on return DOM so we can select result.
    domReturn = nodeReturn.ownerDocument
    domReturn.setProperty("SelectionLanguage", "XPath")
    domReturn.setProperty("SelectionNamespaces", _
     "xmlns:dfs=""" & _
     "http://schemas.microsoft.com/office/infopath/2003/dataFormSolution" & _
     """ xmlns:s0=""http://tempuri.org/PictureBlogService/Service1""")

    ' Get the result from the Web service.
    nodeResult = nodeReturn.selectSingleNode( _
     "/dfs:dataFields/s0:AddOneEntryResponse/" & _
     "s0:AddOneEntryResult")

    Return nodeResult.text
End Function
```

You will notice a few differences between the *AddOneEntryWithSubmitAdapter* method and the *AddEntry* method of the AddPictureBlogEntry form template:

- *AddOneEntryWithSubmitAdapter* uses the *XDocument.DataAdapters* connection instead of the *DataObjects* connection.
- Because *AddOneEntryWithSubmitAdapter* uses a submit connection, the submit parameters are set automatically by InfoPath based on the mapping established when the data connection was created.
- *AddOneEntryWithSubmitAdapter* gets the result from the *OutputLocation* property of the data adapter.
- The XPath to the actual result node starts at the *dfs:dataFields* node because the output is not wrapped in the *dfs:myFields* node, as in a submit data connection.

Error Handling

If you want to trap the errors returned by InfoPath and handle them yourself, call submit using code instead of using rules, and then wrap the submit call in a *Try...Catch* block. In code, using the .NET Framework, the exception is a *System.Runtime.InteropServices.COMException* with an error code of *0x80043032*. If you are using script, the exception will be numbered *0x80043032*, or *-2147209166* decimal. You can parse the exception message to get more information. You can also parse the XML SOAP response by looking at the *ErrorsLocation* property of the *DataAdapter* object.

Note The *ErrorsLocation* and *OutputLocation* properties of a *DataAdapter* are not cleared when Query is called; they are set only when values are returned.

Another technique to get more detailed exception information is to use .NET Web references in place of the InfoPath Web service adapter. If you do that, you can trap the .NET exceptions instead of the InfoPath wrapped exceptions.

Rebinding a Web Service

Two common events require you to change a Web service data connection. One is a change in the interface to the service interface, and other is a change to the service URL. The interface to a service might change during development, and updating the form to match the new interface should be considered a development task. Once a service is finished, the interface should not change.

You might work with a Web service that has multiple potential endpoints. For example, you might have a test Web service and a production Web service that expose the same interface and functionality but have different URLs and different underlying data. In this section, you will learn how to update your form at design time to a different interface, how to change to a different URL for the same interface by editing the manifest.xsf file, and how to change to a different URL for the same interface at run time by using code.

Updating Data Connection Web Service Binding in the Designer

You can update any data source through the Data Connections Wizard. This refreshes the connection, which can be used in a number of scenarios: changing the entire Web service being used to a different one, refreshing the description of a Web service under development, and changing the endpoint of the Web service.

To do this, edit your form template, and then choose Data Connections from the Tools menu. Select the data connection you want to update. If you created your form to receive data from a Web service, the data connection will be called "Main query" by default. If you created your form to send data to a Web service, the corresponding data connection will be called "Main submit" by default. Go through the rest of the Data Connection Wizard, editing parameters such as the URL as necessary.

If the interface of the Web service you are connecting to has changed parameters, you might need to update the data bindings. InfoPath will try to update the binding for you, but it cannot map all changes. You must verify both the binding of controls in each view and the binding of the submit data connection. To rebind the submit data connection, go through the Data Connection Wizard for the submit connection and verify all of the parameters.

Tip If you are changing both the submit data connection and the receive data connection, update the receive data connection first. Otherwise, you will need to update the submit data connection twice in case the receive data connection parameters changed.

You can also use the Convert Main Data Source feature (choose Convert Main Data Source from the Tools menu) to do the same thing, but only with the main data source.

Updating Data Connection Web Service URL Binding in the Manifest

If the only aspect of the Web service that has changed is the URL, you can change it in the manifest. Extract the form files, and edit the manifest.xsf file in a text editor. For every Web service adapter in your form, you will find an *xsf:webServiceAdapter* node. Here is the definition of a Web service adapter that submits to the *AddEntriesAsXml* method of the PictureBlog Web service running on the local computer.

```
<xsf:webServiceAdapter wsdlUrl="http://localhost/PictureBlogService/Service1.asmx?WSDL"
queryAllowed="no" submitAllowed="yes" name="AddEntriesAsXml">
    <xsf:operation name="AddEntriesAsXml" soapAction="http://tempuri.org/PictureBlogService/
        Service1/AddEntriesAsXml" serviceUrl="http://localhost/PictureBlogService/
        Service1.asmx">
        <xsf:input source="Submit.xml">
            <xsf:partFragment match="/dfs:myFields/dfs:dataFields/ns2:AddEntriesAsXml/
                ns2:entryXml" replaceWith="/ns1:PictureBlog" filter="."></xsf:partFragment>
        </xsf:input>
   </xsf:operation>
</xsf:webServiceAdapter>
```

To change the URL, change the *serviceUrl* attribute of the *xsf:operation* node.

Note The *xsf:webServiceAdapter* node can be found in one of four places in the manifest.xsf file. The main query adapter is inside the *xsf:query* node. The main submit adapter is inside the *xsf:submit* node. Secondary data sources (retrieve data connections) are inside the *xsf:dataObjects* node. Secondary data sources (submit data connections) are inside the *xsf:dataAdapters* node.

Because the example uses *http://localhost*, it attempts to connect to the machine where the form is opened, so it probably won't work for anyone except the original developer. The URL must be changed to the absolute URL of the Web service.

Changing the Submit Parameter Mapping in the Manifest

In addition to the *serviceUrl* attribute in the manifest.xsf file, you can change the submit parameter mapping. This is particularly useful if you want to change something that cannot be changed in the Data Connection Wizard. For example, in the *AddOneEntry* adapter in the PictureBlog form template, the *Title* parameter is mapped like this:

```
<xsf:partFragment
 match="/dfs:myFields/dfs:dataFields/ns2:AddOneEntry/ns2:entryTitle"
 replaceWith="/ns1:PictureBlog/ns1:Entry/ns1:Title">
</xsf:partFragment>
```

This selects the title of the first entry in the form if there are multiple entries. If you want to change it to the title of the last entry, you can change the XPath of the *replaceWith* attribute so the selected *Entry* is the last one using *position()=last()*. The resulting *xsf:partFragment* node will look like this:

```
<xsf:partFragment
 match="/dfs:myFields/dfs:dataFields/ns2:AddOneEntry/ns2:entryTitle"
 replaceWith="/ns1:PictureBlog/ns1:Entry[position()=last()]/ns1:Title">
</xsf:partFragment>
```

Don't forget to change all the other parameters of the Web service to match. Other properties of the data connection, such as *soapAction*, can be changed directly in the manifest.xsf file. However, using the Data Connection Wizard, where possible, is the safest way to change these parameters.

Updating Data Connection Web Service URL Binding with Code

You might have a form template that is deployed to multiple locations, such as a test server and a production server. If you want to avoid making changes in the designer at deployment time, you can modify the Web service URL in code. The properties of the *xsf:operation* node are available at run time. The following method can be called from the *OnLoad* event handler to rebind the Web service to a URL on the same server as the publish URL.

```
' Change the service URL for the adapter specified by adapterName
' to the Solution URL + the specified relative URL
Private Sub RebindSubmitAdapter(ByVal adapterName As String, _
                                ByVal webserviceRelativeUrl As String)
    Dim solutionUrl As Uri
    Dim webserviceUrl As Uri
    Dim adapter As WebServiceAdapter2
    Dim xmlOperation As IXMLDOMDocument2
    Dim nodeServiceUrl As IXMLDOMNode

    ' calculate the new URL
    solutionUrl = New Uri(thisXDocument.Solution.URI)
    webserviceUrl = New Uri(solutionUrl, webserviceRelativeUrl)

    ' get the data adapter
    adapter = thisXDocument.DataAdapters(adapterName)

    ' get the operation from the data adapter
    ' this is the manifest's xsf:operation node minus child nodes.
    xmlOperation = thisXDocument.CreateDOM()
    xmlOperation.validateOnParse = False
    xmlOperation.loadXML(adapter.Operation)

    ' change the service URL to the new URL
    nodeServiceUrl = _
     xmlOperation.documentElement.selectSingleNode("@serviceUrl")
    nodeServiceUrl.text = webserviceUrl.AbsoluteUri
```

```
    ' save the operation back to the data adapter
    adapter.Operation = xmlOperation.xml
End Sub
```

In your *OnLoad* event handler, call the method like this: *RebindSubmitAdapter("Submit", "/path/to/webservice.asmx")*. You can also pass in an absolute URL that you have calculated with some other mechanism as the second parameter to the *RebindSubmitAdapter* method.

Setting the Timeout When Calling a Web Service

Web services are calls to remote machines. Network speed is variable, and the processing time for a complex Web service might also be long. By default, the InfoPath Web service adapter times out after 30 seconds. You can change this value in your code. Call the following method in your *OnLoad* event handler or just before you query from or submit to a Web service.

```
Public Sub SetWSAdapterTimeout(ByVal adapterName As String, _
        ByVal seconds As Integer)
    Dim dataObj As DataObject
    Dim wsAdapter As WebServiceAdapter2

    dataObj = thisXDocument.DataObjects(adapterName)
    wsAdapter = dataObj.QueryAdapter

    wsAdapter.Timeout = seconds
End Sub
```

> **Tip** If your data connection is set to retrieve data every time the form is opened, you will not have a chance to set the timeout before the Web service is called. To fix this, first deselect the Automatically Retrieve Data When Form Is Opened check box in the Data Connection Wizard, then, in your *OnLoad* event handler, set the timeout value and call *Query* on the Web service adapter.

Unsupported Web Service Types

InfoPath can send and receive data to and from a wide variety of Web services, but not all types of Web services are supported. This section will discuss some aspects of Web services that are not directly supported in the designer and how to work around those issues.

RPC/Encoded Web Services

The SOAP protocol supports a number of binding styles. The built-in InfoPath Web Service Adapter supports only the document/literal style. If your Web service uses RPC/encoded or another style of binding, you have three options:

First, if you have full control over the Web service, you can generate a new binding using the tool you used to create your Web service.

Second, if you have access to a server, you can create a proxy Web service. The proxy wraps the RPC/encoded Web service and provides a document/literal Web service that the InfoPath designer can use. More information on creating a server-side proxy can be found at *http://msdn.microsoft.com/library/en-us/ipsdk/html/ipsdkRPCEncodingAndWebServices.asp*.

The third mechanism is to use a different client-side (InfoPath) data connection, such as the .NET Web service proxy. This is the most flexible and powerful mechanism and also the most complex to develop. It is covered in more detail later in this chapter.

Web Services That Return Untyped XML

Some Web services return untyped XML, such as a method that is defined to return *xsd:any*. If you know that the Web service always returns data of a particular known schema, you can use a technique similar to that shown in the next section to handle Web services that return XML wrapped in a string.

Web Services That Return XML in a String

Some Web services return XML in a string. This is the other side of the InfoPath feature to submit XML in a string. To use the data as XML, you parse it with code running in the form. Here is one way to create a form that does just that. This is a long procedure that uses a number of temporary files, but the end result is a single, clean template with Visual Basic code-behind. The companion content for this book contains a sample DateTimeWebService that includes a method that returns XML as a string.

Unwrapping an XML String

The form template you are about to create is a temporary template to get a snapshot of the data returned by the Web service.

1. Launch InfoPath, and then choose Design A Form from the File menu.
2. Click New From Data Connection.
3. In the Data Connection Wizard, select Web Service and then click Next.
4. Select Receive Data, and then click Next.
5. Enter the URL to the Web service. If you have installed DateTimeWebService from the companion content on your local machine, the URL will be *http://localhost/DateTimeWebService/DateTimeLiteral.asmx*. Click Next.
6. Select the *GetDateAndTimeAsXmlString* operation, click Next, and then click Finish.

   If your Web service does not have input parameters, skip the next step.
7. Drag and drop the *queryFields* node into the view on top of the “Drag query fields here” placeholder text. When the shortcut menu appears, select Section With Controls.

8. Drag and drop the *dataFields* node into the view on top of the "Drag data fields here" placeholder text. When the shortcut menu appears, select Section With Controls.
9. Preview the form.
10. Click Run Query. All of the data returned from the Web service is displayed in the one bound text box in the *dataFields* section of the form.
11. Select all of the returned text in the Get Date And Time As XML String Result text box, and then copy it.
12. Launch your text editor, and then paste the text into it.
13. Save the resulting XML file to your hard drive, naming it **DateTime.xml**.

    The XML returned by the Web service might contain information about the encoding used by the Web service. Once the .xml file is displayed in InfoPath, Windows will convert everything to Unicode. If you save the .xml file in a text editor, be sure to either save the file using the encoding specified in the XML or delete the encoding. For example, if you are using Notepad as your text editor and the XML has a *<?xml version="1.0" encoding="utf-16"?>* processing instruction, you can remove the *encoding="utf-16"* attribute or you can make sure the Unicode is selected in the Encoding drop-down list in the Save As dialog box.
14. Close the text editor. You now have an XML file that represents a sample snapshot of the data returned by the Web service. This file is temporary and is needed only for the next several steps.
15. Close the preview, and then close the form template. You do not need to save the template.
16. Launch InfoPath, and choose Design A Form from the File menu.
17. Click New From XML Document Or Schema.
18. In the Data Source Wizard, enter the path to the DateTime.xml file you saved, click Next, and then click Finish.
19. When prompted about whether to use the values in the .xml file as the default data in the form, click No. You now have a form that is based on the structure of the data returned by the Web service. However, the new form does not have a connection to the Web service. We will add the connection back as a secondary data connection.
20. Choose Data Connections from the Tools menu, and then click Add.
21. In the Data Connections Wizard, select Receive Data and then click Next.
22. Select Web Service, and then click Next.
23. Enter the URL to the Web service. This will be the same URL that you used before (*http://localhost/DateTimeWebService/DateTimeLiteral.asmx*). Click Next.

24. Select the same operation that you selected before (*GetDateAndTimeAsXmlString*), and then click Next.
25. Deselect the Automatically Retrieve Data When Form Is Opened check box, click Finish, and then click Close. You now have a template with a schema that matches the unwrapped string returned by the data connection, and a secondary data connection that has the parameters of, and a connection to, the Web service. The next step is to hook the two together. We will do this using Visual Basic .NET. The same technique can also be used with script.
26. Save the form template with a temporary name, and then close InfoPath. This form template will be used to build the Visual Basic version of the template.
27. Launch Visual Studio.
28. Create a new Visual Basic InfoPath Form Template project. This will be the final product of this exercise. Name the form **DateTime**.
29. In the Microsoft Office Project Wizard, select Open Existing Form Template, click Browse, locate and select the temporary form template you saved earlier, and then click Open
30. Click Finish, and then click OK. If your Web service does not have input parameters, skip the next four steps.
31. In the InfoPath designer, choose Data Source from the View menu.
32. In the Data Source task pane, select your secondary data connection from the Data Source drop-down list.
33. Drag and drop the *queryFields* node into the view. When the shortcut menu appears, choose Section With Controls.
34. Select Main from the Data Source drop-down list.
35. Add the fields into the view.
36. Open the Controls task pane, and then add a button to the view.
37. Right-click on the button, and choose Button Properties.
38. Change the label to **Query**.
39. Click Edit Form Code. Focus will return to Visual Studio.
40. Add the following method to your form code just above the *End Class* statement:

```
Public Sub XmlStringToData(ByVal adapterName As String, _
                           ByVal nodeDest As IXMLDOMNode, _
                           ByVal replace As Boolean)
    Dim dataObj As DataObject
    Dim dataDOM As IXMLDOMDocument2
    Dim xml As IXMLDOMDocument2
    Dim node As IXMLDOMNode
    Dim nodeClone as IXMLDOMNode
```

```
    dataObj = thisXDocument.DataObjects("GetDateAndTimeAsXmlString")
    xml = thisXDocument.CreateDOM()

    ' Run the query.
    dataObj.Query()

    ' Parse the results as XML.
    ' Use IXMLDOMDocument2 to call setProperty.
    dataDOM = dataObj.DOM
    dataDOM.setProperty("SelectionNamespaces", "xmlns:dfs=" & _
     """http://schemas.microsoft.com/office/infopath/2003/dataFormSolution""")

    ' We are assuming that the entire results are a simple string
    ' stored in the grandchild of the dataFields node.
    node = dataDOM.documentElement.selectSingleNode( _
     "/dfs:myFields/dfs:dataFields/node()/node()")
    xml.loadXML(node.text)

    ' Copy the values into the destination data source.
    ' You could also perform an XSL or other transform at this point.
    ' If replace is true, this will replace nodeDest with the new values.
    ' Otherwise this will add the new values as children of nodeDest.
    nodeClone = xml.documentElement.cloneNode(True)
    If (replace) Then
        nodeDest.parentNode.replaceChild(nodeClone, nodeDest)
    Else
        nodeDest.appendChild(nodeClone)
    End If
End Sub
```

41. Add the following method call in the button *OnClick* event handler:

    ```
    XmlStringToData("DateTime", thisXDocument.DOM.documentElement, True)
    ```

    The name of the data adapter is case-sensitive. You can copy and paste the value from the Data Connection Wizard or directly from the name attribute of the *xsf:dataObject* in the manifest.

42. Save your project, build it, and then test it.

You now have a complete form that connects to a Web service using the standard InfoPath data connection, transforms the data into XML, and updates the main data source. You can extend this technique for a number of similar situations. You can have the results go into a secondary data connection by adding them as a receive data connection based on the temporary XML file you created and then changing the second parameter of the *XmlStringToData* call to reference a node in the data connection. You can do more complex transforms, such using an XSL transform, when moving data between data sources. You can also extend this technique to bring data into your form from the .NET code—we'll do this later in the chapter with .NET Web references.

Using .NET Web References

If you want to have maximum control over how a Web service is called, you can use Web references. Web references are proxy classes generated by Visual Studio to connect to a Web service described by WSDL—similar to the Web service adapter used by InfoPath. The disadvantage of using Web references is that there is no InfoPath designer support for them and you have to handle many issues in code.

The following example walks through using a Web reference in a Visual Basic InfoPath project to read from an RPC/encoded Web service that returns a string. It builds on the techniques demonstrated earlier in this chapter. You'll find an example of submitting to a Web service using a Web reference in the "Creating Items in a SharePoint List" section of Chapter 9.

Creating a Secondary Data Connection with a Web Reference

1. Launch Visual Studio.
2. Create a new Visual Basic InfoPath form template project named WebRefExample.
3. In the Visual Studio Solution Explorer, right-click on the *WebRefExampleFormCode* node, and then choose Add Web Reference.
4. In the Add Web Reference dialog box, type the URL to your Web service, and then click Go. For this example, we will use a sample RPC/encoded Web service on the Oakleaf Systems Web site. The URL to this Web service is *http://oakleaf.ws/AlphaRPC/AlphaRPC.asmx?WSDL*. Visual Studio loads the description of the Web service and then displays documentation about it.
5. Click Add Reference. Your project now has a reference to the Web service that you can call in code. The reference will appear in Solution Explorer, as shown in Figure 7-6. Next you will start to hook it up to the form.

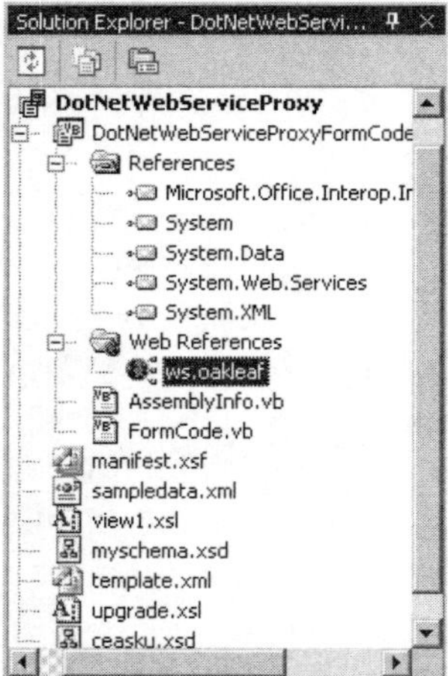

Figure 7-6 Web service reference displayed in the Visual Studio Solution Explorer

6. Choose Open InfoPath from the Project menu.
7. In the Controls task pane, insert a text box into the view. This will be used as a temporary location to copy the XML from the Web service.
8. Insert a Button into the view.
9. Right-click on the button, and then choose Button Properties.
10. In the Button Properties dialog box, click Edit Form Code.
11. Add the following method to your form code just above the *End Class* statement:

```
Public Function QueryAlphaRPCService(ByVal sku As String) As String
    Dim ws As ws.oakleaf.AlphaRPC
    Dim result As String

    ws = New ws.oakleaf.AlphaRPC
    ' The values sent to this example Web service are hard-coded.
    ' See the AlphaRPC Web service documentation for more info.
    result = ws.CheckStock("OAKLEAF-MS7", "AlphaDist", _
                           "AlphaUser", "Alpha#123", _
                           sku, True)
    Return result
End Function
```

12. Add the following code into the button *OnClick* event handler:

```
Dim result As String
' The values sent to this example Web service are hard-coded.
' See the AlphaRPC Web service documentation for more info.
result = QueryAlphaRPCService("SPKF0496")
thisXDocument.DOM.selectSingleNode("//my:field1").text = result
```

13. Press Alt+Shift+F or Ctrl+F5 to preview the form from Visual Studio.
14. In the InfoPath Preview window, click the button. The text field will display some XML as text. Copy this XML to the Clipboard.
15. Launch your text editor and then paste the XML into it.
16. Save the resulting XML file to your hard drive, naming it **ceasku.xml**. This is a temporary file that will be used only to infer the schema of the data, much like the previous string Web service example.
17. Close the text editor, and then close the preview.
18. In the InfoPath designer, choose Data Connections from the Tools menu, and then click Add.
19. In the Data Connection Wizard, select Receive Data, and then click Next.
20. Select XML Document, and then click Next.
21. Enter the path to the ceasku.xml file you just saved, and then click Next.

22. Deselect the Automatically Retrieve Data When Form Is Opened check box, leave the name of the data connection as *ceasku*, and then click Finish.

23. When prompted whether you want to add this file to your form, click No, and then click Close.

24. In the Data Source task pane, select the *ceasku* data source.

25. Insert the *AlphaDistInventory* node into the view as a Section With Controls.

    You now have a data connection with a schema matching the return value of the Web service and some controls on the form to display the data. The data connection has only schema information and is not is not yet hooked up to any data source. The next step is to connect the data to the data source with code.

26. Switch to Visual Studio. A dialog box appears asking if you want to automatically update expressions. Click Yes.

27. Add the following three new lines of code to the button *Onclick* event handler just above the *End Sub* statement:

```
Dim result As String
' The values sent to this example Web service are hard-coded.
' See the Web service documentation for more info.
result = QueryAlphaRPCService("SPKF0496")
thisXDocument.DOM.selectSingleNode("//my:field1").text = result

thisXDocument.GetDOM("ceasku").loadXML(result)
' Updating data connection values doesn't always update the view.
thisXDocument.View.ForceUpdate()
```

28. Save, preview, and then test your solution.

> **Note** If you see the error "This DOM cannot be loaded twice" when you call this function, it means InfoPath has already loaded the DOM. Verify that you cleared the Automatically Retrieve Data When Form Is Opened check box in the Data Connection Wizard when you created this data connection.

You now have a template with a secondary data connection. From the point of view of the InfoPath designer, the data is a static file. The code is what hooks the data to the Web service and makes it dynamic.

You can extend this to any type of Web service, including ones with different parameters, and for both sending and receiving data. You can also use the Web reference without binding it to a particular data connection, and instead use the values from the Web service in other ways, such as copying them to individual items in the main data source or for calculations.

Rebinding Web References at Run Time

To rebind a Web reference at run time, set the *Url* property of the Web service proxy object. You can also control properties such as the credentials, SSL client certificates (for HTTPS), proxy server, and timeout.

Cross-Domain Rules for Calling Web Services

When you call a Web service, you are making a network call. As a result, cross-domain rules come into effect to prevent data from being sent to an undesirable location. In particular, a template using the Domain security model restricts access to InfoPath Web service adapters and certain COM objects, such as the *XMLHTTP* object. Some of these objects are restricted from calling a cross-domain Web service, depending on the user's Internet Explorer settings, which are typically set to Prompt for the Local Intranet zone, Disable for the Internet zone, and Enable for the Trusted Sites zone. A fully trusted form can access cross-domain data.

The SOAP proxy, built by Visual Studio .NET, and the *System.Net.HttpWebRequest* object use the .NET settings. By default, this means you can access services on the same domain only as the form is published. You can use a server-side Web service proxy to control data within a domain, although you must be careful when you consider the security aspects of such a proxy. See Chapter 8 for more information on form deployment and security.

Summary

Web services are a mechanism to connect your rich InfoPath form to logic running on a remote server. You learned how to use this connection to build forms and Web services that can be insulated from database and schema changes, how to connect to existing Web services, how to work with some of the advanced features of the InfoPath Web Service Adapter, and how to use Visual Studio .NET Web references to connect to Web services with even more flexibility than is provided by the InfoPath Web Service Adapter.

Chapter 8

Deployment and Security

In this chapter, we'll take a detailed look at how to deploy InfoPath forms. We'll begin by presenting an overview of InfoPath deployment patterns. Deployment patterns include both a mode and a medium. The *mode* is the form, form template, signed form template, or installation package. The *medium* is the location—for example, local machine, e-mail, Web site (including SharePoint), or a combination of e-mail and Web site.

The InfoPath designer associates a security level with your form based on its design (which features it uses). You can override the automatic setting and request a higher level of security, but the features your form uses determine the minimum level of security required. We will examine how the security level limits the ways in which you can deploy your form. The security level associated with your form specifies which deployment patterns work for which mediums. For example, you cannot deploy a fully trusted form template by sending just a form file.

Recall that the form template is the .xsn package containing various files that describe your InfoPath solution. The form is just the .xml document containing the XML data for the document instance. InfoPath keeps only one copy of the form template corresponding to the most recent download or installation. You can have countless numbers of .xml form files on your computer or Web site. If you send an .xml form in e-mail to a coworker and that person does not have the .xsn form template installed, InfoPath attempts to automatically download the form template from the published location. However, if the form template is fully trusted, InfoPath will prevent automatic installation. You will have to digitally sign the form template or create an installation package for it.

We will also look at how .NET Framework security and InfoPath object model (OM) security differ. InfoPath is not a managed application, but it supports executing managed code. You can simplify your debugging process by defining a custom security policy using .NET Framework configuration tools. However, to call members of the OM that are set to security level 3, you must register the form template.

Next we will examine how InfoPath identifies forms. The identification process is important for caching, security, and version upgrade. If you upgrade your form template and try to open a form created with an old version, InfoPath tries to upgrade it. You can modify how InfoPath upgrades forms by customizing the upgrade.xsl file included in the package or by customizing the *OnVersionUpgrade* event handler. We will step through two examples that show how to do this.

Finally, we will finish the chapter with a section comparing deployment between InfoPath 2003 and InfoPath 2003 SP1.

Deployment

This section presents a high-level summary of the various deployment patterns. InfoPath restricts features depending on the method of deployment you use. For example, e-mail deployment doesn't support automatic version upgrade. Automatic version upgrade requires that the form template exist in a physical location when you load the form, but form templates deployed strictly via e-mail are not associated with a location. The reverse is also true—the features you choose will limit your deployment options. For example, if you have a form that hosts a task pane, InfoPath requires Full Trust security and that means you will need to either sign the form with a digital certificate or create a Windows Installer .msi file. Because of the interdependencies between features, security, and deployment, deciding how to deploy your InfoPath form template is an important step in the forms design process.

Deploying Forms in E-Mail

InfoPath SP1 makes it easier to deploy form templates in e-mail by providing the following techniques.

Send Form Template As An Attachment

From the designer, you can choose File | Send Form As An Attachment. You have to save the form template before you can send it. The save or publish process associates a location with the form and creates a package for it. When you are editing the form within a Visual Studio project, you can't publish it because the form doesn't exist as a package.

In addition, if you don't have Outlook set up, the Send Form As An Attachment item will be missing from the File menu of the InfoPath designer, and the Send To Mail Recipient item will be missing from the File menu of the InfoPath editor.

Sending the form template in e-mail works only for simple forms that do not access external data resources. That restriction rules out forms that use business logic, unsafe ActiveX controls, data connections, custom task panes, and other features for accessing external data. In fact, InfoPath SP1 introduces a new security level, called Restricted, for this e-mail deployment technique.

Send Windows Installer .MSI File As An Attachment

InfoPath ships a command-line tool in the SDK called RegForm that you can run on your InfoPath form template to create a Windows Installer .msi file. The resulting .msi file contains your form template, installation instructions, and a script to register your form template. You can send this .msi file in e-mail. When you open the .msi file, Windows displays an installation wizard. If you choose to install, the script in the .msi file calls InfoPath to register and install the included form template on the computer. The RegForm tool is separate from the InfoPath designer; you will have to run the RegForm tool from a Visual Studio .NET Command Prompt.

Digitally Sign the Form

For deploying a form template via e-mail that is not Restricted, InfoPath SP1 supports signing the form template with a digital certificate. If deploying a digital certificate is not feasible, you can still use the RegForm tool to create an .msi file.

Table 8-1 summarizes the characteristics of the e-mail deployment scenario.

Table 8-1 E-mail Deployment Scenario

Key scenario	Extranet and offline mobile users
Publish methods	Send attachment, digitally sign, RegForm
Collaboration	Send form templates as e-mail attachments
Disadvantages	No automatic version upgrade, forms stored in e-mail

Signing the Form Signing the form is easy. From the Security tab of the Form Options dialog box, available from the Tools menu, you can specify a certificate for your form. Signing a form that is not going to be Full Trust makes sense if you want to prevent people from tampering with it, but most of the time you will probably be signing and making Full Trust at the same time, so don't forget to uncheck the check box labeled Automatically Determine Security Level Based On Form's Design and then select Full Trust. Next select the Sign This Form check box as shown in Figure 8-1. You might have to select and/or create a certificate if you haven't done so previously.

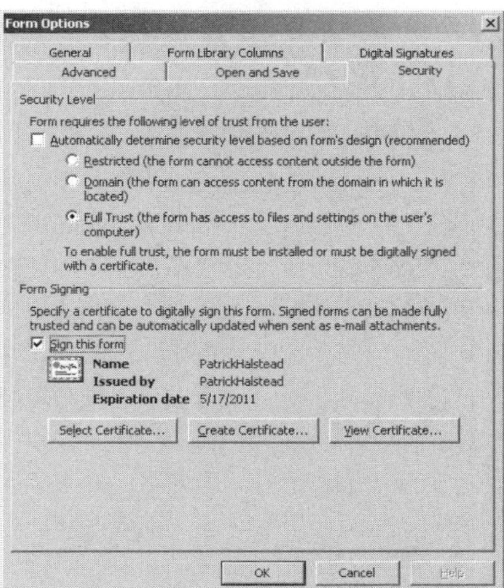

Figure 8-1 Signing a form is simple, but don't forget to mark it as Full Trust.

Installing Digital Certificates for Untrusted Certificate Authorities If you receive a form template that has been signed, you will probably have to install the digital certificate. Digital certificates are the future, but the installation process is still a bit involved. If the author of the form used a digital certificate issued by a trusted certification authority, the installation process is straightforward and similar to accepting the digital certificate for an ActiveX control when you install one from a Web site. This section will cover the more difficult case when the certificate authority is not trusted. If you are developing a form and testing it using your own certification authority, you can use the following instructions to help testers and users install your form.

Assuming you signed and published your form template, users trying to fill out a form or view an existing form might see a dialog similar to the one shown in Figure 8-2.

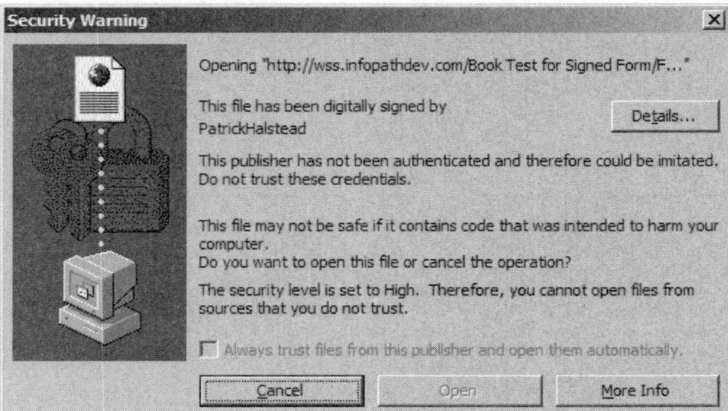

Figure 8-2 If the check box for Always Trust Files From This Publisher And Open Them Automatically is grayed, you will have to trust the certificate authority.

If the check box is not grayed, you can check it, click open, and continue. However, if the check box is grayed, you will have to use the following steps:

1. Click Details and then click the Certification Path tab on the Certificate dialog box that appears. Figure 8-3 shows an example of what you will see.

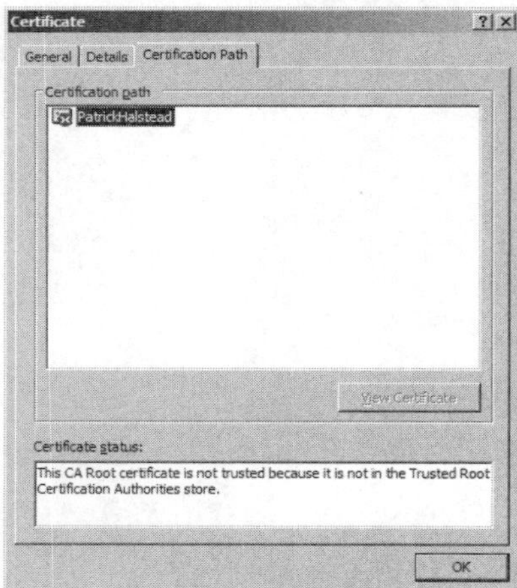

Figure 8-3 The Certificate dialog box

The example in Figure 8-3 corresponds to a digital certificate issued by an individual. If the certificate you receive was issued by a service or process, you will likely see multiple nodes arranged in your certification path. The topmost node in the tree will correspond to a root certificate authority. If this node is untrusted (indicated by a circular red X mark on it), you must select it and click View Certificate. Selecting a digital certificate node farther down the certification path will not result in a trusted root certificate authority, and you won't be able to open the form. If there is only one node in your certification path, you have only one option and you do not need to click View Certificate again.

2. Click Install Certificate. The Certificate Import Wizard appears as shown in Figure 8-4:

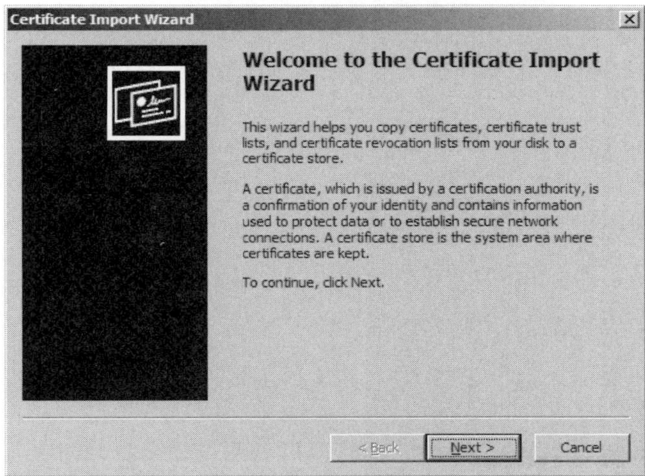

Figure 8-4 The Certificate Import Wizard

3. In the Certificate Import Wizard, click Next. The next page resembles Figure 8-5:

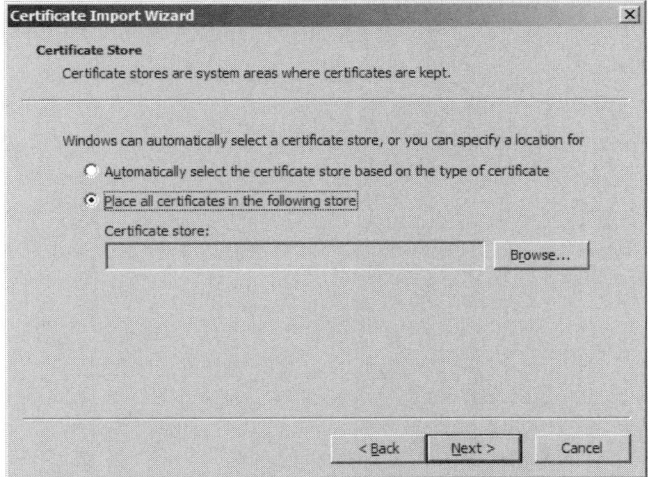

Figure 8-5 Choose a certificate store to place your certificate in.

4. Select Place All Certificates In The Following Store, and then click Browse. You will see a dialog box similar to Figure 8-6:

Figure 8-6 Selecting a certificate store

5. In the Select Certificate Store dialog box, select Trusted Root Certification Authorities, and then click OK.
6. Click Next, and then click Finish. See Figure 8-7:

Figure 8-7 Completing the Certificate Import Wizard

7. A new Security Warning dialog box appears, warning that you are about to install a certificate from a certification authority (CA). See Figure 8-8. Click Yes.

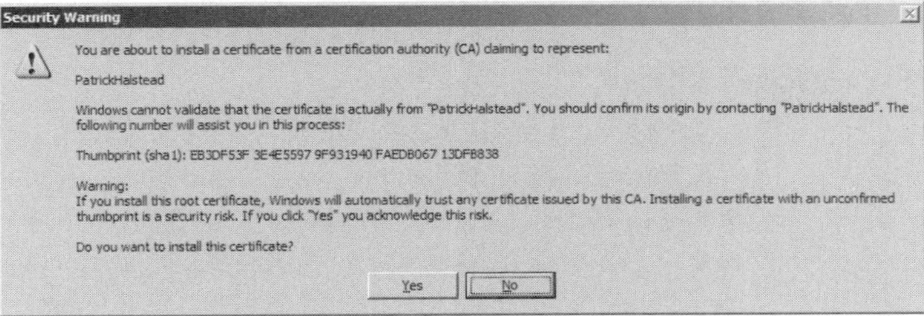

Figure 8-8 Certificate installation warning

8. Click OK to close the Certificate Import Wizard.
9. Click OK to close the Certificate dialog box. If you had more than one certificate dialog open, you might have to do this more than once.
10. Close the Security Warning dialog box by clicking Cancel or the X window control in the top-right corner.
11. Close InfoPath, and then reopen the form.
12. When the Security Warning dialog box appears again, select Always Trust Files From This Publisher And Open Them Automatically, and then click Open.

Deploying Forms to a Web Site or a SharePoint Server

For the best possible collaboration experience, you should deploy your InfoPath forms to a shared Web site or a SharePoint server. By default, when you publish a form to a shared server, the form requires Domain security. To deploy the form as fully trusted, you must digitally sign it. Using RegForm to create an .msi file that can be installed won't work because InfoPath security requires that installed programs not contain a *publishURL* attribute. A later section explains why.

Table 8-2 summarizes the characteristics of the Web site and SharePoint deployment scenarios.

Table 8-2 Web Site and SharePoint Deployment Scenarios

Key scenario	Shared Web site
Publish methods	Publish the form to the Web site
Collaboration	Send links to forms in e-mail
Disadvantages	Requires trusting the site; Full Trust requires signing

Mixed-Mode Deployment: E-Mail and Web Site

If some of your users have access to the shared site but others do not, you can create a mixed-mode deployment and send the form out as an attachment in e-mail. Users who have access can download the latest form from the Web site. Users who are offline can use the form that was sent in e-mail. If you choose to fully trust the form, you must digitally sign it.

Table 8-3 summarizes the characteristics of the mixed-mode deployment scenarios.

Table 8-3 Mixed-Mode Deployment Scenarios

Key scenario	Workflow between extranet/mobile users and internal users
Publish methods	Publish the form to the Web site; send as attachment in e-mail
Collaboration	Attach forms in e-mail to extranet users; send links to internal
Disadvantages	Requires trusting the site; Full Trust requires signing; need to synchronize forms in e-mail and site; no automatic version upgrade

Note Before going on the road, you can use the InfoPath Fill Out A Form dialog box (see Chapter 1) to synchronize your form. Start InfoPath, select your form from the Recently Used Forms list, and click Get Update Of This Form in the Form Tasks list on the right.

Deploying Forms to a Local Machine (My Computer)

Last but not least, you can choose to deploy your forms to your local machine. This scenario is ideally suited for personal forms. If your project requires deploying fully trusted forms, this approach makes forms easier to develop and to deploy and debug locally before digitally signing or installing them in the real deployment environment.

Important To address security concerns, InfoPath SP1 has reduced the permissions granted to forms published locally by making them behave like the ones published on an intranet location. This means that InfoPath will open a form from a local .xsn as if it is coming from the intranet zone, not the My Computer zone. When developing or previewing the form, InfoPath still opens using My Computer zone, e.g., via a *file:///c:* style URL.

Table 8-4 summarizes the characteristics of the local machine deployment scenarios.

Table 8-4 Local Machine Deployment Scenarios

Key scenario	Personal forms; debugging digitally signed or installed forms
Publish methods	Save locally; publish to local Web site or folder
Collaboration	None
Disadvantages	No collaboration

Security Levels

InfoPath supports three levels of trust—Restricted, Domain, and Full Trust. The level of trust determines the security level, and the security level, in turn, determines which methods and properties your form can access from the InfoPath object model (OM). To set your form's security in the InfoPath designer, go to Tools | Form Options and click on the Security tab of the Form Options dialog box. Figure 8-9 shows the security options.

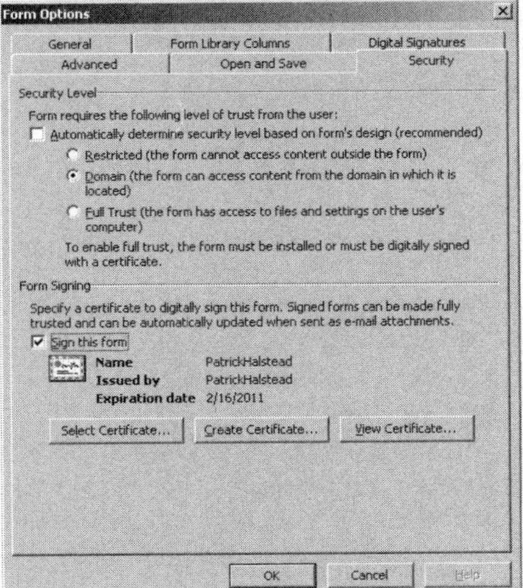

Figure 8-9 The security options for security level and form signing

- **Restricted** Also known as *super-sandbox*, or security level 0, this security level is ideal for simple forms deployed via e-mail. (The e-mail deployment feature was the impetus for this new SP1 security level.) The form can't access content outside of the form, and there is a long list of features that won't work: no managed code, no roles, no custom task pane, no data source adapters, no ActiveX controls, no cocreating XMLHTTP, no BizTalk, no ADO, and no submit adapters (except e-mail).
  - Pros: secure and easy to deploy.
  - Cons: not good if you're updating your form often; many features are not supported.
- **Domain** Also known as *sandbox*, this security level is the default and corresponds to security level 2 in the InfoPath OM. InfoPath restricts the form to a particular security zone. For example, the security zone can be your local file share, intranet site, or Internet site. Code cannot access resources and data on machines outside of the domain specified by the security zone. Managed code in your form gets security permissions corresponding to the Internet Explorer zone. However, this only applies to when the IE zone is *Intranet*. Managed code is not allowed to execute when the IE zone is *Internet*. You can work around this limitation by deploying a .NET custom runtime security policy for the InfoPath Form Templates group (see the Custom Security Permissions section later in this chapter). Note that script-based forms will run when the IE zone is *Internet*.

  By default your form's managed code will run with Local Intranet permissions. This permission set includes Environment Variables (UserName = Read), File Dialog (Unrestricted), User Interface (Unrestricted), etc. The Local Intranet permission set is restricted but it is the maximal set of permissions that can be granted without any risk of escalation to Full Trust. If your managed code were to receive File IO permissions (Unrestricted), the form could be escalated to Full Trust. To give managed code more permissions you can create a custom code group for InfoPath Form Template and deploy at the Machine level. (See the Custom Security Permissions section later in this chapter.)

- Pros: easy to deploy on a trusted domain, supports OM calls for security level 2 (and 0) but not 3 which requires Full Trust
- Cons: any methods that require special security permissions

Note Like most Microsoft Office applications, InfoPath's object model (OM) is implemented in unmanaged code and, as you may know, unmanaged code does not execute with .NET security policies. InfoPath SP1 provides a very important feature in giving you the ability to make calls into this unmanaged OM from your managed code. Most .NET applications interacting with unmanaged Office code through a primary interop assembly (PIA) require Full Trust. However, InfoPath provides a set of managed wrappers on top of its PIA/OM that enable calling into the OM without necessarily having Full Trust. In this way, InfoPath provides more parity with script-based forms than other Office applications.

- **Full Trust** This is security level 3 in the InfoPath object model. Your form must ask for Full Trust, which requires digitally signing the form using a code-signing certificate or creating a standalone deployment package (for example, Windows Installer) that will register the form as Full Trust. Users must choose to trust the form by installing a certificate or by running the deployment package.
  - Pros: unlimited access to the object model, features, and resources; managed code gets Full Trust security permissions.
  - Cons: requires installation.

Tip .NET will override your managed code security permissions when a custom runtime security policy exists. For example, you could have an Enterprise policy that prevents running any managed code from a specific URL. InfoPath managed code will respect the security policy even if the form is digitally signed but has a *publishUrl* that is the same as the URL disabled by the security policy.

Coding Guidelines

The security level controls how your form executes business logic and what methods and properties are accessible from the InfoPath object model. InfoPath tries to determine the security level of your form based on what it contains, but it stops short of parsing your code and figuring out the security level of the methods and properties. Even though Domain is the default security level, you can add calls to security level 3 methods to your code and InfoPath will not warn you. If you run your form, InfoPath will throw an exception when execution reaches the level 3 method.

Restricted

The default trust level is Domain, but form templates can get a Restricted level of trust if they are sent as plain attachments in e-mail. InfoPath supports only script in Restricted mode and runs the script as if it is from an arbitrary Internet URL, i.e., with restricted security permissions. Forms with managed code will not load. In addition, the number of methods and properties that you can call is limited. Refer to the SDK object model reference for details.

Domain Security

Domain trust can actually correspond to several different policies, depending on what the domain is. InfoPath uses the Internet Explorer (IE) zone where your form was published to determine the domain. InfoPath supports only four of the five zones and won't load forms coming from a Restricted IE zone. Only Intranet and Local Machine zones support executing managed code. Table 8-5 summarizes the policies.

Table 8-5 IE Zones and Domain Security

IE Zone	Domain Security
Restricted	InfoPath won't load forms from the Restricted zone.
Internet	InfoPath managed code doesn't run in the Internet zone.
Intranet	InfoPath managed code runs with Local Intranet permissions.
Local Machine	InfoPath managed code runs with Local Intranet permissions.
Trusted Sites	InfoPath managed code runs with Internet permissions. This permission set is very restricted.

Full Trust

Fully trusted forms can access the entire InfoPath object model. Managed code runs with Full Trust inside a fully trusted form.

Creating a fully trusted form requires digitally signing the form or creating a custom installation program to register the form. The InfoPath SDK describes two techniques for creating a custom installation program.

How InfoPath Sets the Security Level

When you open a form, InfoPath grants a maximum security level based on settings in the InfoPath forms cache. The cache is key because it keeps a record of how each InfoPath form came to reside on your computer. Depending on how you install the form, InfoPath will store different information in the cache. For example, if you received your form in e-mail, the cache will contain the name of your form but not a physical location.

In Chapter 2, we introduced the InfoPath form cache and described the two attributes in the form's manifest that are used to identify your form:

- *name* **(URN)** The *name* attribute is a URN that uniquely identifies the form. Every form created using InfoPath SP1 has a URN. However, some old InfoPath 2003 forms might not contain a URN.
- *publishURL* **(URL)** The *publishURL* attribute is a URL that points to the location of your form's template, or where your form lives. The location can be on your local machine, a file share, or a Web server. InfoPath removes the URL for e-mail deployment, which has no corresponding physical location. InfoPath also removes the URL for forms registered using an installation program. The reason for removing the URL in this case is to plug a security hole where a rogue form could have gained access to resources on your computer. (More on that in the next Developer Nugget.)

Table 8-6 shows the maximum trust level that InfoPath grants to forms based on their cached URL and URN entries.

Table 8-6 Automatically Determined Security Level

Cache Info	Full Trust	Domain			Restricted
		Local	Intranet	Internet	
Local URL (FILE:)*			X		
No URL (e-mail)					X
Web URL			X	X	
Domain URL (UNC)			X		
Installed URN with Full Trust	X				
Installed URN without Full Trust		X			
Digitally Signed (URN and URL)	X				
Extracted form files			X		

* See Developer Nugget below on Security Changes for Local Forms in InfoPath SP1.

You can set a security level that is less than the maximum trust level allowed by deselecting the Automatically Determine Security Level check box on the Security tab of the Automatically Determine Security Level check box in the Form Options dialog box. However, this makes sense only for mixed deployment, where you have both extranet and intranet users where you would set the required security level to Domain, and sign the form. Figure 8-9 (shown earlier) depicts this scenario.

Important Digitally signing a form is the only way to deploy a form in e-mail that can be used by mobile users in both offline and online contexts. To safeguard against security attacks, InfoPath refuses to register forms that have a *publishURL* attribute in their manifest, and a Restricted form will not receive the Domain trust level needed for intranet collaboration.

Developer Nugget: Security Changes for Local Forms in InfoPath SP1

In InfoPath SP1, forms running on the local machine do not get *file:* privileges. This is a change from InfoPath 2003. The new restriction is needed to prevent security problems. In InfoPath 2003, applications can drop .xsn files to known locations on your machine, and when you navigate to an .xml file with a processing instruction that points to the dropped .xsn file, InfoPath runs the form as if it were in the Local Machine security zone. This problem is a result of how Internet Explorer redirects .xml file requests to InfoPath.

Getting users to navigate to an .xml file is not hard—just send them a link to an .xml file in e-mail. An .xml file is not considered a security threat because it is just text, but Internet Explorer starts InfoPath if the .xml file contains the *mso-infoPathSolution* processing instruction. (See Chapter 1 for details.) The .xsn file resembles an executable file except that it is more powerful because it can be launched by an .xml page. This is a known problem in InfoPath 2003. InfoPath SP1 mitigates this problem by testing for the *publishURL* attribute in the manifest during installation. If it finds the attribute, installation and registration fail. In addition, InfoPath now sandboxes form templates registered as a local URL to an arbitrary internet URL and executes them with local intranet privileges.

This new policy has implications for how you debug your managed assemblies in InfoPath. Only installed forms will run in the Local Machine zone. Because installation fails if InfoPath finds a *publishURL* attribute, you must sign your form, which is tantamount to creating a fully trusted form anyway (because there is no reason to digitally sign a form that is not fully trusted). The upshot is that there is no longer much use for the Local Machine zone. Preview mode in the designer is the only exception; it runs as Local Machine, but preview mode has limited support and managed code gets less permission in preview mode.

Configuring Security Permissions

In Chapter 2, we showed how to create business logic for your forms using either managed code (.NET Framework) or script. Managed code gets security permissions based on the .NET Framework security policy. Script runs in the context of the form's security level. This section describes how these two security settings interact and how you can configure your development environment to quickly deploy and debug forms that need Full Trust security without having to sign or install them every time you create a new build. When you write managed code, you must consider the form's security level because of two issues:

- **Managed Code Security Permissions May Exceed the Form's Security Level** The .NET Framework governs security permissions for managed code. If you have a runtime security policy that grants Full Trust to forms executed from a folder on your local machine, your managed code can access resources even if the security level is Domain.
- **Access to the InfoPath Object Model May Require a Full Trust Form** InfoPath sets some object model methods to security level 3. Two examples are *XDocument.Save* and *XDocument.UI.ShowModalDialog*. Your form must be fully trusted in order to call those methods. The .NET Framework governs the security permissions for your form's managed code assembly, but not for your form's use of the InfoPath object model, which is unmanaged.

InfoPath requires that you sign or install Full Trust forms. This requirement presents a challenge for the developer because it is obviously impractical to re-sign or reinstall your forms after every code change. Fortunately, InfoPath provides two workarounds to make debugging simple for these scenarios. You can create a custom .NET Framework security policy to give security permissions to managed code, and you can create a script that registers your form template. Then you can more easily debug Full Trust forms.

After showing you the effect of inadequate security permissions, we'll describe several techniques to help you debug code as you are developing it.

Managed Code

Chapter 2 introduced a managed code example to get the username from the environment and populate the name field of a form. Calling *Environment.Username* requires the security permission for environment variables, but developers belonging to the Administrator group will already have these permissions. Let's take a look at an example that even administrators won't have by default. The following code gets the domain and username by using the *Security* object:

```
<InfoPathEventHandler(EventType:=InfoPathEventType.OnLoad)> _
Public Sub OnLoad(ByVal e As DocReturnEvent)
    thisXDocument.DOM.selectSingleNode("/my:myFields/
my:Name").text = Security.Principal.WindowsIdentity.GetCurrent.Name
End Sub
```

To execute this code, you need a form with a root source node named *Name*, which you can create a text box for in your view. Assuming you have not already modified your .NET security permissions, when you preview the form you should see the error shown in Figure 8-10.

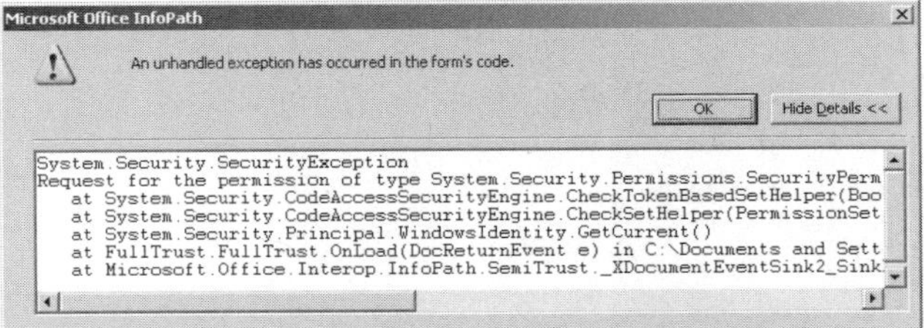

Figure 8-10 Executing managed code without sufficient security permissions.

If you try to change the form's security level to Full Trust, you'll see the warning shown in Figure 8-11.

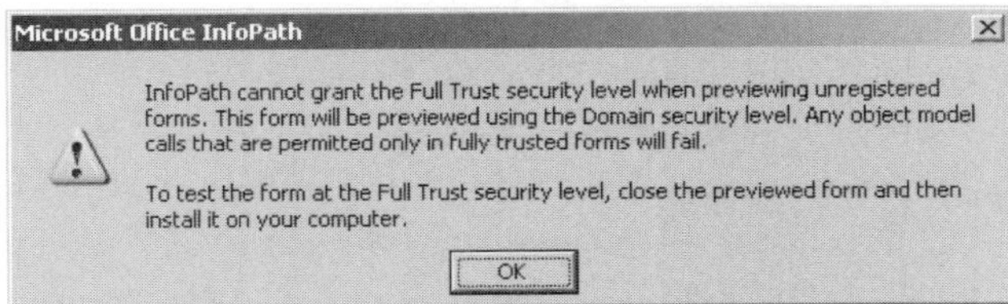

Figure 8-11 You can't preview a form set to Full Trust security level because InfoPath can't sign it at preview time.

For debugging purposes, you can use the .NET Framework 1.1 Configuration tool to assign security permissions to your managed code so that it runs even when your form is not Full Trust. InfoPath SP1 supports custom security policies for managed code. The intent of this SP1 feature is to give developers an easy way to debug Full Trust forms.

Custom Security Permissions You should use the .NET Framework 1.1 Configuration tool (mscorcfg.msc) to create a custom runtime security policy. If you are running Windows Server, this tool is in the Administrative Tools menu. Choose Start | Administrative Tools | Microsoft .NET Framework 1.1 Configuration. Another easy way to access the tool is to start the Microsoft Management Console (mmc.exe). From the Start menu, choose Run, and then type **mmc.exe** and click OK. From the File menu, choose Add/Remove Snap-in. In the Add/Remove Snap-In dialog box, click Add and select .NET Framework 1.1 Configuration, then click Add. Then close the dialog box and click OK to accept the new snap-in.

Expand the tree under My Computer / Runtime Security Policy / Machine / Code Groups. Figure 8-12 depicts the .NET Framework 1.1 Configuration tool with the tree expanded to Code Groups.

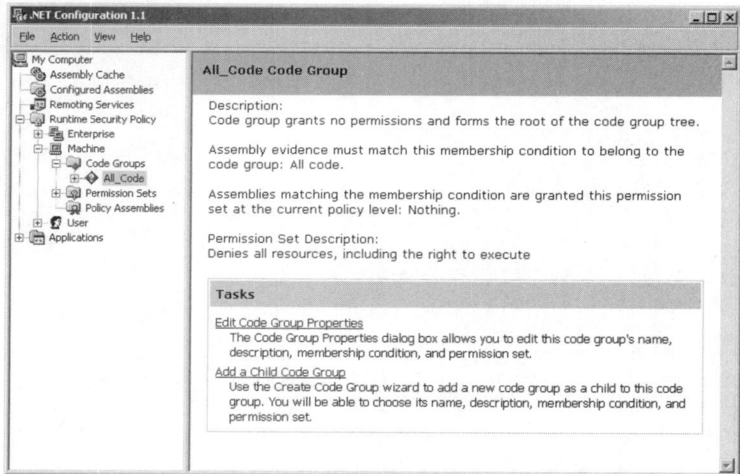

Figure 8-12 Microsoft .NET Framework 1.1 Configuration tool

Creating the InfoPath Form Templates code group The first thing you do is define a code group. Runtime security policies exist for App Domain, Enterprise, Machine, and User. InfoPath SP1 checks for a specific code group named InfoPath Form Templates under the Machine / Code Groups / All_Code subtree. Note that InfoPath checks only under the runtime security policy for Machine. Creating the code group under Enterprise or user has no effect. In addition, you must name the code group exactly as InfoPath Form Templates—otherwise, InfoPath won't find it. InfoPath will load and apply the security policies for child code groups it finds under the InfoPath Form Templates node, regardless of their name. In this section, we will refer to the InfoPath Form Templates code group as the root code group. Figure 8-13 shows the InfoPath Form Templates code group node in this configuration.

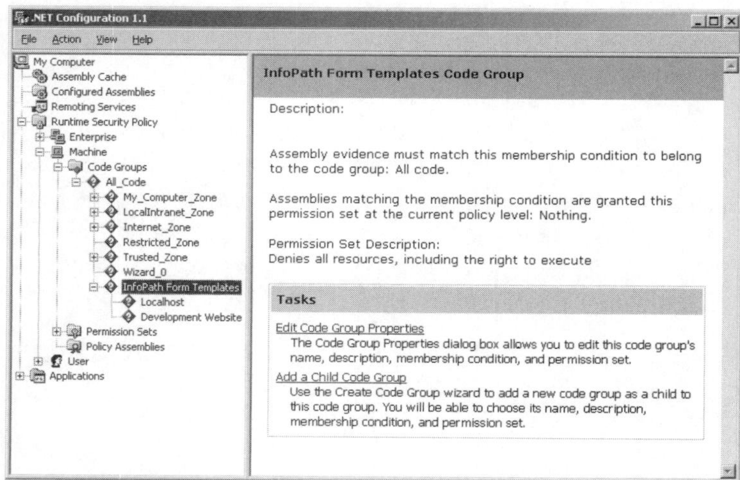

Figure 8-13 InfoPath Form Templates code group in the Microsoft .NET Framework 1.1 Configuration tool

To add the InfoPath Form Templates root code group, expand the Code Groups/All_Code subtree and click the Add A Child Code Group link in the right-hand window. Enter the required name: **InfoPath Form Templates**. InfoPath performs a case-sensitive string match on the code group name, which means you must spell this name exactly as it appears. Figure 8-14 shows this.

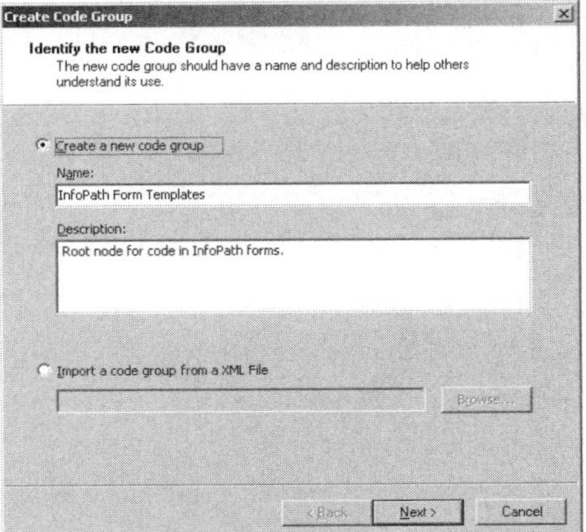

Figure 8-14 Creating a new code group to customize InfoPath security permissions

Add a description which clarifies the purpose of this code group, and then click Next to move to the second step in the wizard. Choose All Code from the Choose The Condition Type For This Code Group drop-down list box. Choosing All Code is the best practice here because it ensures that the code group can be extended using child code groups. Figure 8-15 shows the default condition type.

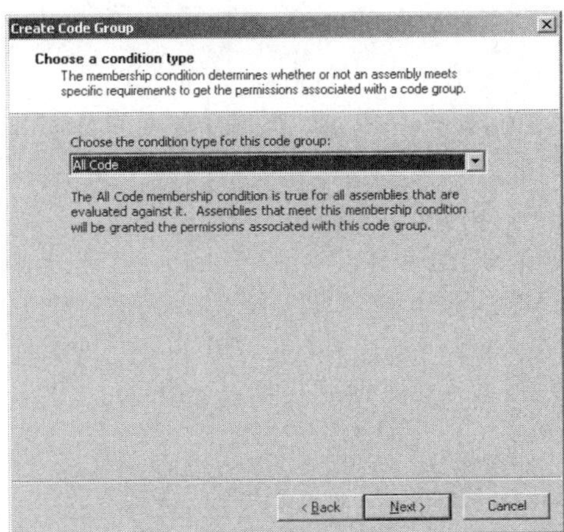

Figure 8-15 Setting the InfoPath Form Templates code group to process All Code

Because the root node is now set to All Code, on the next page you'll want to choose Nothing from the Use Existing Permission Set drop-down list box (as shown in Figure 8-16) to prevent the Common Language Runtime (CLR) from indiscriminately running any assembly. Just because you name the code group InfoPath Form Templates does not mean it is exclusive to InfoPath. The CLR will still apply the custom security policy for this code group and others it finds underneath it.

> **Warning** Do not set Full Trust for the root code group. Setting Full Trust for the root code group will result in a huge security hole because the CLR will grant Full Trust to any assembly that you download.

The best practice is to define the InfoPath root code group to give no permissions to all code and then add child code groups that set Full Trust based on restrictive conditions–for example, trusted folders, Web sites, or security zones.

Click Next and then click Finish to complete the process.

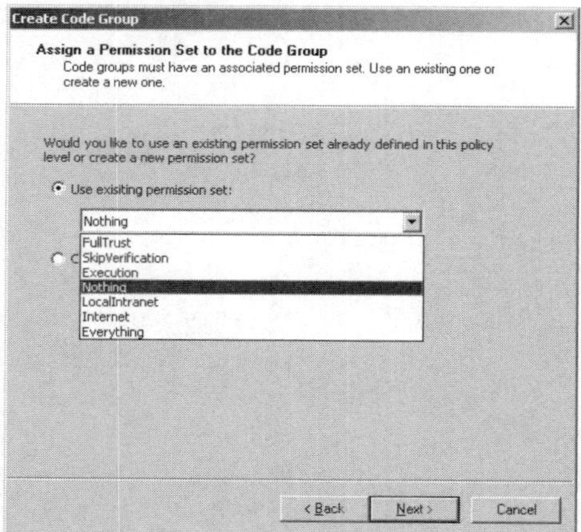

Figure 8-16 Because the new InfoPath Form Templates code group applies to all code, you should assign to it the most restrictive permission set, Nothing.

Extending the code group Now that we have defined the InfoPath root code group, let's extend it with child code groups. Child code groups can be created in the same way as the root. Select the InfoPath root code group, and click the Add A Child Code Group link in the right-hand frame. Create a new code group named Security that applies to all code from the My Computer zone and gets the existing Full Trust permission set. To select the My Computer zone you must first set the condition type for the membership condition to Zone. Then the dialog box will display a Zone drop-down list from which you can select My Computer. Note that you can create a custom permission set, including just the Security permission set. When you are done, click Edit Code Group Properties in the right-hand window. Figure 8-17 displays the General tab of the Security Properties dialog box.

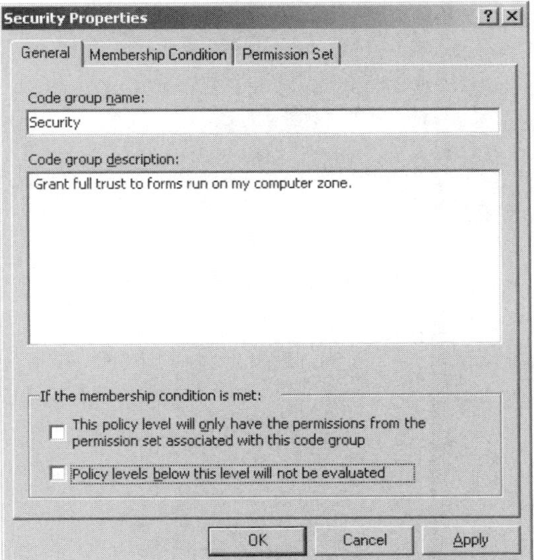

Figure 8-17 Extending the InfoPath root code group with a child code group for Security

Figure 8-18 shows the Membership Condition tab. You can also use the URL condition type to specify code on your local machine. For example, specifying a URL of *file://C:/Documents and Settings/{user}/My Documents/Visual Studio Projects/** sets permissions on all assemblies loaded from underneath the default Visual Studio Projects folder.

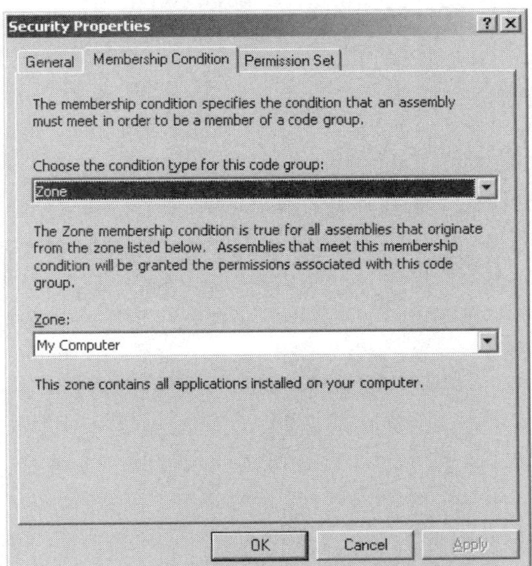

Figure 8-18 The Security code group applies only to code coming from the My Computer zone.

Figure 8-19 shows the Permission Set tab. Because the code group uses a restrictive membership condition, assigning Full Trust permissions is not a problem here, but make sure that you trust the URL and that untrustworthy assemblies cannot be copied into the location. In other words, make sure you know who you are dealing with when you access the URL and that you trust these people or company to safeguard against rogue assemblies.

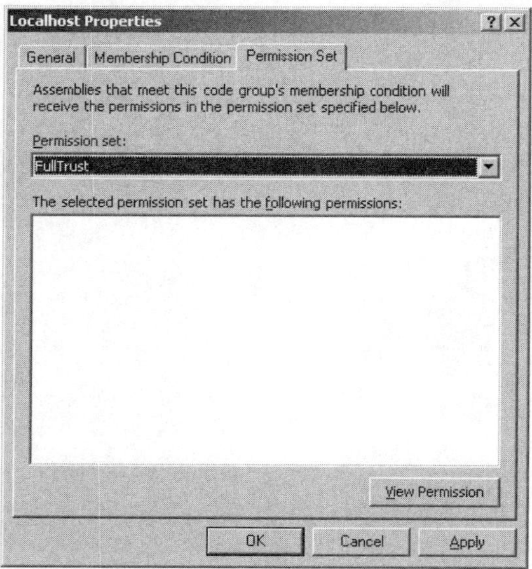

Figure 8-19 Assigning Full Trust permissions to the form templates loaded from the My Computer zone

Once you have created the code group for the My Computer zone, the code in any form that you run from your computer will get Full Trust security permissions. Now try to run the code above that accesses *Security.Principal.WindowsIdentity*.

Deploying .NET Security Policies You can deploy a custom run-time security policy to multiple client machines using a Windows Installer .msi file. An .msi file is a self-contained installation package that supports deployment, installation, and uninstallation. The .NET Configuration tool provides support for creating an .msi file. However, deploying an .msi requires an extra installation step, and installing a security policy on a client machine will replace the entire run-time security policy for the machine policy level. With these two considerations in mind, we recommend using custom security policies only in development environments and not as a general deployment vehicle to client machines.

Creating a custom run-time security policy with the InfoPath Form Templates code group simplifies debugging managed code because you don't have to re-sign or reinstall the form after every change. InfoPath gives permissions to your managed code to run in Full Trust even when it has not been signed or installed. However, when your managed code needs to make calls into the InfoPath OM, and those calls require level 3 security, creating custom .NET security permissions won't work.

Full Trust Forms

You can give your managed code a specific set of permissions by using the InfoPath Form Templates code group described. However, accessing certain methods in InfoPath's unmanaged object model requires executing the entire form as Full Trust.

Registering Form Templates To call security level 3 methods in the InfoPath object model, you must register the form template. Here are the steps:

1. Ensure you have your InfoPath Visual Studio project open.
2. In the InfoPath designer, select Form Options from the Tools menu.
3. On the Security tab of the Form Options dialog box, clear the Automatically Determine Security Level Based On Form's Design check box, and then select the Full Trust option.
4. Click OK, save the form, and then close InfoPath.
5. In Visual Studio, open the manifest.xsf file through Solution Explorer.
6. Remove the *publishURL* attribute from this file. See an earlier Developer Nugget that explains the security reasons for this attribute.
7. Create a script file named **register.js** in the project folder.
8. Edit the register.js file and add the following lines to it:

```
oApp = new ActiveXObject("InfoPath.ExternalApplication");
oApp.RegisterSolution("{path\manifest.xsf}", "overwrite");
```

9. Save and then close the register.js file.
10. Run the register.js file.

The form will be registered as Full Trust from your project location, and you will be able to debug it in the Visual Studio development environment.

Developer Nugget: Additional Security Tips

- **Don't debug with higher security** Custom security policies are useful for debugging Full Trust applications. If you are developing a form to deploy via a trusted domain, you should not grant it Full Trust security permissions using a custom security policy. Doing so is a bad practice because it prevents you from finding code that will fail when run under Domain trust. If you add a Full Trust feature, you will only find out that the form fails when you deploy it in a Domain trust environment. Instead of Full Trust, use Domain.
- **Hash condition doesn't work** The .NET CLR has a bug that prevents the Hash type membership condition from working in InfoPath SP1. The security policy is the result of an intersection of Enterprise, Machine, User, and Applications (App Domain). The App Domain is controlled by code. InfoPath needs to create a tree at the App Domain level. If the code group condition is hash, InfoPath needs to copy the code group to App Domain, but the CLR has a problem serializing the code group copy operation. Therefore, code groups created with the hash condition will fail. However, all of the other conditions should work. As of this writing, there is no known workaround, but please visit the InfoPath 2003 Support Center for up-to-date information: *http://support.microsoft.com/default.aspx?scid=fh;en-us;infopath2003*.
- **Use .NET calls instead of InfoPath security level 3 methods** If you need to access resources that require Full Trust, you must sign your form or create a Windows Installer .msi file for it. If this is not feasible, you can replace the sensitive code with .NET code and use .NET security permissions to let others execute the form. For example, you can use *System.IO.File.OpenWrite* instead of *thisXDocument.FileSaveAs* to save a file.

Version Upgrade

On file open, InfoPath checks the version number of the form template in the cache against the version number of the form template at the published location. InfoPath will check to see if a more recent version of the corresponding form template exists and, if so, download it. Upgrading the template happens automatically and separate from upgrading the form. After upgrading the template, the version of the form to open is compared against the version of the form template. The version comparison results in one of three possible states:

- **Match: form version matches template version** This is the trivial case. In this case, InfoPath just opens the form as it is; no upgrade happens.

- **Upgrade: form version is earlier than template version** This result is common as well and is the case for any form created using an earlier version of the form template. Upgrading the form template creates this condition for all existing forms. By default, InfoPath tries to upgrade forms to match the latest version, but if the schema is significantly different, the form might fail to load.
- **Downgrade: form version is greater than template version** If you receive a form in e-mail and open it offline, you might get into the state where the form version is later than that of the most recently cached form template. When this happens, InfoPath displays the error message shown in Figure 8-20.

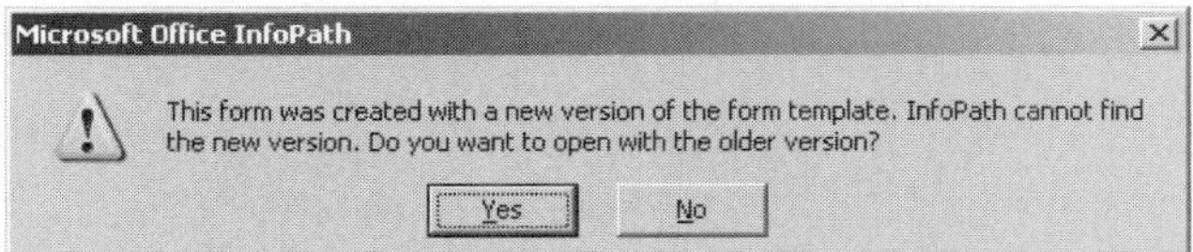

Figure 8-20 InfoPath warns users when the version of the form is later than that of the template.

InfoPath tries to be smart about the upgrade and downgrade case. In the upgrade case, if a newly added schema element is missing from the form, InfoPath adds it. In the downgrade case, however, if there is a new element in the form that does not match an element in the schema, InfoPath fails to open the form.

InfoPath gives you three form upgrade options. In the designer, go to the Advanced tab of the Form Options dialog box and look at the Form Template Version section. Figure 8-21 shows the three options: Do Nothing, Use Custom Event, and Automatically Upgrade Existing Forms.

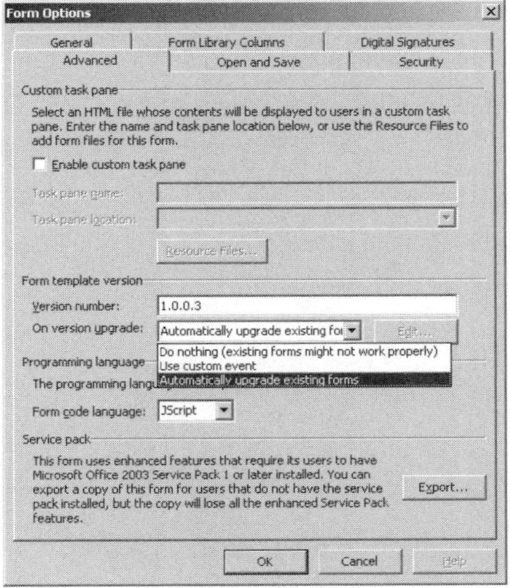

Figure 8-21 InfoPath supports three upgrade mechanisms.

Do Nothing

InfoPath provides the Do Nothing option for optimal performance, security, and data integrity. Selecting this option guarantees that InfoPath will make no structural changes to your document on load. InfoPath cannot automatically upgrade digitally signed forms and will prompt with a dialog box asking to remove the signature. If you use digital signatures, turning off the automatic upgrade may simplify the user experience and reduce the possibility of a digital signature getting removed. For security, auditing and data integrity reasons, you will want to turn off automatic update to prevent InfoPath from changing your form's data on load.

Automatically Upgrade Existing Forms

The default behavior is to automatically upgrade forms that were created with an earlier version of the form template. InfoPath creates an XSL transform file named upgrade.xsl that it applies to all forms created with old template versions. InfoPath specifies the upgrade transform in the manifest.xsf file as follows:

```
<xsf:documentVersionUpgrade>
    <xsf:useTransform transform="upgrade.xsl" minVersionToUpgrade="1.0.0.1"
        maxVersionToUpgrade="1.0.0.10">
    </xsf:useTransform>
</xsf:documentVersionUpgrade>
```

You cannot change the upgrade.xsl file from the InfoPath designer. You must extract the form files or create your solution using Visual Studio to modify the upgrade.xsl file.

InfoPath SP1 creates the upgrade.xsl file by default.

Customizing the Upgrade.xsl File

Let's take a look at how to customize the upgrade.xsl file. Figure 8-22 shows the data source for two versions of a form template created to review webcasts.

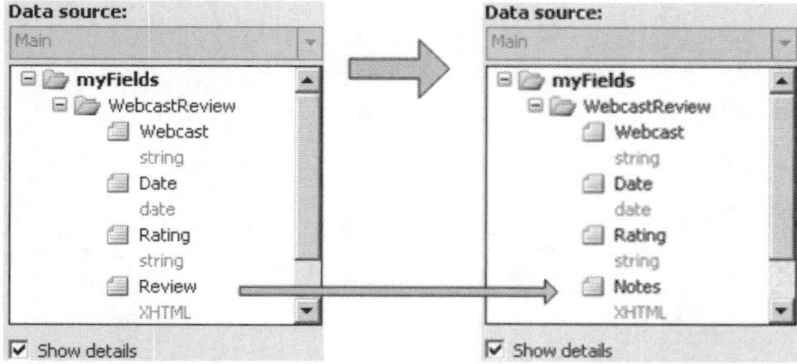

Figure 8-22 Renaming data source nodes requires customizing the upgrade.xsl file.

The first step is to design a form based on the data source appearing on the right in Figure 8-22. Create a new Visual Basic project for InfoPath in Visual Studio. After manually creating the data source, don't forget to drag it into the view so you have something to fill out. When finished, save your form and publish it to your local machine or SharePoint site. We will refer to this as version 1 of your form template. Fill out and save a couple of forms using the published form template.

The next step is to upgrade the form. We will need to refer back to version 1 files later, so create a parallel directory named Webcast Review v2 and copy all files from the original project into it. Open the Visual Studio solution file (.sln) in this directory.

Once you have the InfoPath designer open, go to the Data Source pane. For this exercise, we will make a simple change and rename the Review node to Notes. You can do this by double-clicking on the Review node and typing **Notes**. InfoPath displays the warning shown in Figure 8-23.

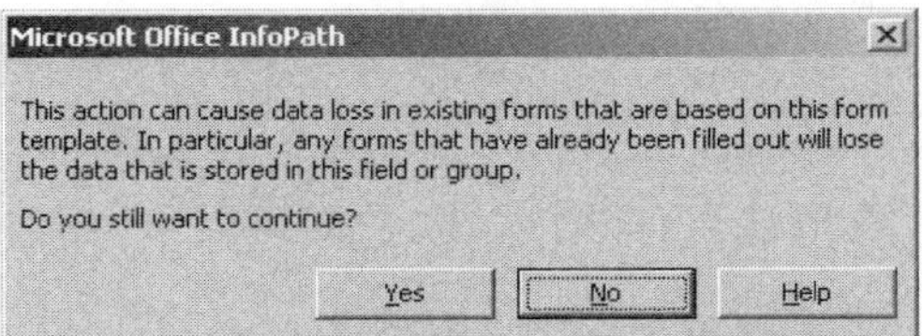

Figure 8-23 Automatic upgrade doesn't support renaming elements.

Click OK to close the dialog box. Switch to Visual Studio to refresh the state of the project and publish the modified form to the same location, and choose to overwrite version 1. We will refer to this revised version of the form template as version 2. Note that the actual version number in the manifest.xsf file might be later. Now try to open one of the forms you saved earlier with version 1 of the form template. InfoPath displays an error message, as shown in Figure 8-24.

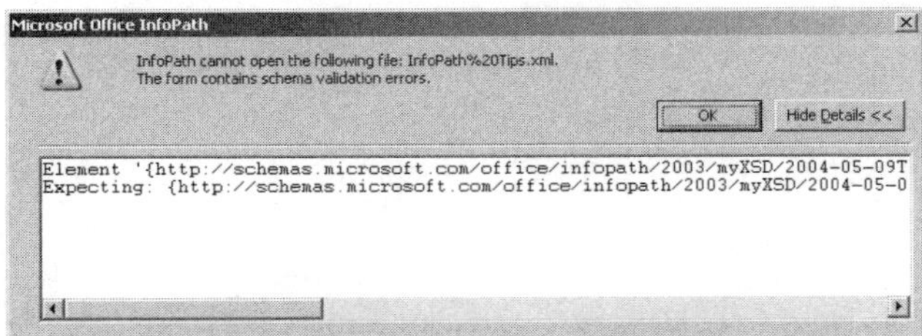

Figure 8-24 Automatic upgrade fails to load old forms when data source nodes have been renamed.

For reference, here's the full text of the error message:

Error Message

```
Element '{http://schemas.microsoft.com/office/infopath/2003/myXSD/2004-05-09T05-12-15}
Review' is unexpected according to content model of parent element '{http://
schemas.microsoft.com/office/infopath/2003/myXSD/2004-05-09T05-12-15}WebcastReview'.
Expecting: {http://schemas.microsoft.com/office/infopath/2003/myXSD/2004-05-09T05-12-15}
Notes.
```

InfoPath expected the Notes node but instead encountered Review. You can modify the upgrade.xsl file to support converting old forms. In most cases, you won't have to worry about this because InfoPath is smart about upgrading forms when there is a schema addition or deletion. However, InfoPath cannot automatically upgrade forms that have been renamed or whose data source nodes have moved.

In our Webcast Review example, the Review node is renamed Notes. Using this simple example, let's look at what it takes to modify the upgrade.xsl file. You can open the file in Visual Studio or Notepad. Before you do that, however, you must close the InfoPath designer if it is open because it locks the file. From Visual Studio, you can double-click on the upgrade.xsl file in Solution Explorer. Recall that InfoPath automatically generates this file, but you can modify it to accommodate upgrading old forms. For this simple exercise, replace the following code:

```
<xsl:element name="my:Notes">
    <xsl:apply-templates select="my:Notes/text() | my:Notes/*[namespace-uri()='http://
        www.w3.org/1999/xhtml']" mode="RichText"/>
</xsl:element>
```

with this new code:

```
<xsl:element name="my:Notes">
    <xsl:choose>
        <xsl:when test="my:Review">
            <xsl:apply-templates select="my:Review/text() | my:Review/*[namespace-uri()
                ='http://www.w3.org/1999/xhtml']" mode="RichText"/>
        </xsl:when>
        <xsl:otherwise>
            <xsl:apply-templates select="my:Notes/text() | my:Notes/*[namespace-uri()
                ='http://www.w3.org/1999/xhtml']" mode="RichText"/>
        </xsl:otherwise>
    </xsl:choose>
</xsl:element>
```

The new *xsl:element* block uses an *xsl:choose* to support processing the old version of the *my:Notes* node named *my:Review*. The *xsl:otherwise* block handles versions of the form that have version numbers later than the *maxVersionToUpgrade* value stored in the manifest. Save the upgrade.xsl file and close the file from Visual Studio so that you can open InfoPath designer. If you try to open the InfoPath designer while the upgrade.xsl file is still open for editing in Visual Studio, Visual Studio will ask whether or not you want to close the files. You should click Yes. You can open the InfoPath designer by right-clicking on the Webcast Request solution in the Solution Explorer pane and choosing Open InfoPath. Republish your form template to the same location, and choose to overwrite the existing form template.

Try again to open one of the forms saved using version 1 of the form template. It should now open. If it doesn't, check the *solutionVersion* attribute in the form and make sure it is less than or equal to the *maxVersionToUpgrade* attribute in the manifest.

By modifying the upgrade.xsl file, you can support upgrading old versions of the form, but there are some limitations:

- **Schemas created outside the designer may not update the upgrade.xsl file** InfoPath will not attempt to automatically upgrade closed schemas created outside of the designer because they cannot be extended. Open schemas developed outside of the designer are OK because they are extensible and InfoPath compliant. The following schema operations are supported:

- Add–OK even with default data
- Delete–OK
- Rename–treated as delete and add; content will be lost

- **Changing schemas from the designer will overwrite the upgrade.xsl file** You can modify the upgrade.xsl file in your form template, but be careful to save a backup copy outside of the package, because when you modify the data source, InfoPath overwrites the upgrade.xsl file. If the name is changed, it will be ignored and a new the upgrade.xsl file will be used instead.
- **The upgrade.xsl file only knows about the current schema** InfoPath will not validate the schema of forms created with older versions of the form template. This can pose problems during upgrade when InfoPath applies the upgrade.xsl file because there is no way to ensure that the old form is valid for the old schema. One workaround is to use a custom event handler.

Using Custom Events

The most powerful upgrade option is defining a custom event handler. When you select Use Custom Event from the On Version Upgrade drop-down list box on the Advanced tab of the Form Options dialog box, InfoPath changes the entry in the manifest to the following:

```
<xsf:documentVersionUpgrade>
    <xsf:useScriptHandler/>
</xsf:documentVersionUpgrade>
```

The *useScriptHandler* element instructs InfoPath to call the *OnVersionUpgrade* event handler. The element name is a carryover from InfoPath 2003, which supports only script. Even though InfoPath SP1 supports managed code, the element name has been left unchanged to provide backward compatibility with form templates authored in InfoPath 2003.

Click the Edit button to jump to the *OnVersionUpgrade* event handler. InfoPath switches to Visual Studio (or the Microsoft Script Editor), and you can add custom logic to the event handler:

```
<InfoPathEventHandler(EventType:=InfoPathEventType.OnVersionUpgrade)> _
Public Sub OnVersionUpgrade(ByVal e As VersionUpgradeEvent)
    ' Write your code here.
End Sub
```

The next two sections present simple examples of how to customize the *OnVersionUpgrade* event handler to upgrade forms.

Upgrading Old Forms

The first example involves transforming the old form to the new form using code. This will have the same effect as creating the custom upgrade.xsl file in the previous example. Instead of using the .xsl file, we'll create code that does the same simple transform. Replace the *OnVersionUpgrade* stub, listed earlier, with the following code:

```
<InfoPathEventHandler(EventType:=InfoPathEventType.OnVersionUpgrade)> _
Public Sub OnVersionUpgrade(ByVal e As VersionUpgradeEvent)
    Try
        Dim oNotes As IXMLDOMNode = e.XDocument.DOM.selectSingleNode("/my:myFields/
            my:WebcastReview/my:Notes")
        If Not (oNotes Is Nothing) Then
            Dim oReview As IXMLDOMNode = thisXDocument.DOM.selectSingleNode("/my:myFields/
                my:WebcastReview").ownerDocument.createElement("/my:Nodes")
             thisXDocument.DOM.selectSingleNode("/my:myFields/
                 my:WebcastReview").appendChild(oReview)
        End If
        e.ReturnStatus = True
    Catch ex As Exception
        thisXDocument.UI.Alert(ex.Message)
        e.ReturnStatus = False
    End Try
End Sub
```

The code gets the old form's *my:Review* node by calling *selectSingleNode* with the passed-in event object variable, *e*. If that succeeds, the code appends the node to the new document.

You can test this code using one of the old forms created with version 1 of the Webcast Review template. You can either update the form template in place or publish it to a separate SharePoint form library. In the latter case, you must upload and relink the old form files. You can upload files from the default form library. The Upload Form button is to the right of Fill Out This Form.

Caution After uploading the old form, you must relink it so the form's *href* points to the new form template's location. Otherwise, the form will continue to execute using the old form template. Please see the section on "Relinking Forms" in Chapter 9 on "SharePoint Collaboration" for details.

Using Merge Forms to Import Old Forms

Another way to upgrade forms is to leverage InfoPath's built-in support for form merging. The key benefit of this approach is support for multiple old versions. You can specify separate transforms for each old version and upgrade and validate even incompatible old versions. In addition, the Merge Forms feature supports XSL annotations that make it easier to transform your old forms. The key disadvantage of the Merge Forms approach is that you must open the form using Merge Forms from the File menu. In other words, double-clicking on the form file won't work.

The following steps describe how to use Merge Forms to import older versions of your forms.

1. First, you need to enable form merging. From the InfoPath designer, go the General tab of the Form Options dialog box, and then select Enable Form Merging (as shown in Figure 8-25). InfoPath selects this option by default, so you probably won't have to do anything, but it's good to double-check.

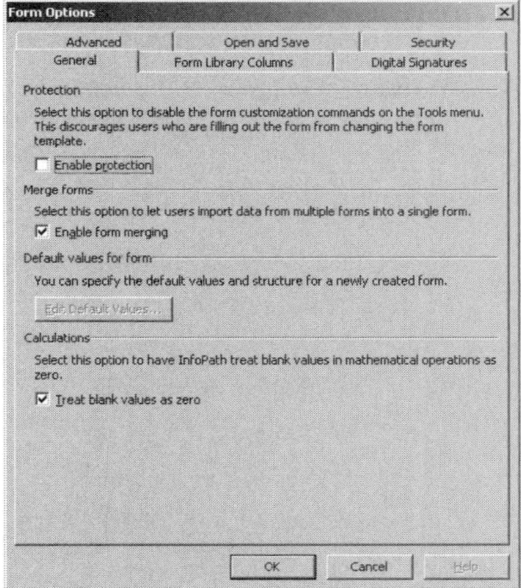

Figure 8-25 Check to make sure Form Merging is enabled.

2. We can repurpose the upgrade.xsl file that we edited earlier. To reuse the upgrade.xsl file for the form merging, you must copy it to a file with a different name. Open a command prompt window, navigate to the project directory, and copy the file. For this example, let's name it **upgrade1.xsl**.

3. Switch back to the designer and add this new file as a resource. Choose Resource Files from the Tools menu, and then add the file to the project.

4. You must also add the schema of the old form as a resource. Recall that we made a copy of the original project before upgrading. Copy the myschema.xsd file from this old project into your new project with a different name—for example, **myschema1.xsd**.

> **Note** If you don't have this old project handy, refer to the Webcast Review directory in the source code for this chapter.

5. Next you have to manually modify the manifest.xsf file. After you have added both the .xsl and the .xsd files as resources, save the form and close the InfoPath designer. That way, Visual Studio won't complain when you try to open the manifest.xsf file.
6. When you switch back to Visual Studio, notice that the new resource files–upgrade1.xsl and myschema1.xsd–appear in Solution Explorer.
7. Double-click on the manifest.xsf file and search for *importParameters*. You should see the following line of code:

```
<xsf:importParameters enabled="yes"></xsf:importParameters>
```

8. Change it to the following:

```
<xsf:importParameters enabled="yes">
    <xsf:importSource name="" schema="myschema1.xsd" transform="upgrade1.xsl">
        </xsf:importSource>
    <xsf:importSource name="" schema="myschema.xsd" transform="upgrade.xsl">
        </xsf:importSource>
</xsf:importParameters>
```

The first *importSource* element in this code instructs InfoPath to test imported files with the myschema1.xsd file and, if it validates against the schema, to apply the upgrade1.xsl transform file. Notice that the *name* attribute is left blank. If specified, the name attribute overrides the schema validation matching. However, for upgrading, all forms will have the same name, so if we want to support upgrading multiple old versions, we want to rely on the schema match.

The second *importSource* element specifies the default form merging functionality for the form. You need this to support default rollup, as you saw in Chapter 1.

> **Important** The order of the *importSource* elements matters. InfoPath goes through the list and attempts to validate the form to import against the schemas in the list. If it succeeds, it stops and uses the corresponding transform. For this reason, if you have two schemas that are structurally equivalent but differ in their restrictions, you must place the less restrictive schema first.

> **Important** Performance is another consideration for the ordering of your *import-Source* elements. If you expect to merge documents from schema A most of the time and documents matching schema B are rare, put A first so that multiple validations do not have to be performed for the frequently imported forms matching schema A.

9. Add the namespace property to the file properties for the myschema1.xsd file definition in the manifest. The fourth line of the following code does this:

```
<xsf:file name="myschema1.xsd">
    <xsf:fileProperties>
        <xsf:property name="fileType" type="string" value="resource"></xsf:property>
        <xsf:property name="namespace" type="string" value="http://
            schemas.microsoft.com/office/infopath/2003/myXSD/2004-05-09T05-12-15">
            </xsf:property>
    </xsf:fileProperties>
</xsf:file>
```

10. Save and close the manifest.xsf file.

11. To test the upgrade, open a blank form by double-clicking on the saved or published .xsn file. (Merge Forms is not available in preview mode.)

12. Select Merge Forms and open a file that was created using an older version of the form.

Merge Forms is a very powerful feature, but debugging the Merge Forms process is practically impossible. You can add code to handle *OnMergeRequest* and *OnAfterImport* events and set breakpoint in both to verify where failure occurred.

Warning Calling ImportDOM is equivalent to performing a merge operation using the Merge Forms command on the File menu. You might be wondering why we didn't call the *ImportDOM* method from the *OnVersionUpgrade* event handler. Yes, that would be very cool, but unfortunately it doesn't work and there is a known issue in InfoPath SP1 where InfoPath will hang when calling ImportDOM inside of the *OnVersionUpgrade* event handler.

Summary

This chapter explored InfoPath deployment, security, and version upgrade. We summarized the various deployment approaches and presented a brief analysis. In the security section, we described the various trust levels and how InfoPath sets the trust level. We also described how to configure the security permissions to make debugging easier. The many tradeoffs between a form's features and its security requirements must be considered when you design a form. If you call methods in InfoPath's object model that require security level 3, you must also fully trust the form. If you restrict the form for e-mail deployment, you cannot use managed code. If you want to support mobile users, you must sign the form.

Version upgrade is inevitable and is often a cost-of-ownership issue. InfoPath supports automatic version upgrade of forms and provides support for custom extensions. When automatic upgrade doesn't work, you can define transforms and event handlers to assist.

Chapter 9

SharePoint Collaboration

InfoPath and SharePoint together make an extraordinarily powerful information management tool. Without any customization at all, you can publish forms to be shared with a group of people, and you can sort and filter information from these forms in a SharePoint view or a view exported from SharePoint to Microsoft Excel or Microsoft Access.

In this chapter, we will cover basic publishing of a form to a SharePoint form library, promoting data from your InfoPath form to columns for use in SharePoint, using views to control the presentation of your data in the SharePoint Web UI, and reading information from and creating items in SharePoint lists within your InfoPath form.

Prerequisites

To use the SharePoint integration features of InfoPath, you must have access to a SharePoint server running on Windows Server 2003 and either Microsoft Windows SharePoint Services or Microsoft SharePoint Portal Server 2003. Windows SharePoint Services can be downloaded from *http://www.microsoft.com/downloads/details.aspx?FamilyID=e084d5cb-1161-46f2-a363-8e0c2250d990&DisplayLang=en*. More information about SharePoint Portal Server 2003 can be found at *http://www.microsoft.com/sharepoint/*.

There are a number of providers of hosted SharePoint services. More information can be found at *http://go.microsoft.com/fwlink/?LinkId=25479*.

> **Important** The SharePoint features in InfoPath cannot be used with earlier versions of SharePoint (SharePoint Team Services and SharePoint Portal Server 2001).

This chapter requires that you have a site set up on a Windows SharePoint Services server or on SharePoint Portal Server 2003. The chapter does not cover any features specific to SharePoint Portal Server.

Publishing to a SharePoint Form Library

A SharePoint form library is designed to store XML documents, and InfoPath is an XML editor. The two together create a powerful combination. The SharePoint form library not only stores the .xml files, but it knows what template to use when editing the file and also which nodes in the XML to promote to columns for displaying and filtering in SharePoint views. In this section, you will see an example of this in action and a discussion of how it works.

In Chapter 1, you saw a brief overview of publishing an InfoPath form to a SharePoint form library. Here we will go over it again and explain each step.

Publishing a Form to a SharePoint Library

1. Launch InfoPath and then click Design A Form.
2. In the Design A Form task pane click Customize A Sample.
3. In the Customize A Sample dialog box, select Meeting Agenda, and then click OK to open a copy of the Meeting Agenda sample in design mode.
4. Choose Publish from the File menu to open the Publishing Wizard, and then click Next.
5. Select To A SharePoint Form Library, and then click Next.
6. Select Create A New Form Library. If you are updating an existing form library, select Modify An Existing Form Library. Click Next.

   You can modify an existing form library that was created via the SharePoint Web interface or created via the Publishing Wizard.
7. Enter the URL of your SharePoint site (e.g., **http://sharepointserver/testsite/**), and then click Next.
8. Enter the name of the form library you want to create–in this case, **Meeting Agenda**–and then click Next.

   The name will be used for both the display name and the URL of the form library. You can change the display name later, but you cannot change the URL.

   The next page displays the list of form library columns to promote. Promotion will be discussed in more detail later in this chapter.
9. Click Finish to accept the list of promoted columns and execute the publishing process.

   After publishing, you will get a final wizard page with the URL to the form. If you have Microsoft Outlook installed, there will be a button to create a blank e-mail message to notify users about the form. This is shown in Figure 9-1.
10. Select the Open This Form From Its Published Location check box, and then click Close to close the wizard and open the SharePoint document library.

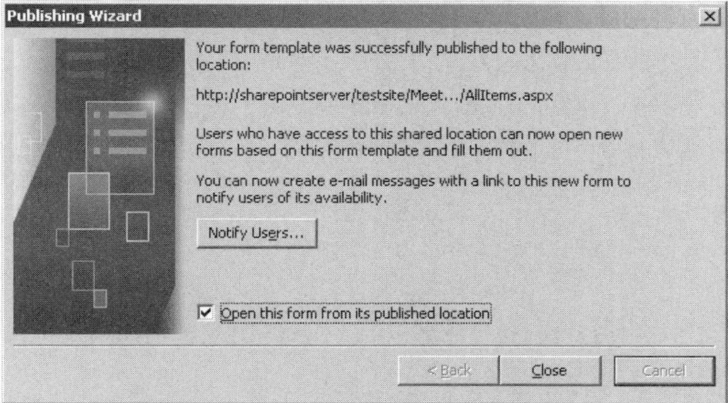

Figure 9-1 Success notification page of the Publishing Wizard

Note There are three ways to review the URL of the SharePoint library you created or updated at the end of the wizard. The first is to check the URL displayed in the wizard. If the URL is too long to fit in the wizard, part of it will be cut off. Second, if you have Outlook installed, you can click the Notify Users button to create an e-mail message to send to others that contains the URL. The third method is to select the Open This Form From Its Published Location check box before closing the wizard, which will open the form library in your browser window.

You now have a SharePoint form library based on the Meeting Agenda template. The library has a number of default settings and has your published template associated with it. Note the URL of the form library so you can access it later to fill out forms using your template and to modify your template as needed.

Caution A SharePoint meeting workspace is a special type of workspace that holds meeting series. You create a meeting workspace by creating a new site in SharePoint and selecting a Meeting Workspace template. Each meeting in a series can have its own independent data. By default, a form library created in a meeting workspace contains separate data for each meeting in the series. For many scenarios, you might want to convert the form library into series items, which will cause all items in the form library to be shared across all meetings. You can then use the form library as if it were not part of a meeting workspace and add information to the form that references the meeting workspace instance.

Caution To convert a meeting workspace list into series items, go to the form library page on your SharePoint site, click Modify Settings And Columns, click Change General Settings, and then in the Share List Items Across All Meetings (Series Items) section, select Yes for Change Items Into Series Items, and then click OK. You cannot undo this operation.

Using a Form in a Document Library

To fill out a form in the SharePoint form library, click Fill Out This Form. After you have filled out or opened a form once on a machine, the template will be cached and show up in the InfoPath Fill Out A Form dialog box. You can also add the form to the InfoPath template cache by using the *CacheSolution* method of the *Application* object. A form filled out from the template will have a reference to the template in the document library and the URN of that template. More information on caching can be found in Chapter 2 and Chapter 8.

Promoting Data to SharePoint Form Library Columns

One of the most powerful features of a SharePoint form library is the ability to promote data from an .xml file to a column in the form library. You can then use your custom data with SharePoint library features such as sorting, filtering, and exporting to Excel. This feature is independent of the editor used to create the .xml files, but we will discuss its use with InfoPath here.

Selecting Form Properties to Promote

There are two places in the InfoPath UI where you can select which form library columns to promote: on a page of the Publishing Wizard and on the Form Library Columns tab of the Form Options dialog box (reached from the Tools menu). Both places allow you to make the same changes. The Form Options dialog box is often a better choice, as explained in the Developer Nugget on "Working with Published Forms."

In this section, we will add some more properties to the base Meeting Agenda form and learn about the features of promoting data.

Promoting Fields in the Meeting Agenda Form

1. Edit the Meeting Agenda template on your SharePoint site by browsing to the form library, clicking Modify Settings And Columns, and then clicking Edit Template on the right side of the Template line in the General Settings section. (See Figure 9-2.)
2. Choose Form Options from the Tools menu.

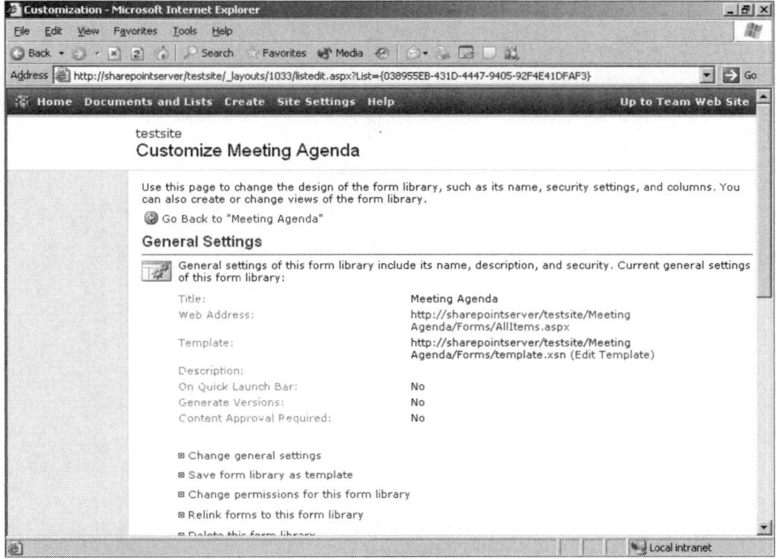

Figure 9-2 Editing the template with Edit Template on the General Settings page in SharePoint

3. In the Form Options dialog box, click on the Form Library Columns tab, and then click Add.
4. In the Select A Field Or Group dialog box, select the *location* node. Note that the column name is filled in with the name of the XML node: *location*.
5. To make the column name consistent with the other promoted column names, change the first letter to uppercase, and then click OK. This creates a single-line text field when the data is promoted.
6. Click Add, select the *objective* node, and then change the column name to **Objective**.

   Note that the Choose A Function To Use On Repeating Data drop-down list box becomes active for this node, and that the list has only one option: Plaintext. This is because *objective* is a Rich Text field that allows XHTML–a data type that SharePoint does not support for promotion. The *plaintext* function tells SharePoint to take all of the text out of the *objective* node, ignore the formatting, and promote it to a multiple-line text field.

7. Click OK, and then click Add again.
8. Expand the *attendees* node and the *attendee* node, and then select the *emailAddressPrimary* node. Change the column name to **Attendees E-mail**.

   Note that the repeating data drop-down list box is active again, this time because the selected node is inside of a repeating group. In this case, the choices are

   - *first*, which creates a single-line column with the first attendee's e-mail address
   - *last*, which creates a single-line column with the last attendee's e-mail address
   - *count*, which creates a number column with the total number of attendee e-mail addresses
   - *merge*, which creates a multiline column with each attendee's e-mail address, separated by line breaks
9. In the Choose A Function To Use On Repeating Data drop-down list box, select *merge* (as shown in Figure 9-3), and then click OK.

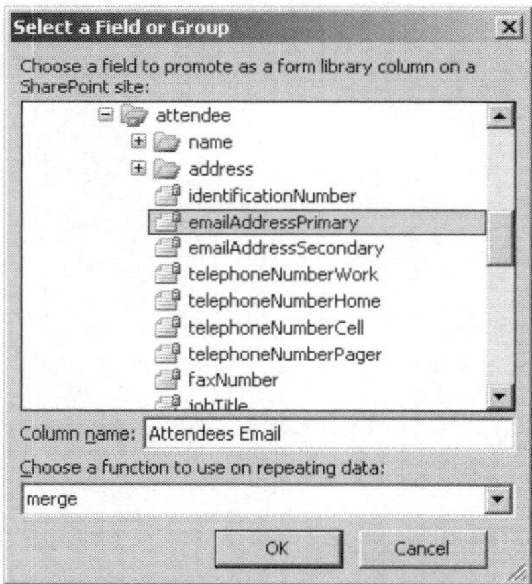

Figure 9-3 Selecting a merged repeating field to promote to SharePoint

10. Click Add. The selection should still be on emailAddressPrimary.
11. Rename the column name to **Attendees Count**, and select the count function from the drop-down list box.
12. Click OK twice to close the Form Options dialog box.
13. Choose Save from the File menu to save your form template back to the SharePoint site.

You have now updated the list of columns on your SharePoint form library (see Figure 9-4). Any new form that is saved to this library will have the data in the new columns exposed. Existing forms will not automatically have their data repromoted to fill in the new columns.

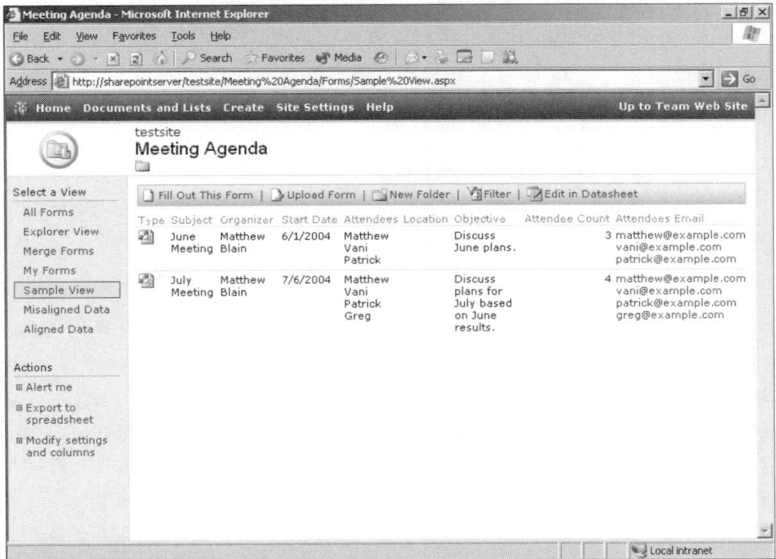

Figure 9-4 Aggregated data in the SharePoint view

Tip To update the promoted data in existing forms in your form library to include the new columns, you must update the individual .xml files. One way to do this all at once is to copy them to your machine and back to the site. Open the form library Explorer view, copy all of the existing files to your local machine, and then copy them back to the SharePoint form library, overwriting the files previously there. This will cause SharePoint to repromote all of the data in the saved .xml files. It will also have the side effect of marking all of the files as being modified by you and setting their date and time to when you copied the files back to the SharePoint site, even though you did not make any changes to the data.

In addition to the *plaintext*, *first*, *last*, *merge*, and *count* options described above for aggregating repeating data, SharePoint can calculate the *sum*, *average*, *min*, or *max* of a numeric field.

Developer Nugget: Working with Published Forms

You have the choice of a few development processes when you create a form for use on a SharePoint site. One method is to work with the form in design mode directly on the SharePoint site. An alternative method, and the primary method used with a Visual Studio project, is to work with the form on your local machine and publish it to the SharePoint site when it comes time to deploy a new release.

Designing the form directly from the SharePoint site is the easiest technique. Once you have created a form library and published the form to it, you have a choice of three methods of reaching design mode. The first is to start design mode from the SharePoint Web site. Go to the form library page, click Modify Settings And Columns, and then click Edit Template. The second method is to start from InfoPath, choose Design A Form from the File menu, select the On A SharePoint site, and then locate your site and form library. The third method is to fill out the form, and then choose Design This Form from the Tools menu. (Notice that you can disable the Design This Form menu item on a per-template basis by selecting Enable Protection on the General tab of the Form Options dialog box.) If you want to make a backup of the template or share the template with others, you can save the template while in design mode to another location, extract the form files while in design mode, or right-click the template link in the General Settings section of your SharePoint form library and save the target of the link to your desired location.

An alternative technique is to save the template extracted locally on your system and publish as necessary to SharePoint. This approach is particularly convenient if you frequently directly edit the individual files of the form, such as the manifest.xsf file, merge .xsl files, or view .xsl files. It is also a good approach to use when storing the template in a source code control system. To work in this mode, extract the form files to a directory on your machine. (More information about extracting form files can be found in Chapter 1.) When it is time to deploy the form to your SharePoint site, save the form to make sure the latest changes are saved locally, go through the Publishing Wizard to publish the form to SharePoint, close the form, and then open it from SharePoint to verify that it has been published correctly.

Why the extra save before publishing and the close after publishing? This is because you are creating two copies of the form, one on your local system and one on SharePoint. It is very easy to accidentally make changes in the copy on SharePoint after publishing and then wonder where the changes went the next time you design the form from your local copy. Similarly, the Form Options dialog box is the recommended place to change form library column promotion settings: the promotion page of the Publishing Wizard only affects the copy of the form on the SharePoint site.

If you are using a Visual Studio InfoPath project, you are using the second technique, with the advantage that Visual Studio manages extracting form files and saving the form for you at the right time.

Caution A Visual Studio InfoPath project contains the form plus the source code behind the form. When you publish the form to SharePoint, or otherwise save the template to an .xsn file, only the form and the compiled assembly are saved. The source code is not saved in the XSN.

Limits on the Number of Promoted Columns

SharePoint lists can have a large number of columns, but there is a limit. Just as InfoPath supports a number of different data types for the nodes in the XML, SharePoint has a similar list of data types for columns. The number of columns allowed for each type is described in Table 9-1, along with the InfoPath data types that map to the corresponding SharePoint column type.

Table 9-1 **SharePoint Column Types and Limits**

SharePoint Column Type	InfoPath Field Type	Maximum Number of SharePoint Columns
Single line of text	Anything not specified in the remaining columns	64
Multiple lines of text	Rich text, merge aggregation	31
Number and currency	Whole number, decimal, aggregation resulting in numbers (e.g., sum)	32
Hyperlink	None	32
Date and time	Date, Date/Time	16
Lookup	None	16
Yes/No	True/False (Boolean)	16
Calculated	None	8

Using Merged Fields to Present Repeating Data

Repeating data must be converted into some other format for SharePoint to store as a single value in the column for a particular form. The functions InfoPath provides to aggregate values–that is, to convert a repeating field to a single value–are those to take the *first*, *last*, *count*, or arithmetic *sum*, *average*, *min*, or *max* of a repeating field. There is also the *merge* function, which concatenates every item of a repeating section separated by line breaks.

If you have only one repeating section in your form, promoting the data using *merge* is straightforward: you can select all of the fields you want to promote and select *merge* for each one. Two other scenarios require more planning: promoting data from two independent groups and promoting data from a repeating group while simultaneously promoting data from a child of that repeating group.

Promoting data from two independent groups requires no special planning when you set up promotion of form data to columns. You can choose a number of fields to promote, and they will all be promoted by SharePoint. For example, with the Meeting Agenda form, you can promote the "title" field under the "action repeating" group (under the "actions" group as Action Items). When you view the form library in SharePoint, the Attendees column will have as many line breaks as there are attendees, and the Action Items column will have as many line breaks as there are action items. You can organize the view such that it is not confusing for the user, or you can create two separate views, one to view attendees and the other to view action items. More information on creating views is included later in this chapter.

Promoting data from a repeating group contained within a repeating group presents a different set of issues. If you want to use only the innermost repeating group, SharePoint will work as you would expect: the text of each innermost item will be put into the column data, separated by a linefeed. If you want to use data from both the innermost group and the containing group, you might have to modify your form slightly. Consider the Guest Speaker section of the Meeting Agenda.

Edit the Meeting Agenda template in the form library you created earlier. Promote two fields with the *merge* function: the *agenda subject* node (meetingAgenda/agendaItems/agenda/subject) as **Agenda Subject**, and the guest speaker *singleName* node (meetingAgenda/agendaItems/agenda/guestSpeakers/guestSpeaker/name/singleName) as **Guest Speaker Name**. Then save your template back to the SharePoint form library.

Note When you use the Meeting Agenda form to insert a guest speaker, click on an agenda item, and then select Subject-Focused Guest Speaker from the Section submenu of the Insert menu.

Now fill out your form with two agenda items, the first with two guest speakers and the second with one guest speaker. Save it to your SharePoint site, and look at the default view, as shown in Figure 9-5. The Agenda Subject column will contain two lines, and the Guest Speaker Name column will contain three. How do you know which agenda item the guest speaker spoke about?

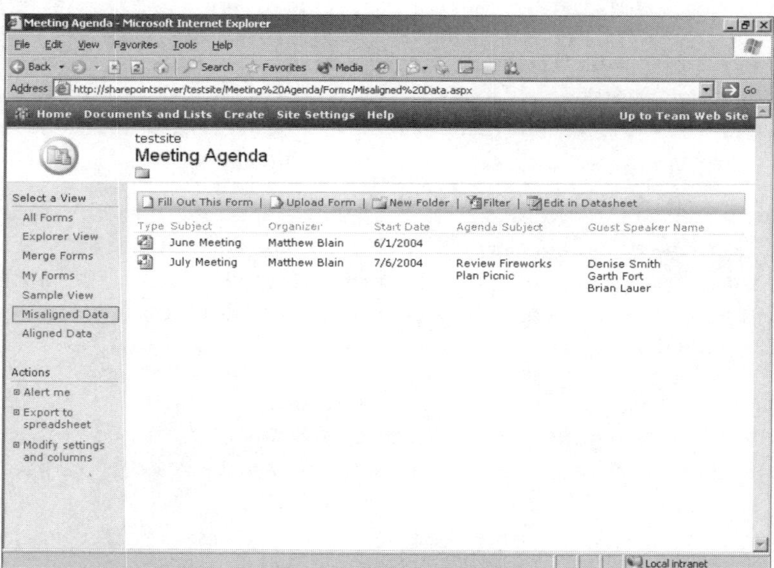

Figure 9-5 Note that the Agenda Subject and Guest Speaker Name fields have mismatched data.

One solution is to repeat the agenda information for each guest speaker, effectively expanding (or joining) the hierarchical information to contain a flat copy. This copy can then be promoted to SharePoint, and everything will line up.

Joining Agenda Information to Guest Speaker for Promotion

1. Edit the Meeting Agenda template on your SharePoint site.
2. Click Select Data Source in the Design Tasks task pane.
3. Navigate the data source to the *guestSpeaker* section (*meetingAgenda/agendaItems/agenda/guestSpeakers/guestSpeaker*). Click *guestSpeaker* to select it.
4. Click Add, enter the name **speakerAgendaSubject**, and then click OK.
5. Right-click on *my:speakerAgendaSubject* in the Data Source task pane, and select Properties.
6. In the Field Or Group Properties dialog box, click the *fx* button to the right of the Value field.
7. In the Insert Formula dialog box, click Insert Field Or Group.
8. Select the *subject* field in the agenda group (which is about two pages above where the dialog box opens to). Click OK.
9. The formula should now read *subject*, as shown in Figure 9-6.
10. Click OK to close the Insert Formula dialog box.

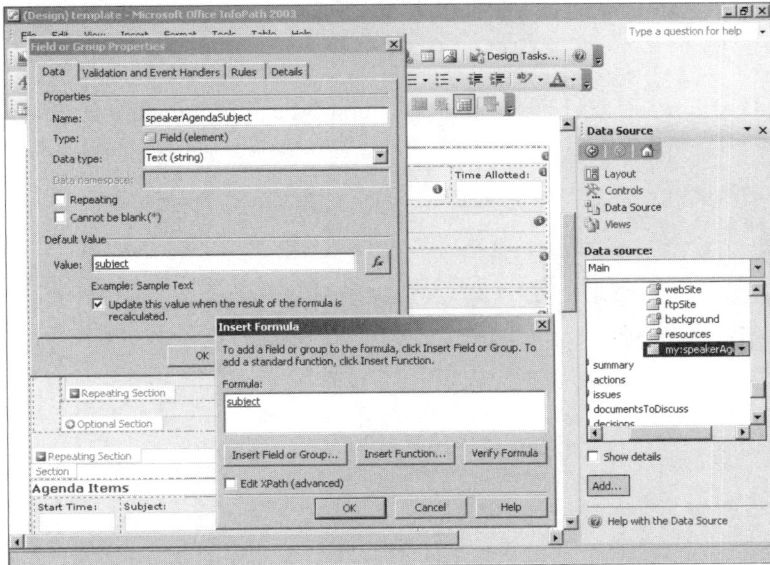

Figure 9-6 Automatically copying the agenda subject to the *guest speaker* node

11. Note that the Update This Value When The Result Of The Formula Is Recalculated check box is selected. This check box is the key to this whole process. When selected, InfoPath will update the value of the field whenever the values the formula depends on change; you don't have to write any rules or form code.

12. Click OK to close the Field Or Group Properties dialog box.

    You have now created a new field in the guest speaker group, which InfoPath will keep synchronized with the agenda the speaker is related to.

13. Go to the Form Library Columns tab of the Form Options dialog box (which is accessed from the Tools menu).

14. Click Add, select the *my:speakerAgendaSubject* node you just created in the guest speaker group, name the column **Guest Speaker Agenda Subject**, select the *merge* function, and then click OK.

15. Click Add, select *singleName* in the name section of the guest speaker group, name the column **Guest Speaker Name**, select the *merge* function, and then click OK twice to close the Form Options dialog box.

16. Save the template to your SharePoint site.

Now when you create a form with your Meeting Agenda template, and create agenda items in the form with multiple guest speakers, the Guest Speaker Agenda Subject and Guest Speaker Name columns will have the same number of lines and will correspond to each other, as shown in Figure 9-7. Note that if there are no guest speakers for an agenda item, there will be no corresponding Guest Speaker Agenda Subject line, so you might also want to continue promoting the Agenda Subject line. When you promote both the *Guest Speaker Agenda Subject* and the *Agenda Subject,* you are now in a situation similar to the case of promoting data from two independent groups: the Guest Speaker Agenda Subject column will have as many line breaks as there are guest speakers, and the Agenda Subject column will have as many line breaks as there are agenda items. You can use these different columns in different SharePoint views.

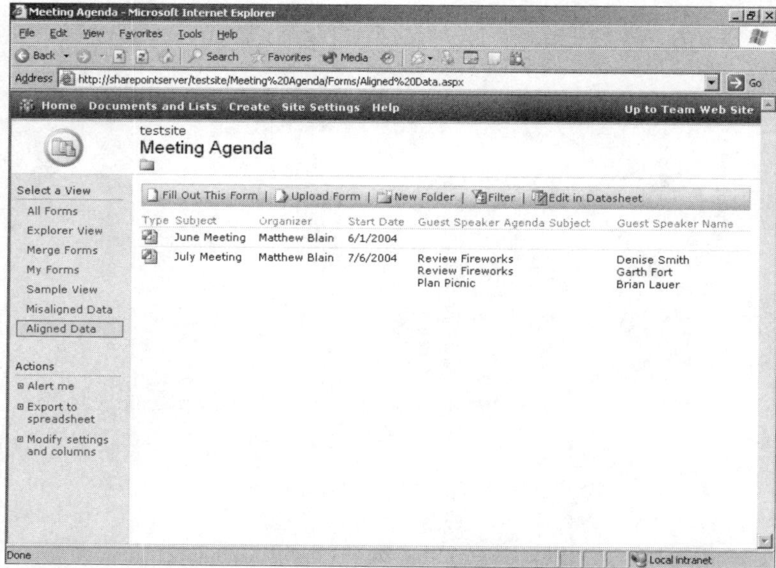

Figure 9-7 Note that the Guest Speaker Agenda Subject and Guest Speaker Name now match.

Promotion Technical Details: The manifest.xsf and properties.xfp Files

The *xsf:listProperties* node of the manifest.xsf file describes what fields in your form will be promoted to columns in SharePoint. The Form Library Columns tab of the Form Options dialog box edits this information. You can also edit the manifest directly, which is a timesaver in editing the display name of multiple fields. Editing the manifest also allows you some level of control over the order and name of internal column names in SharePoint. SharePoint list columns have two names. One is the display name, which is what you see in the UI and what you control with the InfoPath designer, or the *name* attribute of the *xsf:field* node in the manifest.xsf file. The other is the internal name, which is the *columnName* attribute of the *xsf:field* node in the manifest.xsf file.

When the form is published to SharePoint, a file called properties.xfp is created in the Forms directory, along with the template.xsn file. This file lists the promoted properties in the Collaborative Application Markup Language (CAML) format understood by SharePoint. If you work with the internals of SharePoint, the internal name is known as *Name* and the display name is *DisplayName*. The *Node* property points to the node in the .xml file that will be promoted to the associated column. Although it looks like an XPath, it is not. Only the node names are used during the promotion process, while the namespaces are ignored. The sections on working with SharePoint lists later in this chapter will discuss some techniques that use some of this internal information.

SharePoint Views

The goal of promoting InfoPath XML form data to SharePoint columns is to be able to view and filter the data across multiple forms. You can do this with SharePoint views, which can be sorted and filtered based on your data. You can also export the data to Excel or Access. An in-depth discussion of SharePoint itself is outside the scope of this book, but we will briefly cover some of what you can do with a form library.

Creating a New View

1. Go to the Meeting Agenda form library you created earlier. You can also create a form library based on the Meeting Agenda-Full Promotion sample in the companion content.
2. Click Modify Settings And Columns.
3. Click Create A New View, and then click Standard View.

   There are three types of views available. A Standard View shows a list of your forms. A Datasheet View looks like a spreadsheet. With normal lists, you can edit the items directly in the Datasheet View, but data promoted from InfoPath forms cannot be pushed back into the forms by SharePoint, so the fields will be marked read-only. A Calendar View displays a calendar control with the forms displayed at a particular date or range of dates. You can use promoted values (such as the Start Date in the Meeting Agenda) as the date used to display the form.

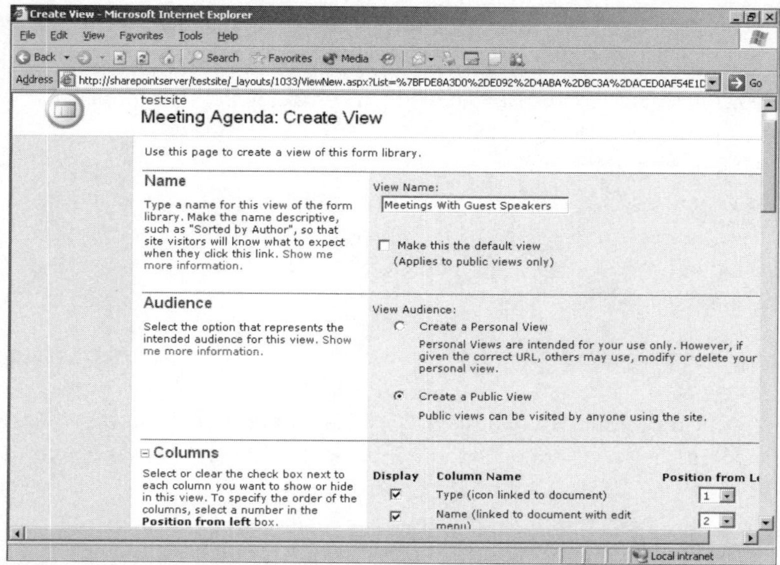

Figure 9-8 Creating a new view

4. Name the view **Meetings With Guest Speakers**.
5. Leave the audience as a Public View.
6. Make sure only the check boxes for Type, Subject, Organizer, Start Date, Attendees, Location, Guest Speaker Agenda Subject, and Guest Speaker Name are selected.

   Figure 9-8 shows the Create View Web page. Look at the Sort and Filter sections. This view uses the default values. Because Guest Speakers is a merged field, you can not check for equality. To limit the view to only forms with guest speakers, you can promote the count of guest speakers as a new column.

   You might choose to set the filter function to a value such as *Start Date is greater than [Today]* to generate a view of future meetings.
7. Click OK to finish creating the view.
8. Click Go Back To "Meeting Agenda". Your view will show up in the list of views on the left.
9. Click Meetings With Guest Speakers to switch to the view.

You have now created a view. You can sort on fields by clicking the field name, or you can filter on fields by clicking the Filter button. Sorting and filtering here only affect the view while you are viewing it; when you return to the view, it will default to the sorting and filtering rules you defined when you created the view.

SharePoint Merge Views

Merge views are unique to form libraries. They let you specify multiple forms to merge. You can create a merge view using the same filtering mechanisms as any other view to display the forms that are likely to need merging. The user can then select items from the list and then click Merge Forms to create a new form from the merged information. You can also include the form library as a Web part on another page along with a content editor Web part to guide the user through the merge process. For more information on merging forms, see Chapter 2.

> **Note** The word *merge* means different things in InfoPath and in this chapter. One meaning is to combine the results of multiple forms into one form, which can be started with the SharePoint merge view, the Merge Forms command on the File menu, or the *ImportDOM* <$I~*ImportDOM* method><$I~methods;*ImportDOM*>method of the InfoPath object model. The second meaning is the *merge* function used when you combine the values of repeating nodes in a single form into a single multiline value during the promotion process on SharePoint.

Exporting to Excel

In Chapter 2, you learned how to export to Excel from within InfoPath. You can also export to Excel from SharePoint. When you export to Excel from InfoPath, you select the list of fields to export and, optionally, additional forms to use as data sources. When you export to Excel from SharePoint, you select a form library view. The first method is excellent for ad hoc data analysis; the second is more suited to recurring analysis and reporting.

To export a view to Excel, browse to your form library on your SharePoint site and select a view. (You might want to create a view just for reporting purposes.) If the view is not a Datasheet view, click Edit In Datasheet. Click the Task Pane button to show the task pane. You will see a number of options for creating reports. Click Export And Link To Excel. This launches Excel and (after presenting the user one or two dialog boxes), creates a new worksheet or workbook with the column information from the view.

The Excel worksheet created will contain a list linked back to your site. The list can be refreshed to get the most recent data from the site. Any fields that are promoted using the *merge* function will show up as multiline fields; if you want to separate the entries, you can use a macro and split the cell data on the line-break character (*Chr(10)*).

> **Caution** The link between the list in Excel and your SharePoint site is two-way. If you delete a row from the linked list and then synchronize the list, the file associated with the deleted row will be deleted from the server. You can prevent this from happening by unlinking the list using Unlink List on the List submenu of the Data menu in Excel.

Other data-linking options include creating PivotTable reports in Excel and linking to a table in Access.

The *OpenXMLDocuments* Control

Microsoft Office 2003 includes the OpenXMLDocuments ActiveX control as part of its install. This is what SharePoint uses to open XML documents, such as InfoPath documents. You can use this control in your own custom ASPX pages created in Microsoft FrontPage or in a content editor Web part. The source in the following code snippet can be used in a content editor Web part on your SharePoint site to provide a convenient shortcut to starting to fill out a Meeting Agenda form.

```
<!-- Create a new InfoPath document from a web page -->
<script language="vbscript">
' Set the URL to the form library.
' Note that it must NOT be URL encoded (e.g. use " ", not "%20").
dim urlLibrary
dim urlTemplate
urlLibrary = "http://sharepointserver/testsite/Meeting Agenda"
urlTemplate = urlLibrary + "/Forms/template.xsn"

Sub CreateNewInfoPathDocument
  dim objOpenXMLDocuments
  Set objOpenXMLDocuments = CreateObject("SharePoint.OpenXMLDocuments")
  objOpenXMLDocuments.CreateNewDocument2 window, urlTemplate, urlLibrary
End Sub
</script>

<button onclick="CreateNewInfoPathDocument()">New Meeting Agenda</button>
```

In addition to the *CreateNewDocument2* method demonstrated in the *CreateNewInfoPathDocument* function shown previously, the OpenXMLDocuments control can be used to open a document for editing (*EditDocument2*), open a template in design mode (*CustomizeTemplate2*), and merge documents (*MergeDocument2*). You can create a custom Web part page with a reference to the merge view in one form library and a button that references a second form library to merge forms based on different templates as part of a workflow scenario.

Relinking Forms

When a form is saved, it references the template it was created with. If you move an .xml file into a different form library or perform another operation that causes the form link to break, you can fix it. Browse to the form library on the SharePoint Web site, click Modify Settings And Columns, and then click Relink Forms To This Form Library. A list is displayed of all the forms that are stored in the form library but are not linked to the template of the form library. Select the forms you want to relink, and then click Relink Forms. This updates the processing instruction in the selected forms to reference the template associated with the form library.

Using SharePoint Lists from InfoPath Forms

You have seen how to create a form library by publishing your form template to SharePoint and how to use some of the UI features of SharePoint to access your data. In this section, you will learn about accessing data stored in SharePoint from within your InfoPath form.

Form libraries, document libraries, and lists are all types of lists in SharePoint. You can access the data stored in the lists through the SharePoint Library Or List data connection, or by calling the SharePoint Lists Web service.

The example that follows is self-referential: the form displays information from its own form library. However, you can read information from any list on your SharePoint site, or even from another SharePoint site if your form template has cross-domain security permissions.

Reading the Form Library as a List

In a number of scenarios, a form might want to read its own form library to present information about other forms in the form library or even metadata about itself. In this section, we will continue expanding the Meeting Agenda sample to display a list of meetings that start on the same date as the meeting being worked on.

Adding a List of Meetings That Start on the Same Date

1. Edit the Meeting Agenda template on your SharePoint site by browsing to the form library, clicking Modify Settings And Columns, and then clicking Edit Template.
2. Choose Data Connections from the Tools menu.
3. In Data Connections dialog box, click Add.
4. In the Data Connection Wizard, select Receive Data, and then click Next.

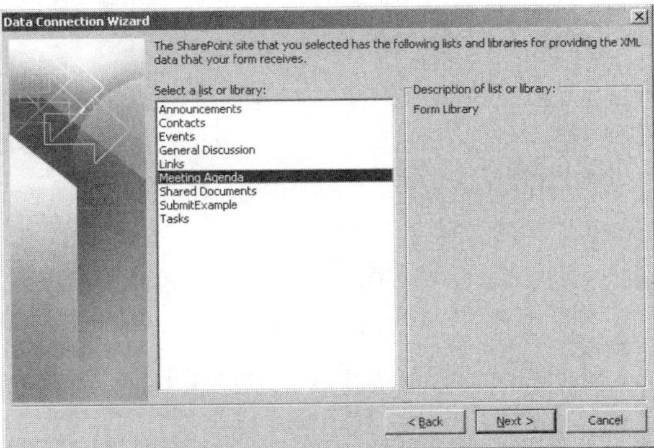

Figure 9-9 Selecting a SharePoint list to receive data from

5. Select SharePoint Library Or List, and then click Next.
6. Enter the URL of your SharePoint site, and then click Next. You should now see a list of all of the form libraries, document libraries, and lists on your site, as shown in Figure 9-9.
7. Select the form library your Meeting Agenda form is published to, and then click Next. You will see a list of all of the fields (columns) in the selected list, including the promoted fields.
8. Make sure only the check boxes for Modified By, Modified, Title, Subject, Organizer, and Start Date are selected (as shown in Figure 9-10), and then click Next.

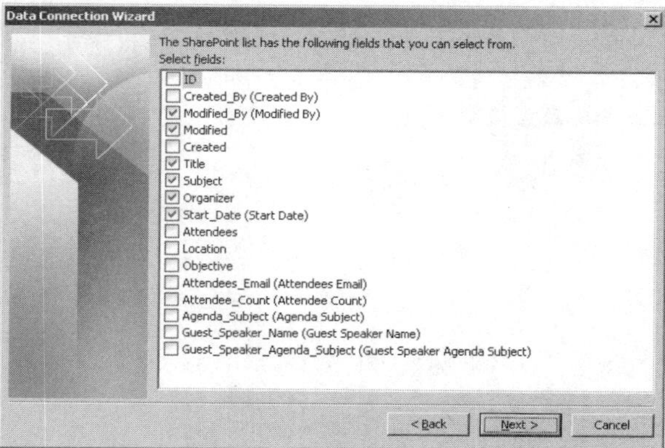

Figure 9-10 Selecting the fields to read

9. Enter the name **Meeting Agenda** for the data connection, leave the Automatically Retrieve Data When Form Is Opened check box selected, click Finish, and then click Close.

   You now have a data connection to the form library's own data. You can now add information about the form library to the form itself.

10. Click in the form view just above Agenda Items to set the insertion point.
11. Press Enter to add some space to the form, and then type **Other Meetings On This Date**.
12. Choose Data Source from the View menu.
13. In the Data Source drop-down list box of the Data Source task pane, select Meeting Agenda (secondary).
14. Expand the items in the data source. You will note that the data source has *myFields*, *dataFields*, and *Meeting_Agenda*.
15. Right-click on *Meeting_Agenda*, and then choose Repeating Section.
16. Click inside the newly inserted repeating section to set the insertion point there.
17. In the Data Source task pane, right-click on *Subject*, and then choose More.

18. Select Hyperlink from the list of available controls, and then click OK.
19. Right-click on the newly inserted Hyperlink control, and choose Edit Hyperlink.
20. In the Edit Hyperlink dialog box, change the Data Source value in the Link To section to the following: **concat('url-to-your-form-library', @Title)**.

    The Title property of the list is in fact the filename, but without the path. The *concat* will concatenate the URL of your form library to the filename, creating a valid link.

> **Note** The *Title* is not actually guaranteed to be the filename. To get a property that is guaranteed to be the filename, you need to modify the .xsf file to add the *LinkFilename* property or the *EncodedAbsUrl* property. Modifying the .xsf file is described later in this chapter in "Reading Columns Not Shown by the Designer Data Connection Wizard."

21. Click OK.
22. Click to the right of the hyperlink to set the insertion point.
23. In the Data Source task pane, right-click on *Organizer*, and then choose More.
24. In the Select A Control dialog box, select Expression Box, and then click OK.

    If you preview the form at this point, you will see that every meeting in your form library shows up in the list, with the subject of the meeting as a hyperlink to the meeting form itself. The next step is to limit the displayed items to just those starting on the same date as this meeting.

25. Right-click on the Repeating Section, and then choose Repeating Section Properties.
26. In the Repeating Section Properties dialog box, click on the Display tab, and then click Conditional Formatting.
27. In the Conditional Formatting dialog box, click Add.
28. In the first drop-down list, select *Start_Date*.
29. In the second drop-down list, select Does Not Begin With.
30. In the third drop-down list, select Use A Formula.

> **Note** Dates in SharePoint form libraries always include the time. Fields that are dates in InfoPath have the time set to Midnight. This means an exact string match will not work. The technique of using *Begins With* is one way you can match a date to a date-time.

31. In the Insert Formula dialog box, click Insert Field Or Group.
32. In the Select A Field Or Group dialog box, change the data source to Main, locate the *startDate* field, and then click OK twice to close the Insert Formula dialog box.

33. Select the Hide This Control check box (see Figure 9-11), and then click OK. This will hide all items in which the start date does not match the start date of the currently open form.

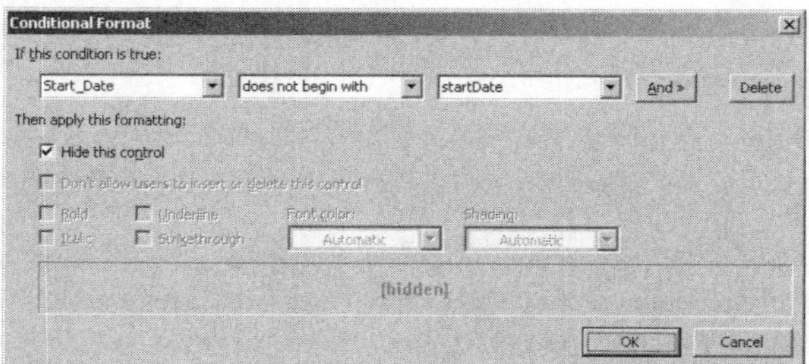

Figure 9-11 Hiding the list items that do not apply to the opened form

34. Click OK twice to close the remaining open dialog boxes.

35. Save your template to your SharePoint site.

You have now updated the template on your SharePoint site. When you create a new meeting or view an existing meeting, you will see a list of all meetings on the same date, with a hyperlink to the relevant Meeting Agenda form. This is shown in Figure 9-12. The entire list is retrieved as the form is opened. This action allows the filtered list items displayed to be dynamic without querying the server again. That is, if you change the date while editing a form, the entries visible in the list will change. However, the list is not aware of changes to other forms, saved on the SharePoint site, while your form is open. The list will be refreshed only when the form is reopened. If keeping the list in sync with the SharePoint site is important, you can call *Query* on the data connection in response to some event.

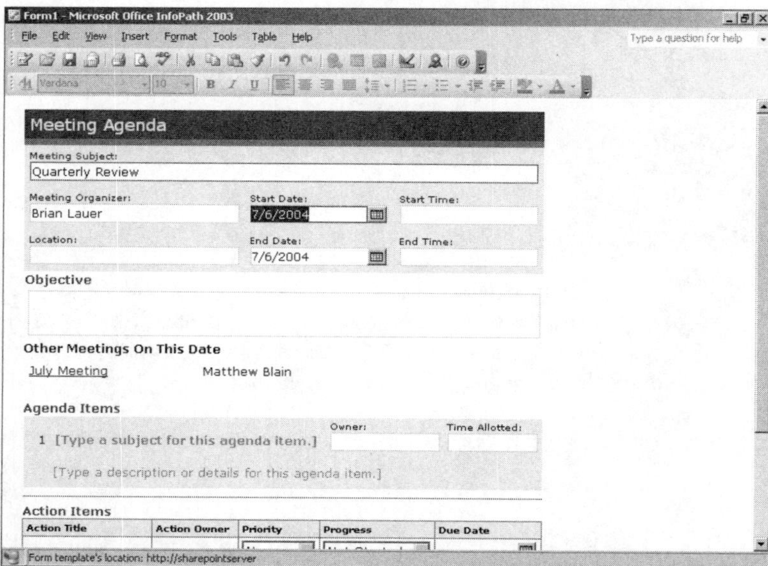

Figure 9-12 The form now displays links to other forms with the same start date.

Important When you use the built-in SharePoint List data connection, the data adapter retrieves the values from the default view of the list. This includes both filtering information and the number of items displayed. The default number of items displayed in a view in SharePoint is 100, as seen in Figure 9-13. If you have more than 100 items, you must ensure that the default view displays all items you wish to use in the form or get the list items using the SharePoint list Web service directly, as described later in this chapter.

Important If you have a large number of items to work with, the performance will degrade. To filter what list items are displayed at run time, you will need to call the Web service directly.

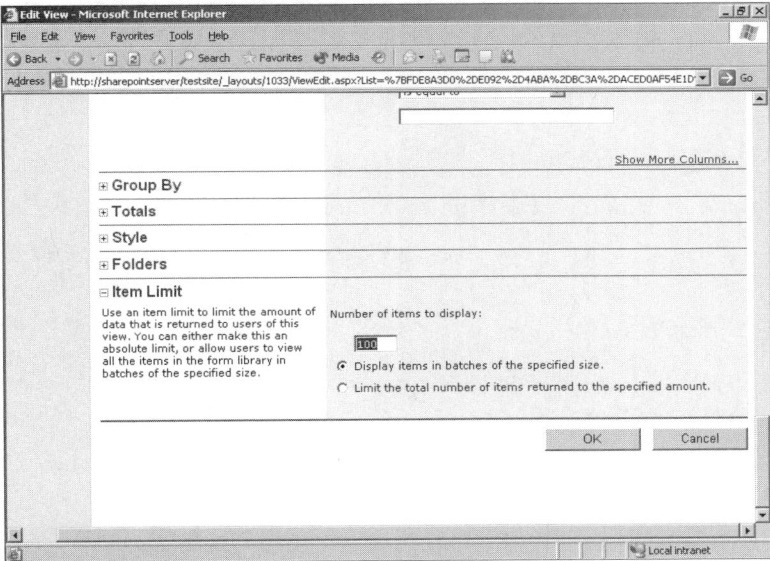

Figure 9-13 Changing the item limit for the default view

Reading the User List

Forms often have fields that identify users, such as Meeting Organizer in the Meeting Agenda sample used in this chapter. Your can create a drop-down list containing the users on your SharePoint site with a SharePoint List data connection. You can also use the User List information for other purposes, such as looking up an e-mail address of the user on your site if you know their logon name.

Note You can add to the User List of a SharePoint site in two ways: by adding individual users to a site or by adding an entire group of users to a site. If you add a domain group, the SharePoint User List will not contain individual users until the particular user has visited the SharePoint site.

Adding a SharePoint-Based User Drop-Down List to the Meeting Agenda Form

1. Edit the Meeting Agenda template on your SharePoint site by browsing to the form library, clicking Modify Settings And Columns, and then clicking Edit Template.
2. Choose Data Connections from the Tools menu.
3. In the Data Connections dialog box, click Add.
4. In the Data Connection Wizard, select Receive Data, and then click Next.
5. Select SharePoint Library Or List, and then click Next.

   Enter the URL of your SharePoint site, and then click Next. You should now see a list of all the lists, form libraries, and document libraries on your site. However, you will not see the UserInfo list because it is a special list.

   Select any form library, such as the one the form template is published to (i.e., Meeting Agenda), and then click Next.
6. In the list of fields, select ID and Title, deselect all of the others, and then click Next.
7. Enter the name **User Info** for the data connection.
8. Ensure that the Automatically Retrieve Data When Form Is Opened check box is selected.
9. Click Finish, and then click Close.

   You have now created a data connection, but it points to the form library instead of the user list. To switch libraries, you must edit the manifest directly.
10. Choose Extract Form File from the File menu, and then extract the files to a folder called **MeetingAgenda**.
11. Close InfoPath to release the lock it has on the extracted files.
12. In the MeetingAgenda folder, locate the manifest.xsf file and open it in a text editor such as Notepad.
13. In the manifest.xsf file, you will find an *xsf:dataObject* node with the attribute *name="User Info"*. This was created when you added the User Info data connection.
14. In this *xsf:dataObject* node is an *xsf:sharepointListAdapter* node with an attribute called *sharepointGuid*. Change the value of this attribute from the GUID saved by InfoPath to the string **UserInfo**. *UserInfo* is the special name for accessing the User Info list in SharePoint.

    The following snippet from the manifest.xsf file is what your changes should look like:

```
<xsf:dataObject name="User Info" schema="User Info.xsd" initOnLoad="yes">
 <xsf:query>
  <xsf:sharepointListAdapter siteUrl="http://sharepointserver/testsite/"
     sharepointGuid="UserInfo" infopathGroup="Meeting_Agenda"
```

```
    queryAllowed="yes" submitAllowed="no" name="User Info">
  <xsf:field sharepointName="ID" infopathName="ID"></xsf:field>
  <xsf:field sharepointName="Title" infopathName="Title"></xsf:field>
 </xsf:sharepointListAdapter>
</xsf:query>
</xsf:dataObject>
```

15. Save and close the manifest.xsf file.
16. Right-click on the manifest.xsf file in the MeetingAgenda folder, and then choose Design to launch your template in design mode.
17. The User List data connection is now hooked up to the user list, but not to the user interface of the form.
18. Right-click on the Meeting Organizer field, and then choose Change To | Drop-Down List Box.
19. Right-click on the Meeting Organizer field again, and then choose Drop-Down List Box Properties.
20. Select the Look Up Values In A Data Connection option, and then change the data connection to User Info.
21. Click the Select XPath button to the right of the Entries field, and then expand the tree of fields.
22. Select the *:Title* attribute, and then click OK twice to close the open dialog boxes.
23. From the File menu, choose Publish, and then publish the form to your SharePoint site as described at the beginning of this chapter, only this time, select Modify An Existing Form Library and Overwrite The Existing Form Template In This Library on the appropriate Publishing Wizard pages to update your form library.

    The meeting organizer is now a drop-down list hooked up to the user information on your SharePoint site.
24. On the last page of the Publishing Wizard, select Open This Form From Its Published Location, and then click Close.
25. On the SharePoint site, click Fill Out This Form to test the drop-down list.

Reading Columns Not Shown by the Designer Data Connection Wizard

Two fields are available when you add the list as in the previous example: ID and Title. ID is an integer and is the internal SharePoint ID for a user of a particular site. Title is the Full Name. Two other fields are also available: Name (login name) and Email (e-mail address). You can add these by modifying two of the extracted files. First add two *xsd:attribute* nodes to the User Info.xsd file. Duplicate the *xsd:attribute* for Title twice, and then change the *name* attribute of one to Name and the other to Email. Second, in the manifest.xsf file, duplicate the *xsf:field* for Title in the *sharepointListAdapter* node twice. Change both the *sharepointName* and *infopathName* attributes from Title to **Name** or **Email** as you did in the previous file. Now your data connection will contain all four fields available from SharePoint.

You can use this technique on any SharePoint list to read the columns not displayed by the Data Connection Wizard, including *LinkFilename*, *EncodedAbsUrl*, and *FileSizeDisplay*. To get a full list of columns for a field, you can use the *GetList* method of the SharePoint lists Web service.

Displaying The Modified Date of an Open Form

You can put together a number of the concepts you have learned in this book to display the modified date of the currently opened form. This requires editing the manifest.xsf file, an .xsd schema file, and an .xsl view file.

Start with the Meeting Agenda sample which has a connection to its own SharePoint form library (created in the section "Reading the Form Library as a List"). Edit the manifest.xsf file and the associated data connection .xsd file to include the *EncodedAbsUrl* property so that your form can retrieve the URL of the forms in the library. Then you can use this data in two ways: in code, or directly in the view by editing the XSL. Edit the view_1.xsl file to include the following XSL template. (You can modify the form template to format the date and time using the Date Picker control; insert one in your view to see the XSL required for those controls.)

```
<xsl:template match="mtg:meetingAgenda" mode="xd:preserve">
    <xsl:if test="function-available('xdXDocument:GetDOM')
     and function-available('xdXDocument:get-URI')">
        <xsl:value-of select="xdXDocument:GetDOM(&quot;Meeting Agenda&quot;)
/dfs:myFields/dfs:dataFields/dfs:Meeting_Agenda/@Modified
[../@EncodedAbsUrl = xdXDocument:get-URI()]" />
    </xsl:if>
</xsl:template>
```

Call the template from somewhere in the main *mtg:meetingAgenda* template by adding the following line:

```
<xsl:apply-templates select="." mode="xd:preserve"/>
```

Now publish your form back to SharePoint and test it. Any opened document should automatically display its modified date.

Submitting Forms to a SharePoint Site

From the user's point of view, a SharePoint form library can be used much like a folder in Windows. A user editing a form can save the form using the regular Save and Save As mechanisms. SharePoint then promotes data from the saved .xml file to columns that can be used in the SharePoint views and elsewhere. The next step is to add custom submit functionality to your form to ensure that the form is saved to SharePoint correctly and so your users do not have to use the Save dialog box.

The simplest approach is to use the built-in SharePoint form library submit data connection. A step up in complexity and flexibility is to submit the form using custom code to a form library. Finally, you can use custom code to create list items in SharePoint lists, which are not form libraries, possibly in addition to using one of the form library submit mechanisms.

Developer Nugget: Controlling Save Filenames

An alternative to using the SharePoint submit data connection or custom code is to use the standard save mechanism but control the requested filename by trapping the *Save* event.

To trap the *Save* event, choose Form Options from the Tools menu, click on the Open And Save tab, make sure that Save And Save As is selected, and then select the Save Using Custom Code check box. This is shown in Figure 9-16. Click Edit to create an *OnSaveRequest* event handler. In the event handler, set the *SetSaveAsDialogLocation* and the *SetSaveAsDialogFileName*, then call *PerformSaveOperation*. An example is as follows:

```
<InfoPathEventHandler(EventType:=InfoPathEventType.OnSaveRequest)> _
Public Sub OnSaveRequest(ByVal e As SaveEvent)
    If (e.IsSaveAs) Then
        Dim uriTemplate As Uri
        Dim uriFolder As Uri
        uriTemplate = New Uri(thisXDocument.Solution.URI)
        uriFolder = New Uri(uriTemplate, "..")
        thisXDocument.UI.SetSaveAsDialogLocation(uriFolder.AbsoluteUri)
        thisXDocument.UI.SetSaveAsDialogFileName("some-calculated-name")
    End If
    e.IsCancelled = e.PerformSaveOperation
    e.ReturnStatus = True
End Sub
```

Submitting a Form Using the SharePoint Submit Data Connection

The simplest way to submit a form to SharePoint without using the Save dialog box is to use the InfoPath submit function hooked up to the SharePoint Submit data connection. This was covered briefly in Chapter 2. You can also use the Submit data connection programmatically for even more control.

Creating a SharePoint Submit Data Connection

1. Create a new Microsoft InfoPath Visual Basic Form Template in Visual Studio. This is not necessary for using the data connection, but you will use it later in this section to control the data adapter programmatically. Name the project **SubmitExample**.
2. Choose Open InfoPath from the Project menu to switch to the InfoPath designer.
3. Choose Text Box from the Insert menu to add a text box to the form.
4. Right-click on the text box, choose Text Box Properties, rename the field to **Title**, and then click OK.
5. Choose Publish from the File menu. This is a Visual Studio project, so the form will be saved to your local computer before the Publishing Wizard starts.

6. Step through the Publishing Wizard and create a new form library named **SubmitExample** on your SharePoint site. Select the Open The Form From The Published Location check box at the end of the wizard to open the form library on your SharePoint site.

   Note the URL from the SharePoint site. When you are looking at the default SharePoint view, the URL will look something like *http://sharepointserver/testsite/SubmitExample/forms/AllItems.aspx*. This is the URL of the All Items view, not the folder where your forms are actually stored.

7. From Visual Studio, again choose Open InfoPath from the Project menu to switch to the InfoPath designer.
8. Choose Data Connections from the Tools menu.
9. In the Data Connections dialog box, click Add.
10. In the Data Connection Wizard, select Submit Data, and then click Next.
11. Select To A SharePoint Form Library, and then click Next.
12. Enter the URL to your form library. The URL will be something like *http://sharepointserver/testsite/SubmitExample/*. You can figure it out by taking the URL to the default view and removing *forms/AllItems.aspx* from the end.

> **Caution** Be sure to enter the correct URL and to test it. The SharePoint data connection is in fact a general-purpose WebDAV data connection, so you can save to any URL that points to a WebDAV-enabled server. This includes directories on your SharePoint site that are not form libraries.

13. In the File Name text box, you can create a function to autogenerate the filename. This is a powerful aspect of this type of data connection.
14. Click the *fx* button to the right of the File Name field.
15. In the Insert Formula dialog box, click Insert Function.
16. Select the *Text* category and the *concat* function, and then click OK. This will create a *concat* statement with three placeholder parameters.
17. Double-click on the first placeholder parameter, select the *Title* field from the data source, and then click OK.
18. Click on the second placeholder parameter, and then type "-", including the quotes.
19. Click on the third placeholder parameter, and then press Delete to remove the existing parameter.

20. Click Insert Function, select the Data And Time category and the Now function, and then click OK twice to return to the Data Connection Wizard. Figure 9-14 shows the wizard at this point.

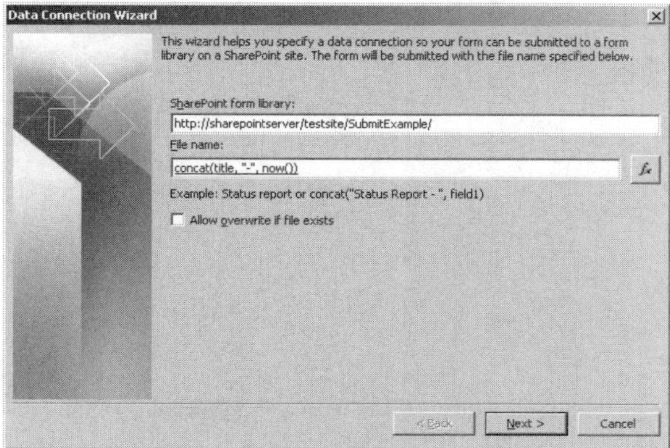

Figure 9-14 Specifying the folder and a dynamic filename for the SharePoint submit data connection

You now have a formula that looks like *concat(Title, "-", now())*. Every time a form is submitted through this data connection, the form filename will include the contents of the Title field, and the date and time the submit was processed.

21. Click Next, click Finish, and then click Close.

You now have a data connection that hooks to your SharePoint form library and names forms as they are created.

Using the SharePoint Submit Data Connection with Basic Submit

1. In the InfoPath designer, choose Submitting Forms from the Tools menu.
2. In the Submitting Forms dialog box, choose Enable Submit Commands and Buttons.
3. Select SharePoint Form Library in the Submit To drop-down list.
4. Make sure the Submit data connection you just created is selected in the Choose A Data Connection For Submit drop-down list, and that the Enable The Submit Menu Item On The File Menu check box is selected (as shown in Figure 9-15), and then click OK.

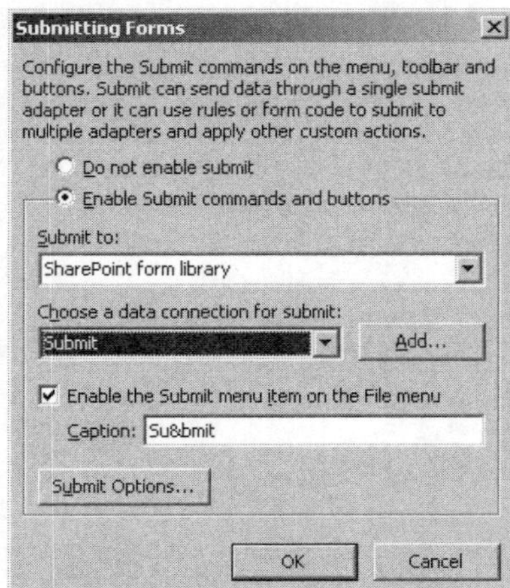

Figure 9-15 Connecting the Submit menu to the SharePoint submit data connection

5. Publish your form back to your SharePoint site.

You have now hooked up the Submit button to the data connection. Test what you have created by visiting your SharePoint form library and clicking Fill Out This Form. Type a title into the Title text box, and then choose Submit from the File menu. You should get a message that the form was submitted successfully. Switch back to your form library, and then click Refresh to see the form you just created.

Troubleshooting the Submit Data Connection

If you do not see the form, it is probably saved to somewhere on your SharePoint site other than the form library. The most likely locations are the Forms directory and the root of the site that the form library is in.

> **Tip** You can view any folder on your SharePoint site using the Web Folders feature of Windows. One way to do this is to click the Explorer View link on a form or document library. Another way is to start from Microsoft Internet Explorer: Choose Open from the File menu, select the Open As Web Folder check box, enter the URL to your SharePoint site or form library, and then click OK to see the folder.

If the filename specified by the formula in the submit data connection would cause it to overwrite the file, the user will see the following error: "InfoPath cannot submit the form. An error occurred while the form was being submitted." Expanding the details will show: "A value in the form may be used to specify the filename. If you know the value in the form that specifies the filename, revise it and try again. Otherwise, contact the author of the form template." You can revise the formula, allow overwrite, or handle this in code. The next section will cover these issues.

Overwriting Existing Files with the SharePoint Submit Data Connection

In the Data Connection Wizard, in addition to the SharePoint Form Library and File Name input boxes, you'll find a check box to specify whether InfoPath should allow an overwrite if the file exists. You can use this with a formula to maintain consistent filename conventions when overwriting is the right approach. For example, you can use the Meeting Agenda sample and set the formula to **concat(mtg:startDate, "-", mtg:subject)**. Any meeting agenda created for a particular date and subject will create the same filename and will overwrite the file when the user submits the form. For more precise control of overwriting, you can write code to control the submit process.

Using Code to Control the SharePoint Submit Data Connection

When you use the form that you have created so far, you will notice that each time you click Submit, a new form is created. If you click Submit twice in a row, two forms will be saved. If you want to control this so that under certain conditions (say, when a blank form is opened) a new .xml file is saved and under other conditions the existing one is overwritten, you can do that in code. In this section, we'll extend the sample form so the Submit button creates a new entry when the form is first submitted but then acts like Save after that.

The SharePoint Submit data connection is known as the DAVAdapter in the InfoPath object model, and we will refer to it that way from here on. It supports both SharePoint and other WebDAV servers. WebDAV is a standard built on top of HTTP to handle common file operations on a Web server. For more information, see *http://www.webdav.org/*.

Adding Save Style Functionality to SharePoint Submit

1. Open the SubmitExample project in Visual Studio.
2. Choose Open InfoPath from the Tools menu to launch the form in the designer.
3. In the InfoPath designer, choose Data Connections from the Tools menu.
4. Select the Submit data connection, and then click Modify.
5. Select the Allow Overwrite If File Exists check box.
6. Click Next, click Finish, and then click Close to save your changes to the data connection and close the Data Connections dialog box.
7. Choose Submitting Forms from the Tools menu.
8. Select Custom Submit Using Form Code in the Submit To drop-down list.

9. Ensure that the Edit Form Code check box is selected, and then click OK to close the Submitting Forms dialog box.

   InfoPath switches to Visual Studio and creates an *OnSubmitRequest* event handler. You will control the existing DAVAdapter inside this event handler.

10. Add the following code to the *OnSubmitRequest* event handler:

```
Dim submit As DAVAdapter
submit = thisXDocument.DataAdapters.Item("Submit")
If thisFilename Is Nothing Then
    thisFilename = submit.FileName
End If

' Always set the filename to the saved one. This prevents
' saving to a different name if the formula contains the current time.
submit.FileName = thisFilename

submit.Submit()
e.ReturnStatus = True
```

11. Now add the following line of code just above the *OnSubmitRequest* event handler, inside the class:

```
Private thisFilename As String
```

Tip The index into *DataAdapters.Item* (Submit above) is case-sensitive. You can copy and paste the value from the Data Connection Wizard or directly from the *name* attribute of *xsf:davAdapter* in the manifest.

This code stores the name of the file that was created the first time the user clicked Submit on the form in the *thisFilename* member variable. The next time the user clicks Submit, the form is saved to the same location. However, the filename is stored only to a member variable with the lifetime of the form being opened. The next step is to set the member variable when the form is opened from the form library.

Note The error "A value in the form may be used to specify the filename. If you know the value in the form that specifies the filename, revise it and try again. Otherwise, contact the author of the form template" means that the data connection is trying to save over a file that already exists but the Allow Overwrite check box is not selected.

Note If you want to trap this error in the code and handle it yourself, wrap the *Submit* method in a *Try...Catch* block. The exception will be a *System.Runtime.InteropServices.COMException* with an error code of *0x800430CF*.

12. Switch to InfoPath, and then choose Programming | On Load Event from the Tools menu. InfoPath will create the *OnLoad* event handler and switch back to Visual Studio.
13. Add the following code to the *OnLoad* event handler:

```
' Check if document has already been saved using the Submit adapter.
If Not thisXDocument.IsNew Then
    Dim submit As DAVAdapter
    submit = thisXDocument.DataAdapters.Item("Submit")
    If thisXDocument.URI.StartsWith(submit.FolderURL) Then
        thisFilename = _
         thisXDocument.URI.Substring(submit.FolderURL.Length)
    End If
End If
```

14. Save and publish your form to your form library.

Your template now has the following submit functionality: any form that is new or was opened from somewhere other than the SharePoint form library will be submitted to a new file. Any form opened from the SharePoint form library will be saved back to itself.

Note URLs are case-sensitive. However, SharePoint is generally case-insensitive. You might need to perform a case-insensitive comparison, such as *thisXDocument.URI.ToLower.StartsWith(submit.FolderURL.ToLower)*, when you are comparing URLs.

Developer Nugget: Preventing Save

Once you have hooked up your submit code, you might want to prevent users from using the normal Save As mechanism. There are two ways of doing this: disabling save entirely and trapping the *Save* event.

To disable save entirely, choose Form Options from the Tools menu, click on the Open And Save tab, and then clear the Save And Save As check box. This will remove all save functionality from your template. Unfortunately, if the form does not have Submit enabled, it will also remove the "save on close" functionality. On a form where Submit is not handled with the standard Submit functionality (e.g., only buttons with custom code are used), a user can close a form and lose all her changes without warning.

To trap the *Save* event, choose Form Options from the Tools menu, click on the Open And Save tab, make sure that Save And Save As is selected, and then select the Save Using Custom Code check box. This is shown in Figure 9-16. Click the Edit button to create an *OnSaveRequest* event handler. In the event handler, do not call *PerformSaveOperation*, but instead display an alert to the user suggesting she use the submit operation, and then set the event *ReturnStatus* to *false*. A more sophisticated approach would determine whether it is in fact a save operation to an existing item in the form library and call

Submit directly. You cannot trap the filename in a *Save As* event, although you can call *SetSaveAsDialogLocation* as described above to suggest a filename to the user.

```
<InfoPathEventHandler(EventType:=InfoPathEventType.OnSaveRequest)> _
Public Sub OnSaveRequest(ByVal e As SaveEvent)
    ' Prevent all Save operations.
    thisXDocument.UI.Alert("Please use Submit instead of Save.")
    e.IsCancelled = True
End Sub
```

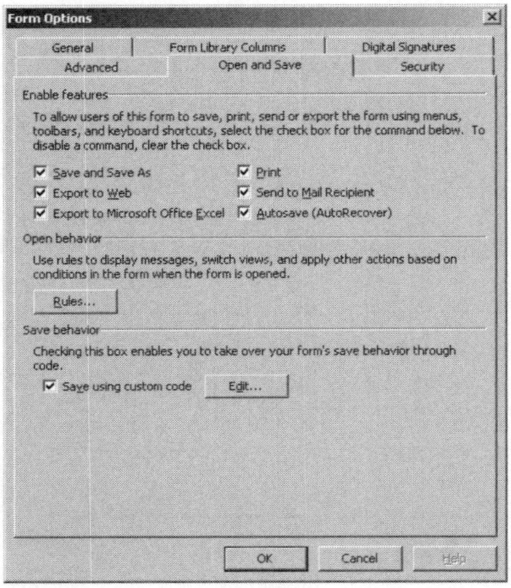

Figure 9-16 Redirecting Save to custom code

Using HTTP WebDAV Directly

The SharePoint submit data connection, or DAVAdapter, handles submitting forms to a SharePoint or other WebDAV-enabled Web site. Sometimes you might want to use HTTP directly—for example, to check whether a file is present using the *HEAD* method of HTTP. To do this with script, you can use the *MSXML2.XMLHTTP* object. In Microsoft .NET, you can use the *System.Net.HttpWebRequest* object. To use the user's current credentials, set the *HttpWebRequest Credentials* property to *System.Net.CredentialCache.DefaultCredentials*. A template with domain-model trust can access data only on the domain where the form is published (e.g., your SharePoint server).

```
' return true if file exists and is OK
Public Function CheckFileExistence(ByVal url As String) As Boolean
    Dim req As System.Net.HttpWebRequest
    Dim resp As System.Net.HttpWebResponse

    req = System.Net.HttpWebRequest.Create(url)
    req.Credentials = System.Net.CredentialCache.DefaultCredentials
    req.Method = "HEAD"
```

```
    Try
        resp = req.GetResponse()
    Catch ex As System.Net.WebException
        resp = ex.Response
        If (resp Is Nothing) Then
            ' The server is probably down or incorrect.
            Throw ex
        End If
    End Try

    resp.Close()

    If (resp.StatusCode = Net.HttpStatusCode.OK) Then
        Return True
    Else
        Return False
    End If
End Function
```

You can also write forms into a data library directly using the HTTP *PUT* method. Forms created before the DAVAdapter was added in SP1 might use this technique. If you want to do this using the .NET Framework, you can use the *System.Net.WebClient* class as an easier alternative to *System.Net.HttpWebRequest*.

Creating Items in a SharePoint List

Form libraries are designed to hold .xml files, but in a number of situations you might want to also create or update another SharePoint list. For example, you can have your Meeting Agenda solution insert an item into the Events list on your site. By reading and writing list items, your solution can use the contact list on your site and modify it on the fly.

The InfoPath SharePoint data connection can read items from a SharePoint list (including form libraries), but it cannot write items to a list that is not a form library. It also has the limitation that the information retrieved by the data adapter reflects the default view of the list, including any filters and the number of items displayed. By connecting directly to the SharePoint List Web service, you have full control over these items.

You can connect to a SharePoint list directly in two ways. One way is to use the SOAP Lists Web service. The other is to use the Windows SharePoint Services remote procedure call (RPC) methods for calling owssvr.dll with the SharePoint URL protocol.

Using the submit data connection described earlier in this chapter is the easiest way to create list items, but it works only for form libraries. To connect to a SharePoint list directly, you need use the Lists Web service with SOAP. The process is complex enough that you must handle all of the code directly. You can do this in script by using a SOAP helper object such as *MSSOAP* or *MSOSOAP* or by coding directly against the server with the *XMLHTTP* objects, but it is much easier to use the SOAP proxies generated by Visual Studio. This section will examine a solution that creates entries in your Tasks list.

Extending the SharePoint Submit Example to Create a Task

1. Open the SharePoint Submit project in Visual Studio. We will first add the Web service reference, and then we will call it from the form.
2. Choose Add Web Reference from the Project menu.
3. In the Add Web Reference dialog box, type the URL to the Lists Web service. This is the URL to your site plus *_vti_bin/Lists.asmx* (e.g., *http://sharepointserver/testsite/_vti_bin/lists.asmx*).
4. Click Go to retrieve information about the Lists Web service.
5. Change the Web reference name to **lists**.
6. Click Add Reference to add the reference to your project.
7. Add **Imports Sytem.Xml** to the top of your FormCode.vb file.
8. Add the following new function to your project that uses the referenced Web service:

```
' return ID of task or 0 for failure.
Public Function CreateTask(ByVal strTitle As String, _
                           ByVal strBody As String) As Integer

    Dim listName As String
    Dim listsservice As lists.Lists
    Dim node As XmlDocument
    Dim res As XmlNode
    Dim resultError As XmlNode
    Dim resultId As XmlNode


    ' listName is the GUID for your tasks list.
    ' You can get the ListGuid by viewing the Web address URL in
    ' Modify Settings And Columns or by adding the list to your
    ' form (receive from a SharePoint list) and viewing the manifest.
    ' listName = "{D4BFA989-7647-4814-BBF9-5CDB1D59270F}"

    listsservice = New lists.Lists
    listsservice.Credentials = System.Net.CredentialCache.DefaultCredentials

    node = New XmlDocument

    node.LoadXml("" _
        + "<Batch OnError='Continue' ListVersion='1' xmlns=''>" _
        + " <Method ID='1' Cmd='New'>" _
        + "  <Field Name='Title'>" + strTitle + "</Field>" _
        + "  <Field Name='Body'><![CDATA[" + strBody + "]]></Field>" _
        + " </Method>" _
        + "</Batch>")

    ' Call the Web service.
    res = listsservice.UpdateListItems(listName, node)
```

```
    ' Parse the results.
    Dim nsmgr As XmlNamespaceManager
    nsmgr = New XmlNamespaceManager(res.OwnerDocument.NameTable)
    nsmgr.AddNamespace("s", "http://schemas.microsoft.com/sharepoint/soap/")
    nsmgr.AddNamespace("z", "#RowsetSchema")

    ' Look for a result of ID "1,New", matching ID="1" and Cmd="New" above.
    resultError = res.SelectSingleNode("s:Result[@ID='1,New']/s:ErrorCode", _
     nsmgr)
    If (resultError Is Nothing Or _
        Convert.ToInt32(resultError.InnerText, 16) <> 0) Then
        Return 0
    End If

    resultId = res.SelectSingleNode("s:Result[@ID=""1,New""]/z:row/@ows_ID", _
      nsmgr)
    Return Integer.Parse(resultId.InnerText)
End Function
```

9. Select Open InfoPath from the Project menu to switch to the InfoPath designer.
10. In the InfoPath designer, add a Rich Text Box control to the form.
11. Right-click on the rich text box, choose Rich Text Box Properties, and then change the Field Name to **Body**.
12. Add a Button control to the form.
13. Right-click on the button, choose Button Properties, change the Label to **Create Task**, and then click Edit Form Code to create the event handler and switch back to Visual Studio.
14. In Visual Studio, add the following code to newly created button event handler to call the *CreateTask* function:

```
Dim id As Integer
id = createtask( _
    thisXDocument.DOM.selectSingleNode("/my:myFields/my:Title").text, _
    thisXDocument.DOM.selectSingleNode("/my:myFields/my:Body").xml)

If (id = 0) Then
    thisXDocument.UI.Alert("Failed to create task.")
Else
    thisXDocument.UI.Alert("Created task with ID " + id.ToString() + ".")
End If
```

15. Save your form.

When you preview this form and click Create Task, the code will contact the SharePoint Lists Web service and create a task. You can add additional fields to the created tasks, such as *Priority* or *AssignedTo*. The value of a user lookup field such as *AssignedTo* must be the SharePoint user ID—you can use a drop-down list with the UserInfo, as described earlier in the "Reading the User List" section, using the ID field from that data source as the data instead of the Title field. You can create multiple items at once by adding additional *Method* nodes to the *Batch* node.

One way to determine the list of possible fields is to add the list to an InfoPath form using the SharePoint Library Or List data connection. You can then extract the form files and look at the *xsf:sharepointListAdapter* node in the manifest.xsf file. The field names will be the *sharepointName* attribute of the *xsf:field* nodes. The list GUID will be in the *sharepointGuid* attribute. You can also retrieve the list information from the *GetListCollection* and *GetList* methods of the SharePoint Lists Web service.

The SharePoint documentation for UpdateListItems *method, other methods in the SharePoint Lists Web service, and CAML can be found in MSDN.*

Reading SharePoint List Items Directly

Using the list adapter is the easiest way to read lists, and it works for all types of SharePoint lists, including form libraries. Next in complexity for reading lists is to use the *Display* method of the URL RPC protocol.

Add a secondary data connection to your form using an .xml file, with a location of **http://sharepointserver/testsite/_vti_bin/owssvr.dll?Cmd=display&XMLDATA=true&Query=*&List={ListGuid}**. The *Query=** parameter will return all columns and all rows of the list data, not just the values in the default view. You can get the *ListGuid* by viewing the Web address URL in Modify Settings And Columns. To do additional filtering, see the documentation on this method in MSDN.

To execute more complex queries, you can use the *GetListItems* method of the Lists Web service, which is similar to using *UpdateListItems* described earlier. It returns the same CAML-formatted data as the display method of the URL RPC protocol. With the *GetListItems* method, you can specify the filter, number of items to return, and columns to return. You can parse the returned data in code, or see the "Creating a secondary data connection with a web reference" section procedure in Chapter 7 to learn how to bind the results of the Web service call to a secondary data source. For the GetListsItems Web service, the results are XML, not a string as in the example in Chapter 7. Use the *OuterXml* method of the returned *XmlNode* to get a snapshot of sample data to create the temporary data file to pass to InfoPath.

Summary

This chapter covered publishing your InfoPath form template to a SharePoint site, promoting columns so you can use list views in SharePoint, automating the submit process to a SharePoint site, reading SharePoint lists from within InfoPath, and creating list items from within InfoPath. The next chapter will build on some of these techniques to create forms-based workflow scenarios.

Chapter 10

Forms-Based Workflow

This chapter shows how to build workflow processing into InfoPath forms using e-mail and Microsoft SharePoint. (If you don't have SharePoint, you can substitute a shared folder to store your forms.) Implementing workflow logic in an InfoPath form is a simpler alternative to deploying a server-based solution such as Microsoft BizTalk. This chapter is an introduction to forms-based workflow using just InfoPath; Chapter 11 will address InfoPath support for BizTalk on the server.

In Chapter 2, we implemented a simple workflow example using e-mail, user roles, open rules, and default merge to create a book purchase form. The form included views for requesting, approving, and reporting book purchases. This chapter extends the book purchasing sample to support the following features:

- Multiple approvers and managers
- Assigning the form to oneself
- Submitting forms to a forms library (SharePoint)
- Controlling write access to forms based on assignment
- Tracking workflow history in the form
- Deploying the form to external requesters (outside of the domain)

You can implement these features using just InfoPath, e-mail, and SharePoint, but with the following limitations:

- Submit and notify are separate steps (not fail-safe). Workflow logic has to submit the form and send e-mail notification in two separate steps. If the submit succeeds but e-mail fails, rewinding the submit operation can be hard or impossible. BizTalk supports transaction-based submit and notify.
- It's hard to upgrade forms to include workflow. Workflow data requirements can affect the schema, causing versioning headaches. Workflow process requires state information–who the form is assigned to and what stage it is in. Auditing might require logging of the actions. State and actions must be associated with the form. BizTalk stores some of this information in a database and uses an identifier in the XML form to look up the data on demand. (Note: The form still must store usernames for assignees.) Without a database, you have to store the workflow data with the form's data, which requires modifications to its schema.

- Workflow data must be secured. By default, InfoPath stores XML data as plain text, which means users can view the contents using non-InfoPath editors such as Notepad. Signing the form ensures that the data hasn't been changed, but it doesn't address privacy. You must implement encryption to obfuscate workflow state and other sensitive information. Web services in BizTalk's Human Workflow Services encode forms in Base64 binary by default.
- Incomplete support for converting forms. When you need to create a workflow around existing forms and don't have the option of modifying their schemas to enable workflow, you can use the powerful Merge Forms feature in InfoPath. Merge Forms lets you import data from existing forms. You can craft your own custom transform to import the data using various aggregation verbs to control how the items are inserted. Unfortunately, InfoPath doesn't support debugging custom transforms in the designer, which might explain why this feature isn't used more. The BizTalk mapping tool is a great alternative here.

To summarize, InfoPath comes with many features that support forms-based workflow. For example, using out-of-the-box data connections for e-mail and SharePoint, you can create workflow that notifies teammates and routes forms to them. With user roles and open rules, you can implement form assignment and control access to the form. Storing access control lists (ACLs) in resource files or secondary data sources gives you an alternative to defining your own Active Directory groups (more on that later), and InfoPath supports deploying forms via e-mail and on domain Web sites. This chapter extends the Book Purchase example that we started in Chapter 2 to take advantage of these features.

The Approval Process

A simple approval process can involve many people. InfoPath has built-in support for user roles and open rules, and you can use the e-mail adapter in InfoPath to attach the XML form to an outgoing e-mail message. When the internal users click on the attached XML form, InfoPath launches the form and switches to the Approve view. We'll use the views in our existing Book Purchase form to do this and then extend the form to support submitting the form to SharePoint upon approval.

Figure 10-1 shows the Book Purchase workflow that we defined in Chapter 2.

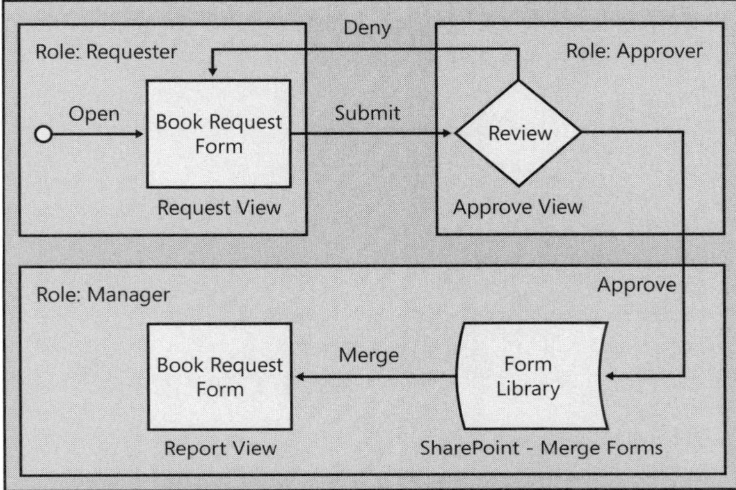

Figure 10-1 Book Purchase workflow

Controlling Access

Forms that implement workflow need to control user access. Consider the following scenario: User A opens the Book Purchase form and assigns it to himself. In this chapter, we'll refer to setting ownership to oneself as "taking ownership." The form sets user A as the owner and saves the form. User A now has write access to the form. User A can review the purchase details and approve or deny the request. For the Book Purchase example, this step might not take much time, but for most workflow scenarios we have to assume the possibility of a processing delay. User B opens the form after user A has taken ownership but before user A has routed the form to her. If the form lets user B modify its data while user A is reviewing it, the result is a chaotic workflow situation where actions can be duplicated, resulting in user distrust of the process and possible data loss. The workflow should support assignment and control access and actions based on it. While the form is assigned to user A, InfoPath should prevent user B from approving or denying it.

The Take Ownership Section

The first feature to implement is Take Ownership, which supports form assignment. Figure 10-2 shows a diagram of the Take Ownership process.

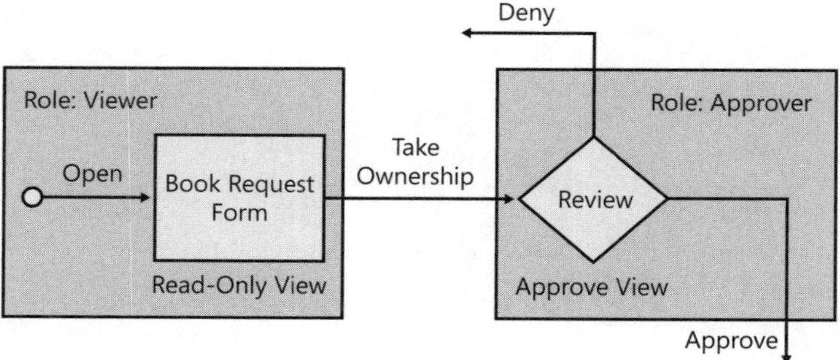

Figure 10-2 The Take Ownership process

The requester fills out a form and clicks Submit. InfoPath sends the form in e-mail to a distribution list. User A, who is a member of this distribution list, opens the form by double-clicking the attachment. The InfoPath form switches to a read-only view with a Take Ownership section. User A can review the request or take ownership and decide whether to approve it.

The Book Purchase sample in Chapter 2 contained no code. In this chapter, we will add a lot of code to the Book Purchase sample. Let's create a new Visual Basic InfoPath Form Template project in Visual Studio from the existing Book Purchase sample. Name this new project **Book Purchase with Workflow**. Once you have the project open, switch to the InfoPath designer and add the read-only view, which we'll conveniently name **View**. Figure 10-3 shows this view.

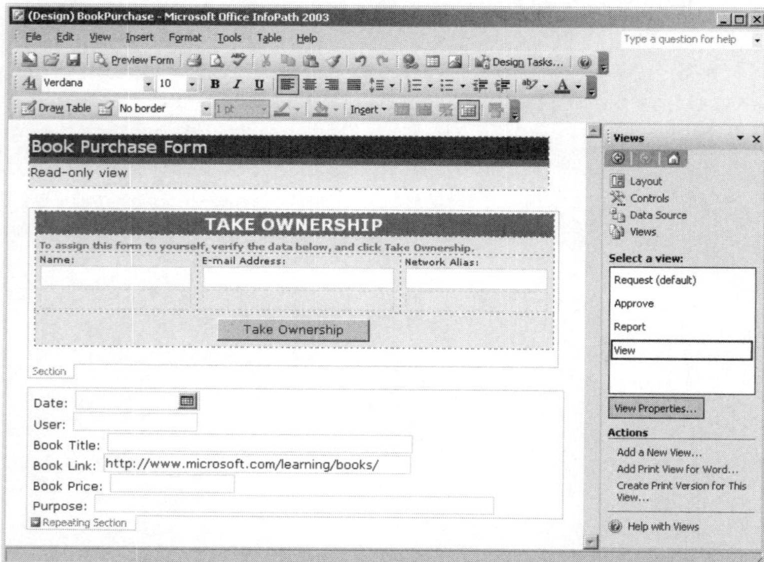

Figure 10-3 The Take Ownership section controls form assignment.

We could have added a task pane to the form and displayed the Take Ownership control as part of it, but putting it in the view garners more screen real estate and makes it more noticeable. Later we will see how to use the task pane to implement similar functionality.

Conditional Visibility for Approvers

Using conditional formatting, we can hide the section if the user who opens the form is not a member of the Approver group. In the InfoPath designer, double-click on the Section label that appears below the Take Ownership section, click on the Display tab, and then click Conditional Formatting. Figure 10-4 shows the condition to add.

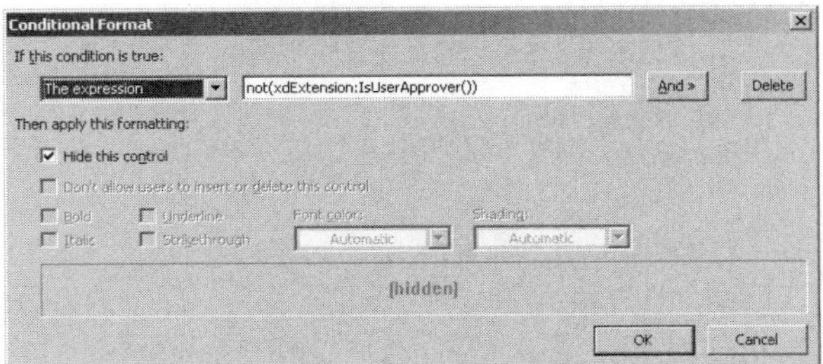

Figure 10-4 The workflow will hide the Take Ownership section if the user isn't an approver.

You will recall from Chapter 5 that the way to call into your managed code from the view is to use *xdExtension*. In this case, we will hide the entire section if the user is not an approver. You're probably wondering how the form determines the current user and the list of valid approvers. The Take Ownership section is just the tip of the iceberg. First let's look at the code for *IsUserApprover*:

```
Public Function IsUserApprover()
    With thisApplication.User
        If .IsUserMemberOf("DOMAIN\Approvers") Then
            Return True
        Else
            Return False
        End If
    End With
```

InfoPath provides the *IsUserMemberOf* method as a member of the *thisApplication.User* object; it is a fine solution, but only if you can create the Active Directory group DOMAIN\Approvers for your domain and populate it with the required people. If you do not have permissions to change your Active Directory groups, you will have to define your own list. Using a secondary data source is one way to do this:

```
Public Function IsUserApprover() As Boolean
    Dim sAlias As String = GetLoggedInUser("Alias")
    Dim sContact As String = String.Format("//Roles/Approvers/{0}[@alias=" & _
        Quote & "{1}" & Quote & "]", sAlias)
    Dim oUser As IXMLDOMNode = _
        thisXDocument.GetDOM("Form Data").selectSingleNode(sContact)

    Return Not (oUser Is Nothing)
End Function
```

In this example, the form relies on a list of valid approvers stored in the Form Data secondary data source. The code creates an XPath query expression using the current logged-in user's username (referred to as "Alias" in the code). If the query returns a result, the user is in the list of approvers. The file formdata.xml stores the contents of Form Data:

```
<FormData>
    <Roles>
        <Approvers>
            <ContactInfo alias="AUTONOMYSYSTEMS\UserA"
                email="DevelopingSolutionsWithInfoPath@InfoPathDev.com"
                name="User A"/>
            <ContactInfo alias="AUTONOMYSYSTEMS\UserB"
              email="patrick.halstead@InfoPathDev.com" name="User B"/>
        </Approvers>
        <Managers>
            <ContactInfo alias="AUTONOMYSYSTEMS\UserC"
                email="patrick.halstead@InfoPathDev.com" name="User C"/>
        </Managers>
    </Roles>
    <ViewOptions>
        <LoggedInUser>
            <Name/>
            <Email/>
            <Alias/>
        </LoggedInUser>
        <ShowTakeOwnership>false</ShowTakeOwnership>
        <ShowDeniedMessage>false</ShowDeniedMessage>
    </ViewOptions>
</FormData>
```

The *Roles* node contains static data to be used in the form's workflow conditions. The *ViewOptions* node is used as temporary storage during run time to set various workflow values. Recall that setting values in a secondary data source at run time is allowed, but the values will not be persisted in the solution when the form closes. We will come back to *ViewOptions* later.

Hardcoding the list of approvers in a secondary data source isn't very elegant. It is especially impractical if the list of approvers or managers changes often because you will have to republish the solution every time the list changes. Another solution is to store the list of approvers on SharePoint and define a receive data connection that queries the SharePoint list adapter in your form's *OnLoad* event handler. However, the SharePoint list adapter points to a fixed location (URL), and it won't work when the user is offline. A hybrid option can work well here. Create a Web service that provides a list of contacts, and use a hardcoded resource file in the form to provide backup for disconnected users. For our simple workflow example, we'll show just the latter and will continue using the secondary data source. See Chapter 7 for information on how to connect to a Web service.

Conditional Visibility for Read-Only

If someone opens the form who is not a user, conditional visibility will hide the Take Ownership section. Similarly, if the user doesn't have permission to save the form, it doesn't make sense to taunt her with the Take Ownership section. The most common example of this is when the form is read-only. You can add another *xdExtension* condition–*not(xdExtension:IsFormReadOnly())*–to hide the form when InfoPath marks it as read-only. Here's the code:

```
Public Function IsFormReadOnly() As Boolean
     Return thisXDocument.IsReadOnly
End Function
```

Unfortunately, InfoPath might report false positives, depending on your Outlook cache settings, so you can't rely on *IsReadOnly* for forms attached to e-mail. You must detect whether the form was opened from e-mail. Here's some code to determine whether your code is an attachment:

```
Private Function getFormPath() As String
    Dim sFormUri As String = thisXDocument.URI
    Dim iPosition As Integer = sFormUri.LastIndexOf("/")

    ' if path is to the outlook file cache, then this will return ""
    If (iPosition <> -1) Then
    ' Just return path
        Return sFormUri.Substring(0, iPosition + 1)
    Else
        Return ""
    End If
End Function

Private Function getSharePointFolder() As String
    Dim sUri As String = thisXDocument.Solution.URI
    Dim iPosition As Integer = sUri.LastIndexOf("/Forms/")
    If (iPosition <> -1) Then
        Return sUri.Substring(0, iPosition + 1)
    Else
        iPosition = sUri.LastIndexOf("/")
        If (iPosition <> -1) Then
            Return sUri.Substring(0, iPosition + 1)
        End If
    End If
    Return ""
End Function

' FormPath will be different from SharePointFolder when the form is opened from e-mail
isOpenedLocally = (0 <> String.Compare(getFormPath(), getSharePointFolder()))
```

The functions *getFormPath* and *getSharePointFolder* return strings corresponding to the currently loaded form's path and the current form template's publish location (or URL). The property *thisXDocument.URI* refers to the form, and *thisXDocument.Solution.URI* refers to the publish location of the form template. *getFormPath* calls *LastIndexOf* to look for a file path delimiting slash (/) character. Lack of a slash character means the file is new or was opened from the Outlook e-mail cache. *getSharePointFolder* calls *LastIndexOf* to look for the Forms folder, which designates the location as a SharePoint form library. If there is no match for */Forms/*, the publish URL must point to a shared folder and the code looks for a trailing file path delimiter instead. Finally, a single line of code that is separate from the functions shows the comparison.

Getting the Current User

We've seen how the form stores the list of approvers, but how does it determine the current user? The *GetLoggedInUser* method reads the value of the current user from the *ViewOptions* node in the secondary data source:

```
Public Function GetLoggedInUser(ByVal sNode As String) As String
    Dim oLoggedInUser As IXMLDOMNode = thisXDocument.GetDOM("Form Data").selectSingleNode("
        /FormData/ViewOptions/LoggedInUser")
    Dim oNode As IXMLDOMNode = oLoggedInUser.selectSingleNode(sNode)
    If oNode Is Nothing Then
        Return ""
    End If
    Return oNode.text.ToString()
End Function
```

Recall from the formdata.xml listing above that the *LoggedInUser* values are not static. Our form sets these in its *OnLoad* method:

```
Dim sLoggedInUser As String
Dim iFormat As EXTENDED_NAME_FORMAT = EXTENDED_NAME_FORMAT.NameSamCompatible

' First, get the size of the string buffer
GetUserNameEx(iFormat, Nothing, uiSize)
sbBuffer = New StringBuilder(Convert.ToInt32(uiSize), Convert.ToInt32(uiSize))
GetUserNameEx(iFormat, sbBuffer, uiSize)

' Decompose the buffer
sLoggedInUser = sbBuffer.ToString()
iBreak = sLoggedInUser.IndexOf("\")

sLOGGED_IN_DOMAINNAME = sLoggedInUser.Substring(0, iBreak)
sLOGGED_IN_USERNAME = sLoggedInUser.Substring(iBreak + 1)

Dim sAlias As String = sLOGGED_IN_DOMAINNAME & "\\" & sLOGGED_IN_USERNAME
SetLoggedInUser(getDelegateInfo(sAlias, sName, "name"), getDelegateInfo(sAlias, sEmail,
"email"), sAlias)
```

In a nutshell, this code is getting the user and domain information from *GetUserNameEx*, which is declared earlier in the code as

```
Declare Unicode Function GetUserNameEx Lib "Secur32.dll"
(ByVal NameFormat As EXTENDED_NAME_FORMAT, ByVal lpNameBuffer As StringBuilder, ByVal nSize
As System.UInt32) As Boolean
```

The type *EXTENDED_NAME_FORMAT* is just an enum defined as follows:

```
Enum EXTENDED_NAME_FORMAT
    NameUnknown = 0
    NameFullyQualifiedDN = 1
    NameSamCompatible = 2
    NameDisplay = 3
    NameUniqueId = 6
    NameCanonical = 7
    NameUserPrincipal = 8
    NameCanonicalEx = 9
    NameServicePrincipal = 10
    NameDnsDomain = 12
End Enum
```

In .NET, you can obtain the logged-in username in a variety of ways. You can use *Environment.UserName* and *Environment.UserDomainName*, or you can use *System.WindowsIdentity*, as we did in Chapter 2. We use *GetUserNameEx* here because it returns the correct value for the domain even when the domain controller isn't accessible and you log in with cached domain credentials. In that scenario, *Environment.UserDomainName* returns the local machine name, which is not what we want. Unfortunately, all of these require security permissions—see Chapter 8 for details.

Take Ownership Logic

Let's look at the code behind the actual Take Ownership button. The Book Purchase workflow example supports two methods of submitting forms: e-mail and SharePoint. When an approver opens a form and takes ownership, the code has to determine whether the form was opened locally from e-mail or from the form library on SharePoint:

```
' The following function handler is created by Microsoft Office InfoPath. Do not
' modify the type or number of arguments.
<InfoPathEventHandler(MatchPath:="btnTakeOwnership",
    EventType:=InfoPathEventType.OnClick)> _
Public Sub btnTakeOwnership_OnClick(ByVal e As DocActionEvent)
    Dim sName As String = GetLoggedInUser("Name")
    Dim sEmail As String = GetLoggedInUser("Email")
    Dim sAlias As String = GetLoggedInUser("Alias")

    Dim iLastStatus As Integer = Convert.ToInt32(getNodeValue( _
        "//my:myFields/my:Actions/my:LastStatus"))

    Try
        ' FormPath will be different from SharePointFolder when the
        ' form is opened from e-mail
        isOpenedLocally = (0 <> String.Compare(sFormPath, sSharePointFolder))
        ' If form is out of date, switch to separate view
        sharepointFormExists = FormExists(sSharePointFileName)
```

```
If isOpenedLocally Then
    If sharepointFormExists Then
        ' Form is out of date. Hide the "Take Ownership"
       ''section.
        ' The "Form Is Out Of Date" section will now appear.
        setNodeValue(thisXDocument.GetDOM( _
            "Form Data").selectSingleNode( _
            "//ViewOptions/ShowTakeOwnership"), "false")
    Else ' Form does NOT exist on SharePoint.
        ' Set assigned to and current contact.
        setAssignedTo(sName, sEmail, sAlias)
        setCurrentContact(sName, sEmail, sAlias)

        ' Force a save to SharePoint to keep track of who took
        ' ownership.
        completeLastAction(L_sTakeOwnership_Text, _
            iLastStatus, sName)
        submitToSharePoint()
        OpenSharePoint()
    End If
Else ' Form was opened from SharePoint
    If sharepointFormExists Then
        ' Set assigned to and current contact.
        setAssignedTo(sName, sEmail, sAlias)
        setCurrentContact(sName, sEmail, sAlias)
        ' Force a save to SharePoint to keep track of who took
        ' ownership.
        completeLastAction(L_sTakeOwnership_Text, _
            iLastStatus, sName)
        submitToSharePoint()
        insertAction()

        ' Set role and switch to the appropriate view.
        thisXDocument.Role = aRoleName(iLastStatus)
        thisXDocument.View.SwitchView(aViewName(iLastStatus))

        ' Reset the take ownership button.
        setNodeValue(thisXDocument.GetDOM( _
            "Form Data").selectSingleNode( _
            "//ViewOptions/ShowTakeOwnership"), "false")

        ' Force a node change in the main DOM to get error
        ' board to refresh.
        thisXDocument.DOM.selectSingleNode("//my:myFields/my:Actions/my:Action
            /my:Description").text = ""
    Else ' Form is no longer on SharePoint.
        ' Set assigned to and current contact.
        setAssignedTo(sName, sEmail, sAlias)
        setCurrentContact(sName, sEmail, sAlias)

        ' Force a save to SharePoint to keep track of who took
        ' ownership.
        completeLastAction(L_sTakeOwnership_Text, _
            iLastStatus, sName)
        submitToSharePoint()
```

```
                OpenSharePoint()
            End If
        End If
    Catch ex As Exception
        Debug.WriteLine(ex.ToString())
        thisXDocument.UI.Alert(L_sTakeOwnershipFailed_Text)
        isReadOnly = True

        ' Reset the take ownership button.
        setNodeValue(thisXDocument.GetDOM( _
            "Form Data").selectSingleNode( _
            "//ViewOptions/ShowTakeOwnership"), "false")
        ' Force a node change in the main DOM to get error board to
        ' refresh.
        thisXDocument.DOM.selectSingleNode("//my:myFields/my:Actions/my:Action
            /my:Description").text = ""
    End Try
End Sub
```

The *btnTakeOwnerhsip* method uses the member variable *isOpenedLocally* to determine whether the user opened the form locally–i.e., from the e-mail cache. We use the string comparison to check whether the path to the form is not the same as the SharePoint URL, and if so *isOpenedLocally* gets a value of *True*.

Coordinating E-Mail and SharePoint

E-mail is ubiquitous, but team Web sites can improve collaboration by centralizing resources. The forms in your workflow are an example of one such resource. Storing forms in a centralized document repository, or SharePoint form library, enables centralized status and reporting. Some users might not have access to your team site because they are offline or because they are not allowed access. For those users, submitting forms via e-mail is a requirement. This section shows how your workflow solution can bridge e-mail submissions and notifications with a centralized team site and document repository such as SharePoint forms library.

Opening via Attachment vs. Opening from SharePoint

The workflow submits the form to SharePoint when the user takes ownership. With more than one approver, you can have cases where one approver opens the form from e-mail after another approver has taken ownership and submitted it to SharePoint. The code will check to see if a more recent copy of the form exists on SharePoint and will set the member variable *sharepointFormExists*. Chapter 9 included a code example showing how to check whether a form exists on SharePoint. (See "Adding Save Style Functionality to SharePoint Submit.") The Book Purchase example includes the *FormExists* method, which performs the same check but using the RPC protocol instead of the more common DAV. Using a DAV adapter to check whether a form exists is preferred, due to its simplicity. We provide the RPC example for Book Purchase to show another technique.

The two Boolean member variables *isOpenedLocally* and *sharepointFormExists* describe four possible states:

- Opened from e-mail and the form already exists on SharePoint
  - Values: *isOpenedLocally* is *True*, *sharepointFormExists* is *True*
  - Description: Approver opens the request form by double-clicking the attachment in e-mail; the form already exists on SharePoint. This is the case when another approver has already taken ownership of the form.
  - Actions: Hides the Take Ownership section and displays the Open Latest section, including a message that the form is out of date and a button to enable opening the latest form from SharePoint. Figure 10-5 shows this new section. As with the Take Ownership section, we hide the Open Latest section when the following expression is *True*: *not(xdExpression:isFormOutOfDate())*. The code for *isFormOutOfDate* is as follows:

```
Public Function IsFormOutOfDate() As Boolean
    Return isOpenedLocally AndAlso sharepointFormExists
End Function
```

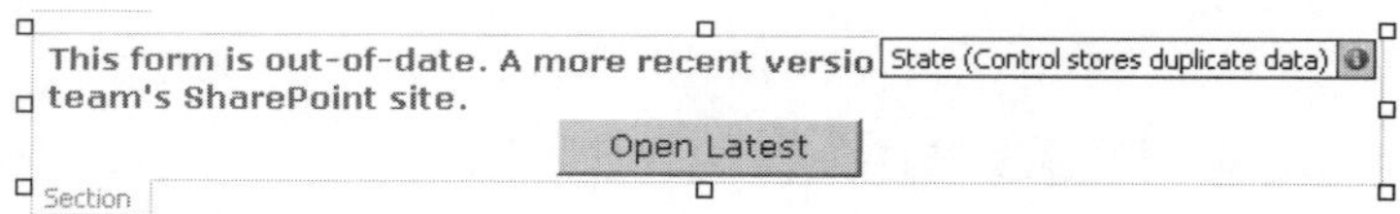

Figure 10-5 The Open Latest section appears when the form is out of date.

- Opened from e-mail and the form does not exist on SharePoint
  - Values: *isOpenedLocally* is *True*, *sharepointFormExists* is *False*
  - Description: Approver opens the request form by double-clicking the attachment in e-mail; the form does not exist on SharePoint. This is the normal case when the approver is first to take ownership.
  - Actions: Set the ownership and submit the form to SharePoint; open the submitted form from SharePoint. Opening from SharePoint has the added benefit of switching to the Approve view because the user who is opening the form is now the one assigned the form. We'll review open rules shortly.
- Opened from SharePoint and the form still exists on SharePoint
  - Values: *isOpenedLocally* is *False*, *sharepointFormExists* is *True*
  - Description: Approver opens the form from SharePoint. In this case, the form was submitted directly to SharePoint without using e-mail.
  - Actions: Set ownership, save updated form to SharePoint, set role, and switch to the Approve view. The code does not have to open the form from SharePoint because it already did. In the previous case, the code had to open the form from

SharePoint to reset form identity; otherwise, InfoPath would still treat the form as local. We'll talk about the *thisXDocument.Role* property in the next section.

- Opened from SharePoint but the form was later deleted from SharePoint
  - Values: *isOpenedLocally* is *False*, *sharepointFormExists* is *False*
  - Description: Approver opens the form from SharePoint; however, before the approver clicks the Take Ownership button, the form was somehow deleted from SharePoint. This is a corner case. When a user opens a form from SharePoint, SharePoint locks the form to prevent deleting, but administrators can still delete the form, and if the user goes offline or lets the short-term lock expire (10 minutes by default), the form becomes deletable.
  - Actions: Set ownership, save and reopen the form from SharePoint.

Submitting to SharePoint

The *submitToSharePoint* method creates a data adapter object using the *DAVAdapter* class. Chapter 9 covered this in greater detail. The sample code accompanying the book comes with a method that implements exception handling. In the following code, we remove the exception handling to specifically highlight the functionality:

```
Private Sub submitToSharePoint()
    Dim oSharePoint As DAVAdapter = _
        CType(thisXDocument.DataAdapters("SharePoint Submit"), DAVAdapter)
    oSharePoint.FileName = sSharePointFileName
    oSharePoint.FolderURL = sSharePointFolder
    oSharePoint.Submit()
End Sub
```

You have to define the SharePoint Submit adapter first and then refer to it in your code. From the designer, select Data Connections from the Tools menu and then add a data connection named SharePoint Submit. Your code can override the defaults that appear in the dialog box. For example, setting the *FolderURL* as shown in the preceding code snippet lets you dynamically redirect the saves based on the currently deployed form. While the Data Connections dialog box forces you to hardcode the location, the code above overrides the hardcoding.

Opening from SharePoint

Let's take a look at the *OpenSharePoint* method.

```
Public Sub OpenSharePoint()
    Dim sForm As String = sSharePointFolder & sSharePointFileName
    thisApplication.XDocuments.Open(sForm,
        CType(XdDocumentVersionMode.xdCanOpenInReadOnlyMode,
        Integer))
    exitApp()
End Sub
```

This code is pretty simple. It opens a new InfoPath form from SharePoint and closes the current form. The effect is to switch from a local version to the SharePoint version. If the user opens the form from SharePoint, the call to *thisApplication.XDocuments.Open* will fail with an access denied error because you have the form open. However, the Book Purchase logic should never call this method if the form is opened from SharePoint.

To close the current form, we define the method *exitApp* as follows:

```
Private Sub exitApp()
    thisXDocument.View.Window.Close(True)
End Sub
```

Passing a value of *True* to the *View.Window.Close* method instructs it to close without prompting the user with a Save dialog box.

The *btnTakeOwnership* method makes calls to several other helper functions–for example, *setNodeValue*, *setAssignedTo*, *setCurrentContact*, *CompleteLastAction*, and *InsertAction*. These methods set values in the XML. The workflow logs action history in the XML document, too. For more details about the helper functions, see the sample code available on the book's companion Web site.

Uniquely Naming the Form

If your workflow submits the form to SharePoint and sends out e-mail notifications to your teammates that include a link to the form, you must make sure the link to the form persists. Creating a name for the form based on some value in its XML is a bad idea because that value might change, and if the form name changes, links sent in e-mail will no longer refer to valid file locations. The following example shows how to use the *Guid* object (which stands for globally unique identifier) to create a unique name for your form.

```
Private Shared ReadOnly sFORMAT_FILENAME As String = "BookPurchase-{0}.xml"

Private Function getFormName() As String
    Dim oFileName As IXMLDOMNode = getNode("//my:myFields/my:State/my:Filename")
    Dim sFileName As String = getNodeValue(oFileName)

    If "" = sFileName Then
        setNodeValue(oFileName, getEscapedFileName(String.Format(sFORMAT_FILENAME,
            Guid.NewGuid().ToString())))
    End If

    Return getNodeValue(oFileName)
End Function
```

Developer Nugget: Creating a *Guid* in Script

With the .NET Framework, you can use the *Guid* object to generate unique identifiers for your forms. If you have a script form and would like to use a unique identifier, you have to generate your own. Here's an example of how to do this using JScript:

```
function generateGuid()
{
    var sGuid = "";
    for (var i = 1; i <= 32; i++)
    {
        var n = Math.floor(Math.random()*16).toString(16);
        sGuid += n;
        if((i == 8) || (i == 12) || (i == 16) || (i == 20))
            sGuid += "-";
    }
    return sGuid;
}
```

The above function, *generateGuid*, uses the JScript *Math* object to get a sequence of 32 random numbers that are concatenated together with dashes to form a pseudo-unique identifier.

Uniquely naming your forms in this way solves the broken link problem, but it creates a problem, too. Locating forms based on the name becomes impossible. On SharePoint, you can change your view to hide the filename (default Title column) and display other columns for the form. On a shared folder, you don't have this option.

Schema Changes for Workflow

Workflow requires additional data to describe who is working on the form, what state it's in, and what has happened to it. This data can live separately in a database on the server (for example, in a BizTalk Server database), or it can live in the document. Storing the workflow status in the form data is less secure than storing it in a server database because users can view the contents outside of InfoPath and see who the form was assigned to or even modify the workflow data. By allowing sections to be digitally signed, you can guard against surreptitious modifications to the form's workflow data, but your users will have to install digital certificates. To prevent viewing, you can encrypt the workflow data, but that requires installing encryption keys.

In addition to security concerns, extending your form to include workflow data requires modifying its schema. To XML purists, modifying the form's schema to include extraneous data such as view state violates the essence of XML, which was designed as a means to separate data from its presentation. With the exception of logging, workflow data is transitory: it describes the workflow process. When the workflow process ends, the form no longer needs the workflow data.

You can use the techniques discussed in Chapter 6 to define a secondary data source and store your workflow data in a database on a server. Later in this chapter, we will discuss an example that uses BizTalk Server 2004 to further simplify storing and retrieving workflow data. However, for our Book Purchase example, we will store the workflow data in the actual form.

The workflow for our Book Purchase schema needs two additional root nodes–one named *State* and another named *Actions*.

State

The workflow state describes where the form is in the workflow process. In Figure 10-1, shown earlier, the dashed boxes represent the states of the Book Purchase form. State includes status, assignment, and filename. Figure 10-6 shows the new data source elements when the Show Details option in the Data Source task pane is checked.

- **Status/Id** Integer representing the workflow status–Request (0), Approve (1), Report (2), and View (3); useful for comparisons in code.
- **Status/Name** String representing the workflow status–"Request", "Approve", "Report", and "View"; useful for reporting and e-mail notifications. Status is also useful when promoted as a property in SharePoint form libraries because it can quickly show form status.
- **Roles/Approver** Contains *Name*, *Email*, and *Alias* elements corresponding to the approver of this form. Note: The Book Purchase example supports only one approver; to support more than one approver, you can make the schema element and view section repeating.
- **Roles/Requester** Contains *Name*, *Email*, and *Alias* elements corresponding to the Requester of this form.
- **AssignedTo** Contains *Name*, *Email*, and *Alias* elements corresponding to the person the form is currently assigned to.
- **Filename** Name of the form; needed to bridge e-mail and SharePoint scenarios.

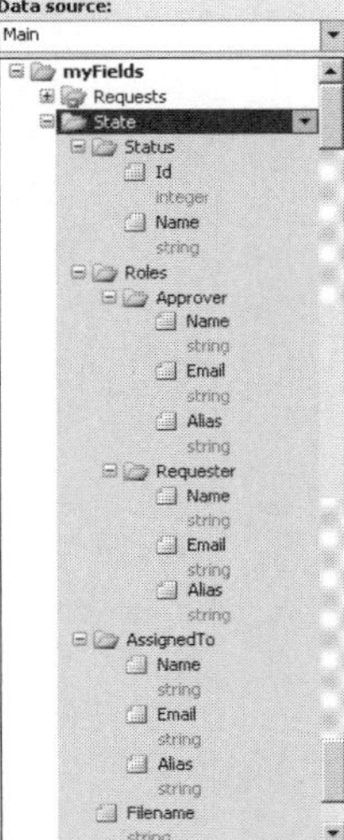

Figure 10-6 Adding workflow state to the Main data source

Actions

The Book Purchase form uses the *Actions* node to keep a log of the actions performed during the workflow processing. The *Action* node underneath *Actions* is repeating. Figure 10-7 shows the new data source elements. For readability, the *my:* namespace has been removed from the following *XPaths*.

- ***Action/Date*** The date when the action took place.
- ***Action/Time*** The time when the action took place.
- ***Action/Description*** The description of the action. This can be as detailed or simple as required.
- ***Action/Id*** A status identifier for the action. This is used for filtering in SharePoint views to see, for example, all book purchases that are not approved, where a condition can be simply written as "*Id* is less than 2."
- ***Action/PerformedBy*** The *PerformedBy* element has four attributes describing who performed the action: *name, email* address, domain *alias*, and what *role* the user played.
- ***Action/LastStatus*** Stores the last status identifier for the form; as we saw in the sample code for this chapter, the Book Purchase form uses *LastStatus* for various checks in the form's workflow logic.

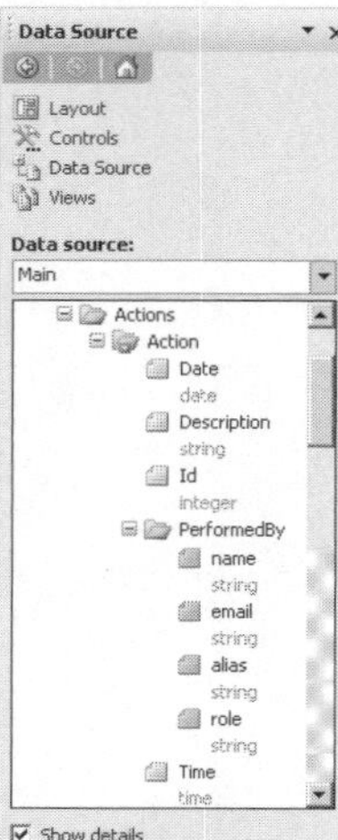

Figure 10-7 Adding workflow action logging to the Main data source

User Roles

In Chapter 2, we defined two user roles for the Book Purchase example–one for Requester and another for Approver. We set the Requester role as both the *default* and the *initiator* and hardcoded the Approver role to the local user account (in the author's case, AUTONOMYSYSTEMS\PatrickHalstead). We will show how to extend the user roles to support multiple approvers. In addition, we will add two new roles to the form, one for Viewer and another for Manager. Figure 10-8 shows the Manage User Roles dialog box with these changes.

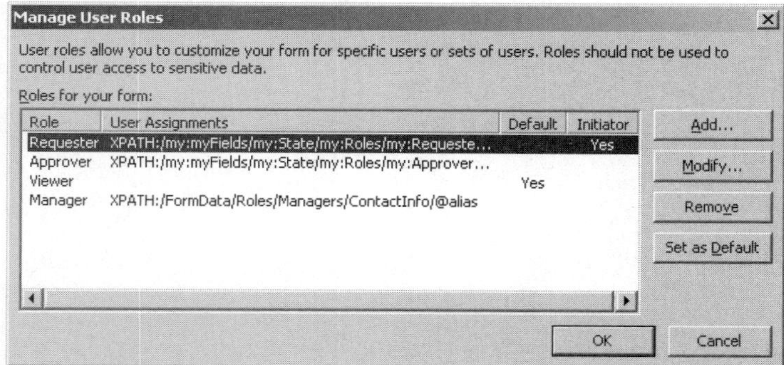

Figure 10-8 Adding user roles for workflow

- **Requester** The Requester continues to be the initiator, which means it is the default role for new forms. For existing forms, Viewer is the default role. When the Approver denies a book purchase request and sends the form back to the Requester, we need to set the user role to Requester based on the user names from the form. Select the Requester role, click modify and then select User Names From The Form. Click the

Select A Field In The Data Source button to the right of the text field. Expand the tree to select the *Alias* field under the *State/Roles/Requester* node. Next we'll do the same for the Approver user role.

- **Approver** To extend the Approver role to support multiple users, select the Approver role, and click Modify. Deselecting the User Names check box will disable editing in the text control and leave the hardcoded value from Chapter 2. Delete the hardcoded value first, and then deselect the check box. Select User Names From The Form. Click the Select A Field In The Data Source button to the right of the text field. Expand the tree to select the *Alias* field under the *State/Roles/Approver* node. You have just mapped the role to the workflow state data. (See Figure 10-9.) The Approver is now defined as the person who took ownership because the act of taking ownership sets the Approver information in the main DOM. Be careful to not confuse this with the list of approvers defined in the FormData.xml file, which the form uses to conditionally hide or show the Take Ownership section.

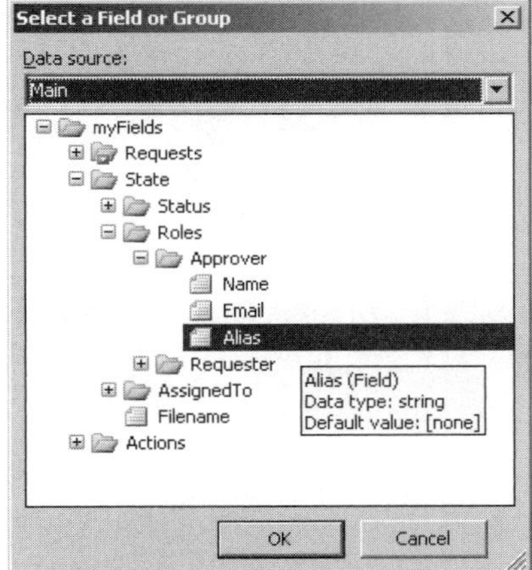

Figure 10-9 Mapping the Approver to the form's data

- **Viewer** The Viewer is the new default role for the form but has no user assignments.
- **Manager** In the Book Purchase workflow, the role of Manager is different from that of Approver. The manager's role is about reporting, not approving. Managers don't participate in the approval process. The workflow logic should let any manager open the form at any time. Instead of checking against the workflow data, we'll check the list of managers stored in the Form Data secondary data source. If you haven't added the Manager user role to the form, click Add to do so. Type the name for the role and select User Names From The Form. Click the button to the right of the text field to select a field from the data source. Unlike with Approver, we'll use the secondary data source for Manager, so select Form Data from the Data Source drop-down list. In the tree view that appears, expand Roles/Managers/ContactInfo and select the *alias* attribute. That's it—click OK to accept the change.

Order of User Role Evaluation

InfoPath evaluates the role of the user in the order in which the user roles appear in the dialog box. Unfortunately, InfoPath provides no way of changing the order. To change the order, you can manually modify the form's manifest (.xsf) file. The *<xsf:roles>* element for the Book Purchase workflow example is as follows:

```
<xsf:roles default="Viewer" initiator="Requester">
    <xsf:role name="Requester"></xsf:role>
    <xsf:role name="Approver"></xsf:role>
    <xsf:role name="Viewer"></xsf:role>
    <xsf:role name="Manager"></xsf:role>
    <xsf:membership>
        <xsf:getUserNameFromData select="/my:myFields/my:State/my:Roles/my:Approver
            /my:Alias" memberOf="Approver"></xsf:getUserNameFromData>
        <xsf:getUserNameFromData select="/FormData/Roles/Managers/ContactInfo/@alias"
            dataObject="Form Data" memberOf="Manager"></xsf:getUserNameFromData>
    </xsf:membership>
</xsf:roles>
```

When a user belongs to two roles and the form's open rules are using the role as a condition, you can run into problems. For example, in the Book Purchase form, if the Manager is also an Approver, when the Manager opens the form, InfoPath sets the role of the current user to Approver because Approver appears first in the user roles list. However, in this case, if your open rules have a condition that checks for the Manager and controls switching to the Manager view, and if the user role is Approver, InfoPath will not execute the action. In the upcoming section on open rules, we describe how to work around this problem.

Setting the User Role

Recall that we added a new view, called View, for read-only viewing of the form. This view includes the Take Ownership section. When the user clicks the Take Ownership button, four scenarios are possible, as described in the earlier "Opening via Attachment vs. Opening from SharePoint" section. When the user opens the form from SharePoint and takes ownership, the code switches the view and has to change the role from Viewer to Approver. At form startup, InfoPath evaluates the user roles and initializes the *thisXDocument.Role* property. However, you can modify the property later by setting it to the string value of one of the roles defined in the Manage User Roles dialog box.

Adding Open Rules

In Chapter 2, we defined two open rules for the Book Purchase form. The Approver rule switched to the Approve view if the *Purpose* was not blank and the user role was Approver. The Reporting rule switched to the Report view if *Approved* equaled *True* and the user role was Approver. These rules were very simple. To implement our workflow, we will have to add rules with conditions based on the workflow state.

Using Status to Control Workflow State

Open rules for workflow typically involve switching views and setting state. You will have at least one rule for each step in your form's workflow. For the Book Purchase sample, we'll define the following open rules:

Approve—Assigned

Conditions

- *LastStatus* is equal to 1.
- User role is Approver.

Actions

- Switch to view: Approve.
- Stop processing rules.

Figure 10-10 shows the dialog box defining this new rule.

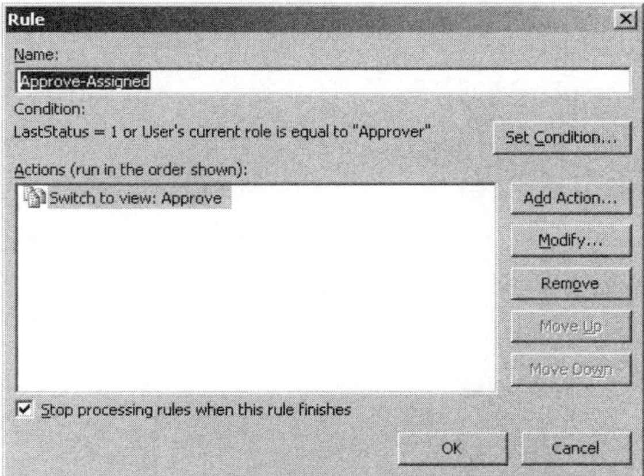

Figure 10-10 Defining open rules using workflow status

Approve—Unassigned

This rule must appear after the Approve–Assigned rule. Order is important because this rule will be the default handling for forms opened with *LastStatus* equal 1 but without an assigned approver.

Conditions

- *LastStatus* is equal to 1.
- (Implied) Conditions for Approve–Assigned rule failed.

Actions

- Switch to view: View.
- Stop processing rules.

Approved-Reporting

Conditions

- *Approved* is equal to *True*.
- *LastStatus* is equal to 2 (corresponding to Reporting).
- User role is Manager.

Actions

- Switch to view: Report.
- Stop processing rules.

Approved-ReadOnly

Conditions

- *LastStatus* is greater than 2.
- (Implied) All previous rules failed.

Actions

- Switch to view: View.
- Stop processing rules.

Users with Multiple Roles

The Book Purchase workflow example assumes that the manager is different from the approver. Suppose one of the users is both a manager and an approver. InfoPath will set the user role to the first one that matches, which in this case is Approver. If the user role is Approver, however, there is no way to open the form in the Report view because the open rule switches to that view only if the user role is Manager.

Specifying Assignment for Manager

Workflow doesn't work well when there is no specific assignment because the rules have no data on which to define conditions. If you set up your workflow to require a manager's assignment, you can check to see if the approver is in fact the same person as the manager.

Modify the workflow to designate a single manager for the reporting step. In this scenario, the manager takes ownership of the form and in so doing assigns himself to it. You have to add a node to your schema to hold the manager's details and insert an open rule after the Approved–Reporting rule, as follows:

Approved-Reporting-ApproverIsManager

Conditions

- *Approved* is equal to *True*.
- *LastStatus* is equal to 2 (corresponding to Reporting).
- User role is Approver.
- Approver's alias is equal to manager's alias.

Actions

- Switch to view: Report.
- Stop processing rules.

The fourth condition is what makes this solution work. InfoPath will set the user role to Approver because the user is actually playing both roles. The fourth condition checks to see that the Manager is in fact the same as the Approver.

Specific assignment solves the problem, but it is unnatural to require form assignment when the manager merely wants to create reports. In addition, it doesn't work when multiple forms are aggregated into one report.

To Restrict or Not to Restrict

Leaving the Read-Only view unrestricted while restricting access to the Reporting view to managers is contradictory. The manager doesn't need to change the data. If he did, the first solution to set assignment makes sense because in essence it locks ownership while the manager makes a change. An easy solution is to let everyone generate reports, and thus all users can view the forms in the Read-Only view. If you have data that is sensitive and want to provide mixed viewing based on role, you can use conditional formatting to control access to views.

Using Conditional Formatting

Another solution is to add a Reporting button to the Read-Only view and only show it if the user's alias exists in the list of managers. Clicking on the button switches to the Report view. The modifications that enable this are left to the reader as an exercise. Conditional formatting is a simple solution but does not prevent users from opening the XML file in Notepad and viewing the contents.

Controlling Access to SharePoint

Yet another solution is to prevent users from accessing your SharePoint form library (or shared folder) and provide a Web part (or Web page) to filter the data from the form library. This prevents users from actually accessing the XML contents, and you can make the Report view open to all approvers and managers.

Controlling Access in Code

One last idea is to allow access only to the Report view when a *merge* event happens. You can define an event handler for *OnMergeRequest* that checks to see whether the user is a member of the Manager list, and if not, redirect her to a warning view. This limits access to the Report view and works around the one role per user limitation in InfoPath.

Developer Nugget: Execution Order at Startup

When InfoPath loads a form, the processing options include user roles, open rules, and the *OnLoad* and *OnSwitchView* event handlers. The execution order is important because it affects the downstream options. If you make the wrong assumption–for example, thinking the *OnLoad* event handler happens before open rules–debugging open rules can be very difficult. Actually, debugging open rules is currently impossible without the InfoPath source code.

The order of processing at startup of a form is:

1. User roles
2. Open rules
3. *OnLoad* event handler
4. *OnSwitchView* event handler

InfoPath must process the user roles first so the open rules can use the current role in the rule conditions. Although open rules have an action to switch the view, the View object doesn't exist yet–nor does it exist during the *OnLoad* event handler. Thus any call to *thisXDocument.View.SwitchView* will fail during the *OnLoad* event.

The open rules Switch Views action suggests an *OnSwitchView* event will occur, but in reality the action is setting the default view at startup. This is the same action that can be taken during the *OnLoad* event to establish the initial view. After the *OnLoad* event is complete, the *View* object is created and InfoPath fires an *OnSwitchView* event.

Stepping Through the Workflow

In this section, we'll put the various workflow pieces together and walk through the workflow scenario for when a user opens a submitted form from e-mail.

User Roles

When the Book Purchase form opens, InfoPath processes the user roles. These check for membership by comparing the current user's credentials (DOMAIN\username) with the results of the *select* attribute's *XPath* as defined in the manifest.xsf file. Here's an example:

```
<xsf:getUserNameFromData select="/my:myFields/my:State/my:Roles/my:Approver/my:Alias"
memberOf="Approver"></xsf:getUserNameFromData>
```

In this case, if the user's credentials match the value of the *Alias* node, InfoPath sets the role to Approver. As soon as InfoPath finds a match, it stops processing user roles. Remember, the first match wins. If no match is found, InfoPath sets the user role to either the initiator, if this is a new form, or default. The initiator for Book Purchase is Requester, but the default is Viewer. Let's assume that the Requester has just submitted the form and that it is unassigned. In this case, the user role will be Viewer.

Open Rules

Next up are the open rules. InfoPath runs through the open rules (in top-down order), checking conditions and performing actions. For the submitted form, *Actions/LastStatus* is equal to 1, which corresponds to the Approve state, but the user isn't an Approver. The *Approve-Unassigned* rule condition succeeds after the *Approve-Assigned* rule condition fails. The action switches the default view to the Read-Only view, named View (a confusing name in the context of the designer).

OnLoad Event Handler

InfoPath calls the *OnLoad* event handler, which has to get the user credentials separately for use in the code. Unfortunately, there is no way to get the user credentials from InfoPath during load even though the user roles use them. In addition to getting the user credentials, the *OnLoad* event handler calculates whether the form was opened locally from the Outlook cache and stores the Boolean result in the *isOpenedLocally* member variable. It also checks to see if the form exists on SharePoint and sets the Boolean result in the *sharepointFormExists* member variable. For our workflow state, *isOpenedLocally* returns *True* and *sharepointFormExists* returns *False*.

Conditional Formatting

Mercifully, our Book Purchase form does not use the *OnViewSwitch* event handler. InfoPath creates the View object and executes the conditional formatting rules it finds. *View* has two conditional formatting sections—one for the Take Ownership section and another for the Open Latest section. For the Take Ownership section, the conditional formatting expression is *not(xdExtension:isUserApprover())*, which evaluates to *False* because the user is in the list of approvers in the Form Data secondary data source. For the Open Latest section, the conditional formatting expression is *not(xdExtension:isFormOutOfDate())*, which evaluates to *True* because the form doesn't exist on SharePoint so it can't be out-of-date, and *not(False)* is *True*. The result: InfoPath displays Take Ownership but hides Open Latest.

Take Ownership

When the user clicks Take Ownership, InfoPath calls the *btnTakeOwnership OnClick* event handler, which executes the appropriate clause based on the two member variables: *isOpenedLocally* and *sharepointFormExists*. In this case, the user opened the form from e-mail (locally) and the form was not on SharePoint (first time open). The code in *btnTakeOwnership* sets the new user as the assigned approver, saves the form to SharePoint, opens the saved form in a new editor, and closes the existing e-mail form.

OnLoad Event Handler (SharePoint Form)

InfoPath starts up again, and we start a new process of user roles, open rules, and the *OnLoad* event handler. This time, however, the user matches the Approver role and the *ApproveAssigned* rule succeeds, resulting in the user seeing the Approve view.

Visualizing a workflow process by analyzing each part is difficult because the workflow process is invariably the sum of its parts. Without an understanding of the user roles and open rules, it's difficult to see the value of the Take Ownership logic. Now that we have finally put all of these pieces together, the workflow should make more sense.

Tracking History Through Event Logging

To see who approved or denied a request, you'll want to keep an audit trail. We have already described how to extend our Book Purchase schema to include an *Actions* group. This section takes a look at the logic needed to keep an action history. We'll create two methods—one for inserting an action, and another for completing an action. First let's look at the *insertAction* method:

```
Private Sub insertAction()
    ' If there is already an Action that hasn't been completed, do not add another one
    ' as it will only cause problems later due to invalid data.
    Dim oActions As IXMLDOMNode = getNode("//my:Actions")
    Dim oFirstAction As IXMLDOMNode = getNode("//my:Actions/my:Action[1]")
    Dim sActionDate As String = getNodeValue("//my:Actions/my:Action[1]/my:Date")
```

```
    If (Not oFirstAction Is Nothing) AndAlso "" = sActionDate Then
        Return
    End If

    Try
        Dim sXml As String = "<my:Action xmlns:wcr=" & Quote & _
            "http://www.InfoPathDev.com/BookPurchase/" & Quote & ">" & _
         "<my:Date/>" & _
         "<my:Description/>" & _
         "<my:Status><my:Id/><my:Name/></my:Status>" & _
         "<my:PerformedBy name=" & Quote & Quote & " email=" & _
             Quote & Quote & " alias=" & Quote & Quote & _
             " role=" & Quote & Quote & "/>" & _
         "</my:Action>"

        Dim oXml As IXMLDOMDocument = thisXDocument.CreateDOM()
        oXml.async = False
        oXml.loadXML(sXml)

        Dim oNewAction As IXMLDOMNode = _
            oActions.insertBefore(oXml.documentElement, oFirstAction)
        setNil(oNewAction.selectSingleNode("my:Date"))
        setNil(oNewAction.selectSingleNode("my:Time"))
        setNil(oNewAction.selectSingleNode("my:Status/my:Id"))
    Catch ex As Exception
        Dim s As String = ex.ToString()
        ' Add specific logic to handle exception
    End Try
End Sub
```

The method creates the XML for the *my:Actions/my:Action* node by first composing a string and then using XML support in InfoPath to load it into an XML DOM.

Inserting the action happens during the *OnLoad* event handler and when the user clicks Take Ownership for a form opened from SharePoint. Because the form has not yet been finalized, the *insertAction* method cannot set *my:Date*, *my:Time*, and *my:Status/my:Id* values. Setting those values happens when the form is submitted to SharePoint in a call to the *completeLastAction* method.

Notice that the code initializes *my:Date*, *my:Time*, and *my:Status/my:Id* by calling the private method *setNil*.

```
Private Sub setNil(ByVal oNode As IXMLDOMNode)
    If oNode Is Nothing Then
        Return
    End If

    Dim oElement As IXMLDOMElement = CType(oNode, IXMLDOMElement)
    If Not (oElement.getAttribute("xsi:nil") Is Nothing) Then
        ' Create xsi:nil attribute with the proper namespace.
        Dim oNil As IXMLDOMAttribute = _
            CType(oNode.ownerDocument.createNode(DOMNodeType.NODE_ATTRIBUTE, _
            "xsi:nil", "http://www.w3.org/2001/XMLSchema-instance"), _
            IXMLDOMAttribute)
        oNil.text = "true"
```

```
        ' The order is important.
        If "" <> oNode.text Then
            oNode.text = ""
        End If
        oElement.setAttributeNode(oNil)
    End If
End Sub
```

The *setNil* method comes in handy when you deal with XSD types that require *xsi:nil*—for example, *my:Date* and *my:Time*. Any schema elements that define the *nillable* attribute as true require *xsi:nil*. For types requiring *xsi:nil*, you must set the *xsi:nil* value to *true* before you can nil the value of the node.

```
Private Sub completeLastAction(ByVal sDescription As String, ByVal iStatus As Integer, ByVal
 sPerformedByRole As String)
    thisXDocument.View.DisableAutoUpdate()

     setNodeValue("//my:myFields/my:Actions/my:Action[1]/my:Date", _
        getDateString())
    setNodeValue("//my:myFields/my:Actions/my:Action[1]/my:Description", _
        sDescription)
    setNodeValue("//my:myFields/my:Actions/my:Action[1]/my:StatusId", iStatus)
    setNodeValue("//my:myFields/my:Actions/my:Action[1]/my:PerformedBy/@role", _
        sPerformedByRole)

    If STATUS.REQUEST = iStatus Then
        Dim oRequester As IXMLDOMNode = _
            getNode("//my:myFields/my:State/my:Roles/my:Requester")
        Dim sName As String = _
            getNodeValue(oRequester.selectSingleNode("my:Name"))
        Dim sEmail As String = _
            getNodeValue(oRequester.selectSingleNode("my:Email"))
        Dim sAlias As String = _
            getNodeValue(oRequester.selectSingleNode("my:Alias"))

        setNodeValue("//my:myFields/my:Actions/my:Action[1]/my:PerformedBy/@name", sName)
        setNodeValue("//my:myFields/my:Actions/my:Action[1]/my:PerformedBy/@email", sEmail)
            setNodeValue("//my:myFields/my:Actions/my:Action[1]/my:PerformedBy/
                @alias", sAlias)
    Else
        setNodeValue("//my:myFields/my:Actions/my:Action[1]/my:PerformedBy
            /@name", GetLoggedInUser("Name"))
        setNodeValue("//my:myFields/my:Actions/my:Action[1]/my:PerformedBy
            /@email", GetLoggedInUser("Email"))
        setNodeValue("//my:myFields/my:Actions/my:Action[1]/my:PerformedBy
            /@alias", GetLoggedInUser("Alias"))
    End If

    thisXDocument.View.EnableAutoUpdate()
End Sub
```

In addition to setting the value of the nodes making up the action history, *completeLastAction* also sets the *my:Requester* values under the *my:State/my:Roles* node when the Requester submits the form. The *setNodeValue* helper method is included in the sample code for this book.

Security

InfoPath saves forms in XML format as plain text files. Nefarious users with access to your workflow's form library can sabotage the audit trail by opening forms in a text editor and manually changing values. To guard against such spoofing, you should use partial signing on the Actions section. Add a section to each view that is editable (Request and Approve for Book Purchases), and bind it to the *Actions* node. Double-click the section and go to the Digital Signatures tab and enable digital signatures for the *Actions* group. Figure 10-11 shows the dialog box with the *Actions* node selected for signing.

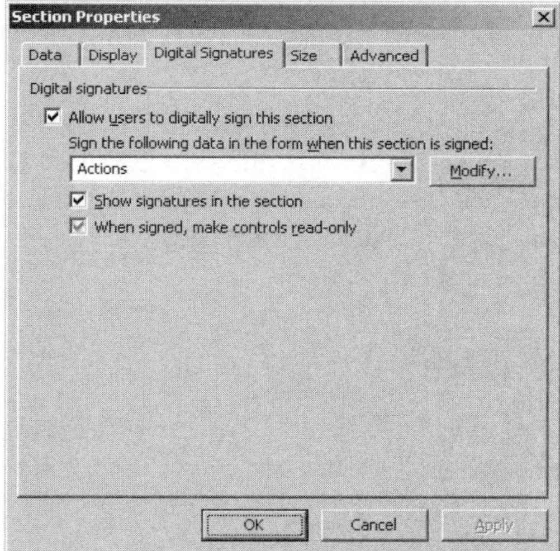

Figure 10-11 Partial digital signatures prevent spoofing of actions.

Make sure the digital signature that you add supports subsequent signing (i.e., counter-signing) so users can sign a form that has already been signed. Figure 10-12 shows the Set Of Signable Data dialog box with the countersign signature option selected.

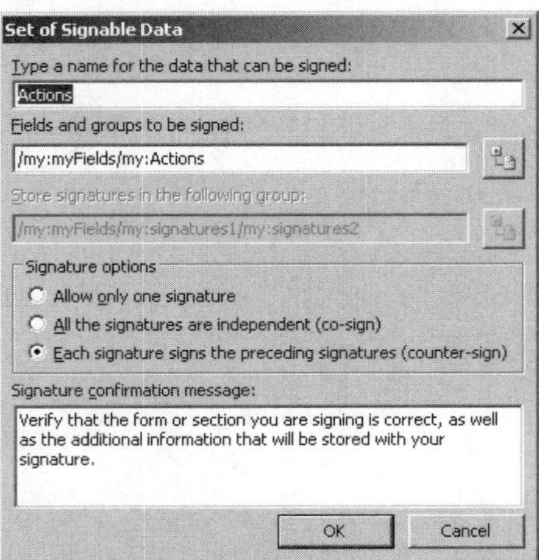

Figure 10-12 Set your digital signature options to enable countersigning so forms can be signed in an additive fashion.

When you change the properties of a section to make it digitally signable, InfoPath creates a corresponding *signatures* node in your main data source (appended at the end). To force signing the *signatures* node during submit, add code in *completeLastAction* to call the *Sign* method on the *signatures* data block. We'll leave this as an exercise for the reader. Chapter 4 covers digital signatures in more detail.

Deploying Forms to External Users

Many workflow scenarios originate with users that are not connected to the corporate Web site, either because they are offline or because they are outside the company's firewall. In these scenarios, external users submit requests via e-mail to an internal approval process. Creating an InfoPath form that bridges the external submission and internal approval process is desirable.

InfoPath supports three options for deploying a one-form solution that will work on both external clients and internal clients as well as interoperate between them:

- Send a restricted form to external requesters
- Send a full trust form to everyone
- Send RegForm packages to everyone

Sending a Restricted Form to External Requesters

The first option is to create a one-off restricted form that you attach to e-mail and send to your external requesters.

Publish your form to SharePoint, close the InfoPath designer, navigate to the form library, click on Modify Settings and Columns, and then click Edit Template. The form will open in the designer. Set the security level to restricted (Tools | Form Options | Security), and send the form as an attachment in e-mail (File | Send Form As Attachment) to your external requesters. (Recall from Chapter 8 that you must have Outlook 2003 installed to enable the Send Form As Attachment menu item on the InfoPath File menu; not only must Outlook be installed, but it must be set as the default e-mail client or the menu item will not be present.) Change the security level back to Automatic, and resave the form.

If you don't perform the last save step, the version of the form attached to e-mail will be later than the form on SharePoint. This will result in version warning messages for the internal users because they will receive forms that have a more recent version number than the form saved to SharePoint.

An alternative solution is to ensure that the version of your SharePoint form template is always greater than 1.0.0.1, and then when you send out the e-mail copy, set its version to 1.0.0.1 and set its security level to Restricted. Because the version of the e-mail copy of the form template is always lower than that of the SharePoint copy, there is no need to resave to SharePoint. This method is cleaner and safer because you cannot make inadvertent modifications to the SharePoint form template.

Pros

- No digital certificates.

Cons

- Restricted security level means you can't do much on the external client, though InfoPath does support submit via e-mail for restricted forms.
- Managed code won't work. InfoPath does not support running managed code for restricted forms. You must use script instead.
- External users can view workflow data stored in the form template.

Sending a Full Trust Form to Everyone

The second option is to set the security level for your form to full trust. Full trust security requires signing the form and having your users install a digital certificate.

Publish your form to SharePoint, close the InfoPath designer, navigate to the form library, click on Modify Settings and Columns, and then click Edit Template. The form will open in the designer. Set the security level to full trust (Tools | Form Options | Security), and select the check box to Sign This Form. InfoPath will prompt you to add a digital certificate. When you are done, exit from the Form Options dialog box by clicking OK, and save your form. Then send the form as an attachment in e-mail (File | Send Form As Attachment).

Pros

- Uses same form for everyone.
- Supports managed code.
- Form has access to everything.

Cons

- Digital certificates aren't easy to install.
- Full Trust forms have access to the user's machine, and this can pose a security risk.
- External users can view workflow data stored in the form template.

Sending RegForm Packages to Everyone

Chapter 2 introduced the RegForm tool, and we discussed it again in Chapter 8. The RegForm tool creates an install package that users can run to install an InfoPath form on their computer. During the installation process, RegForm calls InfoPath's *RegisterSolution* method using the *ExternalApplication* object. *RegisterSolution* does what you would expect–it registers the solution in the user's registry. But in the process it removes the *href* attribute from the form's manifest. Recall that the *href* attribute holds the publish location information. Forms with no *href* attribute are referred to as URN-based. When the requester fills out a form using this URN-based form template, the resulting XML contains no *href* attribute. Without an *href* attribute in the XML for the form, internal users won't be able to open the forms attached to e-mail unless they have the same URN-based form installed on their machine. Basically, this has the result of turning the SharePoint form library into a shared folder with a dummy template and no support for automatic upgrade.

Pros

- No digital certificates.
- Managed code support.

Cons

- No automatic upgrade.
- Breaks interop with SharePoint features. Must hardcode form library or shared folder.
- External users can view workflow data stored in the form template.

Sending a Separate Form for External Requesters

An alternative to the one-form deployment solution is to deploy two separate forms. You use one form for the internal workflow and another for the external submission. The internal form accesses your team's Web site as domain-level trust or full trust. (Recall that it must be domain-level to access the Web site). The external form is sent out in e-mail as a RegForm package.

The two-form solution is complicated by the fact that it requires interop between two forms. The internal users that bridge the workflow step between external users and the internal workflow must install both solutions. The external form must invoke the internal one using the *NewFromSolution* method. To execute the *NewFromSolution* method, the form must have a security level of 2 or higher–i.e., it must be domain-level trust or full trust.

At the time of this writing, InfoPath has a bug where the target form can't access domain resources unless it is cached before running, as the result of *NewFromSolution*. In other words, the internal user must pre-cache the internal form (simply opening it will work) to allow it to access the SharePoint site. If the internal user fails to pre-cache the form, she will have to remove the form from the cache using the Fill Out A Form dashboard and try again.

Pros

- No digital certificates.
- Internal users get automatic upgrade.
- External form can exclude sensitive data.

Cons

- More work to implement.
- More complicated.
- Must work around caching bug in InfoPath.

Summary

In this chapter, we explored InfoPath's support for forms-based workflow. We looked at conditional formatting, user roles, open rules, and business logic for supporting both e-mail and SharePoint submit. In the process, we extended the Book Purchase example we started in Chapter 2 to include access control, workflow data, and edit history. Finally, we saw various options for deploying forms to mixed teams of internal and external users.

Forms-based workflow differs from server-based workflow in that workflow logic is placed in the actual form. InfoPath's support for forms-based workflow provides compelling solutions for some workflow processes, but there are limitations. Forms-based workflow has to keep workflow data somewhere. Modifying the schema to hold the workflow data might not be feasible, and the alternative of putting the data on the server requires a lot of work. E-mail notifications and SharePoint submits cannot be transactioned together as an atomic operation, and this presents robustness issues. Finally, if the workflow's business logic changes, forms saved using the old workflow might no longer work. This is a consequence of hardcoding the workflow process in the business logic.

The next chapter will offer an overview of the InfoPath and BizTalk story and show how integrating InfoPath with BizTalk can address many of the limitations of forms-based workflow. Needless to say, if you don't have the option of deploying BizTalk Server, the forms-based workflow presented in this chapter is a good place to start.

Chapter 11

Advanced Workflow with BizTalk

Chapter 10 showed how to create simple forms-based workflow where the form included the status of the workflow. This chapter shows how to create more powerful server-based workflow solutions using Microsoft BizTalk Server 2004 and Human Workflow Services (HWS).

BizTalk Server 2004 includes support for human-oriented workflow via a component called Human Workflow Services, which InfoPath now supports in Service Pack 1. A good example of human-oriented workflow is an approval process, which can include actions for approving, denying, or delegating forms. Approving a form routes it forward, denying a form routes it backward, and delegating a form routes it sideways to another person. You can combine these actions in many ways, which makes sense because human workflow is often ad hoc. Each form can conceivably travel a different path through the workflow.

Figure 11-1 shows an architectural diagram of form processing using InfoPath and HWS. When you enable HWS for an InfoPath form template, InfoPath uses a built-in submit data connection to send instances of your form to HWS Web services. When HWS receives the message, it executes the specified action. Each action defines a BizTalk orchestration. Orchestrations specify workflow between people or processes given the context of the form data. You can develop orchestrations that perform a variety of tasks. Orchestrations define workflows using conditions, rules, logic, and processing by external components–to name just a few of the features.

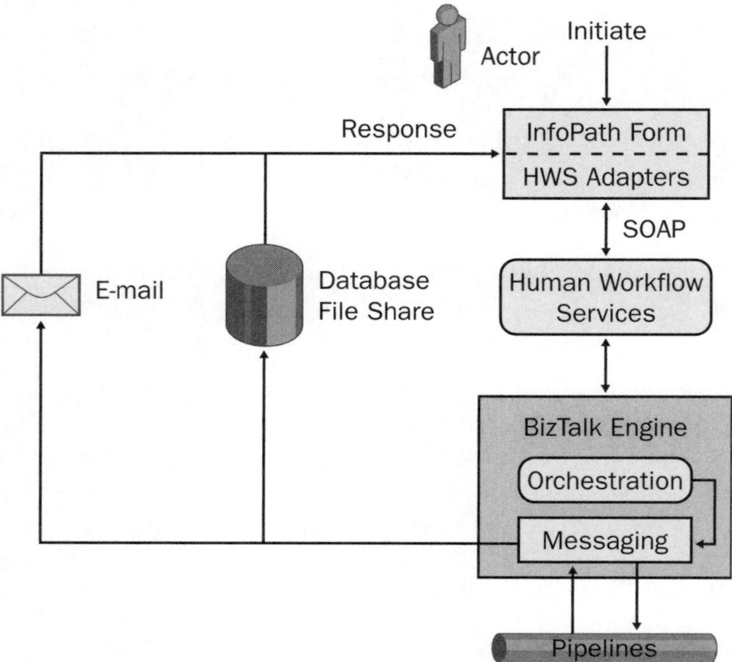

Figure 11-1 InfoPath integrates with BizTalk via HWS.

The InfoPath SDK comes with an HWS Pipeline Component, which inserts special identifiers in the processing instruction of the form's XML data. InfoPath relies on these identifiers to query workflow state from BizTalk. Any action that you define where the outcome is an InfoPath form must use the Pipeline Component to reinsert, or *rehydrate*, the HWS processing instruction. More on that later.

In addition to sending forms to HWS Web services, InfoPath supports a task pane to display workflow status and action buttons. Unfortunately, the InfoPath designer does not have a user interface for enabling support for HWS integration, so you must manually modify the manifest to enable these HWS features. You must add an *hwsWorkflow* section to enable the task pane and one or more *hwsAdapter* sections to define workflow actions for it. Modifying the manifest by hand might seem onerous, but it is straightforward compared with developing BizTalk orchestrations.

This chapter presents an overview of the steps needed to integrate your form with BizTalk and HWS. In spite of the manual editing requirements, the good news is that integrating InfoPath with HWS is rather simple. The bad news? If you don't have BizTalk installed and configured, be prepared to spend some time up front on those tasks. Of course, this book does not cover installation and configuration of BizTalk—see the BizTalk Server 2004 release documents. In addition, if you don't have HWS orchestrations defined, you must set aside time to develop actions or repurpose samples that already exist. For this chapter, we will refer you to sample HWS actions provided in the BizTalk Server 2004 SDK. Keep in mind that you will likely spend more time preparing BizTalk and HWS than actually integrating InfoPath.

HWS and InfoPath

HWS adds human-based workflow support to BizTalk by exposing a number of Web services. InfoPath accesses these Web services to submit and retrieve forms and query the status of the form in the workflow process. Before jumping into the implementation details of adding HWS support to your InfoPath form, we need to cover some of the HWS bases. This section gives a basic overview of HWS and how InfoPath integrates with it.

HWS Objects

The HWS platform exposes five objects for describing the state of a form in a workflow process:

- **Activity model** An *activity model* enforces an order on a series of actions in a business process. InfoPath does not support activity models. For more information about activity models, see the following URL: *http://msdn.microsoft.com/library/default.asp?url=/library/en-us/sdk/htm/ebiz_design_hws_dacm.asp*.
- **Activity flow** An *activity flow* is a series of related actions, or a *workflow*. By default, InfoPath forms support only one activity flow per form, which works fine for business processes with workflows in series—for example, a purchase order process followed by an invoice process. Business processes requiring parallel workflows are not uncommon, but they are complex. An example is a broadcast request process for a radio station that involves two workflows—one for reviewing the content of the broadcast and another for scheduling the broadcast. In practice, such parallel processes can be serialized. However, if you need activity flows in parallel for the same form, you can still do this with InfoPath, but you must implement your own support for HWS.
- **Action** An *action* is the smallest unit of workflow and usually involve two or more actors and multiple steps. Examples include *approve* and *delegate*.
- **Tasks** A *task* is an individual step in an action. Examples include *send* and *notify*.
- **Actors** *Actors* map to roles in the workflow process. Examples include *initiator*, *approver*, and *delegate*. HWS roles are not the same as the roles supported in InfoPath.

Figure 11-2 depicts an activity flow involving two actions, three actors, and several tasks (represented by boxes inside the actions).

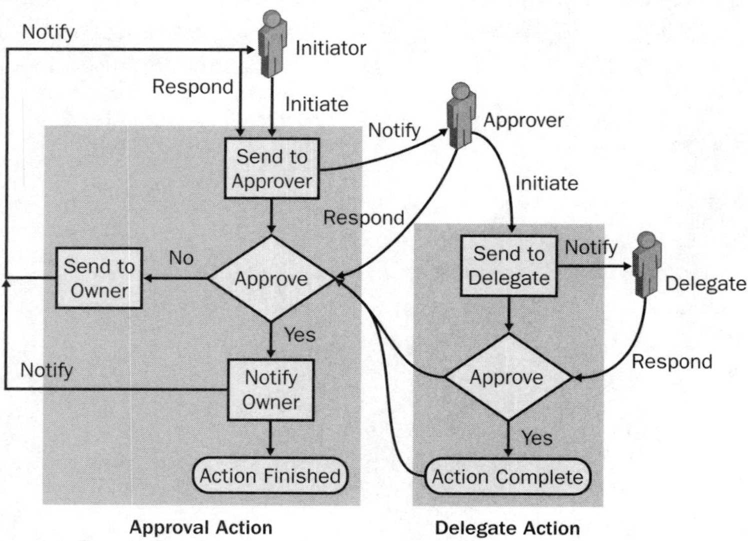

Figure 11-2 An activity flow for an approval process.

InfoPath Maps Forms to HWS

The activity flow, action, and task combine to identify the workflow *state* for an InfoPath form in BizTalk. They determine where the form is in the workflow process. The actor is important when responding to a task because it specifies notification. InfoPath must refer to these objects when it queries BizTalk to get the state for the form or submits a form to the workflow process. Because InfoPath is a rich client supporting offline scenarios, this state must be stored in the actual form data; otherwise, InfoPath has no way of querying the state when the user reopens the form or regains connectivity to the network. For all forms supporting HWS, InfoPath saves a special processing instruction (PI) in the XML instance of each form:

```
<?mso-infoPathSolution solutionVersion="1.0.0.6" productVersion="11.0.6357"
PIVersion="1.0.0.0" href="file:///
C:\Development\Training\InfoPath\Lab12\HWS%20Sample\HWS%20Sample.xsn" name="urn:schemas-
microsoft-com:office:infopath:HWS-Sample:-myXSD-2004-08-17T20-34-10" ?>
<?mso-application progid="InfoPath.Document"?>
<?mso-infoPathHWSWorkflow activityFlowID="F5272259-6A74-4C28-90FF-7291E966DF39"
actionInstanceID="51789349-0448-4d33-8b0f-362d4e841d02" taskID="" taskResponses="" ?>
```

The *?mso-infoPathHWSWorflow* PI encodes three identifiers, which map to corresponding HWS objects. These HWS objects specify the workflow state of your form. In the code above, InfoPath uses GUIDs for the identifiers *activityFlowID* and *actionInstanceID*. However, *taskID* is blank. Why is that? HWS creates a *taskID* for each form, but only after they have been submitted to the workflow process.

The PI tracks the workflow, action, and task, but InfoPath specifies different attributes depending on whether the form was created by the action initiator or action recipient. For the initiator, InfoPath creates only the *activityFlowID* and *actionInstanceID*. This is true even after the initiator submits the form. The recipient's form will have the *activityFlowId*, *actionInstanceID*, and *taskID*. The *taskID* tells InfoPath to show the workflow pane for the task recipient. When *taskID* is nil, InfoPath shows the initiator pane. The initiator and target can be the same person–for example, in an extended workflow where the actor is both the target of the previous task and the initiator of a new task. In that scenario, the *taskID* will be non-nil, but the *actionInstanceID* will refer to the new action.

The preceding code example is for a form that has been saved before submitting. Each HWS-enabled form must define activity flow and action instance in advance so InfoPath can save values for those IDs. InfoPath uses the fourth attribute, *taskResponses*, to synchronize display of the form's status–more about that later.

Note For details about the *?mso-infoPathSolution* and *?mso-application* PIs, see Chapter 2 and Chapter 1, respectively.

Figure 11-3 shows how the HWS object hierarchy and leaf nodes map to identifier attributes stored in the HWS PI. When a task is extended with an action (for example, Action Instance 2 underneath Task a), InfoPath encodes the ID of the extended action and not the parent. The delegate action shown earlier in Figure 11-2 is a good example of an extended action.

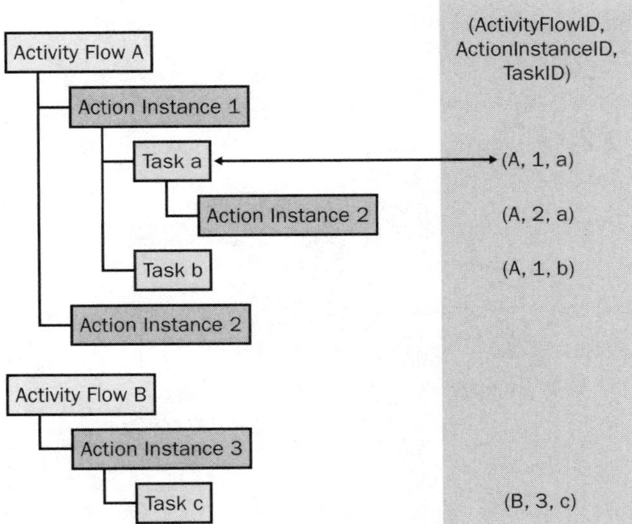

Figure 11-3 InfoPath tracks the workflow state of a form using three identifiers: *ActivityFlowID*, *ActionInstanceID*, and *TaskID*.

The HWS Web services receive SOAP messages. When you enable HWS for a form, you have to define receive data connections for *GetActivityFlowInfo*, *GetActionInstance*, *GetTaskInfo*, and *GetActivityList*. You can use the InfoPath designer to specify these data connections. Figure 11-4 shows an example of the Data Connections dialog box with the required definitions.

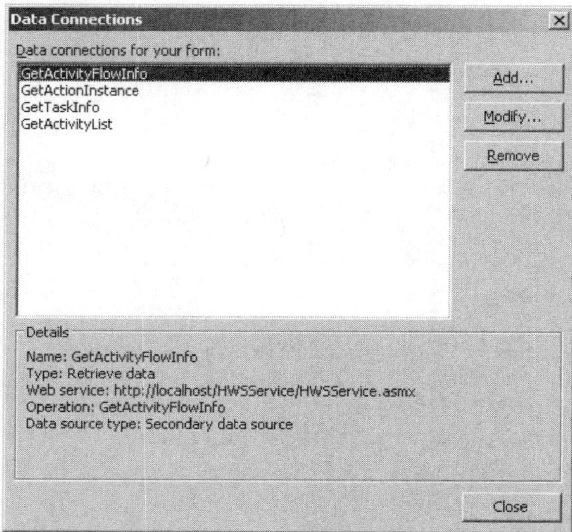

Figure 11-4 Defining data connections to receive data from HWS Web services

In addition to the receive data connections, you must manually define special HWS data adapters for submitting data from the form to HWS. An upcoming section describes how to extract your form files to a folder and manually add the HWS data adapters.

InfoPath provides built-in support for mapping the HWS PI in the form to an HWS section in a SOAP message. The data for the InfoPath form itself is encapsulated in the SOAP message's payload. Figure 11-5 shows this HWS submit process.

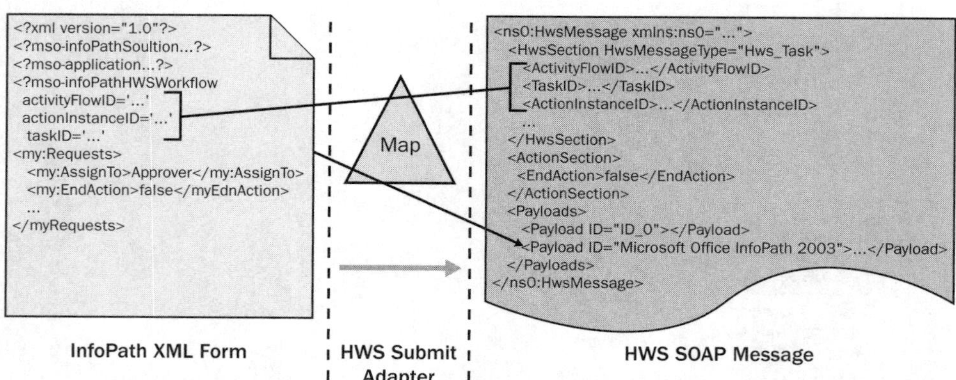

Figure 11-5 The HWS submit process: InfoPath automatically maps the PI, but HWS submit adapters must be defined manually.

BizTalk Generates InfoPath Forms

When the HWS workflow task is complete, BizTalk sends the form to a port. You can define any number of port outputs for your business process. BizTalk has extensive support for adapters. The port can be an e-mail message, a Web/file folder, line-of-business application, and so forth. To output a file in a format that is InfoPath-friendly, BizTalk needs a pipeline adapter. Not only does the pipeline adapter extract the payload for the InfoPath form, but it must also map the new *taskID* and *actionInstanceID* because the action or task might have changed as a result of the prior workflow. Figure 11-6 shows the process. The pipeline component converts the HWS SOAP message back into an InfoPath form.

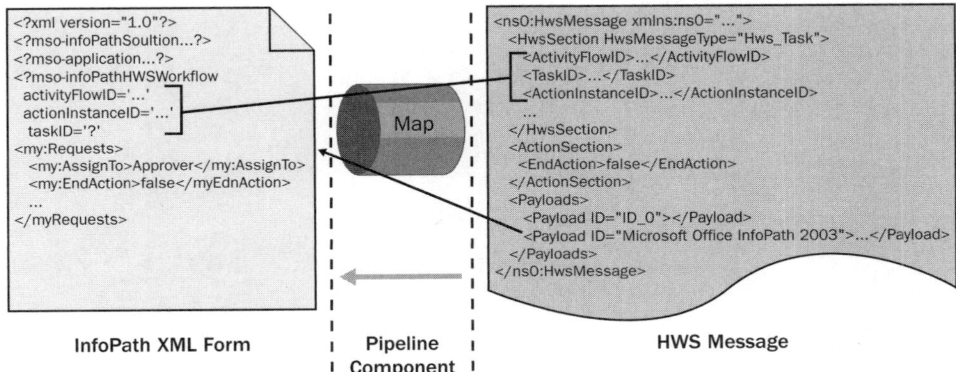

Figure 11-6 After the orchestration task, the HWS pipeline component for InfoPath extracts the form's XML data from the payload and inserts updated attributes back into the HWS PI.

The pipeline component is the recommended way of unpacking the InfoPath form's XML from the payload, updating the HWS PI attributes in it, and repacking it into the payload. However, that is not the only way. For InfoPath to understand and interact with Human Workflow Services, the steps that the pipeline component performs must happen but you don't need to do them in the pipeline. In fact, the location of the logic that performs the steps depends on the orchestration designer. For example, you could have custom code within the orchestration itself that handles these operations. The pipeline component is the recommended way but not the only way of preparing a BizTalk message to work with InfoPath.

The pipeline component is specific to InfoPath but must be installed and deployed from within BizTalk. We will describe where to get it and how to install it in the upcoming section titled "Programming Prerequisites."

Task Pane Workflow

InfoPath supports displaying workflow state in the task pane. To enable the HWS workflow task pane, you have to manually modify the manifest for your form template. The layout of the workflow status in the task pane is fixed, but you can specify buttons for your tasks. You can specify button captions only for the buttons that initiate or respond to an action. Figure 11-7 shows an example of the HWS workflow layout in the task pane. This example corresponds to an approval process where the requester and the approver are the same user, namely WIN2K3\Administrator.

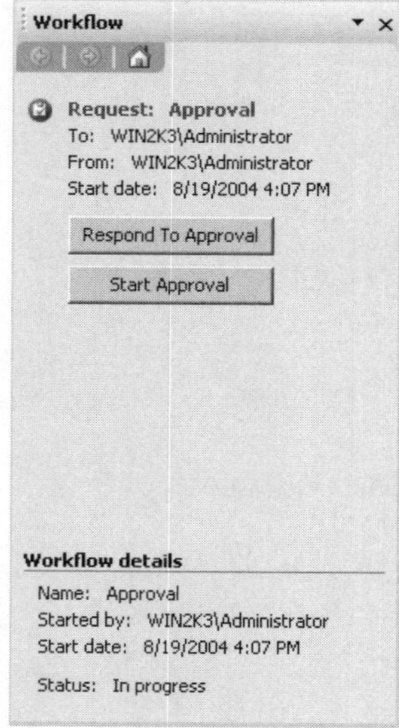

Figure 11-7 InfoPath has built-in support for displaying HWS workflow status in the task pane.

Developer Nugget: Custom HWS Forms

Instead of relying on InfoPath's built-in support, you can write managed code that talks directly to the HWS Web services. The advantage of "rolling your own" is that you have more control over what is displayed in the task pane. You can expose more data, including multiple targets, and show other responses. However, if you want to use managed code to do this, you have to deploy your form as Full Trust. Forms using managed code and task panes must be Full Trust.

You can create a custom task pane that works with HWS. Managed code solutions present many options for the InfoPath forms designer. For example, you can combine code that accesses HWS, InfoPath's object model, and other business applications in the same form.

Status Synchronization

By default, when InfoPath submits a message to a Web service, it waits for the Web service to respond. That means it blocks user input. If the Web service doesn't respond in a fixed period of time, InfoPath displays an error message. Submitting to a Web service is synchronous by default. You can define your own asynchronous logic in .NET and do all of the submit yourself, but you'll probably have to block on submit anyway because it is such an important operation. HWS implements Web services, but BizTalk uses a queue for incoming messages. When the queue is deep, BizTalk might not process the message for some time. The HWS Web services can't wait for that to happen, so they return quickly and report success–the message was queued successfully. InfoPath informs the user that the form was successfully submitted, but because the form might be waiting in the BizTalk queue, the status is not immediately available. Clicking the Get Status button in the task pane seemingly has no effect. How does InfoPath know when to display the status?

InfoPath uses the *taskResponses* attribute in the HWS PI to keep track of the response level for the form. At the start of an approval process, there are no responses, so the attribute is nil. InfoPath calls the *GetActionInstance* Web method to query the status of the form's workflow. The return message contains action instance and task data. Each *task* node contains a *responses* element that counts the number of processed responses for that task. InfoPath displays the status only if the value of the *responses* element in the returned SOAP message is greater than or equal to the value of the *taskResponses* attribute in the HWS PI. Otherwise, the workflow task pane resembles Figure 11-8.

Figure 11-8 InfoPath encodes the number of responses for a task in the HWS PI so it can tell when to refresh the status in the workflow task pane.

Programming Prerequisites

Successful mountain climbers use a checklist to prepare for every climb. The same should be true when you set off to develop an InfoPath form for BizTalk. This section covers crucial preparation steps.

> **Warning** Installing BizTalk Server 2004 and working through the online lab described in this section will take several hours—at least. BizTalk is a complex server product, so there is no shortcut. If you don't have time now, skip these steps and return to them later.

BizTalk Server 2004

You will need to install BizTalk Server 2004, which includes Human Workflow Services. There are ample online resources describing the ins and outs of installing and configuring BizTalk. Check out the MSDN link for comprehensive information: *http://msdn.microsoft.com/library/en-us/deploying/htm/ebiz_deploy_intro_metn.asp*.

> **Tip** Installing BizTalk on a domain controller or on a server that already has SharePoint complicates configuration. BizTalk requires a dozen or so components. Consider using a Virtual PC image if you have to install from scratch. Virtual PC images isolate the installation environment, reducing the variables and the related risk of encountering an installation error.

HWS Pipeline Component

As discussed earlier, BizTalk supports inserting adapters into the routing pipeline. These components are used to convert the output message to a format that is useful for the receiver. Dropping the output message to a file share or sending it as an attachment in e-mail requires extraction of the XML payload and insertion of the updated workflow identifiers. The HWS pipeline component does both.

Downloading the Component

The HWS Pipeline Component is included as an uncompiled source file in the InfoPath online lab titled "Lab 12: Workflow Support in InfoPath 2003" at *http://msdn.microsoft.com/library/default.asp?url=/library/en-us/odc_ip2003_tr/html/odc_INF_Lab_12.asp*. You can also find a complete project at *http://home.comcast.net/~sdwoodgate/InfoPathTaskPatchingPipeline.zip*.

The upcoming section titled "Integration Steps" details how to install, configure, and deploy the pipeline component.

BizTalk Server 2004 SDK

The SDK contains several sample HWS actions. In particular, InfoPath's MSDN Lab 12 training lab relies on the *Assign* and *Delegate* actions. Install the SDK from the following URL: *http://www.microsoft.com/downloads/details.aspx?familyid=8A1CA3AF-790C-4261-838A-9F0661C72887&displaylang=en.*

Lab 12: Workflow Support in InfoPath 2003

InfoPath's MSDN Lab 12 is one of the most thorough examples of InfoPath and BizTalk 2004 integration. The lab contains step-by-step instructions to walk you through the development of a sample BizTalk orchestration and InfoPath form. The majority of steps in the lab involve configuration and deployment of the BizTalk orchestration. This chapter is not a lab and does not give step-by-step instructions for creating and deploying BizTalk orchestrations, so Lab 12 is a must read.

To install Lab 12 files and download instructions, go to *http://msdn.microsoft.com/library/default.asp?url=/library/en-us/odc_ip2003_tr/html/odc_inf_lab_12.asp.*

Caution Installing Windows Server 2003 automatically enables Internet Explorer (IE) Enhanced Security. This will cause problems when you attempt to view the HWS Web service using the URL for your machine name. For example, *http://WIN2K3/HWSService/HWSService.asmx* will display a logon dialog box if you have IE Enhanced Security installed. Interestingly, *http://localhost/HWSService/HWSService.asmx* will display no such logon prompt. Enhanced Security also causes problems when InfoPath queries the Web service. Your best bet is to disable Enhanced Security. In Control Panel, go to Add Or Remove Programs, and then select Add/Remove Windows Components in the left pane. Make sure the check box for Internet Explorer Enhanced Security Configuration is cleared. Click Next to uninstall the component.

Installing on a standalone machine can result in HWS problems. InfoPath checks to see if the machine is online before executing HWS queries. If your machine is a Virtual PC without network connectivity or a standalone machine at home, you might experience problems.

Integration Steps

We need a workflow describing how to create workflow! This section gives an overview of the steps required to create an HWS orchestration. For the InfoPath-specific components, we'll provide more details.

Creating HWS Orchestration

The first step is to create an HWS orchestration. This will likely take the longest time to complete. For an in-depth example showing how to do these steps, refer to Lab 12 described in the previous section.

The following list summarizes the steps:

1. **Define and deploy component actions.** The BizTalk SDK includes sample HWS actions and a command-line script named DeployActions.cmd to deploy them. See Lab 12 for more information.
2. **Create a BizTalk Server Human Workflow project for your main action.** Visual Studio includes a template for HWS projects under BizTalk Projects.
3. **Strong sign the action.** All BizTalk orchestrations must be strong signed.
4. **Update schemas to match the InfoPath workflow.** Customize the schemas to meet the needs of your new InfoPath-based workflow. Add nodes for any form state that you will need in the orchestration. To stop orchestration, for example, you must define a node in your form that sets the condition for stopping. Define an *endAction* node and add a node to the HWS schema to map it.

   The flag that determines when an action is finished may not be as declarative as an *endAction* node. For example, your BizTalk orchestration could include logic that checks for a finish condition such as when the FirstName and LastName are populated.
5. **Create the Activation XML file used by InfoPath.** HWS actions require Activation XML instances so InfoPath needs to use an instance of the HWS activation schema when it constructs the outbound SOAP message containing the form.
6. **Edit the Payload section for the Activation XML.** InfoPath can handle only one *Payload* element without any nodes.
7. **Create a map.** Map the incoming HWS activation message into the HWS task message used for orchestration. Use a Scripting functoid to create a GUID for the TaskID. See the box marked *S* in Figure 11-9.

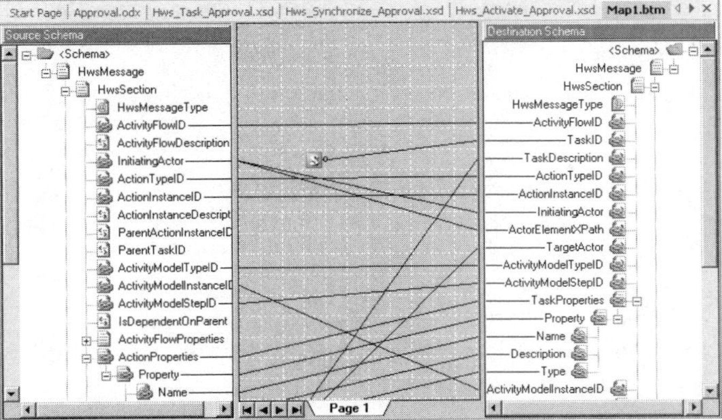

Figure 11-9 BizTalk includes a powerful schema mapping tool.

8. **Create the InfoPath forms orchestration.** A simple workflow could involve a send block to create an outbound message including the form. If your orchestration does not involve routing the form data, you can have an action that does not contain send ports. To allow successive submissions, you will need a receive block with a loop condition to accept form updates until some end state is true. You need a transform to map the incoming message into the schema for the action. Figure 11-10 shows an example of a simple orchestration. See Lab 12, described earlier, for more details.

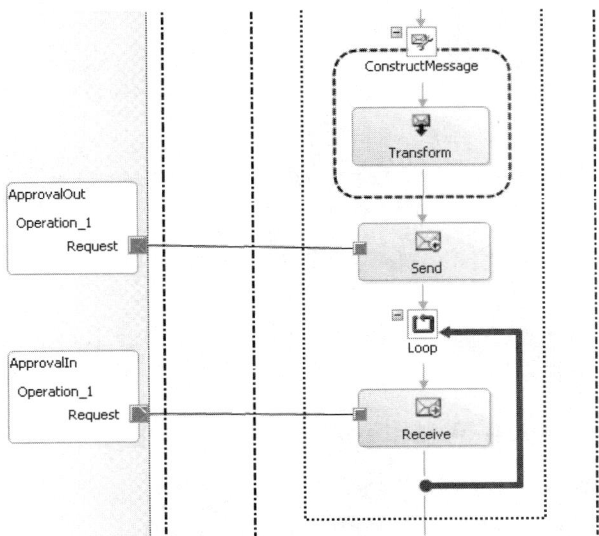

Figure 11-10 This small excerpt from a much larger BizTalk orchestration shows how to orchestrate InfoPath forms for an Approval process.

9. **Deploy the action.** You must deploy BizTalk actions before you can create and bind ports and start the workflow.
10. **Bind ports, start action, register action, and add constraints.** BizTalk has many steps to perform!

The process of creating an orchestration is complex, but it leverages subactions for assigning and delegating forms. Lab 12 also reuses these stock actions–and it still takes 100 individual steps to complete the orchestration.

If you are new to BizTalk, you'll definitely want to look at the BizTalk lab. If you have experience working with BizTalk, you will be familiar with the complexity hinted at in the above summary.

Attaching the HWS Pipeline Component

The HWS Pipeline Component is unique to InfoPath, so we'll spend some time describing how to install it. If you downloaded the C# file (HWSInfoPathPipelineComponent.cs) for the pipeline component, you must create a project from scratch:

1. Start Visual Studio .NET, and create a Visual C# Class Library project named **InfoPathPipelineComponent**.
2. Add the HWSInfoPathPipelineComponent.cs file to the project, and delete the default class1.cs file.
3. Add a reference for the Microsoft.BizTalk.Pipeline.dll assembly in your BizTalk installation directory. The default install location is C:\Program Files\Microsoft BizTalk Server 2004\Microsoft.BizTalk.Pipeline.dll.
4. Strong sign the assembly. Use the sn.exe tool to create a strong key file. From a Visual Studio command prompt, type **sn –k mykey.snk**.
5. Open the AssemblyInfo.cs file from Solution Explorer, and insert the full path to the mykey.snk filename between the double quotes.
6. Build the solution, and copy the resulting DLL to the Pipeline Components folder in the BizTalk installation directory.

Building the Send Pipeline Adapter

To deploy the pipeline component in BizTalk, we need to wrap it in a BizTalk send pipeline assembly. The following steps describe this process:

1. Create a new BizTalk project from the Empty BizTalk Server Project template. Name it **InfoPathPipelineAssembly**.

2. Add a send pipeline to the project. From the Project menu, choose Add New Item. In the Add New Item dialog box, select BizTalk Project Items in the left pane and double-click Send Pipeline template in the right pane (or select and click Open).
3. From the Tools menu, choose Add/Remove Toolbox Items, select the BizTalk Pipeline Components tab, and click Browse to enter the path to the Pipeline Component DLL you created in the previous section (e.g., C:\Program Files\Microsoft BizTalk Server 2004\InfoPathPipelineComponent.dll). Click OK. Visual Studio should have added a new item to the toolbox named BizTalk 2004 HWS – InfoPath SP1 Integration Component.
4. Drag the new component into the preassemble stage of the pipeline component. Your pipeline should resemble Figure 11-11.

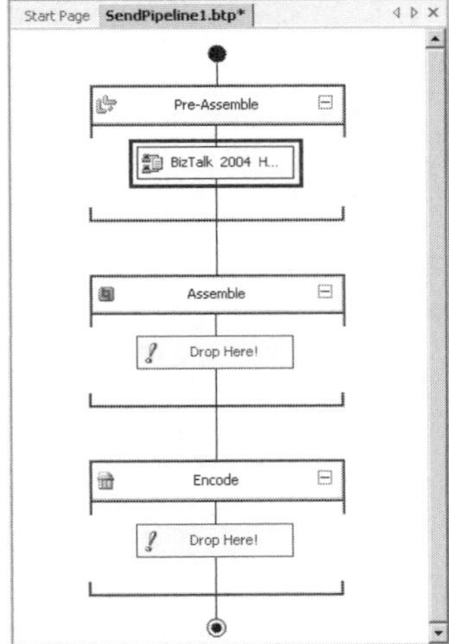

Figure 11-11 Adding the HWS pipeline component to your BizTalk orchestration.

5. Add the assembly key file to the list of common properties. From the Project menu, choose Properties | Common Properties | Assembly, and in the Strong Name field type the location of the assembly key file you added in the previous section. Click OK.
6. Choose Build Solution from the Build menu.
7. Right-click on the InfoPathPipelineAssembly project in Solution Explorer, and select Deploy.

Attaching to Orchestration

The following steps explain how to attach the pipeline to your orchestration's send ports.

1. Open the BizTalk Server Human Workflow project that defines your orchestration.

2. Choose BizTalk Explorer from the View menu, and click the Refresh button (shown in Figure 11-12).

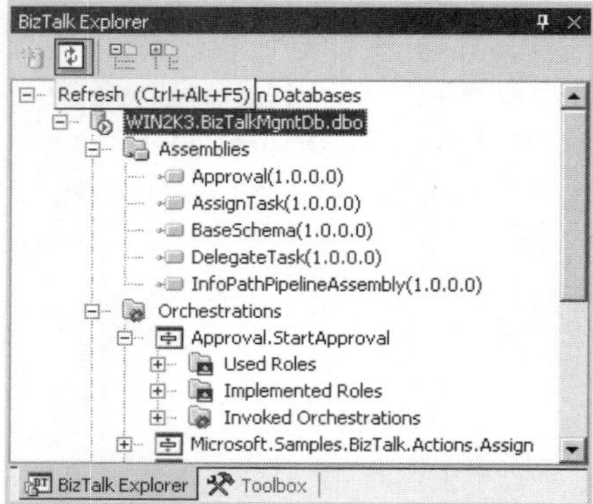

Figure 11-12 Refreshing the BizTalk Explorer

3. Expand Send Ports, and double-click the port defined for your orchestration. The Send Port Properties dialog box appears.
4. Select Send underneath the Configurations node in the left pane.
5. Click the value drop-down list for the Send Pipeline field, and select InfoPathPipelineAssembly.SendPipeline1.
6. Click OK.

Enabling HWS in InfoPath

To enable the default HWS support for your InfoPath form, you must implement the following, as detailed in the following sections:

1. Extract the form files.
2. Add receive data connections.
3. Modify the schema to support workflow.
4. Activate the HWS workflow in the manifest.
5. Add a resource file for action activations.
6. Add HWS data adapters for the actions.
7. Add event handlers for workflow buttons.

Extracting the Form Files

You must extract the form files to allow manual editing of the manifest.xsf.

1. Open the form template in the InfoPath designer, and choose Extract Form Files from the File menu.
2. Specify a folder to use.
3. Open Windows Explorer, and navigate to the folder.
4. Right-click on the manifest.xsf file, and choose Design.

Adding Receive Data Connections

InfoPath uses four receive data connections to query the HWS Web services and get workflow status for the form:

- GetActivityList
- GetTaskInfo
- GetActionInstance
- GetActivityFlowInfo

You must define these four data connections to enable HWS for your form. Here are the steps:

1. Choose Data Connections from the Tools menu.
2. Click the Add button to add a connection.
3. Select Receive Data From A Web Service.
4. Enter the URL for the HWS Web service (for example, *http://localhost/hwsservice/hwsservice.asmx?WSDL*).
5. Select GetActivityList from the list of operations.
6. Click Next, and accept the default values.
7. Disable the check box labeled Automatically Retrieve Data When the Form Is Opened.
8. Click Finish.
9. Repeat the above steps for GetTaskInfo and GetActionInstance.
10. Repeat the above steps for GetActivityFlowInfo, but in the Parameters list box, select s0:detailLevel and click Set Value.
11. In the Parameter Details dialog box, select ActionInstanceLevel from the Sample Value drop-down list.
12. When you are done, your data connections should resemble Figure 11-4.
13. Save the form, and close the designer.

Modifying the Schema to Support Workflow

Most forms require the addition of data elements to control workflow. Here are three common examples:

- *endAction* A Boolean field that controls when to stop processing a form. The loop control in the workflow tests the value, and if it is *true*, the loop aborts, which stops form updates.
- *target* A string field that specifies form assignment.
- *status* A string that describes the status of the form. Map this to the Task Status node in the HWS message to set the status that InfoPath displays in the workflow task pane.

Activating the HWS Workflow in the Manifest

For this step and the next, you must open the manifest in Notepad and make manual modifications.

1. Right-click the manifest.xsf file and choose Open With | Notepad.
2. Insert an *<xsf:hwsWorkflow>* section after *</xsf:views>*. Here is a sample of what this section might look like:

```
<xsf:hwsWorkflow taskpaneVisible="yes">
    <xsf:location url="abc"></xsf:location>
    <xsf:allowedActions>
       <xsf:action name="Approval" actionTypeID="B78376F4-E786-AAA6-733A-E19A6261EEA6"
canInitiateWorkflow="yes" caption="Start Approval"></xsf:action>
    </xsf:allowedActions>
    <xsf:allowedTasks>
        <xsf:task name="RespondToApproval" taskTypeID="http://tempuri.org/
Hws_Task_Approval" caption="Respond To Approval"></xsf:task>
    </xsf:allowedTasks>
</xsf:hwsWorkflow>
```

<xsf:location> contains the URL for the HWS Web service. *<xsf:allowedActions>* contains the HWS actions enabled for this form. At run time, InfoPath takes this list of actions and compares them with the actions made available to the user via the *GetActivityList* call. The intersection of these actions is what gets displayed in the workflow task pane.

Tip The HWS Constraint Service can block individual actions per user on the BizTalk Server. To view constraints, start HWS Server Administration and click Constraints.

<xsf:allowedTasks> contains the HWS tasks enabled for this form. The *taskTypeID* attribute holds the target namespace for the schema associated with the task. *actionTypeID* contains a GUID string identifying the HWS action.

To get the GUID for your action, do the following:

1. Start SQL Server Query Analyzer.
2. Select the server where the BizTalk database resides.
3. In the Database drop-down list, select BizTalkHwsDb.
4. Enter **select * from hws_actions**, and press F5.
5. Copy the *ActionID* value from the results window.

Adding a Resource File for Action Activations

InfoPath needs an XML instance file to create an appropriate HWS message to start actions. For each action that your form will initiate, you must add a corresponding XML file.

Creating the Activation XML from Visual Studio

1. Open the HWS orchestration project.
2. In Solution Explorer, right-click on the XSD schema file corresponding to the activation task, and choose Properties.
3. In the General section of the Property Pages dialog box, type **C:\activation.xml** in the Output Instance Filename field.
4. Click OK.
5. Right-click on the XSD schema file, and choose Generate Instance.

Adding the Resource to Your InfoPath Form Template

1. Right-click on the manifest, and choose Design.
2. From the Tools menu, choose Resource Files.
3. Click Add and browse to the C:\activation.xml file.

Adding HWS Data Adapters for the Actions

You must define a special HWS submit adapter for each action that you will expose on the form or in the workflow task pane. The only way to do this is by manually modifying the manifest.xsf file.

1. Right-click manifest.xsf file, and choose Open With | Notepad.
2. Insert an *<xsf:dataAdapters>* section after *</xsf:dataObjects>*.

> **Caution** If your form already has a *dataAdapters* section, just add the individual data-Adapter nodes.

The following code shows a sample of what this section might look like:

```
<xsf:dataAdapters>
    <xsf:hwsAdapter name="Approval" wsdlUrl="http://localhost/hwsservice/
        hwsservice.asmx?WSDL" submitAllowed="yes" queryAllowed="no">
        <xsf:hwsOperation type="addActionToNewActivityFlow" typeID="B78376F4-E786-AAA6-
            733A-E19A6261EEA6" serviceUrl="http://localhost/hwsservice/
            hwsservice.asmx?op=GetActivityList">
            <xsf:input source="Activation.xml">
                <xsf:partFragment match="ActionSection/Target" replaceWith="/my:myFields/
                    my:Target"></xsf:partFragment>
                <xsf:partFragment match="ActionSection/Status" replaceWith="/my:myFields/
                    my:Status"></xsf:partFragment>
                <xsf:partFragment match="ActionSection/EndAction" replaceWith="/my:myFields/
                    my:EndAction"></xsf:partFragment>
            </xsf:input>
        </xsf:hwsOperation>
    </xsf:hwsAdapter>
…
</xsf:dataAdapters>
```

The *<xsf:input>* node contains the source instance as well as the nodes in the data source to map. Each *<xsf:partFragment>* node specifies a mapping from the form's main data source to the HWS message. The *replaceWith* attribute contains an XPath query string for the main data source, and the *match* attribute contains an XPath to insert the value into the HWS message schema.

Adding Event Handlers for Workflow Buttons

Last, you have to bind workflow buttons in your form to the submit data adapters described earlier. Double-click on the button control in your view, and select Edit Code. Here's an example of a simple event handler that calls Submit, which in turn submits a message to HWS:

```
<InfoPathEventHandler(MatchPath:="Approval", EventType:=InfoPathEventType.OnClick)> _
Public Sub Approval_OnClick(ByVal e As DocActionEvent)
    thisXDocument.DataAdapters.Item("Approval").Submit()
End Sub
```

Important You must create the entire event handler from scratch because the InfoPath designer does not show the HWS workflow pane. Make sure that you use the button name from the manifest in the *OnClick* name for the event handler.

Developer Nugget: Debugging Tips

Integrating InfoPath with HWS is complex, and the risk of an error resulting from a configuration mistake is high. If something is wrong with your workflow, here are some tricks to try:

- **Event Viewer** When you have an error, the first place to look is in Event Viewer. From the Start menu, click Run and type **eventvwr.exe**. Select Applications in the left pane, and look for errors for HWS or BizTalk.
- **Pipeline component** Use two outbound ports. One specifies the pipeline, the other does not. Compare the output.

  Check out the trace utility on MSDN: *http://support.microsoft.com/default.aspx?scid=kb;en-us;835451*.
- **HWS Administration** You can monitor activity flows using this tool. (See Figure 11-13.)

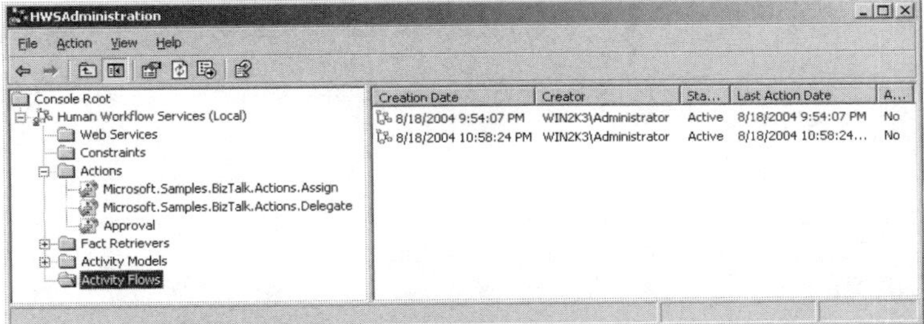

Figure 11-13 Monitoring activity flows with the HWS Administration tool

> **Note** You can also use the Health and Activity Tracker tool provided by BizTalk to monitor activity flows.

- **BizTalk Administration Console** Use this tool to stop and start the BizTalk server application. (See Figure 11-14.)

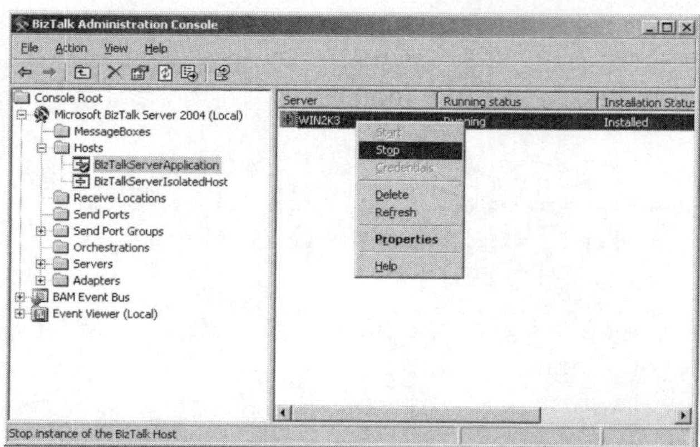

Figure 11-14 Using the BizTalk Administration Console to stop and start BizTalk

- **Rebuilding requires redeploying** From the BizTalk Explorer, right-click on the action and choose Stop. Then right-click on it again and choose Unenlist. (See Figure 11-15.)

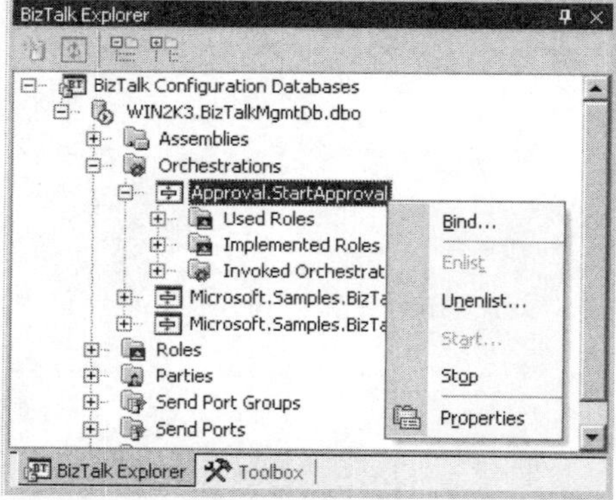

Figure 11-15 Using BizTalk Explorer to stop and unenlist actions

- Use the BizTalk Deployment Wizard to remove and undeploy a BizTalk assembly. (See Figure 11-16.)

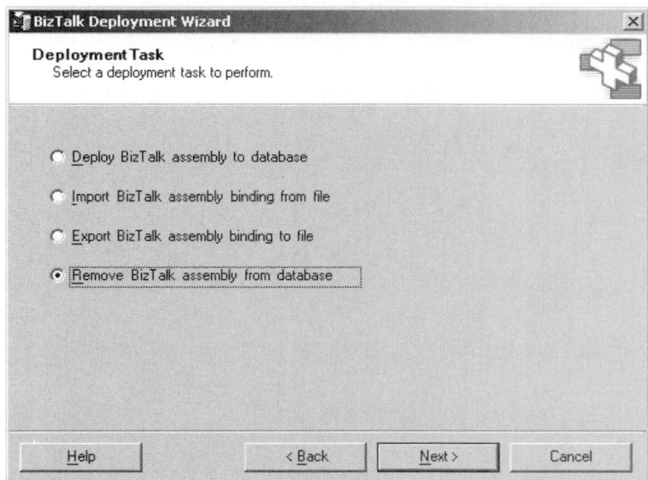

Figure 11-16 Using the BizTalk Deployment Wizard to remove and undeploy assemblies

When you remove the assembly, don't forget to select the check box to remove it from the global assembly cache. (See Figure 11-17.)

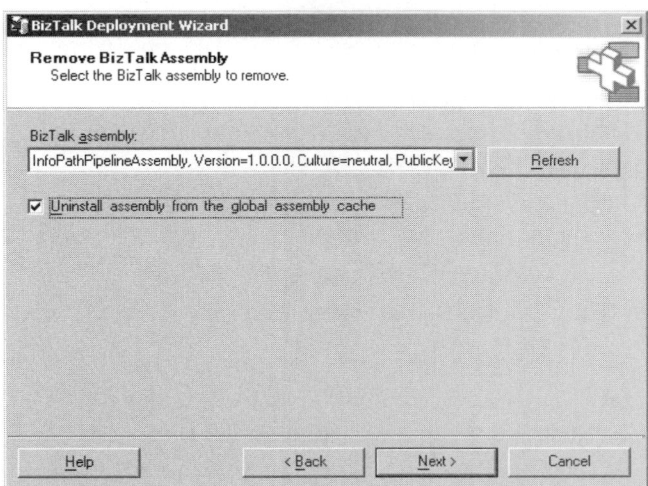

Figure 11-17 Don't forget to remove the assembly from the global assembly cache when undeploying.

- After rebuilding, bind and start the action.
- Right-click on the solution in Solution Explorer, and choose Deploy.

Additional Resources

As an XML forms editor, InfoPath is an ideal down-level client for BizTalk business processes. Numerous online resources showcase integration scenarios for this happy marriage. BizTalk itself ships with InfoPath templates for managing the Business Activity Services component. See the following URL for more details: *http://msdn.microsoft.com/library/default.asp?url=/library/en-us/operations/htm/ebiz_ops_bas_admin_mfmt.asp*.

Earlier, you learned about the online MSDN lab titled "Lab12: Workflow Support in InfoPath 2003." Unless you are a seasoned BizTalk guru, Lab 12 is undoubtedly your best resource for learning about BizTalk. We'll highlight two additional resources and another resource that will be available in the near future.

BizTalk Adapter for SharePoint Libraries

As you saw in Chapter 9, Windows SharePoint Services 2 provides support for XML Form Libraries and is an easy-to-use yet powerful back-end file server for your InfoPath forms. As you saw in Chapter 10, you can use SharePoint form libraries to implement a forms-based workflow. When you outgrow forms-based workflow, you can easily extend it to use BizTalk with the BizTalk Adapter for SharePoint Libraries: *http://www.gotdotnet.com/workspaces/workspace.aspx?id=0d1aa85c-cf8d-497e-84f4-3ffec8db115f*.

The BizTalk Adapter for SharePoint Libraries contains the following two components:

- **Receive Adapter** Polls SharePoint folders, checks out files, submits files to BizTalk Message Box, and calls Web methods to delete files from SharePoint. You can specify a view that acts as a filter for the adapter to poll which forms are submitted. The Receive Adapter is not an event handler, and that means it's easier to deploy. Event handlers offer better performance but are difficult to deploy because they require separate configuration for each form library by a system administrator.
- **Send Adapter** Sends forms back to SharePoint using a Web method on the SharePoint server.

Figure 11-18 shows the high-level architecture for using InfoPath, SharePoint, and BizTalk to implement workflow. Note that this architecture assumes that you implement forms-based workflow in place of HWS. The main benefit of using this architecture is that it provides a simple upgrade path from forms-based to server-based workflow. If you have already implemented a forms-based workflow using SharePoint, you can easily extend it to receive the benefits of BizTalk without drastic changes to your form template. The main benefit of server-based workflow in this scenario is that you will have robust transactions. You can rid your form of the problems when the file save succeeds but e-mail doesn't. BizTalk enables atomic transactions. When you save the form to your SharePoint site, BizTalk picks it up, sends it through orchestration, and sends e-mail as a result. Of course, you still have to implement an orchestration in BizTalk, but you get a more fail-safe workflow because BizTalk handles saving and notifying in one step.

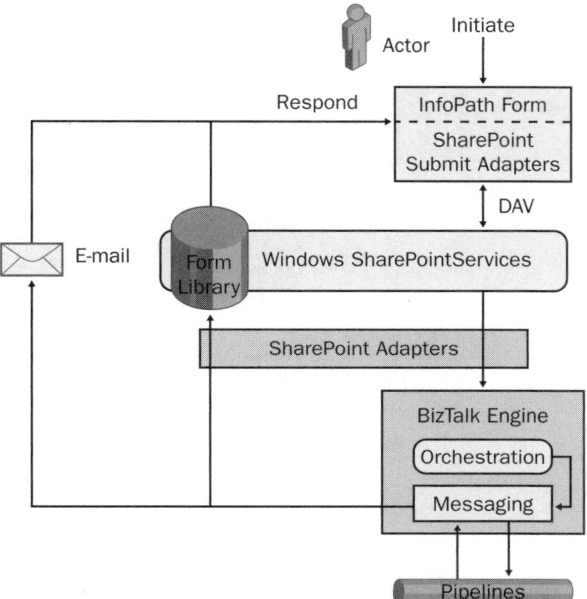

Figure 11-18 InfoPath integrates with BizTalk via HWS.

FabriKam Solutions Kit

Microsoft spent a year developing FabriKam, and it shows. FabriKam is the most comprehensive resource out there. In fact, it is a Microsoft Office System Solutions Learning Platform. The FabriKam platform addresses several enterprise business scenarios using numerous technologies: Web services, SharePoint, BizTalk, Active Directory, and of course InfoPath and Smart Documents (Word and Excel) on the client. You can learn more about it at *http://msdn.microsoft.com/office/understanding/officesystem/fabrikam/introfabrikam/*.

To simplify setup and installation for its many components, FabriKam uses Virtual PC images. These images are huge (many gigabytes) and can't easily be downloaded from the Web. See Microsoft's Web site for details on how to order a DVD containing the Virtual PC image.

Information Bridge Framework

Like FabriKam, Information Bridge Framework (IBF) is another platform for building Office solutions, but it does not target learning. IBF is more like a platform accelerator–it helps you build enterprise solutions using Office by providing a "bridge" from Office documents to business processes. The result is a vastly simplified deployment story. Smart Documents must be installed on each client. IBF provides a generic smart document that can be dynamically updated and changed via a metadata cache on a server. For more details, see *http://msdn.microsoft.com/office/understanding/ibframework/default.aspx*.

Version 1.0 includes support for Word and Excel. So where's InfoPath? Version 1.1 will support InfoPath and should be available in the near future.

Summary

Let's summarize the tradeoffs of integrating HWS in your InfoPath forms:

Benefits

- **More powerful** BizTalk orchestration supports extensive customization and integration with other business processes and applications.
- **More secure** Storing workflow status in your BizTalk server (vs. the form's data) is more secure.
- **More robust** Workflow is transactional, which means setting status and routing forms happen as an atomic operation.

Costs

- **Steep learning curve** Installing and configuring BizTalk is not trivial; developing orchestrations requires familiarity with BizTalk.
- **More complexity** Server configuration is much more complex. BizTalk has many pieces that need to be synchronized.
- **More work** You must manually modify the InfoPath form to support HWS. To expose more information, you must create your own task pane.
- **More components** You must insert steps into the BizTalk orchestration to unpack, update, and repack your form's XML. The pipeline component that comes with the SDK is one way of doing this, but you can also do it as logic in the orchestration itself.

You must have BizTalk actions that support InfoPath workflow.

Appendix

Resources

The following are lists of resources that are useful for solutions development using InfoPath:

On Your Computer

In InfoPath, press F1 to launch the InfoPath Help system.

- **End User Help** *C:\Program Files\Microsoft Office\OFFICE11\1033\IPMAIN11.CHM*
- **InfoPath Dev Reference** *C:\Program Files\Microsoft Office\OFFICE11\1033\INFREF.CHM*
- **XML and Unmanaged Code Reference** *C:\Program Files\Microsoft Office\OFFICE11\1033\MSE10.CHM*

Visual Studio includes the InfoPath 2003 Toolkit for Visual Studio .NET documentation.

Microsoft Online

Office Online

- *http://office.microsoft.com/infopath/*

Developer Center

- *http://msdn.microsoft.com/office/understanding/infopath/default.aspx*

InfoPath Support Center

- *http://support.microsoft.com/default.aspx?scid=fh;EN-US;infopath2003*

Blogs

- InfoPath Team Blog *(http://blogs.msdn.com/infopath)*
- Office Zealot *(http://www.officezealot.com/BlogHome.aspx)*
- InfoPath Tips and Tricks *(http://radio.weblogs.com/0131777/categories/infopath-TipsAndTricks)*
- Jan Tielens' Bloggins *(http://weblogs.asp.net/jan/category/2442.aspx)*
- LauraJ's Weblog *(http://weblogs.asp.net/lauraj/category/2785.aspx)*

Newsgroup

- *news://msnews.microsoft.com/microsoft.public.infopath*
- *http://groups.yahoo.com/group/InfoPath*
- *http://groups.google.com/groups?&meta=group=microsoft.public.infopath*

SDK

- *http://www.microsoft.com/downloads/details.aspx?FamilyId=351F0616-93AA-4FE8-9238-D702F1BFBAB4&displaylang=en*

Other

Standards

- *http://www.w3c.org*

External InfoPath sites

- InfoPathDev (*http://www.infopathdev.com*)
- InfoPathFAQ (*http://www.infopathfaq.com*)
- Serriform Tips (*http://tips.serriform.com*)
- Office Zealot (*http://www.officezealot.com*)

Books

- *Introducing Microsoft Office InfoPath 2003* by Roger Jennings and Acey Bunch (Microsoft Press, 2004)
- *Programming Microsoft InfoPath (Programming Series)* by Thom Robbins and Thomas Robbins (Charles River Media, 2004)
- *How to Do Everything with Microsoft Office InfoPath 2003 (How to Do Everything series)* by David McAmis (McGraw-Hill Osborne Media, 2004)
- *Professional InfoPath 2003* by Ian Williams and Pierre Greborio (Wrox, 2004)

Index

C

D

E

G

J-K

L

M

P

Q

R

S

T

U

V

W

X

Z

Patrick Halstead

Patrick Halstead is the founder of Autonomy Systems LLC, a software consulting company dedicated to helping companies streamline data handling costs and improve data analysis using solutions based on Microsoft Office. Patrick worked for many years at Microsoft as a developer and led solutions development for the first version of Microsoft InfoPath. He is a 2004 Microsoft MVP for Office Systems–InfoPath. On a personal note, Patrick reads and writes Japanese and enjoys watching Japanese movies on a region-free DVD player. Patrick's other hobbies include half marathons, numbers and mnemonics, and wine identification. He moved to Kirkland, Washington, with his wife, Naoko, and cats, Skaredy and Indy, to be closer to the sunset.

Vani Mandava-Teredesai

Vani Mandava-Teredesai is a member of the InfoPath test team at Microsoft. She has worked on InfoPath since its inception and is excited about the impact of XML technologies on software. She joined Microsoft in 2000, after attending graduate school at SUNY Buffalo. She moved to the United States six years ago from Mumbai, India. Vani lives in Redmond, Washington with her husband, Ankur, and fish, Nemo. She is thankful for her siblings and grateful to her wonderful family for their support.

Matthew Blain

Matthew Blain is the Director of Software Development for Serriform LLC, a Seattle software consulting company that designs and delivers enterprise-class software solutions. He previously worked at Microsoft as a developer for Internet Explorer and the team that later developed Microsoft InfoPath. Matthew has traveled extensively, having visited five of the seven continents, though only two of the great seas.

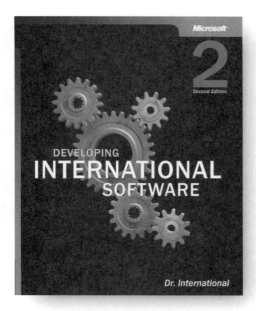

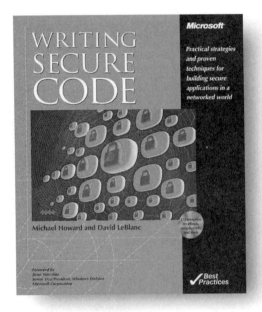

What do you think of this book?
We want to hear from you!

Do you have a few minutes to participate in a brief online survey? Microsoft is interested in hearing your feedback about this publication so that we can continually improve our books and learning resources for you.

To participate in our survey, please visit:

www.microsoft.com/learning/booksurvey

And enter this book's ISBN, 0-7356-2116-0. As a thank-you to survey participants in the United States and Canada, each month we'll randomly select five respondents to win one of five $100 gift certificates from a leading online merchant.* At the conclusion of the survey, you can enter the drawing by providing your e-mail address, which will be used for prize notification *only*.

Thanks in advance for your input. Your opinion counts!

Sincerely,

Microsoft Learning

Learn More. Go Further.

To see special offers on Microsoft Learning products for developers, IT professionals, and home and office users, visit: *www.microsoft.com/learning/booksurvey*

* No purchase necessary. Void where prohibited. Open only to residents of the 50 United States (includes District of Columbia) and Canada (void in Quebec). Sweepstakes ends 6/30/2005. For official rules, see: *www.microsoft.com/learning/booksurvey*